Learn

FONTLAB

FAST

A Simplified Guide to Creating Fonts with
FontLab, TypeTool,
ScanFont *and* **AsiaFont Studio**

D1295287

Learn **FONTLAB** *Fast*

A Simplified Guide to Creating Fonts
with FontLab, TypeTool, ScanFont and AsiaFont Studio

Written and Designed by
Leslie Cabarga

Technical Editor:
Adam Twardoch

Thanks to Ted Harrison, Yuri Yarmola, Sasha Petrov, Lisa Devlin, and the FontLab team.
Also, thanks to Thomas Phinney, Stuart Sandler, Mark Simonson, Steve Zafarana, Hrant Papazian,
Sammy Or, James Grieshaber, Jill Bell, Eric Olsen, Jeff Holtzman, Zuzana Licho, John Hudson,
David Barlia, Ray Larabie, David Berlow, Erik van Blokland, Christian Schwartz, Brian Sooy.
Special thanks to Adam Twardoch for his expertise, and for tolerating my endless questions.

This book is composed in Adobe Palatino, and in Amplitude, designed by Christian Schwartz for The Font Bureau

ISBN 0-9657628-5-8

Published by
ICONOCLASSICS Publishing Co.
253 S. Orange Dr.
Los Angeles, CA 90036
Tel: 323 549 0700   email: lescab@flashfonts.com
website: www.logofontandlettering.com

To order additional books direct from the publisher, call or visit:
www.logofontandlettering.com
Please inquire about bulk and educational discounts.

Contents

1 Preliminaries

8 *Creating a font: Basic procedure* • **10** *Launch FontLab* • **11** *Start a new font* • **12** *The Glyph window* **13** *The enhanced Glyph window* • **14** *What's different in FontLab?* • **15** *Font encodings: Latin-based* **16** *Choosing Encodings for designing and generating fonts* • **17** *Non-latin font encodings* • **18** *Save the font* • **19** *The Font Info dialog box* • **23** *Cap height comparison*

2 Starting a Font

23 *Getting Characters Into FontLab* • **26** *Open an existing font* • **27** *Selecting the right font to open* **27** *Open a Fontographer .fog file* • **28** *Import glyphs from Illustrator* • **30** *Import bitmap scans from Photoshop* • **31** *In depth: Preparing scanned images* • **33** *Make an outline into a background* • **34** *Make bitmap scans with ScanFont* • **39** *Autotraced characters in FontLab* • **40** *Creating glyphs with a digital pen* • **41** *The Brush tool and digital pen* • **43** *Vector Paint tools* • **45** *Tracing with Pen tool and digital tablet* • **46** *How to trace a scan*

3 Drawing a Font

48 *Glyph Window details* • **49** *Alignment Zones* • **50** *Making points with the Drawing tool* • **52** *Making and Breaking connections* • **54** *How to select points and paths* • **55** *Selecting, Deselecting; the Magic Wand* • **56** *Working with nodes and paths* • **58** *Drawing Glyphs* • **61** *How to Preview your drawing* • **65** *Pop-up Menus* • **67** *Transform, Transforming, Transformation* • **71** *Letter spacing 101* **72** *Check progress in the Metrics Window* • **73** *Working suggestions* • **74** *Optional drawing tools: Sketch mode* • **75** *Working in Sketch mode* • **76** *Drawing with off-point curves* • **77** *The Grid and off-point curves* • **78** *Meter mode*

4 Generating, Installing and Printing a Font

81 *Making a usable font; Comparing font formats* • **83** *Generate a Mac Type 1 font* • **84** *Generate a Mac Type 1 font and install it into Mac OS X.3* • **85** *Generate a Mac or PC TrueType font* • **87** *Install TrueType, OpenType or Type 1 fonts for Mac into Macintosh OS 8.x or 9.x* • **88** *Install TrueType, OpenType or Type 1 fonts for PC into Windows XP or 2000* • **89** *Printing test documents in FontLab* **90** *Printing tests from installed fonts* • **91** *FontLab Studio 5's expanded printing*

5 Spacing, Kerning and Hinting a Font

93 *The Metrics window* • **96** *Spacing and Kerning* • **97** *Using the Metrics window* • **98** *Auto Metrics* **99** *Kerning* • **100** *Kerning and the Kerning Info panel* • **101** *Remove existing Kerning* • **102** *Transform Metrics* • **103** *The Metrics window in Studio 5* • **104** *Time-saving class-based kerning* • **106** *Hinting* **108** *Auto-hint a Type 1 font* • **109** *Font Audit* • **110** *Type 1 hinting; Alignment Zones* • **112** *Type 1 hinting; The Preview panel* • **114** *Links, Replacement hints, Auto stems* • **116** *Beginning TrueType hinting*

6 Accents and Composite Characters

119 *Making Accented characters* • **120** *Using Anchors to set up composites* • **121** *Composite an accent glyph with Components.* • **121** *Making composites with Generate Glyphs.*

7 Making a family of fonts

123 *About font families* • **124** *Change weights in the Transform window* • **126** *Making families with Effects* **127** *Automate Effects with Transform Range* • **128** *Family naming set up for Mac Type 1 and TT* **129** *Family naming for OT, TT, and Win Type 1* • **130** *Typical naming plan for an OpenType family*

8 Making OpenType fonts

132 *About OpenType* • **132** *Using OpenType in Adobe InDesign CS* • **133** *Using OpenType in Adobe Illustrator CS* • **134** *Add OpenType features to an existing font* • **136** *Add OpenType features using Classes* **138** *Why OpenType failure?* • **139** *Some OpenType features*

9 Features, Tips & Tricks

141 *Find/Replace; Center Components* • **142** *Paste Special; Contiguous selections* • **143** *Mark cells; Noncontiguous selections; Annotate cells; Enlarge cells* • **144** *Primitives (Smart Shapes) panel: Grid and Star* • **145** *Add/Subtract shapes with contour tools* • **146** *Envelope; Setting Family Metrics*

10 What's NEW in FontLab Studio 5

148 *Latest features and improvements*

11 Using Asia Font Studio

152 *How AFS differs from FontLab*

154 Index

Don't waste time reading this **INTRODUCTION**
if you want to Learn FONTLAB Fast!

50% ILLUMINATION

FontLab is a program that has been evolving and gaining ground for ten years. Fontlab Ltd., the parent company, remains small and friendly. For users, this has meant a high degree of accessibility and openness to outside suggestions.

The beauty of FontLab is its ability to perform a dizzying array of font-related tasks—perhaps everything a font designer could wish for in a font creation software program. And yet, this very complexity can seem somewhat daunting to the beginning user, especially one familiar with other font-creation or computer drawing programs.

The purpose of this book is to illuminate that 50% of FontLab that will likely be the only portion ever needed by 90% of us. For the rest—you intrepid techies—FontLab provides a free 700-page manual—choose Mac or Windows—that is downloadable as a .pdf file. A bound, hard-copy is also available for purchase from www.ondemandmanuals.com.

I have always found that computer manuals only become comprehensible after I've learned the basics of the program. If you can relate to that statement, I recommend that after becoming familiar with FontLab through this mini-manual, and gaining some practical experience with the program, that you peruse the Big manual to learn of FontLab's full capabilities.

OBJECT ORIENTED

Presumably you bought this book because you want to find out how to make a font in FontLab. This book is designed to provide the answers you need, as you need them, for the specific tasks you want to accomplish. I have tried to avoid making you memorize program details that you might never use. Skip around; use the Table of Contents or Index to find what you're looking for on a need-to-know basis. Later, use the Index to locate any information you may have missed.

FASTER IS BETTER

This book takes the position that time is of the essence and the faster we are able to accomplish each task, the better off we are. Given the super redundancy of FontLab—admirably designed to provide different users the widest range of options for accomplishing the same task—we feel that there still are certain ways of doing tasks that are faster than other ways, and we show you these as we go along, rather than mentioning every single available option.

VERSION ?

This book was completed just as FontLab Studio 5 neared release. Most of the features discussed here are so basic that they have not been altered much through versions 4.5, 4.6 and Studio 5. However, we point out the major areas in which Studio 5 does differ from earlier releases. Check my website, www.logofontandlettering.com for updates to this book. (You can also check www.fontlab.com for program updates.)

MAN VS. MACHINE

As the brainchild of a programmer, FontLab allows us to accomplish every task with minute precision. Let us not forget though, that whereas imprecision is to be avoided, the emphasis of the technical aspects of a font—the ability to move glyph cells in a font window to custom positions, the ability to imbed more voluminous copyright information into a font than ever before, the ability to automate tasks with Python scripting—all of these must never override the fact that a font is a work of art. Therefore, the approach of this book is to avoid technical details as much as possible to show you how to easily produce fonts that are, hopefully, works of art.

Before we begin...

• *Some notes on Mac/Windows differences*

This book was created from a Macintosh computer perspective. Throughout the book, we have noted those instances in which differences exist between the Mac and PC versions. When key combinations are listed, the Mac always leads, followed by Windows. You will see each instance written in one of the following ways:

"Cmd-B (Mac) or Ctrl-B (Win)" or "Cmd-/Ctrl-B" or "Option-Cmd- or Alt-Ctrl-B"

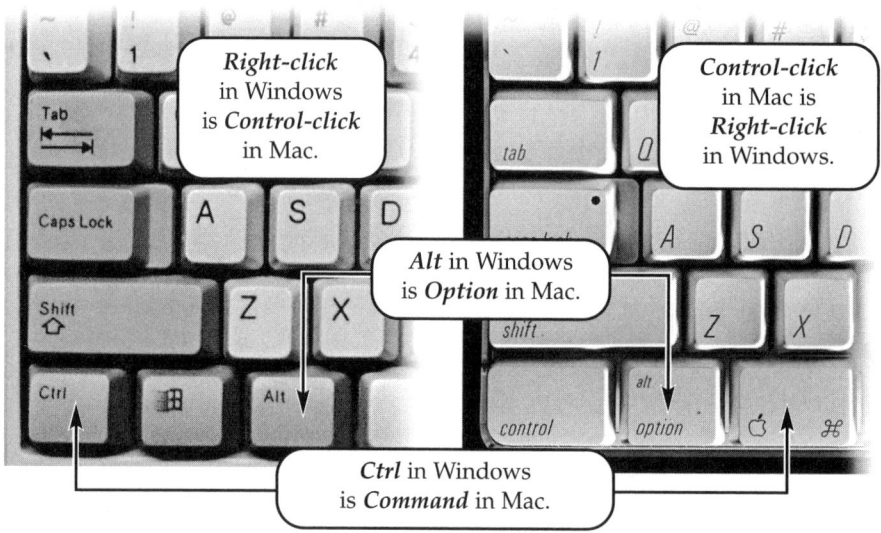

Right-click in Windows is Control-click in Mac.

Control-click in Mac is Right-click in Windows.

Alt in Windows is Option in Mac.

Ctrl in Windows is Command in Mac.

• *The Mac* Preferences *dialog is called* Options *in Windows.*

• *The* Preferences *dialog is described as being located under the* TOOLs *menu throughout this book. In MAC OSX it is located under the* FONTLAB *menu.*

• *TypeTool users:*

TypeTool is the pared-down, simplified version of FontLab, meant as a lower-cost entree into font-creation software for students and beginners. When you see the following symbol, it indicates that the FontLab features described are not available in TypeTool.

• *About clutter:*

If the layout of this book seems overly busy or cluttered in places, just be glad there are only 160 pages to read and not 700. I'm actually saving you time by limiting text in favor of pictures that are worth 1000 manuals. I did this because I have no patience for manuals; its the only time I ever experience dyslexia. Frankly, I believe dyslexia is not so much neurological, as it is part of a complex (that includes ADD and Tourette's), which I call SPSD (Self-Protective-Shutdown syndrome). It's a protective maneuver by the mind causing a shutdown or malfunctioning of certain senses to avoid submitting to outside coercion. I'm sure that Dr. A.M. Skeffington, considered the father of behavioral optometry, would have concurred. He laid the blame for many visual problems on what he termed "socially compulsive near-point tasks." Unfortunately, when SPSD is subconsciously invoked on a sustained and habitual basis (such as in reaction to authoritarian tutelage), it can indeed effect a lingering physical dysfunction. Dyslexics rejoice; you're not sick, you've just refused to sacrifice your ethos. But anyway, just read this book like a comic book: from top to bottom, left to right and it'll all make sense (I hope).

PRELIMINARIES

Page **8** *Creating a font: Basic procedure*

10 *Launch FontLab*

11 *Start a new font*

12 *The Glyph window*

13 *The enhanced Glyph window*

14 *What's different in FontLab?*

15 *Font encodings: Latin-based*

16 *Choosing encodings for designing and generating fonts*

17 *Non-Latin font encodings*

18 *Save the font*

19 *The Font Info dialog box*

23 *Cap height comparison*

CREATING A FONT: Basic Procedure

How should you begin creating a font? What do you do, first? Following are some practical and labor-saving guidelines that can help you to streamline the font-making process and avoid backtracking and duplicating of tasks, which waste time. Here are the words of five font designers explaining their own approaches to font creation. Although many differences are apparent, it seems safe to say that the basic procedure is relatively similar. And it is upon such basic guidelines as these that we shall proceed in this book to outline the process by which you may create fonts using FontLab.

Zuzana Licho; Emigre, Inc.

1. Start experimenting with the concept; draw characters in my preferred glyph-drawing program, decide on ascent and descent.

2. Set background guidelines and alignment zones, including overshoots.

3. Finish rough idea of alphabetic characters (*a–z* and *A–Z*). (The order depends on the design.)

4. Experiment with weights and styles.

5. Finish rough idea of numbers, then punctuation, and all other non-accented characters.

6. Decide on the weights and styles to be included in the family. (*Steps 1–6 = 12 months*)

7. Finalize all the above, including proofs with high resolution Linotronic printouts. Check both small sizes (for evenness of texture) and very large sizes for smooth curves. (*Step 7 = 2 months*)

8. Spacing: check and finalize side bearings (fit) (*Step 8 = 1 month*).

9. Check and finalize kerning. (*Step 9 = 2 months*)

10. Set up accented characters as composites and check alignment.

11. Decompose Composites.

12. Run Python scripts to kern accented characters. Don't do double accents, but do include common collisions. Then check collisions manually.

13. Run Python scripts to check consistency of side bearings and kern pairs for ligatures and other derivative characters (for example: *æ Æ ø Ø fi fl*).

14. Run Python to check for common problems: overlapping outlines, suspect side bearings, etc.

15. Verify Underlines.

16. Verify Font Names, Family Names, PostScript and NFNT IDS, etc.

17. Verify copyright notice.

18. Check hinting.

19. Generate font files.

20. Merge Mac font families.

21. Iconize Mac files.

22. Add MS font properties to TrueType fonts (*Steps 10–22 = 1 month*).

Stuart Sandler; The Font Diner

1. Scan in reference material (sketch or inspirational ephemera). Usually it's one word, sometimes as few as two letters.

2. Enlarge reference on the pasteboard about 500% and autotrace outlines in Adobe Illustrator.

3. Clean up reference outlines, make judgements about glyph shapes and establish rules for the typeface. Establish guides if precision is necessary (many of my faces are *display*, or headline fonts, meant for larger point sizes and are non-exacting).

4. Start from reference outline and flesh out the entire lowercase and uppercase, then numbers.

5. Draw currency figures, fractionals, foreign glyphs, math glyphs, then punctuation. I usually compare glyphs in each sub-family for consistency (Currency: Yen, Euro, Dollar, Cent, Florin, etc.).

6. Copy glyphs to a new document, scale down and print out drawings as a "waterfall" to see glyphs at different sizes (usually 12, 60, and 200-point) on a letter size page horizontally formatted.

7. Standardize glyph shapes by fixing any inconsistencies in my glyph forms, correcting for weight, color, thicks and thins, appropriate shape, and I use guides to ensure consistent proportions including height and width.

9. Final standardization to correct for any glyphs that are bugging me in the face (this is usually pretty picky, subjective opinion stuff).

10. Import the glyphs into font-creation program from Illustrator.

11. Once all glyphs are in their appropriate slots, I space the font completely and create all the composite and reference characters.

12. Kern the entire font, key in all the font info, set the ascent and descent, and the Euro via unicode.

13. Hint the font if it's appropriate.

14. Generate the font.

James Grieshaber; P-22 Type Foundry

1. INSPIRATION. I get inspired from historical letterforms or some thing I've seen or just something I think I want to see. This usually takes the physical form of pencil roughs, sketches and redrawing.

2. DIGITIZATION. Sometimes I can construct directly in an illustration application, but more often than not I have to scan in my sketches to use as templates. Do test print outs.

3. FONTIZATION. Then I try to get the outlines of the upper and lowercase into a font generation application (FontLab) to see if the letters play well together. Do test print outs of words.

4. REFINEMENT. Create the all punctuation and diacritical characters, this is where spacing and kerning happens, along with tweaking of the letterforms so that they work well with each other. Do more test print outs.

5. FINISHING. Make sure all the info in the head-er is correct. Generate and test versions for Mac and PC. Do more test print outs of every version, from every application, on both platforms.

Thomas Phinney; Adobe Systems, Inc.

1) Scan my sketches, if any. (I often work directly on the computer. This seems to be much more common with the younger type designers.)

2) Do a basic keyword, especially of the lower case. "hamburgefonstiv" or equivalent, plus, say, a few caps.

3) Do initial printouts. Refine spacing, and designs, for the keyword letters. Almost every step after this includes making refinements to outlines.

4) Add period and comma, and gradually expand the alphabetic coverage, while repeating the refinement process of step 3. This is the point where I'm generating my first actual working test fonts, incomplete though they are.

5) Start kerning (but I always make sure that my spacing is done). The number one error made by beginning type designers is to start kerning too early. Never start kerning until the spacing is finalized! Otherwise you're using kerning to fix underlying spacing problems, and just digging yourself a big hole. If you make any significant spacing changes later, you'll have to throw out all your kerning.

6) Do the ligatures, numerals and additional punctuation.

7) If I'm doing extended language coverage, this is when I start experimenting with extended Latin and non-Latin letterforms.

8) Generate test fonts for print out. Continue making refinements.

Sumner Stone; Stone Type Foundry, Inc.

My ways are many. All mysterious. I have said too much already.

Launch FONTLAB

When you launch FontLab by double-clicking its icon, a start-up window, right, will appear and then the program will open. FontLab can also be opened by dragging and dropping a TrueType, OpenType or Type 1 font (use the screen font since it contains the metrics) onto its program icon. You'll know FontLab is open when the menu bar, icon panel bar and toolbar, below, appear on your desktop.

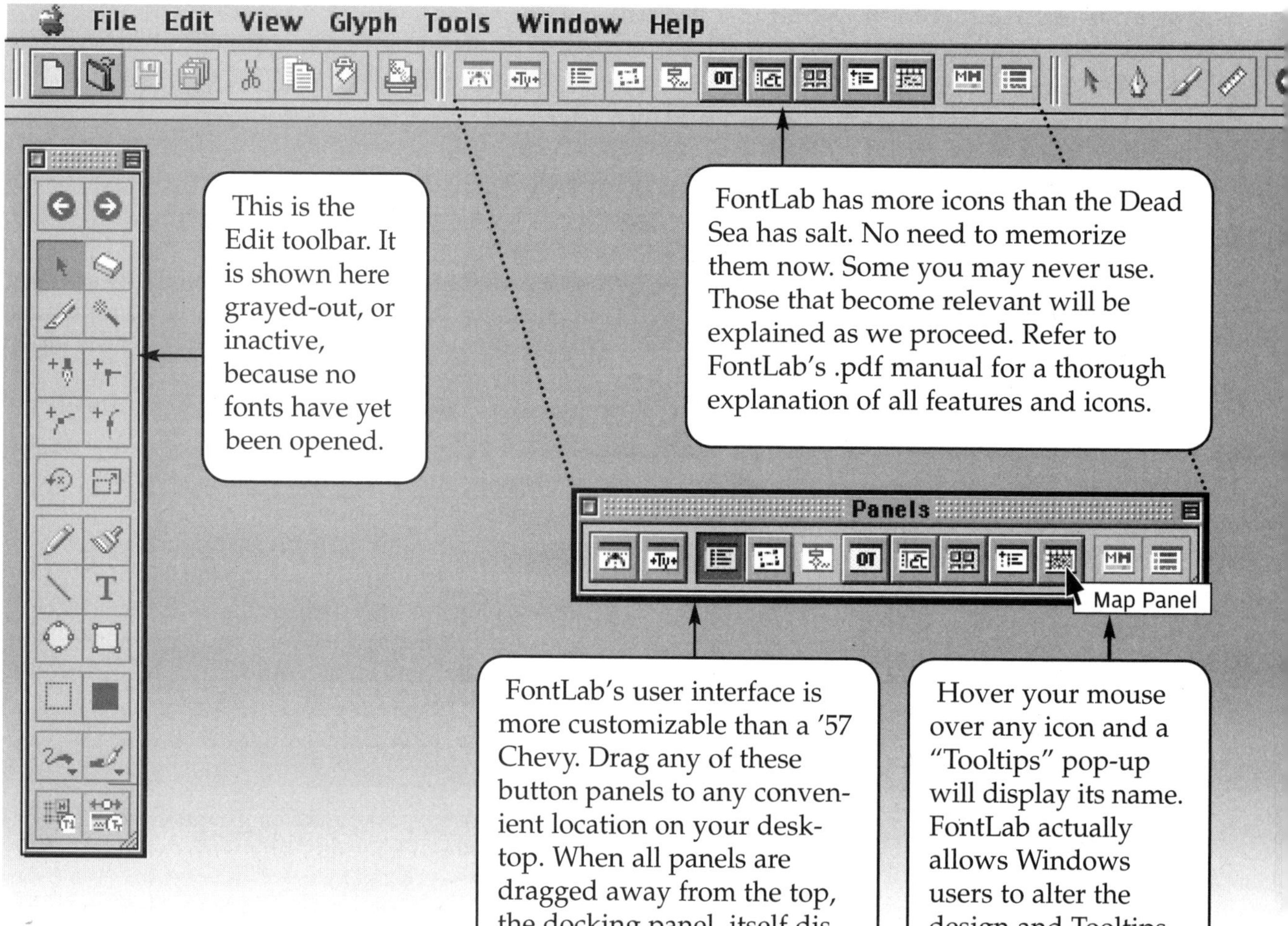

File   Edit   View   Glyph   Tools   Window   Help

This is the Edit toolbar. It is shown here grayed-out, or inactive, because no fonts have yet been opened.

FontLab has more icons than the Dead Sea has salt. No need to memorize them now. Some you may never use. Those that become relevant will be explained as we proceed. Refer to FontLab's .pdf manual for a thorough explanation of all features and icons.

Panels

Map Panel

FontLab's user interface is more customizable than a '57 Chevy. Drag any of these button panels to any convenient location on your desktop. When all panels are dragged away from the top, the docking panel itself disappears until one or more panels are dragged back to the top dock.

Hover your mouse over any icon and a "Tooltips" pop-up will display its name. FontLab actually allows Windows users to alter the design and Tooltips content of any icon. But for now, let's design a font, not redesign FontLab.

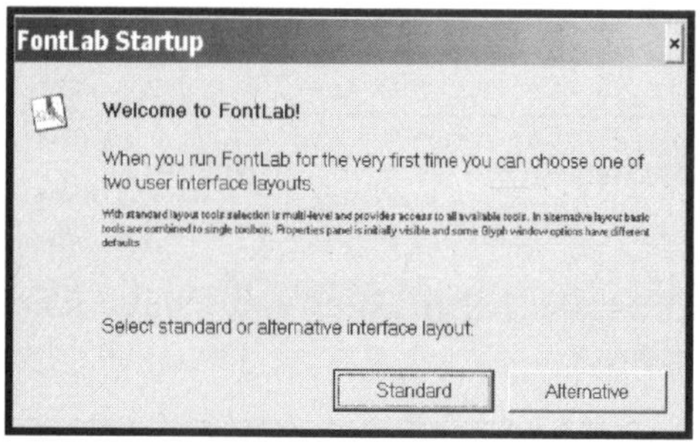

FontLab Startup

Welcome to FontLab!

When you run FontLab for the very first time you can choose one of two user interface layouts.

With standard layout tools selection is multi-level and provides access to all available tools. In alternative layout basic tools are combined to single toolbars. Properties panel is initially visible and some Glyph window options have different defaults.

Select standard or alternative interface layout.

[Standard]   [Alternative]

Windows users:
The first time you start up FontLab 4.6, choose the "Alternative" interface layout to be compatible with this book. If you've already opened FontLab, simply go to VIEW>Toolbars>Edit *to open the essential Edit toolbar. (In FontLab Studio 5, The default interface layout is the Alternate one.)*

Start a NEW FONT

Do you prefer pulling down menu bars, clicking icon buttons, or hitting key combinations to accomplish a task? For many tasks, FontLab offers all three choices.

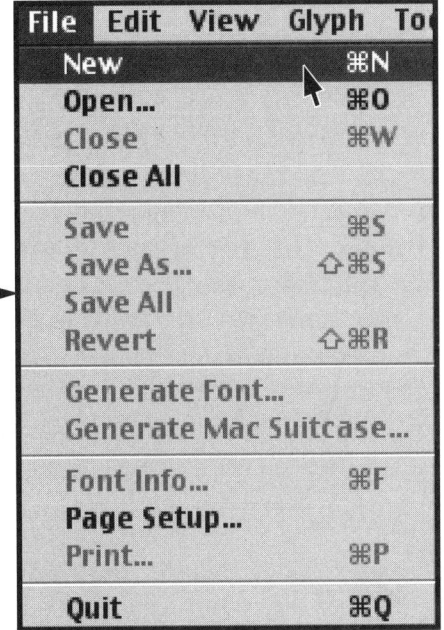

To begin working on a New font, click the mouse button on FILE and scroll down to New.

Or, click the New Font icon in the top toolbar.

Or, hit Command-N (Mac) or Control-N (Windows)

The New command opens a new Font window containing a slot or cell for every character in a standard Adobe Latin-Encoded font, which is the default font encoding. Your job, should you choose to accept it, is to fill each and every cell, in the encoding of your choice, with its designated glyph.

Character vs. Glyph: What's the difference?

A character is an encoded slot in a font that is assigned a number when in codepage or Unicode view. A glyph is the contents of that slot: the outlines you've drawn in FontLab. Some glyphs are unencoded—that is, they don't get a number assigned in any codepage or in Unicode. Some characters can relate to multiple glyphs, such as when you make alternate forms of a given character and associate them with OpenType layout features. For example, the letter *A* is Unicode U+0041. But you might also have a swash cap *A* and a small cap *A* and an alternate version of the *A*, all in the same font: one character, but four different glyphs.

—*Thomas Phinney*

Click here to enlarge or reduce cell sizes in the Font Window.

...or here.

Note that the Font Window displays the Names of every character because this is the default Title mode for new fonts.

The Glyph Window

Double click any cell in the Font Window. Then double click again (four clicks total) and a Glyph Window for that glyph will open. The Glyph Windows are where we'll draw the characters for our font. After a Glyph Window has been opened, or if it already contains a drawing, a mere double-click will open it the next time.

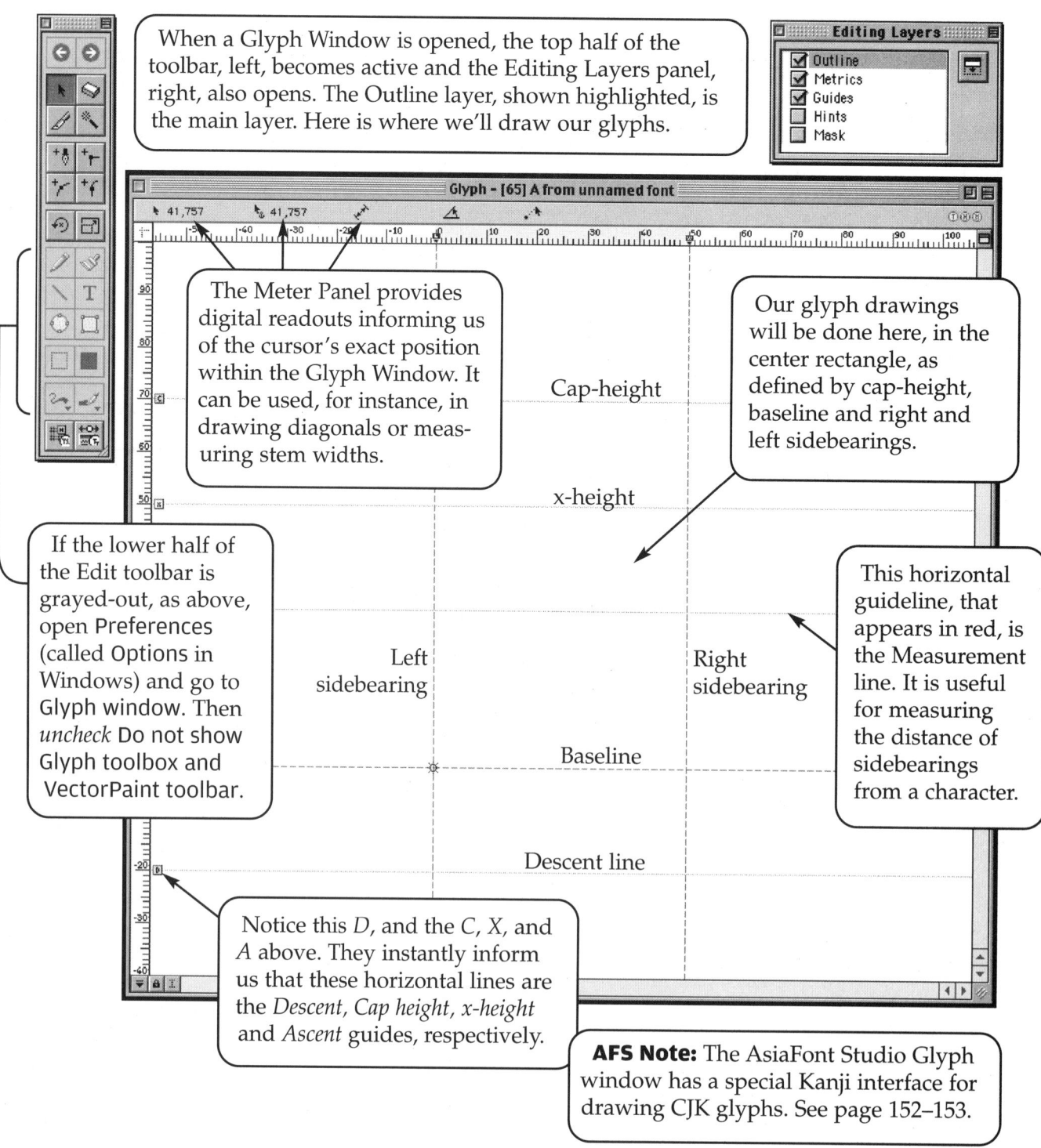

When a Glyph Window is opened, the top half of the toolbar, left, becomes active and the Editing Layers panel, right, also opens. The Outline layer, shown highlighted, is the main layer. Here is where we'll draw our glyphs.

Editing Layers
- ☑ Outline
- ☑ Metrics
- ☑ Guides
- ☐ Hints
- ☐ Mask

Glyph - [65] A from unnamed font

The Meter Panel provides digital readouts informing us of the cursor's exact position within the Glyph Window. It can be used, for instance, in drawing diagonals or measuring stem widths.

Our glyph drawings will be done here, in the center rectangle, as defined by cap-height, baseline and right and left sidebearings.

If the lower half of the Edit toolbar is grayed-out, as above, open Preferences (called Options in Windows) and go to Glyph window. Then *uncheck* Do not show Glyph toolbox and VectorPaint toolbar.

This horizontal guideline, that appears in red, is the Measurement line. It is useful for measuring the distance of sidebearings from a character.

Cap-height

x-height

Left sidebearing

Right sidebearing

Baseline

Descent line

Notice this *D*, and the *C*, *X*, and *A* above. They instantly inform us that these horizontal lines are the *Descent, Cap height, x-height* and *Ascent* guides, respectively.

AFS Note: The AsiaFont Studio Glyph window has a special Kanji interface for drawing CJK glyphs. See page 152–153.

The Enhanced Glyph Window

*If the first Glyph Window you open does not look like the one below, just click the expand button, **a**, to add toolbars to the top, and then click the expand button at **b**, to open the Glyphs Bar that provides a slightly quicker way of accessing characters in the Font Window without having to leave the Glyph Window environment to click back on the Font Window.*

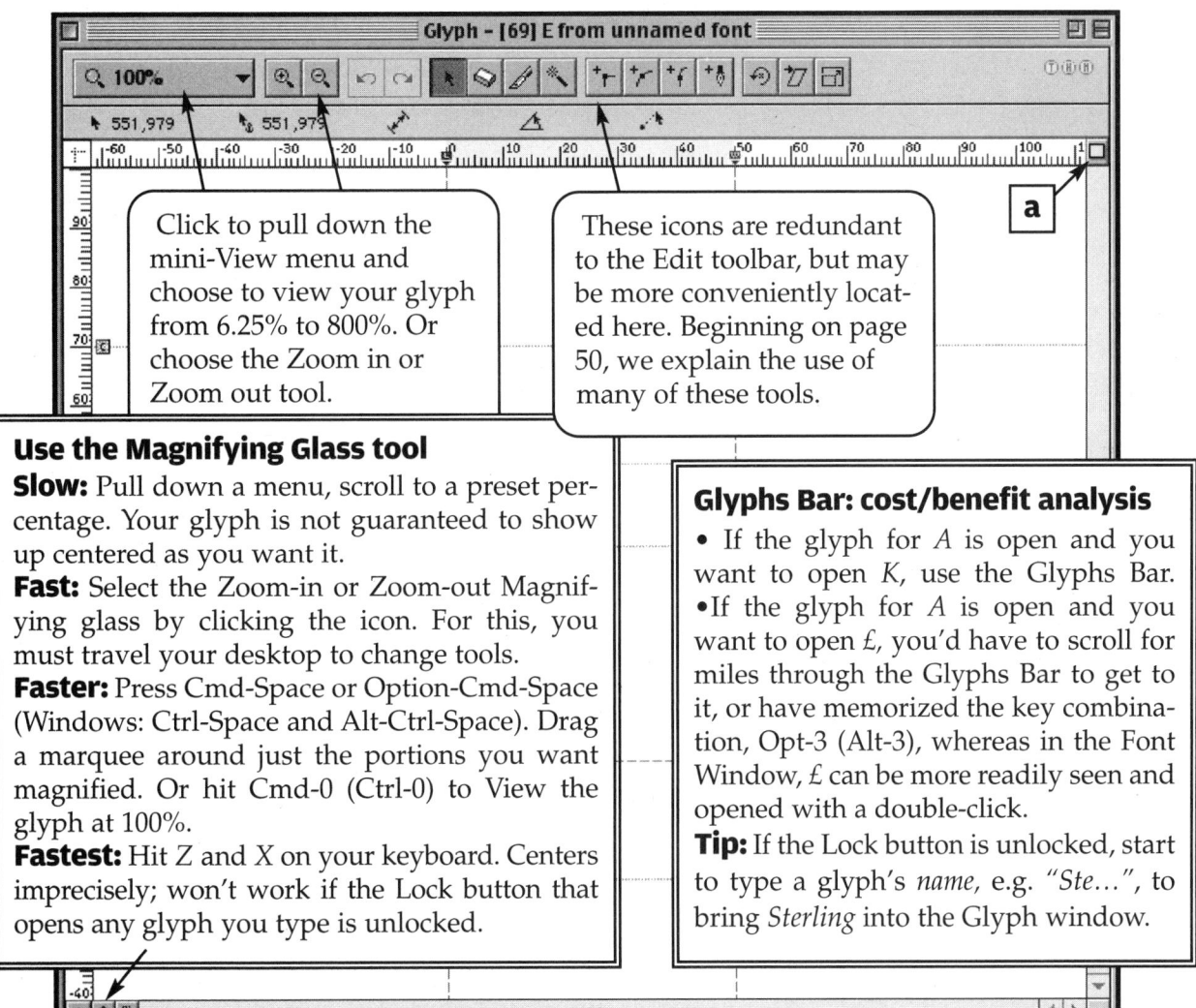

Click to pull down the mini-View menu and choose to view your glyph from 6.25% to 800%. Or choose the Zoom in or Zoom out tool.

These icons are redundant to the Edit toolbar, but may be more conveniently located here. Beginning on page 50, we explain the use of many of these tools.

Use the Magnifying Glass tool

Slow: Pull down a menu, scroll to a preset percentage. Your glyph is not guaranteed to show up centered as you want it.

Fast: Select the Zoom-in or Zoom-out Magnifying glass by clicking the icon. For this, you must travel your desktop to change tools.

Faster: Press Cmd-Space or Option-Cmd-Space (Windows: Ctrl-Space and Alt-Ctrl-Space). Drag a marquee around just the portions you want magnified. Or hit Cmd-0 (Ctrl-0) to View the glyph at 100%.

Fastest: Hit Z and X on your keyboard. Centers imprecisely; won't work if the Lock button that opens any glyph you type is unlocked.

Glyphs Bar: cost/benefit analysis

• If the glyph for *A* is open and you want to open *K*, use the Glyphs Bar.
•If the glyph for *A* is open and you want to open *£*, you'd have to scroll for miles through the Glyphs Bar to get to it, or have memorized the key combination, Opt-3 (Alt-3), whereas in the Font Window, *£* can be more readily seen and opened with a double-click.

Tip: If the Lock button is unlocked, start to type a glyph's *name*, e.g. *"Ste..."*, to bring *Sterling* into the Glyph window.

In a New font, untouched, empty cells—both here, in the Glyphs Bar, and in the Font Window—stay gray until they are opened and filled with glyphs. Then our glyph appears within the cell and the cell background color becomes white.

What's different in FontLab?

If you've just switched to FontLab from Fontographer, the first things you'll notice are the many differences in the FontLab interface—some of which may seem overwhelming to the eye. Below we'll outline a few of these features and also tell you how to turn them off if they make you nervous. But you may soon find that FontLab's "differences" represent, on the whole, a quantum leap in technology and in the capabilities afforded the user.

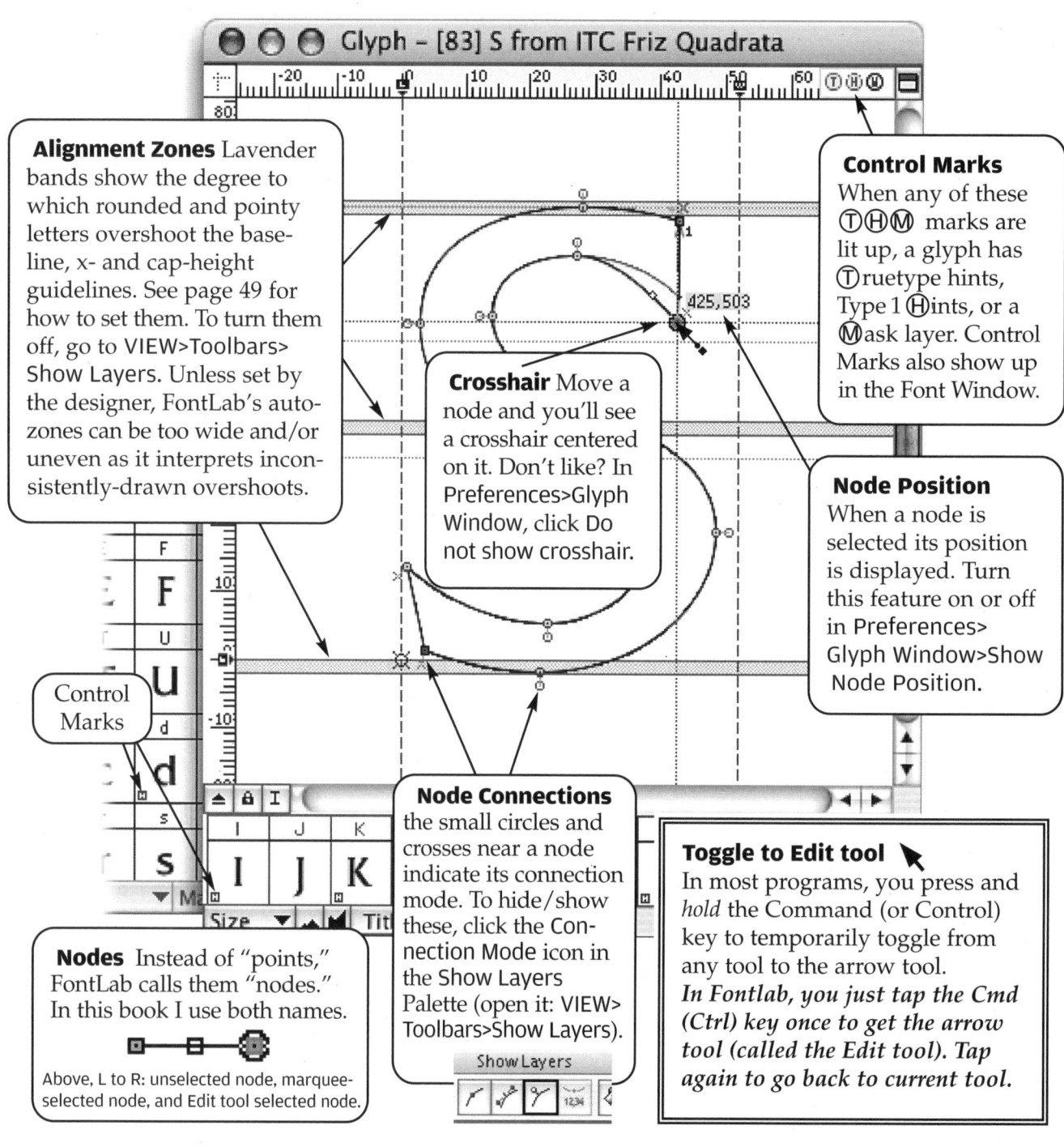

Alignment Zones Lavender bands show the degree to which rounded and pointy letters overshoot the baseline, x- and cap-height guidelines. See page 49 for how to set them. To turn them off, go to VIEW>Toolbars> Show Layers. Unless set by the designer, FontLab's auto-zones can be too wide and/or uneven as it interprets inconsistently-drawn overshoots.

Control Marks
When any of these ⓉⒽⓂ marks are lit up, a glyph has Ⓣruetype hints, Type 1 Ⓗints, or a Ⓜask layer. Control Marks also show up in the Font Window.

Crosshair Move a node and you'll see a crosshair centered on it. Don't like? In Preferences>Glyph Window, click Do not show crosshair.

Node Position
When a node is selected its position is displayed. Turn this feature on or off in Preferences> Glyph Window>Show Node Position.

Control Marks

Node Connections the small circles and crosses near a node indicate its connection mode. To hide/show these, click the Connection Mode icon in the Show Layers Palette (open it: VIEW> Toolbars>Show Layers).

Toggle to Edit tool ↖
In most programs, you press and *hold* the Command (or Control) key to temporarily toggle from any tool to the arrow tool.
In Fontlab, you just tap the Cmd (Ctrl) key once to get the arrow tool (called the Edit tool). Tap again to go back to current tool.

Nodes Instead of "points," FontLab calls them "nodes." In this book I use both names.

Above, L to R: unselected node, marquee-selected node, and Edit tool selected node.

Font Encodings: Latin-based

Before beginning work on your font, you'll need to choose an encoding. If your font is for the English language, or for most European languages, and it contains the characters "ABCDEFG; abcdefg…" with or without the addition of accents, it is a Latin-based font. For most Latin-encoded fonts, the Macintosh Roman encoding shown below provides all the required glyph cells. Its character cell positions are very similar to those of earlier font creation software programs, with which you may already be familiar. Mac Roman just refers to the layout of the characters in the Font Window. For PC users the default encoding is "Default Encoding"—a general purpose encoding which makes the most compatible fonts, however "Macintosh Roman" will work for PC, too.

If your font will be non-Latin, such as Cyrillic, Arabic, Hebrew, Kanji or Bengali, see page 17.

The gray "Template" images in Font Window cells provide a basic idea of how each glyph looks. The gray images disappear once a cell is opened or filled with a character drawing of your own.

Click on **Mode** to choose Names, Unicode or other encodings that may be applied to fonts. Each Mode listed provides different options, as discussed on the next page.

Whether your font will eventually become Type 1, TrueType or OpenType to be used on Windows or Macintosh is not important now. These issues need only be considered at the time of completion, when you generate the font for use. Then we can easily generate the same font for use in all formats including OpenType, which is discussed on page 131. How we draw a font is basically the same for every format.

Choosing encodings for designing and generating fonts

By Adam Twardoch

Q: *Should both Mac and Windows users choose the Default Encoding in the Font Window?*

A: In choosing an encoding, consider these three aspects:

I. **Design process:** *Planning the glyph coverage; What glyphs will be in my font?*

During the design (drawing) process, encoding and font format are unimportant. My recommendation: If you're making a Western font—whether on Mac or Windows, and regardless of the final font format—work in "Macintosh Roman" encoding. This will always provide the glyph coverage (or range) you'll need.

II. **Encoding:** *What sequence (codes) will be assigned to my glyphs?*

Leave "Macintosh Roman" selected in the Names mode for your fonts regardless of the font format you're making. After finishing the design, choose Glyph/Glyph Names/Generate Unicode/Standard Table/OK. When making a Western font, regardless of the font format, make sure that you've set the following parameters:

1. For a type 1 font, go to Preferences (called Options in Win)>Type 1>Type 1 Export>Encoding Options and select Always write Standard Encoding in the pulldown, as below.

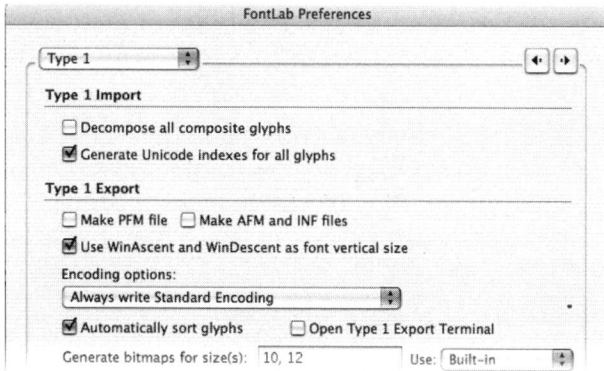

2. For a TrueType font, go to TrueType>TrueType Export> check to enable Use Unicode indexes as a base for TrueType encoding. *(See the screenshot on top of this page.)*

a) Under Use following codepage for first 256 glyphs, select Do not reencode first 256 glyphs (and therefore, Export only first 256 glyphs will be disabled, as it should).

b) Still in the TrueType>TrueType Export> section, disable Put MS Char Set value... by unchecking it.

c) Under Use following codepage to build cmap(1,0) table, select MacOS Roman (default) from the pulldown.

3. Go now to the Font Info window (Cmd- or Ctrl-F).

a) In the page called Encoding and Unicode, look down

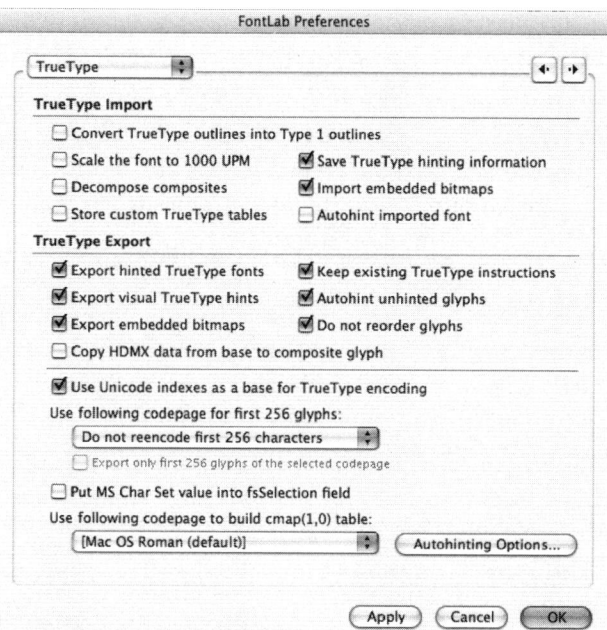

toward the bottom for Microsoft Character Set and select Western (Latin 1) CP1252/ANSI.

b) Under Mac script and FOND ID, choose Roman.

c) In the Available codepages column above, select: 1252 Latin 1 and scroll down to select Macintosh Character Set. Click the right-pointing arrow to include these selections in the Supported codepages field.

d) Go to the Font Info page "Unicode Ranges" *(not pictured)*. Click to enable both Basic Latin and Latin-1 Supplement.

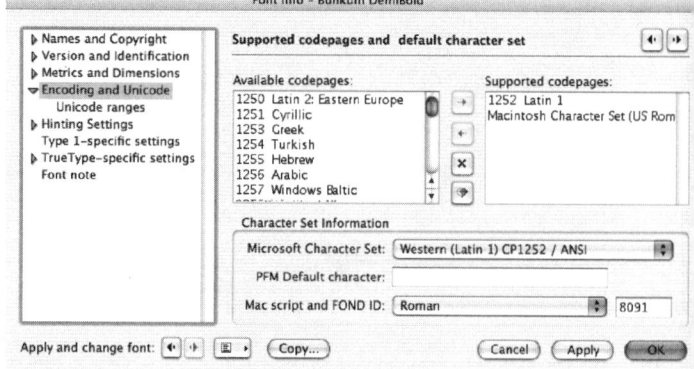

III. **Font format:** *In which font format will I generate my font?*

When making a Mac Type 1 or Win Type 1 font, switch font to Names mode. When making a TrueType or OpenType-CFF font, switch font to Codepages mode.

For more info, see Generating and installing a font, pages 81–88.

Non-Latin font encodings

Most likely, the font encoding for the script of your language is among the hundreds listed in the Encoding pull-down menu shown below. If you are not certain which encoding to choose, use FontLab to open up an existing font in your language that works correctly on your computer. **In general, it is a good idea to open an existing font or two—in whatever language—and study them.** *You'll find clues about bezier construction, character spacing and more. And the font will contain encoding information upon which to base your own font. "However," cautions font designer Hrant H. Papazian, "It may be dangerous to rely on encodings of third-party font designs. There's no guarantee *they* know what they're doing. So choose the source carefully."*

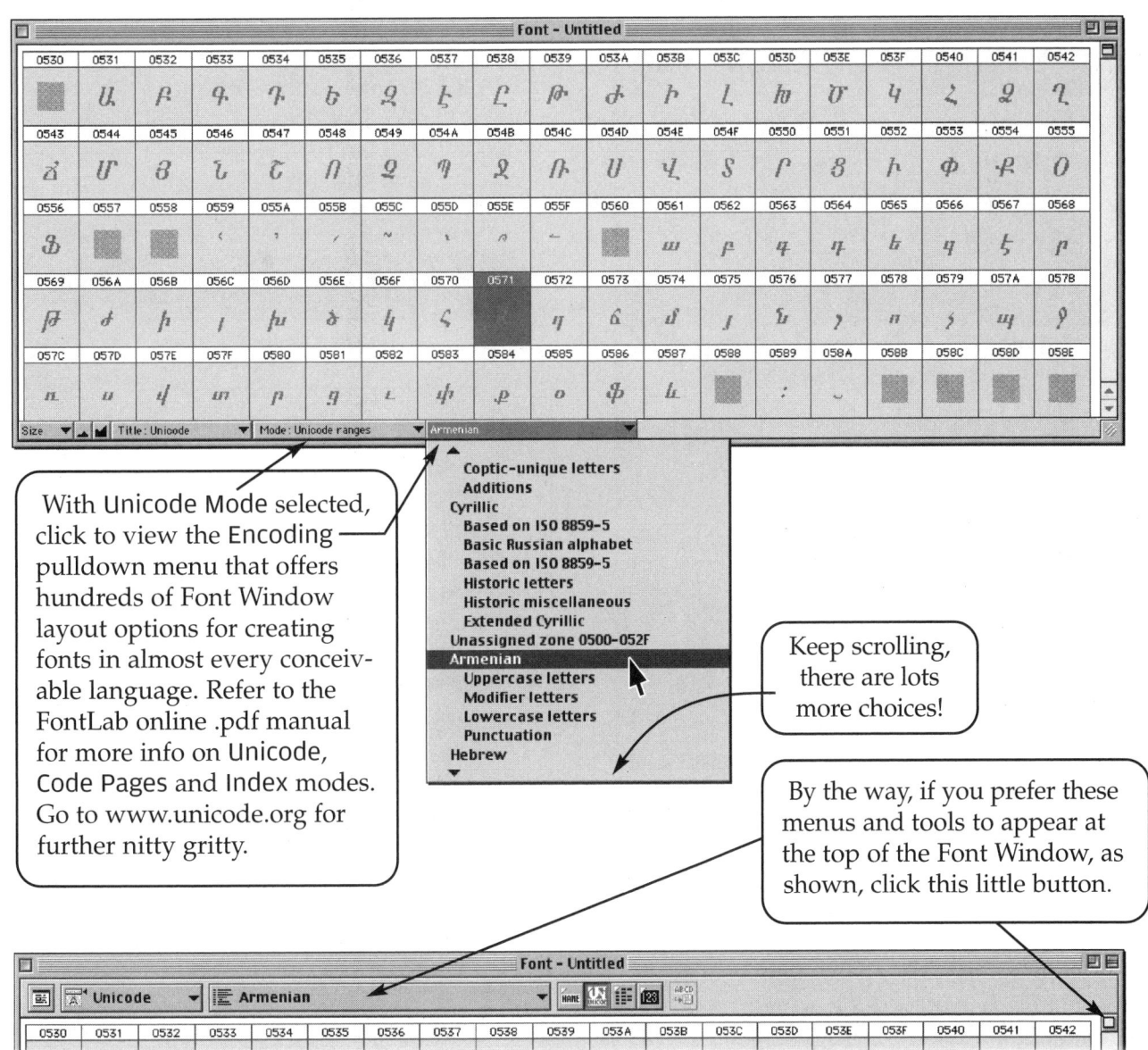

With Unicode Mode selected, click to view the Encoding pulldown menu that offers hundreds of Font Window layout options for creating fonts in almost every conceivable language. Refer to the FontLab online .pdf manual for more info on Unicode, Code Pages and Index modes. Go to www.unicode.org for further nitty gritty.

Keep scrolling, there are lots more choices!

By the way, if you prefer these menus and tools to appear at the top of the Font Window, as shown, click this little button.

Save the font

Saving your new font can be done now or later, but it ought to be done soon in case a crash should interrupt your progress. FontLab itself is fairly stable, but computer crashes can happen for many reasons. After Saving the font file, as explained below, we'll run-through FontLab's Font Info Dialog Box with its many sections. A potentially huge amount of information may be added to your font data in these sections, though not all of it is necessary. Therefore, we have chosen to explain only the most important fields. If you plan to market your fonts through an established font foundry, you need only concern yourself with adding the most basic info and letting the foundry fill in the rest with its standard boilerplate (small print) and naming conventions.

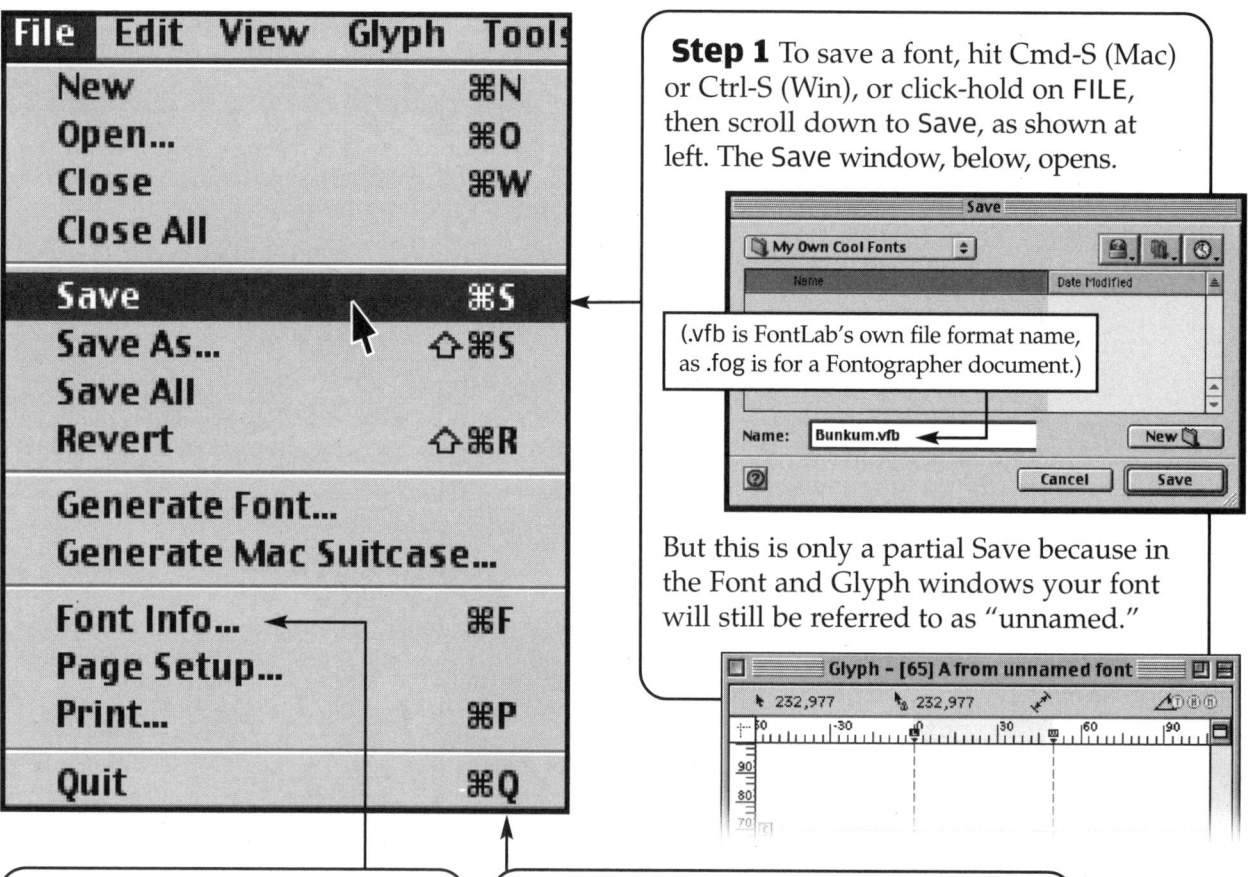

Step 1 To save a font, hit Cmd-S (Mac) or Ctrl-S (Win), or click-hold on FILE, then scroll down to Save, as shown at left. The Save window, below, opens.

(.vfb is FontLab's own file format name, as .fog is for a Fontographer document.)

But this is only a partial Save because in the Font and Glyph windows your font will still be referred to as "unnamed."

Step 2 of the Saving process is to click once again on FILE, then Scroll all the way down to Font Info. In the dialogue box that opens (see next page), you will input the rest of the information needed to properly identify and save your font.

How to Quit
Discouraged already? Hit Cmd-Q (Alt+F4) whenever you want to Quit FontLab or Scroll down to Quit. But come on, show some spunk, keep at it. I thought your dream was to be a font designer!

The Font Info dialog box

You've just saved your new master .vfb font file, but no parameters have been established to identify it or differentiate it from other fonts when it is loaded into a fonts folder. That's where **Font Info** comes in. Click on FILE>Font Info, as shown on the previous page or just hit Cmd-F (Mac) or Ctrl-F (Win). **Font Info** opens to the **Names** section, which is perhaps the most important of those listed in the column at left. Many fields are self-explanatory. The others that are most relevant will be explained here.

Technically, you should go through each and every item here and fill in all fields to define your font. But actually, many sections can be left at default, as we'll see.

Type the basic font name here, For now, we'll name a single font, rather than a family.

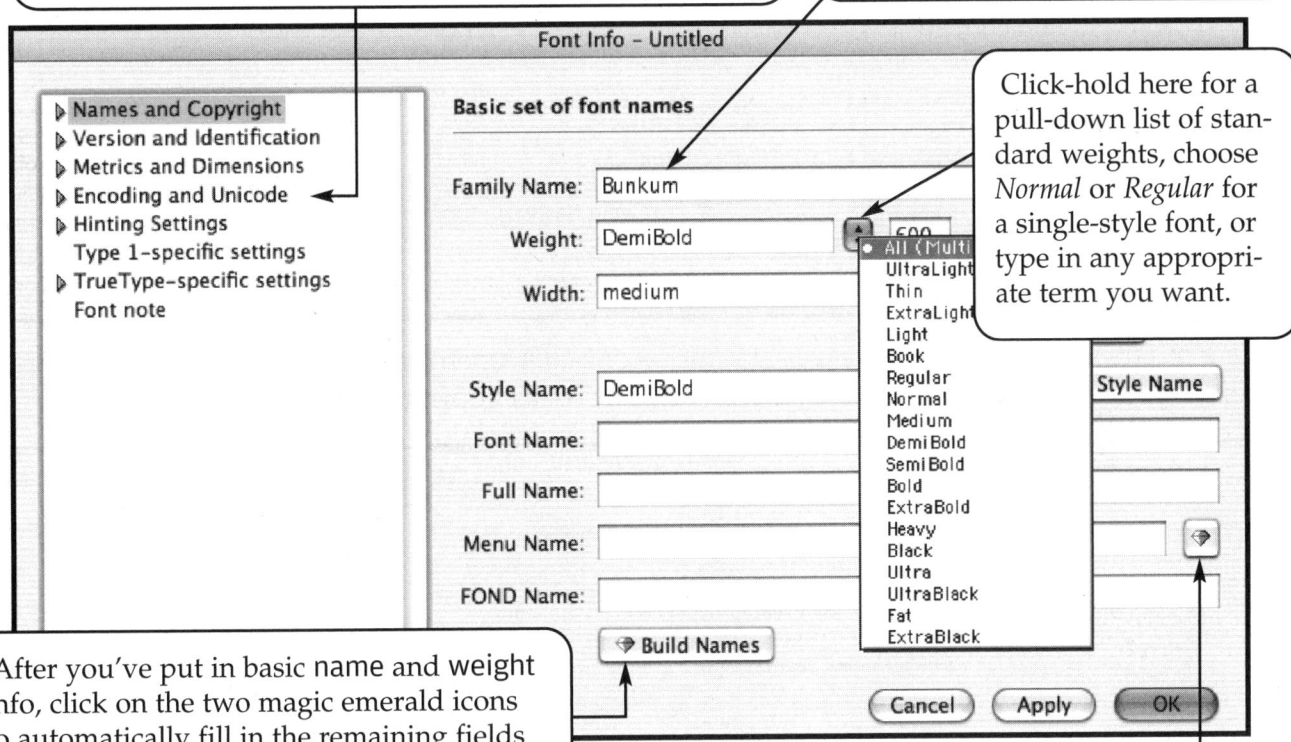

Click-hold here for a pull-down list of standard weights, choose *Normal* or *Regular* for a single-style font, or type in any appropriate term you want.

After you've put in basic name and weight info, click on the two magic emerald icons to automatically fill in the remaining fields according to proper naming conventions.

Now that you've filled in the *Names* section of the Font Info Dialog box, above, you could click OK to close the box and start actually drawing your font. However, the following pages explain a few other important areas of the Font Info Dialog box that really should be filled in before proceeding. ⟶

How to Name Fonts in a Font Family

After you've completed your "key" font in what will be an extended family of different weights and styles, go to FILE>Save As and re-save the key font with a different Style Name such as *Bold, Black, Italic, etc.* Then hit Cmd- or Ctrl-F to open The Font Info window and make changes to reflect the name of the new family member. See page 128 for complete info.

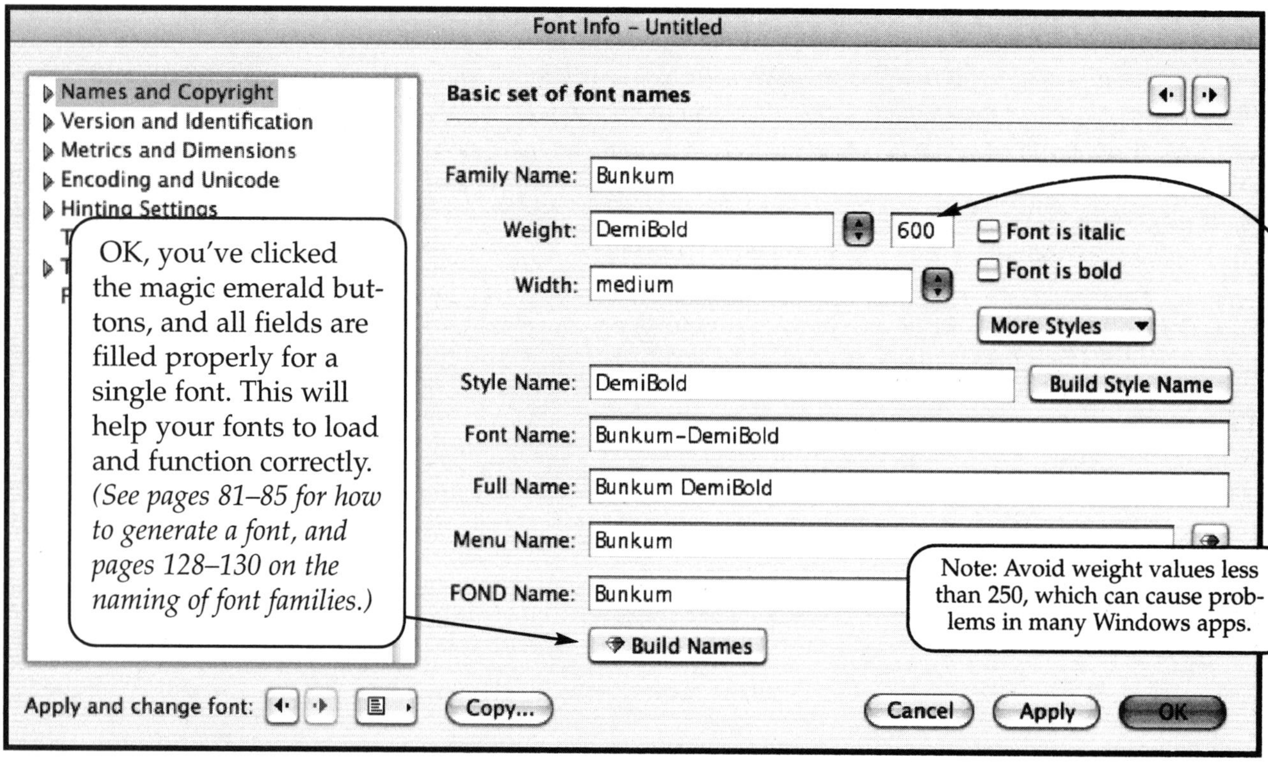

Font Info – Untitled

▷ Names and Copyright
▷ Version and Identification
▷ Metrics and Dimensions
▷ Encoding and Unicode
▷ Hinting Settings

Basic set of font names

Family Name: Bunkum

Weight: DemiBold   600   ☐ Font is italic

Width: medium   ☐ Font is bold

More Styles ▼

Style Name: DemiBold   **Build Style Name**

Font Name: Bunkum–DemiBold

Full Name: Bunkum DemiBold

Menu Name: Bunkum

FOND Name: Bunkum

⬧ **Build Names**

OK, you've clicked the magic emerald buttons, and all fields are filled properly for a single font. This will help your fonts to load and function correctly. *(See pages 81–85 for how to generate a font, and pages 128–130 on the naming of font families.)*

Note: Avoid weight values less than 250, which can cause problems in many Windows apps.

Apply and change font: ◀· ·▶ ▤ ·   (Copy...)   (Cancel) (Apply) ● OK ●

Click this triangle to reveal other pages in this category. Skip the OpenType names *pages for now (we cover these in the family naming section on pages 128–130) and click on* Copyright Information.

Font Info – Untitled

▽ Names and Copyright
   OpenType–specific names
   Additional OpenType names
   Copyright information
   Embedding
   Designer information
   License information

Font copyright information

Created by: Frederick Bunkum

Creation year: 2005

Copyright: Copyright Frederick Bunkum, 2005. All rights reserved.

Trademark: Bunkum DemiBold is a trademark of Frederick Bunkum.

⬧ **Build Copyright and Trademark records**

Notice Description: Copyright Frederick Bunkum, 2005. All rights reserved.

Type your name or company name and year the font was created into the top two fields.

Click the magic emerald to automatically create properly formatted text in the rest of the fields.

This field can contain a repeat of the copyright notice.

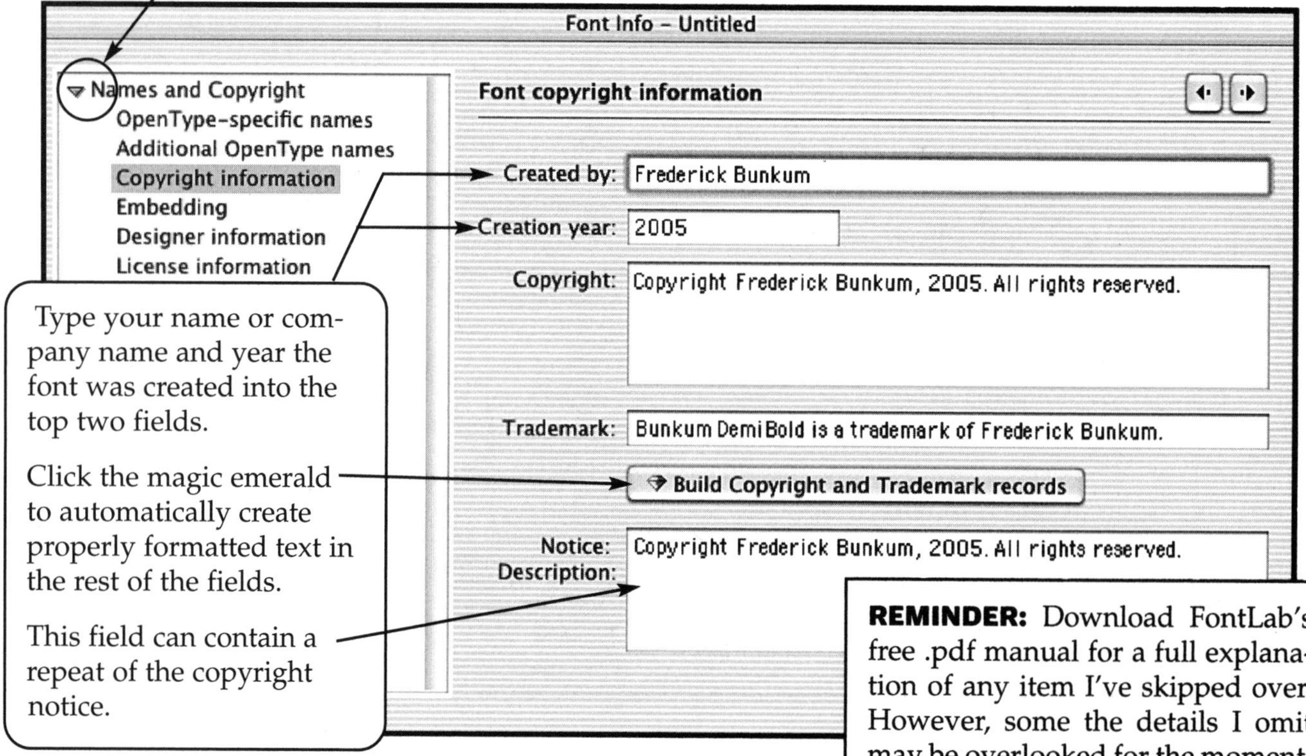

REMINDER: Download FontLab's free .pdf manual for a full explanation of any item I've skipped over. However, some the details I omit may be overlooked for the moment.

Click on Embedding *in the left column. To allow your font to be embedded in documents like Acrobat .pdf files is helpful to users, but doing so makes it possible for a font pirate to extract your font from the document. Of course, the beauty of a .pdf is that users can view the doc as you designed it, fonts and all. Click* **a** *to view embedding choices. The one below would be our choice for general use.*

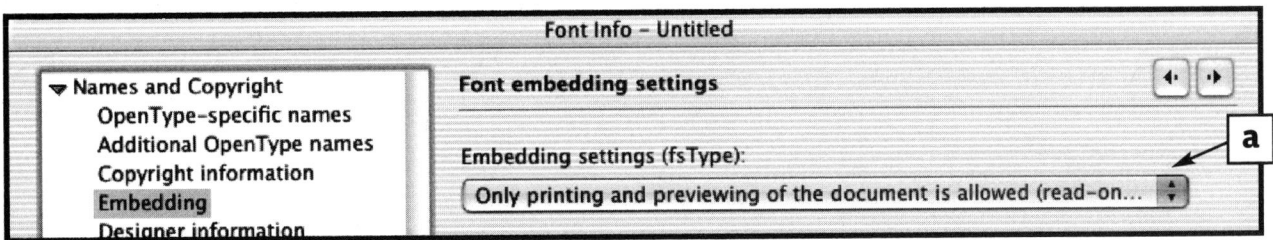

Now click Designer Information *in the left column. The backwards/forwards buttons at* **b** *will also take you from page to page. Personalizing a font by adding your name and website url not only gives credit where it's due, but allows users to find you, buy your fonts and/or hire you for custom work. Knowing that a real person, not just a faceless corporation, has created a font may dissuade some potential font pirates. If you want, under* Vendor URL, *type the website address such as myfonts.com or veer.com where users can purchase your fonts.*

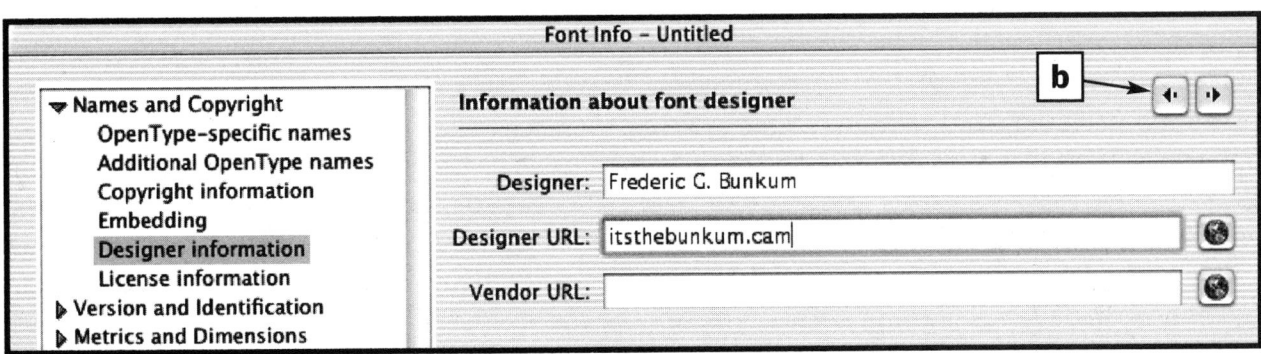

Click License Information. *Type here the terms of your legal agreement with the purchaser of the font. Typical font license agreements state that the font is not to be altered, resold, or given away and that it is to be used on just one computer, unless negotiated otherwise. Type in the* License URL *where the text of the full agreement may be found on your website (if you've got a website, otherwise leave blank).*

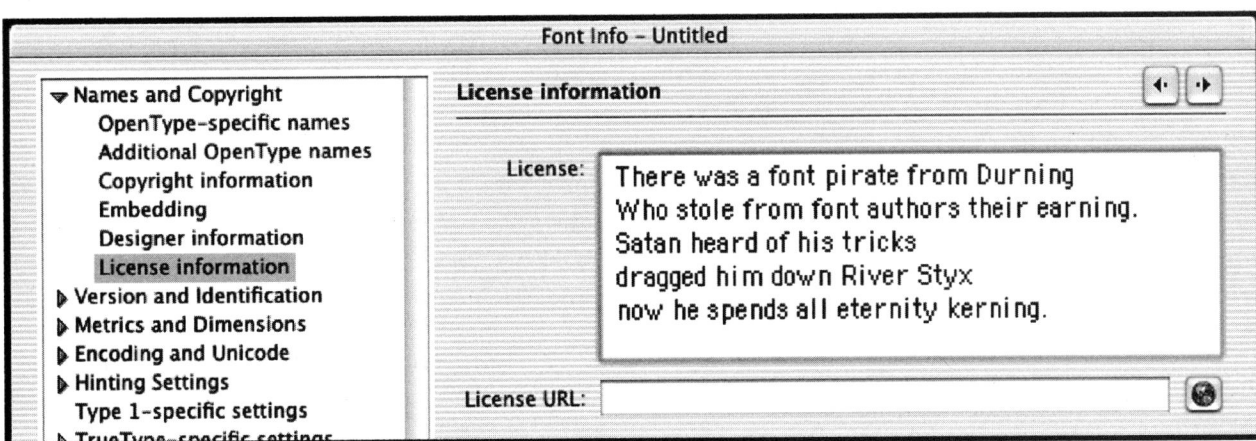

The next important section in the Font Info window is Key Identification Settings. The numbers and codes you put here will enable computer operating systems to distinguish between your font and others. Ultimately you will want to supply your font in a variety of formats to suit various users. That's why we usually include Type 1, TrueType, and OpenType data in our fonts to cover all bases when we finally generate them.

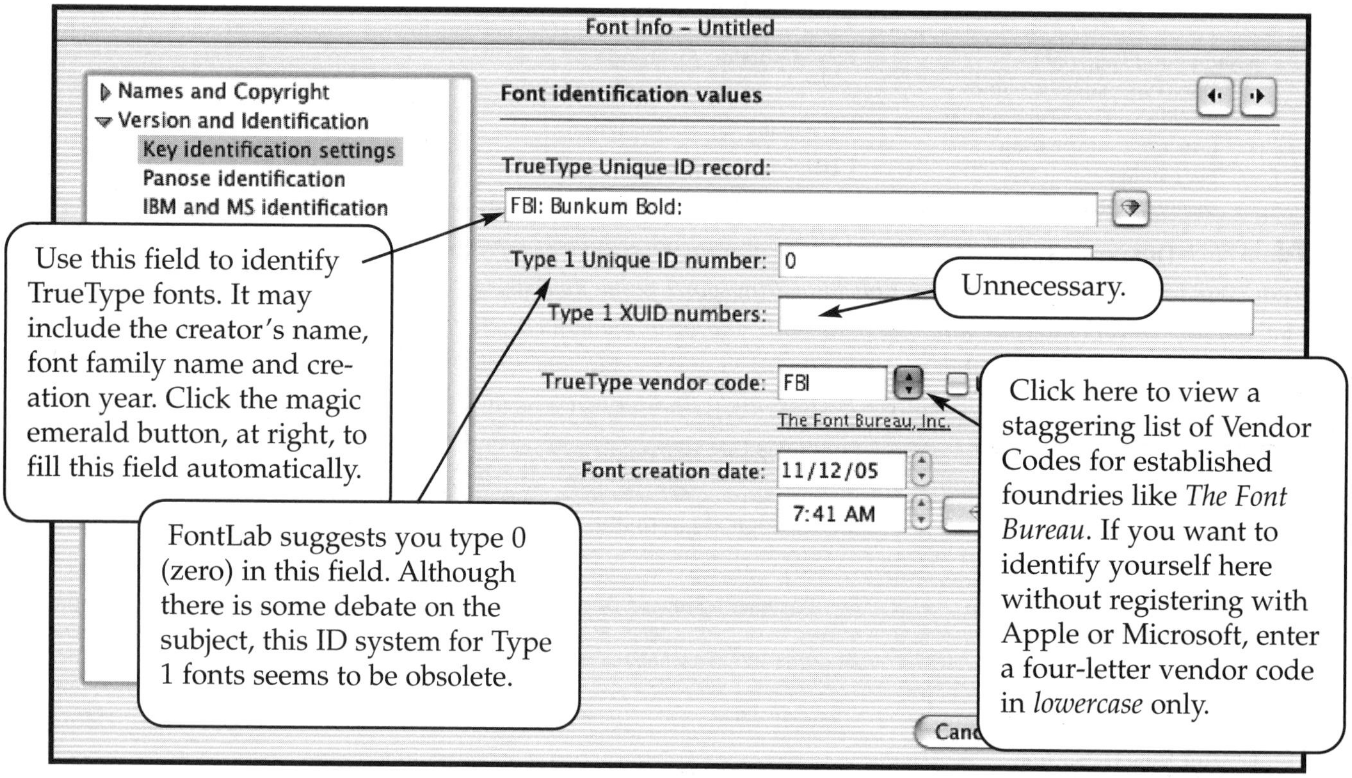

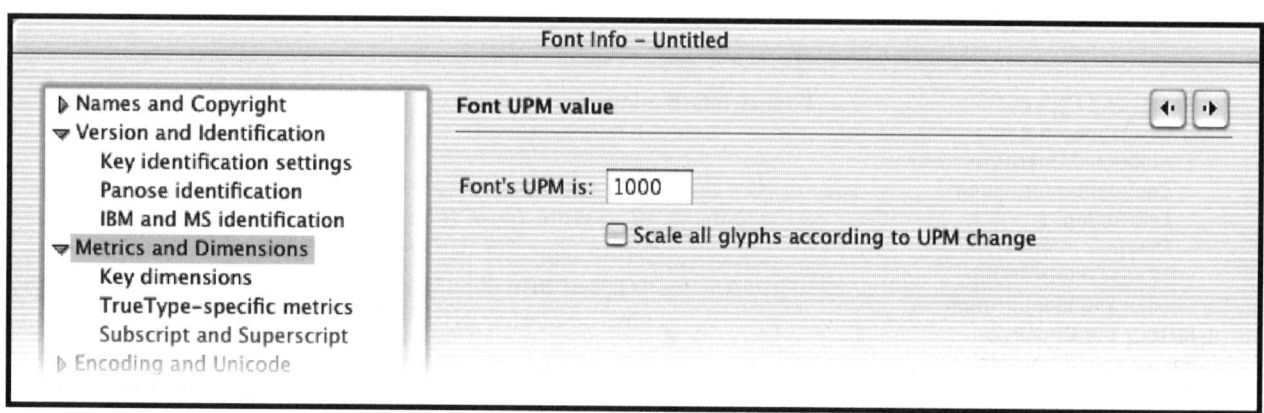

Move along to Metrics and Dimensions. UPM means "units per em." It refers to the size of the basic square in which we draw our glyphs. Just leave this at 1000 UPM regardless of the format you're creating. Only if you are specifically requested to do so by a client, for example, should you change the UPM to a different one, e.g. 2048. For information on TrueType font generation, see page 85.

Key Dimensions *shows mostly vertical measurements like how high our capital letters will extend compared with height of lower case letters, and how low our descenders, like the tails of g and y, will fall beneath the baseline. If you use a cap height standard of about 700, it'll mean that at a given point size, your font will most likely be the same height as other standard fonts so, in a paragraph setting, all fonts will appear at about equal size.*

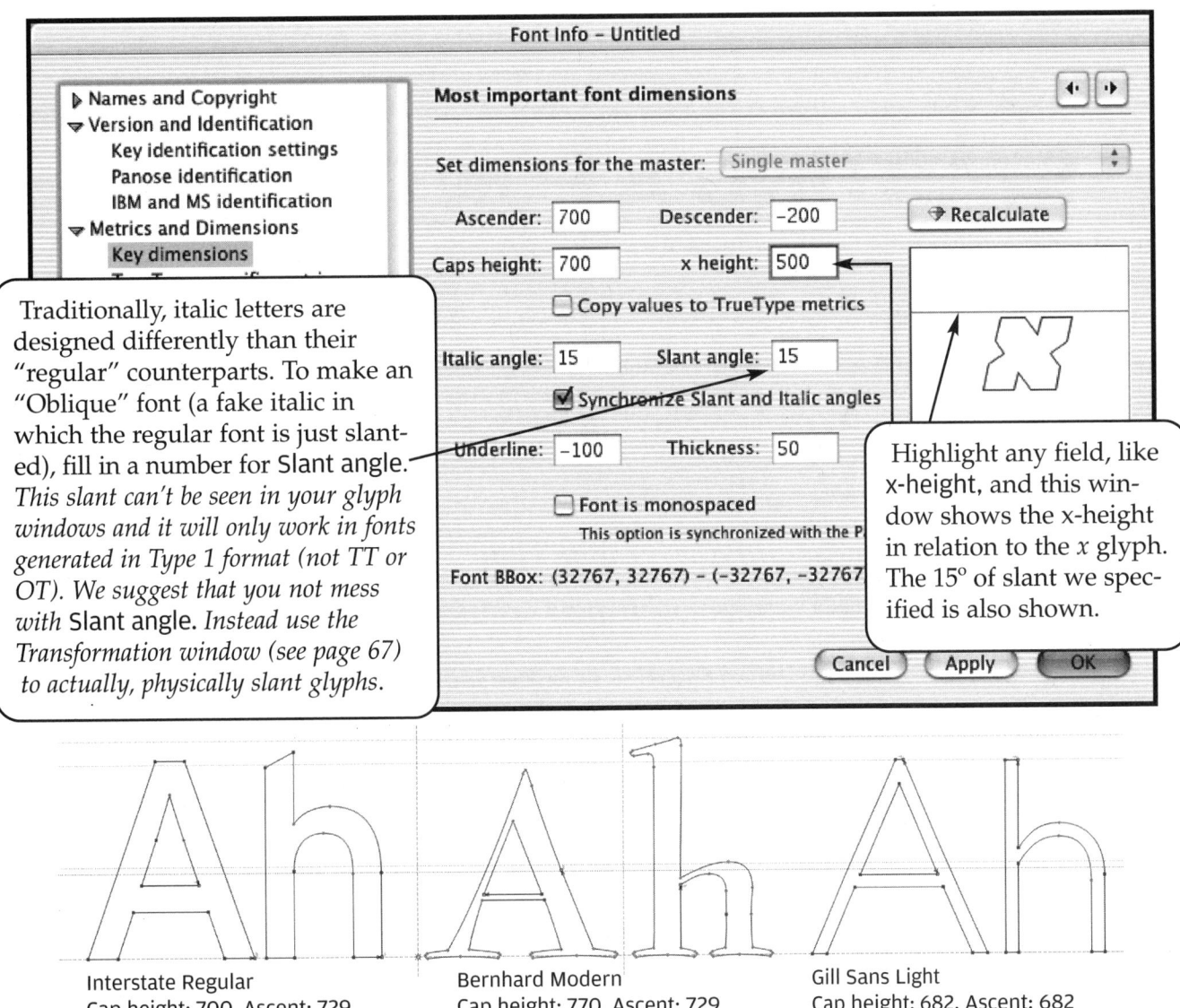

Traditionally, italic letters are designed differently than their "regular" counterparts. To make an "Oblique" font (a fake italic in which the regular font is just slanted), fill in a number for Slant angle. *This slant can't be seen in your glyph windows and it will only work in fonts generated in Type 1 format (not TT or OT). We suggest that you not mess with* Slant angle. *Instead use the Transformation window (see page 67) to actually, physically slant glyphs.*

Highlight any field, like x-height, and this window shows the x-height in relation to the *x* glyph. The 15° of slant we specified is also shown.

Interstate Regular
Cap height: 700, Ascent: 729

Bernhard Modern
Cap height: 770, Ascent: 729

Gill Sans Light
Cap height: 682, Ascent: 682

Cap height comparison
Characters from three different fonts were pasted into one Glyph Window. All three hover around the 700 cap height standard, but the chosen heights of ascent reveal interesting considerations of design. The highest point of Interstate's lower case vertical stem is slightly higher than cap A, but that's only to make both appear optically equal in height. Bernhard Modern's ascenders exceed cap height. In Gill Sans, cap and ascender height are the same. A font's key dimensions are never set in stone. Changes may be made later, either in the Font Info window shown above, or by dragging bars in the Metrics layer of a Glyph Window.

STARTING A FONT

Page **23**   *Getting Characters Into FontLab*

26   *Open an existing font*

27   *Selecting the right font to open*

27   *Open a Fontographer .fog file*

28   *Import glyphs from Illustrator*

30   *Import bitmap scans from Photoshop*

31   *In depth: Preparing scanned images*

33   *Make an outline into a background*

34   *Make bitmap scans with ScanFont*

39   *Autotraced characters in FontLab*

40   *Creating glyphs with a digital pen*

41   *The Brush tool and digital pen*

43   *Vector Paint tools*

45   *Tracing with Pen tool and digital tablet*

46   *How to trace a scan*

Getting character drawings into FontLab

Most likely you will use one of the following methods to input character drawings, or "glyphs" as FontLab calls them, into your font. Decide upon how you want to get character drawings into FontLab and skip right to the appropriate section. Another time, when you may want to use another method to import or initiate drawings, you can go to that appropriate section and fill in your understanding of an additional process.

Open An Existing Font
A great way to become familiar with FontLab applications is to open an existing font to study its structure and play around. If the font is one of your own that was designed with older font creation software, you can generate it in such a way as to bring it in to FontLab while still preserving its spacing and kerning.
See page 26

Import scans from Photoshop
Many of us like to start with something to guide us when we draw letter shapes. We may scan our own tight or rough sketches, top, or we may scan letters from an older source, like a book or magazine. If you base a font upon a type or lettering sample that is not your own, be sure you are not infringing upon someone else's property.
See page 30

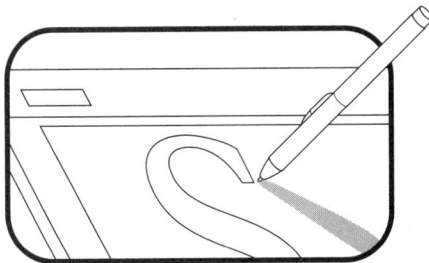

Create glyphs with a digital tablet and FONTLAB's Pen or Brush tools
Digital pen tablets offer a means to achieve freehand flourish and drawings that can resemble pencil, pen and brushwork drawn by hand. We may also use the digital pen to roughly trace our pencil sketches into FontLab, instead of scanning them.
See page 45

Import drawings from Illustrator
For those who are most comfortable drawing glyphs in a drawing program rather than in FontLab, there are just a few simple steps you must take to get your outline drawings pasted into FontLab.
See page 28

Import scans with ScanFont
ScanFont is a separate program from the folks at FontLab that lets you can scan alphabets, optimize the scans, automatically separate individual characters, and Autotrace them for export into FontLab, TypeTool or AsiaFont Studio.
See page 34

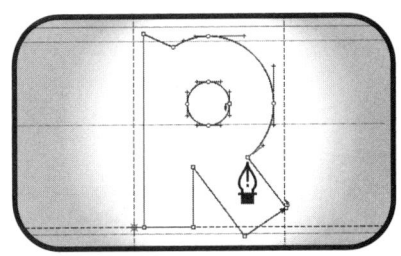

Draw glyphs in FontLab
The process of drawing, whether with pencil, digital pen tablet or mouse, usually involves previsualization. That is, we must start with some idea in our minds of the shapes we wish to create. This section explains the Drawing tool, bezier curves, selections and other aspects of drawing glyphs in FontLab applications.
See page 47

Open an existing font

We've suggested that opening a few preexisting fonts and studying them is a great way to get familiar with the FontLab environment. Remember, however, that it's illegal and/or immoral to modify, distribute or sell under a different name an existing font that isn't yours. That said, here are a few ways to open fonts.

The simplest way to open a font is to drag its icon on top of the FontLab icon, as seen at right. It doesn't matter whether the font itself or the FontLab icon or its alias is on the desktop or within a folder.

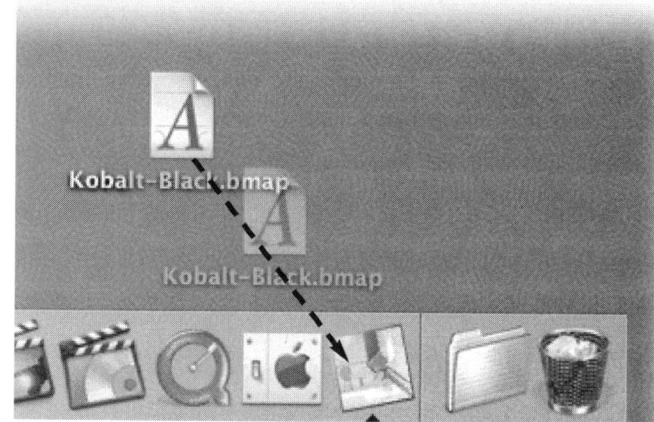

The most common way to open an existing font is to Open FontLab then go to FILE>Open (or Cmd-O Mac/Ctrl-O Win), locate your fonts folder (or wherever else you've stored fonts) and double-click to open a selected font.

Type 1 fonts contain two parts, either of which FontLab can open. However, the better choice may be to open the .bmap screen font (Mac) or .pfb (Win). See top of next page.

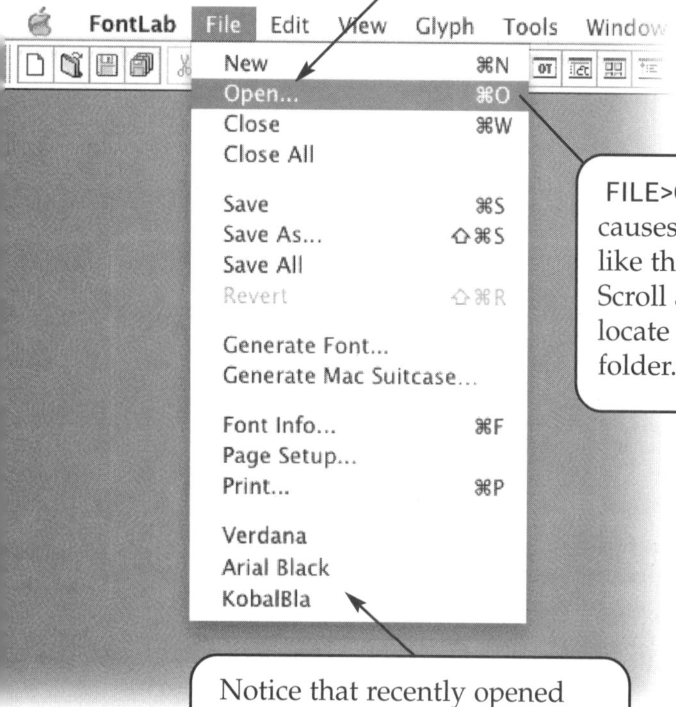

FILE>Open causes a window like this to open. Scroll around to locate your fonts folder.

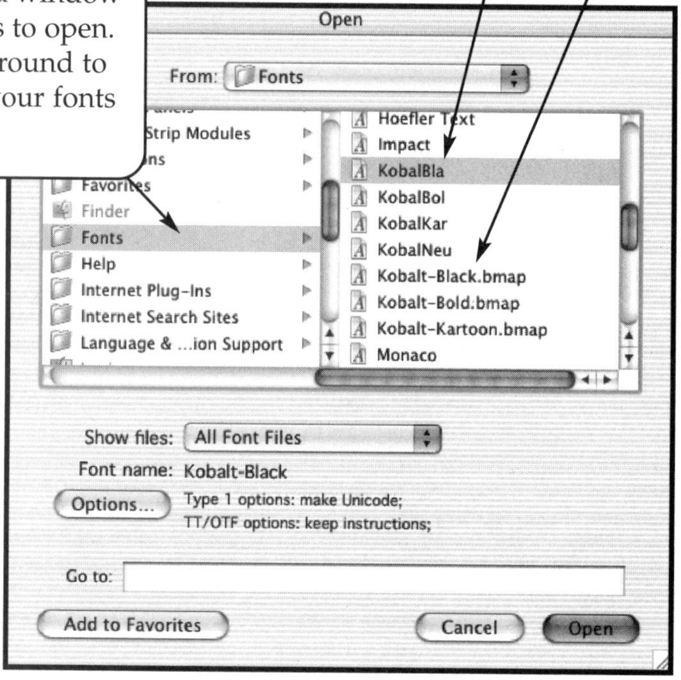

Notice that recently opened fonts and .vfb files are listed at the bottom of this menu. Reopen one by scrolling down to the font name.

Selecting the right font to open

If you're attempting to open an existing Mac Type 1 font in FontLab, it's better to open the screen font (.bmap, suitcase) rather than a printer font. When you open a Windows Type 1 (.pfb) font, be sure the corresponding .pfm or .afm file is in the same folder. Opening other formats is easy since they only have one file per font. In the Preview/Metrics window, shown below left and right, spacing and kerning are assigned. At **a**, only the M button is depressed so no kerning is displayed. At **b**, the K button has been depressed so kerning snaps into place closing up the huge gaps between letters. If you open an existing font from its printer half, depressing the K button will reveal that no kerning is present. For more about using the Preview/Metrics window, see pages 93-103.

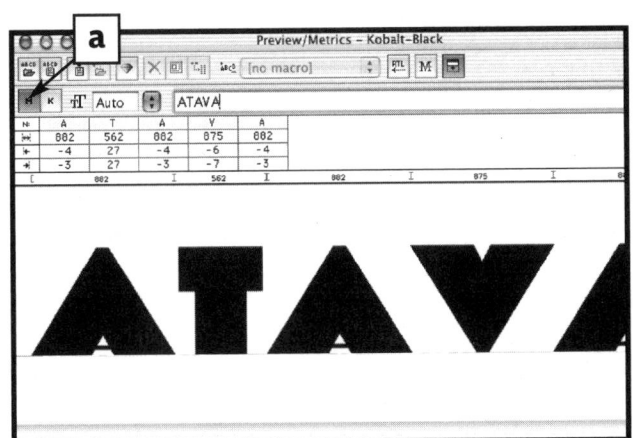
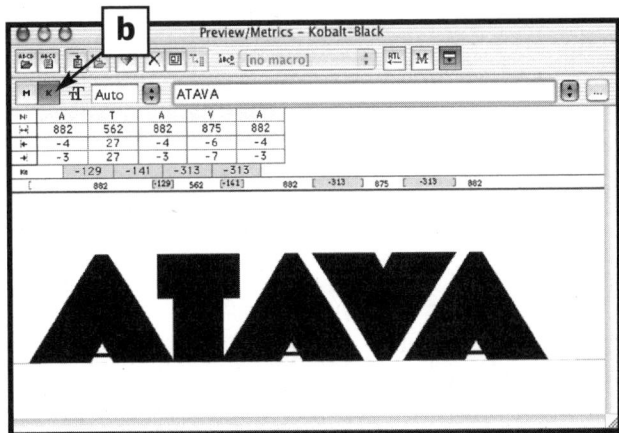

Open a Fontographer .fog file in FontLab

Macromedia's Fontographer font creation software, once the dominant force in the industry, has not been upgraded since 1996 and has become incompatible with Apple's OSX software. Many designers therefore want to convert old .fog files into FontLab's equivalent .vfb files. Unfortunately, Fontographer files cannot be directly imported into FontLab. But here's the workaround: Open a .fog file then go to FILE>Generate Font Files. Use the Fontographer settings as shown, left, to export a Postscript type 1 font for PC. Fontographer will generate four files of which only the .pfb will be useful to us. Open this .pfb file in FontLab and all the point information, along with spacing and kerning, will be preserved, though bitmap scans in the original .fog are not salvageable. However, BitFonter, a separate application from FontLab, Ltd. is designed to open and save bitmaps as separate fonts or as parts of outline fonts.

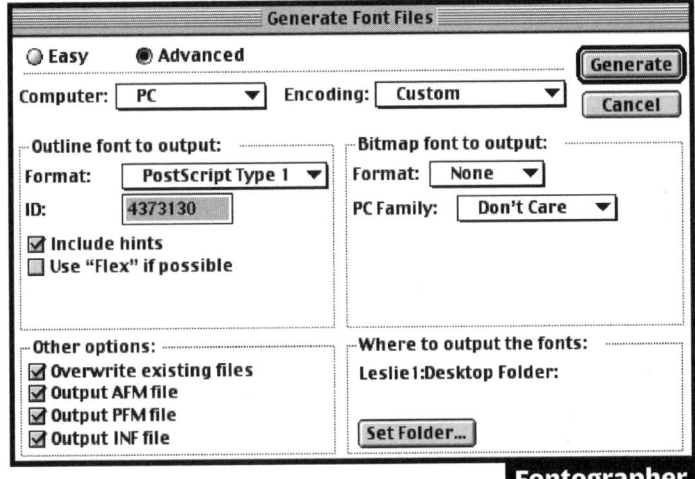

Import art from Illustrator: wrong way

If you are a font designer who prefers to draw characters in Adobe Illustrator, here's how to paste Illustrator art into FontLab. First, the following are some of the wrong ways to import Illustrator art into FontLab.

Illustrator

If you Copy drawings from Illustrator, left, then go to FontLab, right, open a Glyph window and Paste, the Illustrator art imports as a weird bitmap, too lousy even to be traced with the Pen tool.

Instead, go to Illustrator's Preferences file, right, (EDIT>Preferences> Files & Clipboard) and change the Clipboard to AICB; Preserve Paths.

This is a step in the **right** direction toward importing art from Illustrator into FontLab, but it is not the only necessary step.

> **Preferences**
> File Handling & Clipboard
> **Version Cue and Files**
> ☐ Enable Version Cue   (Tell Me More)
> ☑ Use Low Resolution Proxy for Linked EPS
> Update Links: [Ask When Modified]
> **Clipboard on Quit**
> Copy As: ☐ PDF
> ☑ AICB (no transparency support)
> ⦿ Preserve Paths
> ○ Preserve Appearance and Overprints
>
> (OK) (Cancel) (Previous) (Next)
>
> **Illustrator**

Now Copy from Illustrator, then go to FontLab, open a character window and Paste. As you can see, the characters import as vector paths, but in a seemingly arbitrary size and position in relation to the em square.

One solution to the problem of pasted art being too small might be to drag the characters to the baseline, **a**, select FontLab's Scale tool, **b**, and begin to scale the art to cap height, **c**. But this is not ideal. After all, you'd have to scale every subsequent character you paste into FontLab to that exact degree, so scaling or positioning inconsistencies might result.

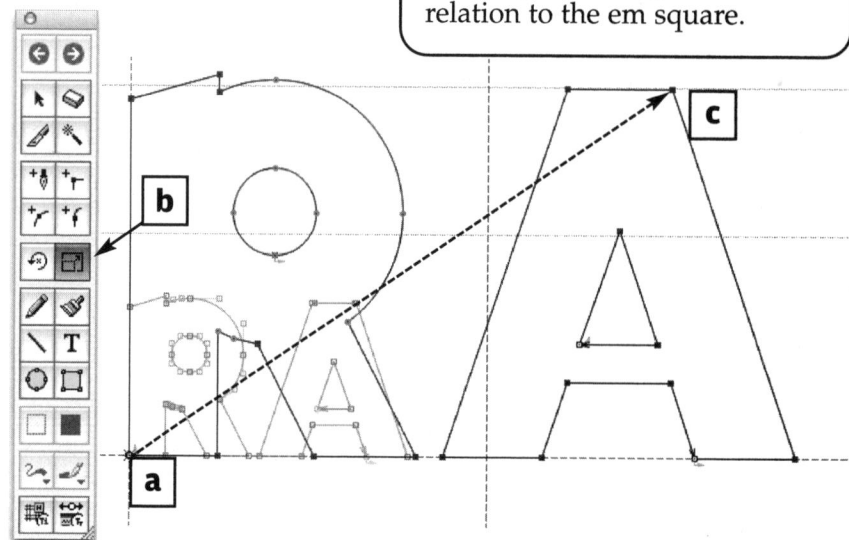

Right way: 1. In FontLab, below, draw a box with the Rectangle tool*, **a**, (or just draw

a line) from baseline to cap height, **b**. The width of the box is not important. Copy this box and Paste it into Illustrator, **c**. The box from FontLab pastes tall—almost as high as an 11"x 8.5" page in landscape.

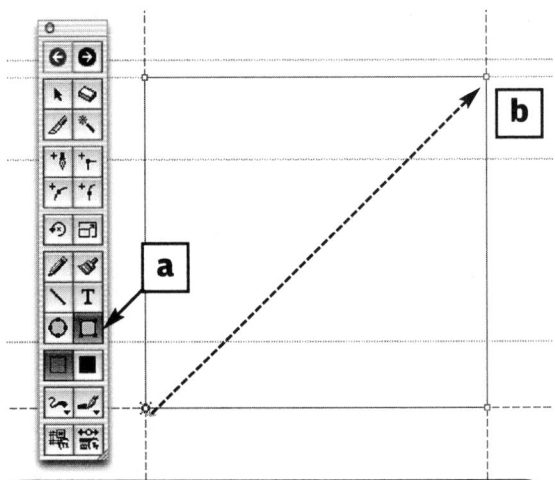

(***Rectangle tool disabled?** *For constant access to the full toolbar, open* Preferences>Glyph Window *and* **enable** Do not show Glyph toolbar and Vector Paint toolbar. *Checking the box means toolbars* **will** *show.*)

2. In Illustrator, select the characters to be pasted into FontLab and move them into alignment with the lower left corner of the big rectangle. Use the Scale or Free Transform tool (hold the Shift key to maintain proportions) and drag the letters, **d**, up to cap height, which is the top of the rectangle. Copy the character art and Paste into FontLab, **e**. The art will come in at cap height. Draw all subsequent letters in Illustrator to the same scale, they'll paste into FontLab at the proper size.

Note: *Drag the 0-point of Illustrator's rulers to the letters' baseline so they will paste to FontLab's baseline.*

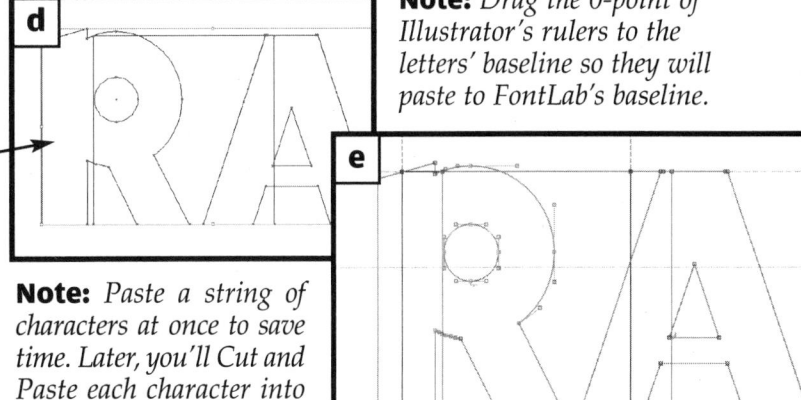

Note: *Paste a string of characters at once to save time. Later, you'll Cut and Paste each character into its own Glyph window.*

Illustrator into FontLab

Here's a slightly different method for importing art from Illustrator CS (or Illustrator 9+).

1. In FontLab, go to Preferences>General and click to enable Do not rescale EPS files.

2. In Illustrator CS, go to Preferences>Units & Display Performance. Change General units to points *(1 point is equal to 1 unit in FontLab).*

3. Also in Illustrator's Preferences go to File handling & Clipboard and change the Clipboard to AICB/Preserve Paths.

4. In Illustrator, make a rectangle 700 x 700

points and scale your drawings to that height.

5. Assign any kind of fill to all your Illustrator drawings (FontLab won't import paths with neither fill nor stroke).

6. Press Cmd-/Ctrl-R to show Illustrator's Rulers. Drag the rulers' 0-point to the baseline of your letters so they will paste at FontLab's baseline. Select then Copy your Illustrator art.

7. Open a FontLab Glyph window and Paste.

You can now Copy/Paste between FontLab and Illustrator without re-scaling your outlines.

(Import Illustrator files with ScanFont, see page 36.)

Import bitmap scans from Photoshop

Many font designers find it easier to base their drawings of font characters on a scan or sketch than to begin blindly placing points in mid-space. Here's how bitmap scans may be added to Glyph windows for tracing.

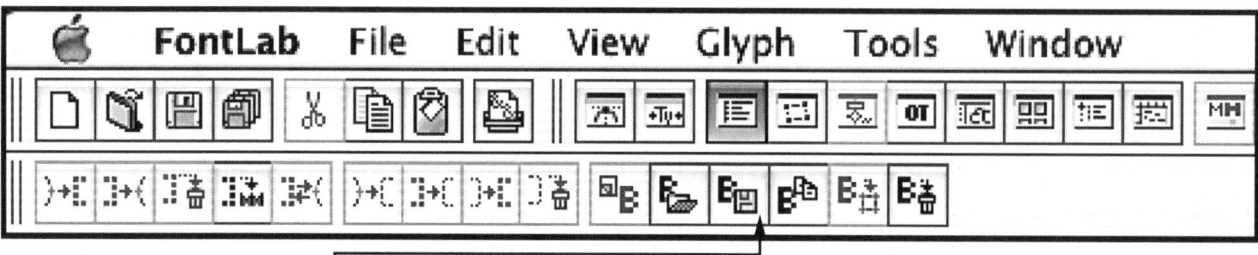

When a Photoshop image, such as a .tiff, .bmp or .jpeg, is pasted into FontLab, it is automatically placed in the Background layer. Go to VIEW>Toolbars>Templates to open the palette of icons (above, with all the bitmap *B*s) relating to the Background layer.

Next, you'll need a scan of something, like these initials, below, taken from an old book. First, straighten the scanned image so you won't be bringing crooked characters into FontLab. Use guides to ensure the baseline of all letters are straight. (more about preparing scans can be found in my book, *Logo, Font and Lettering Bible*).

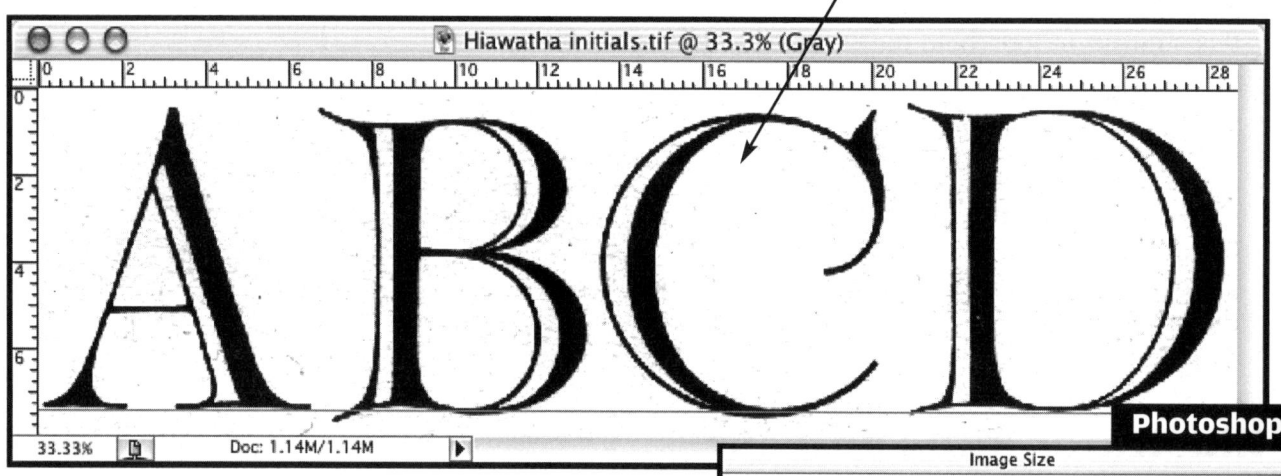

Note: When scanning an image, let the height of caps come out at 700 pts (9.722 inches). However, like the fancy serifs above, many parts of letters stick out beyond the base and cap lines. Therefore, the total height of your Photoshop scan should be more than 700 points—like perhaps 975 points—as in the Photoshop Image Size window (IMAGE>Image Size), right. Though a 72 dpi scan resolution would be too low for print usage, if a scan is the right height, 72 dpi produces an amply sharp and clear bitmap in FontLab.

In depth: Preparing scanned images

Images intended for tracing must be scanned at a large-enough size and resolution to ensure fairly smooth edges. Otherwise we are always wondering which part of the bitmappy, stair-stepped edge is true. Right, at **a**, smoother image than **b**, which was scanned too small then scaled up to cap height in FontLab.

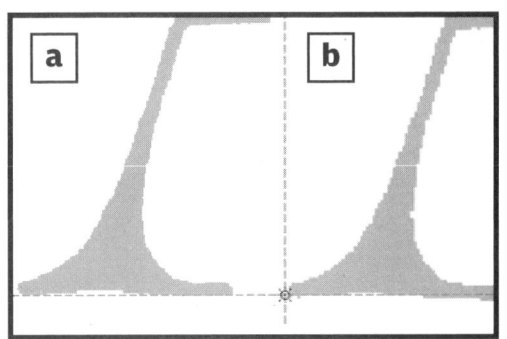

Above, wood type from an old ad will succumb to the scanner's nondiscriminating gaze; the letters to become bitmap background images for tracing in FontLab. I plan to use the smaller, underlined caps as my lower case. Of course, I will have to invent the missing letters

1. Before scanning, measure cap height of original. Ours is less than one inch (25.4 mm). It will eventually have to be almost 10 inches tall at 72 dpi. to paste into FL at proper cap height. Your original art may be larger, but shouldn't be smaller or detail will suffer, as my own murky example above reveals.

The idea is to set the scanner's resolution high enough so that the scan may later be enlarged to FontLab cap height, and res decreased to 72 dpi without increasing file size much or at all.

2. Open your scanning software. Marquee only the area you want to scan. Omit superfluous margin area as it needlessly increases file size.

3. Scan in gray scale, **a**, at sufficient resolution, **b**, for later enlargement (see chart, far right). Don't scan below 300 dpi because the pixel information gathered may be insufficient to ensure a good image (even though dpi will be automatically reduced to 72 when the scan enters FontLab).

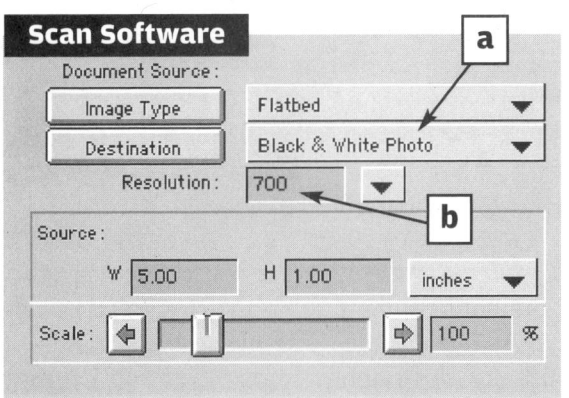

Cap height	scan res,
1"/25.4 mm	700
2"/50.8 mm	350
3"/76.2 mm	300

(Never scale up a scan, e.g.: 200%, without also increasing scanning resolution. Excess file info can be discarded, but insufficient info makes the image quality suffer.)

Preparing Scans continues on next page

VULCANITE EMRY WHS.

4. When the scan is made, as above, adjust it by using Photoshop's Curves or Brightness/Contrast filter to remove gray background, pump up the contrast and maybe add some Unsharp Mask to sharpen it. I compacted my scan by removing redundant letters in order to reduce file size and conserve hard drive space.

5. Now press Cmd- or Ctrl-N to open a blank New Document in Photoshop. Make the width and height 700 points and the resolution 72 dpi, as at right. Hit OK. *The idea is to establish actual cap height, then paste our scan in and scale it by eye to this height (without resorting to higher mathematics!).*

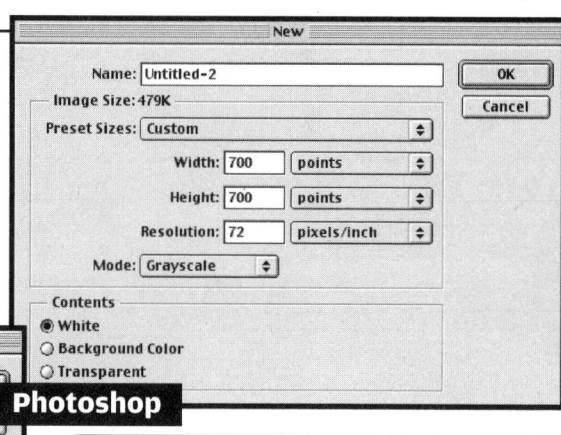

6. In the new Photoshop document, Select All, then Fill it with any gray. Go to IMAGE>Canvas Size and increase the height and width of the document to allow ample room for pasting your scan.

7. Paste your scan into the new document. Press Cmd- or Ctrl-T to scale your scan to cap height, below, according to the height of the 700-point (cap-height) gray rectangle, **a**. Hit Return to complete the Transform. In the Layers Option palette, Flatten Image. Marquee-select one or more letters, Copy them and Paste them into FontLab.

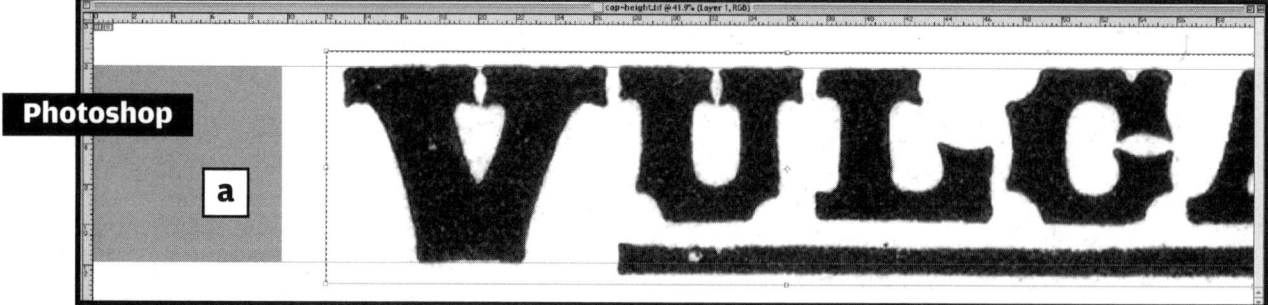

Notes: If you require several scans to get your characters into the computer, make sure you follow the same procedure—using the same numerical settings—in processing each scan. Paste the contents of each scan into the document with the gray cap-height box, as above. It is usually preferable to paste strings of letters, rather than one at a time, and perhaps even to draw all letters in the string in the same Glyph window to compare them as you draw, then paste them individually into their own cells.

Make an outline into a Background

This might be useful if you wanted to refer to the original character shape while altering its contour or if you were using the existing font as a template to create a different style of font, but with similar proportions. This would also be a way to get Illustrator drawings, pasted into FontLab, to become bitmap backgrounds.

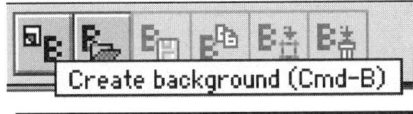

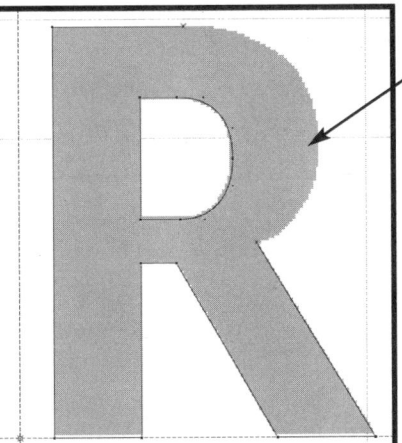

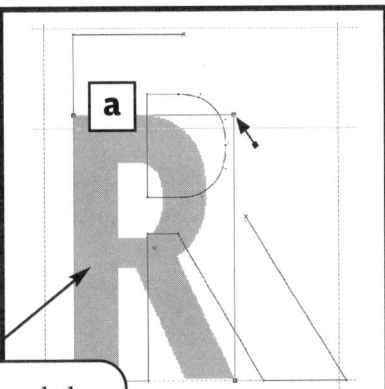

1. Click the Create Background icon and a bitmap copy of the Character drawing in the Outline layer forms in the background layer. Notice that the bitmap is rough and doesn't seem to perfectly adhere to the contour of the outline. Let's fix it. Double click anywhere on the bitmap background.

2. A four-handled box forms around the bitmap. Grab a handle and drag to scale the background, but to retain original proportions—unlike at **a**—hold down Shift.

3. Here is the "refitted" bitmap. The scaling method described is the same for any bitmap background, whether created from the outline layer, as above, or from a Photoshop scan.

Bitmap scan tips

Flatten Photoshop files containing layers or the resulting paste into FontLab, **a**, will be unusable. Images that are not 100% black, **b**, will paste funky. Darken up grayed images with Photoshop's Brightness/Contrast and they will paste nicely, **c**. A Background bitmap, **d**, created in FontLab from an outline drawing (as described at the top of this page) with Create Background will be rendered at a less satisfactory resolution than a bitmap background pasted from Photoshop (**c**). One way to tighten **d**'s res would be to scale the outline to 400%, hit Create Background, then scale both background and outline back down to 25%.

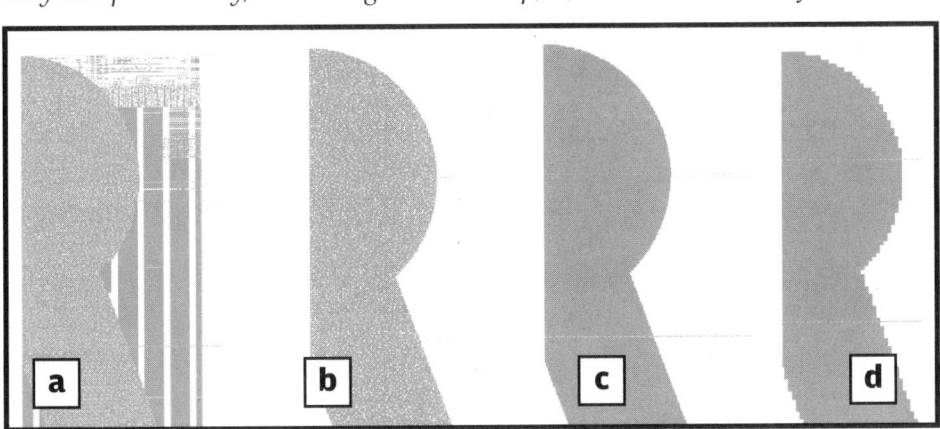

Make bitmap scans with ScanFont

*F*or automatization of the scan/import process, there is no faster method than through ScanFont, a separate product from FontLab. The following instructions do not include mention of all ScanFont's many sophisticated capabilities. Our goal is to show how to simply and quickly scan, prepare, and export bitmap character images into FontLab apps.

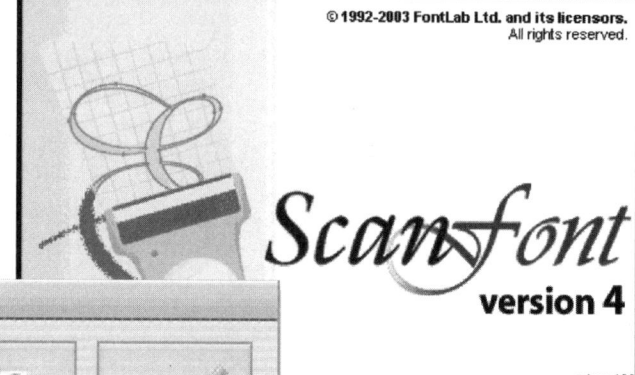

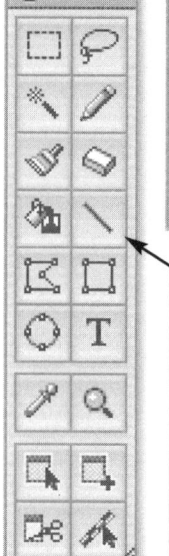

Double-click the The ScanFont icon to open the program. The toolbar, left, contains drawing tools and image editing tools such as eraser and paintbrush to create or improve scanned images before importing them into FontLab. These tools are similar to those found in Photoshop and Illustrator, which could be preferred choices for accomplishing these same tasks, especially if you are already familiar with the Adobe products.

This is the intuitive SCANFONT Workflow toolbar, a brilliant concept with endless possibilities for emulation by other software programs. This toolbar makes using the program as easy as **a**, **b**, **c**.

Tips for Preparing images to be scanned

• Carefully line up the book page or paper sheet straight against the scanner's glass edge. If you're scanning an image that is printed crooked on the page (not uncommon), try turning the page slightly. Trick: Xerox a book page, then draw a thin, straight line (not touching any characters) on the page. Use a bleed-through marker or press hard with a ballpoint pen so the line can be seen on the reverse of the sheet and then line it up with the scanner edge. Or, if the image on the page is not aligned with the paper itself, trim one edge of the paper straight in alignment with the characters.

• Size of original character image can be as small as 0.5 inch (1.25 cm). Larger characters will produce a cleaner image but making letters larger than 4 inches (10.16 cm) is not necessary for good results. Scan smaller characters at 600 dpi, larger ones at 300 or 400 dpi.

• Paper should be white with a strong black image, pencil or thin-point pen sketches won't show up well and the resulting scan may have a broken-up image. Trick: play with the density settings on a copier to darken the lines of a weak image or to lighten a gray background before scanning.

• Scan in gray scale, not RGB color, for a smaller file. Color is irrelevant, anyway, in outline fonts.

• Make sure no two characters in your image-to-be-scanned touch or overlap one another because ScanFont will assume them to be a single character.

Use ScanFont to access your regular Twain scanning software:

1. Place your original in the scanner and hit Scan-Font's New button (in Mac OS X) or Scan button (OS 9) to start up your Twain scanning software.

Note: ScanFont can't scan in Mac OSX. So Quit ScanFont, click on its icon, hit Cmd-I to open the Info window. Then check the "Open in the Classic environment" box.

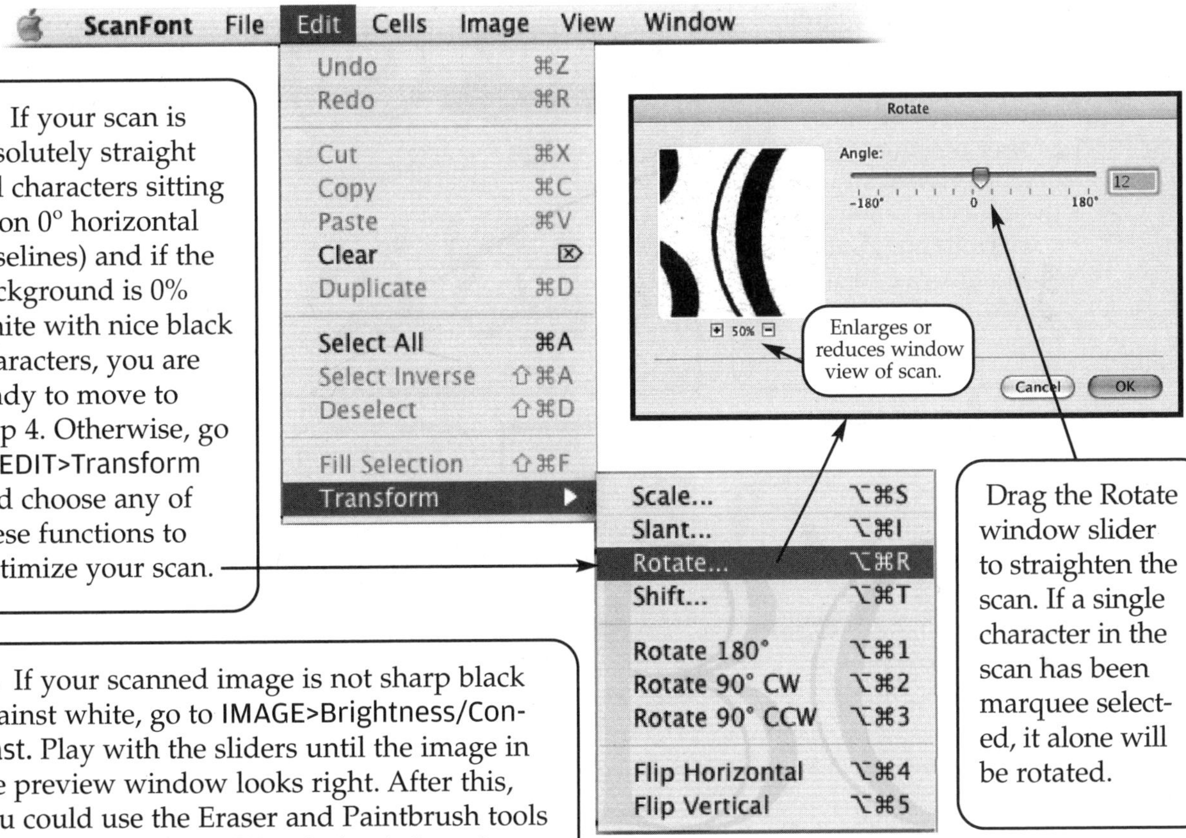

![apple]	**ScanFont**	File	**Edit**	Cells	Image	View	Window

Undo	⌘Z
Redo	⌘R
Cut	⌘X
Copy	⌘C
Paste	⌘V
Clear	⌫
Duplicate	⌘D
Select All	⌘A
Select Inverse	⇧⌘A
Deselect	⇧⌘D
Fill Selection	⇧⌘F
Transform ▶	

2. If your scan is absolutely straight (all characters sitting upon 0° horizontal baselines) and if the background is 0% white with nice black characters, you are ready to move to step 4. Otherwise, go to EDIT>Transform and choose any of these functions to optimize your scan.

Rotate window: Angle: 12, –180° ... 0 ... 180°. 50%.

Enlarges or reduces window view of scan.

Scale...	⌥⌘S
Slant...	⌥⌘I
Rotate...	⌥⌘R
Shift...	⌥⌘T
Rotate 180°	⌥⌘1
Rotate 90° CW	⌥⌘2
Rotate 90° CCW	⌥⌘3
Flip Horizontal	⌥⌘4
Flip Vertical	⌥⌘5

Drag the Rotate window slider to straighten the scan. If a single character in the scan has been marquee selected, it alone will be rotated.

3. If your scanned image is not sharp black against white, go to IMAGE>Brightness/Contrast. Play with the sliders until the image in the preview window looks right. After this, you could use the Eraser and Paintbrush tools to remove spots and fill in holes (otherwise, a spot may end up in its own cell, autotraced).

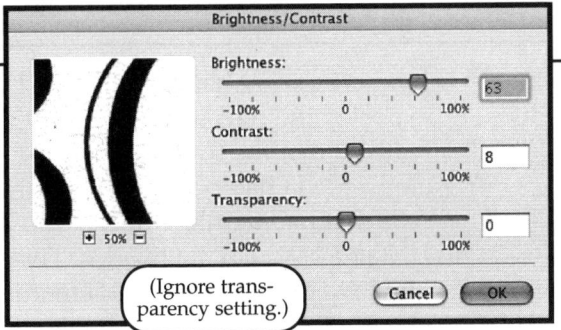

Brightness/Contrast — Brightness: 63, –100% 0 100%. Contrast: 8, –100% 0 100%. Transparency: 0, –100% 0 100%. 50%.

(Ignore transparency setting.)   Cancel   OK

Skip steps 1 through 3 by hitting "Open" in the Workflow palette and scrolling to a previously-scanned and optimized Photoshop image (tiff, pict or png) to import into ScanFont.

Note: *An abundance of practical and arcane details concerning ScanFont may be had by downloading the free ScanFont .pdf manual from www.fontlab.com.*

Using ScanFont continues on next page

4. If your scan is optimized, hit Separate in the Workflow palette to "auto split" the individual characters in the scan into separate cells as shown below. The Separate Shapes window (not shown) will open. In the Separation Method pulldown, select Book Smart (try other options too, or read about them in the ScanFont .pdf manual). Click OK.

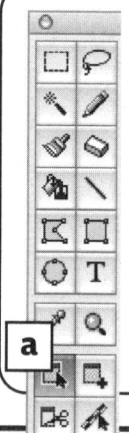

5. Choose the Cell tool, **a**, so you can drag the baseline bars appearing under each cell to a proper position so all characters will sit upon the baseline when imported into FontLab. Shift-click two or more cells to drag their baselines simultaneously.

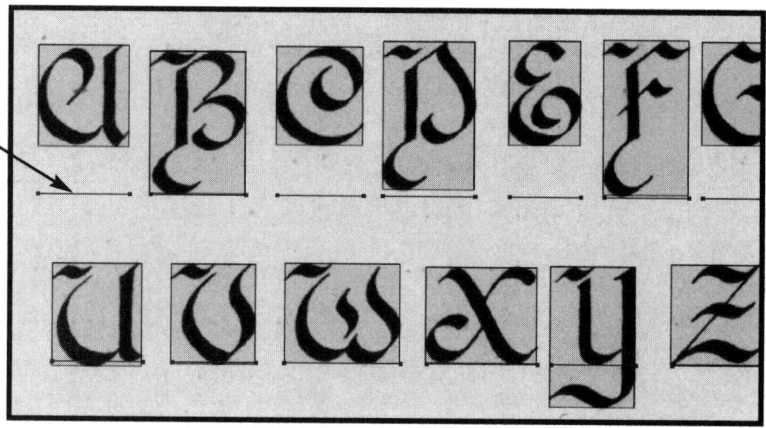

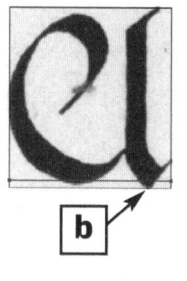   

Left, a few letters with their baselines raised. The Cell tool is seen under letter *D*. Allow for "overshoot," the degree to which pointy shapes, **b**, and rounded shapes, **c**, should extend past baseline and cap height to visually appear level with characters whose stem ends align square and flat against those guidelines.

ScanFont can recognize that the letter *i* and its dot belong in one cell as a single character. But beware of the occasional oversight. For example, at right are Adobe Illustrator vector letters brought into ScanFont. (Save the Illustrator doc as .eps, click Open in the ScanFont Workflow palette. ScanFont does not autotrace in this case because the vectors already exist; it just exports your paths into correct FontLab slots.)

But here's what happened: After I'd exported the cells to FontLab, left, I realized that the two narrow bars alongside H had been given separate cells that had naturally fallen into the *H, I* and *J* slots in the FontLab Font window. Back in ScanFont, I marqueed *H* with its three cells and went to Cells>Merge cells and then I re-exported to Fontlab, this time successfully.

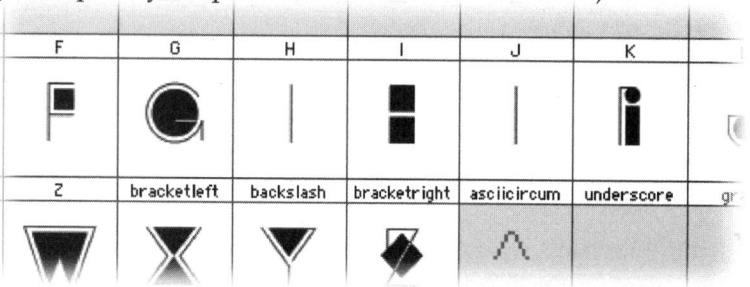

F	G	H	I	J	K

z	bracketleft	backslash	bracketright	asciicircum	underscore	gr

Placing ScanFont characters into FontLab.

6. Choose the **Scale** tool, **d**, to check cap height relative to font height. Drag the tool so its 0 point aligns with your chosen baseline. If the number 7 is not aligned with cap height, place your cursor within the bar at number 10 til it becomes an arrow and (hold the Shift key) drag the bar up or down, **e** until the 7 aligns with tops of caps.

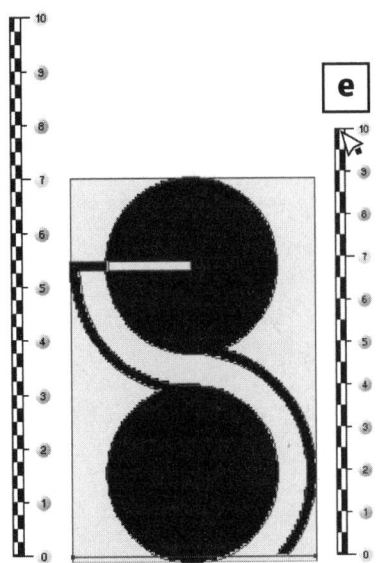

To Scale one or more letters differently than the others (for instance, if one letter was drawn too large and needs reduction), click a cell to select it, then drag the **Scale** tool up or down.

So: When *no* cells are selected, changes to the Scale tool apply to all cells. But when one or more cells are selected and the Scale tool is adjusted, the change applies just to those characters. The rest retain the scaling applied to the "group."

7. Before you finally Export you must tell SCANFONT where its seeds will be sewn. Go to FILE>Preferences>FontLab Server. Click Use and hit the Select button. This will allow you to search your hard drive for FONTLAB, TYPETOOL or ASIAFONT STUDIO and Choose one of them as the program to receive the SCANFONT Background bitmaps and autotraced contours. Then click OK.

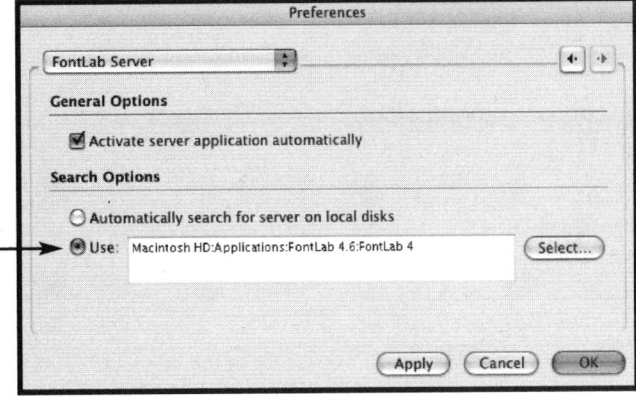

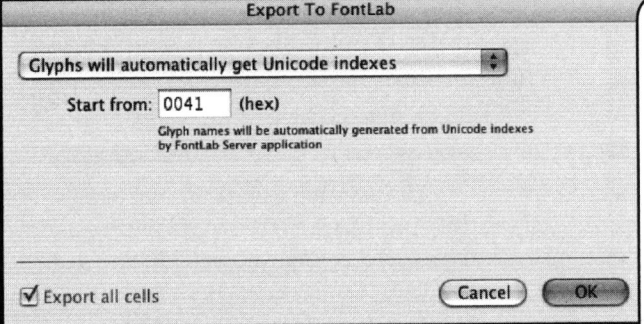

8. Hit Export button in the Workflow palette. The Export To FontLab panel, left, comes up offering the possibility to assign names to the cells for identification when exported. This means that each of the characters will end up in its own correct slot in the Font window.

The most reliable way to do this is to choose the top selection, Glyphs will automatically..., shown at left, and type in the unicode that the first character in your scanned sequence will "Start from." For example, the unicode for character *A* is 0041; *a* is 0061; and *!* is 0021.

Note: If the characters in your scan are in random order—not sequential like *A, B, C,* or *5, 6, 7,* etc.—you can always manually move them around to their proper Font Window slots, so the above step is not essential (though it is an efficient timesaver).

Using ScanFont continues on next page

9. The final step before your scans get exported is the Tracing Options window, right. Skip Luminosity unless your scan is RGB (scanning in grayscale is always preferable).

Under the little preview window, Click **+** to enlarge the image to 200%. Then, when you experiment with Trace tolerance and other sliders you'll be better able to observe which arrangement seems best. These sliders may also be left at their default settings. Click OK.

Happy Medium: The more points (also called "nodes") in your autotraced outlines, the more accurate will be the tracing. However, too many excess nodes can be a pain to remove.

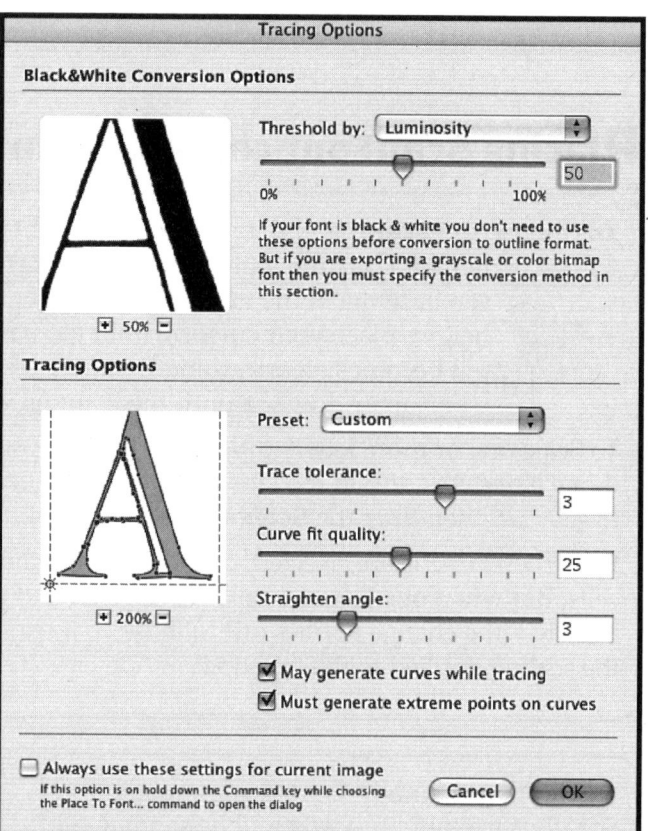

SCANFONT will now Open the target FONTLAB application, and create a new font with the new characters and their bitmaps in place in the font window, as shown below. Or you can have ScanFont export into any currently open font.

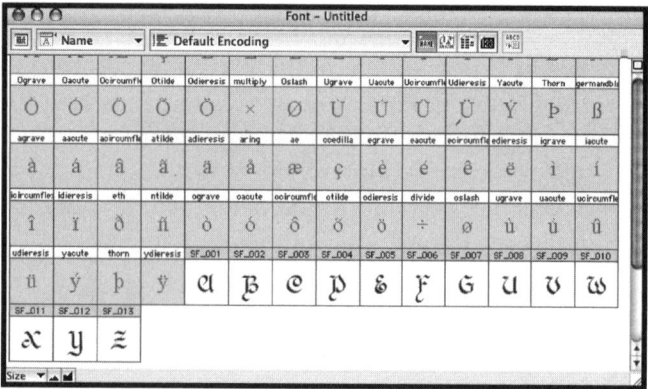

Will two or more scans be required to get all your characters into the FontLab application? Just be sure to scan each time at the same size and resolution, follow the same steps, and use the same settings as you export additional character cells.

10. If you filled in the Start From field in the Export To FontLab window (page 37), your autotraced sequence of cells—and their accompanying bitmap scans in the Background layer—will fill the appropriate FontLab slots, as shown above.

If you left the Start From field blank, your characters will appear at the bottom of the Font window, left. Then drag (or cut and paste) them into their proper slots.

Drag/Drop Option for exporting:
In ScanFont, click on a cell to select it, then drag and drop it onto a character slot in an open FontLab Font window.

Autotraced characters in FontLab.

Despite the resolution quality of the Background image, **a**, that ScanFont imports into FontLab, the program's autotraced vector outlines, **b**, are excellent. Using only the default trace settings has resulted in very few excess nodes , and those present are correctly placed in "extrema" (that is, at the extreme NORTH/SOUTH/EAST/WEST edges of the curves), so our editing of the outline will now be relatively easy.

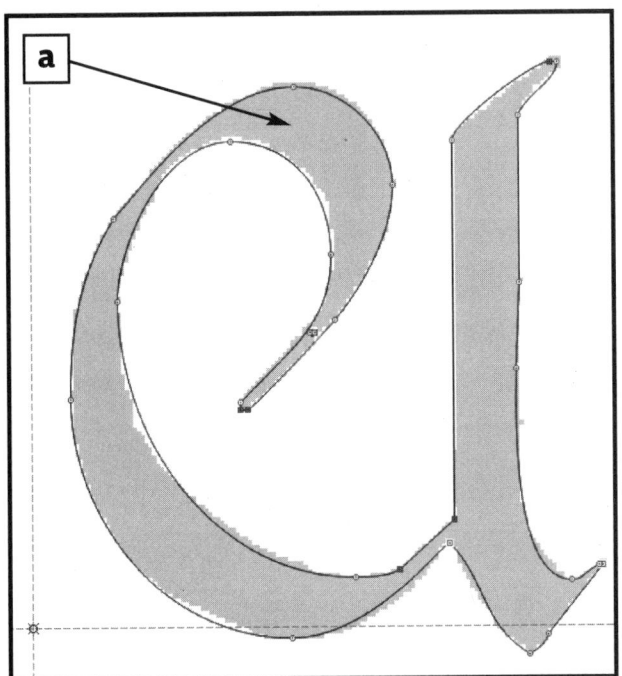

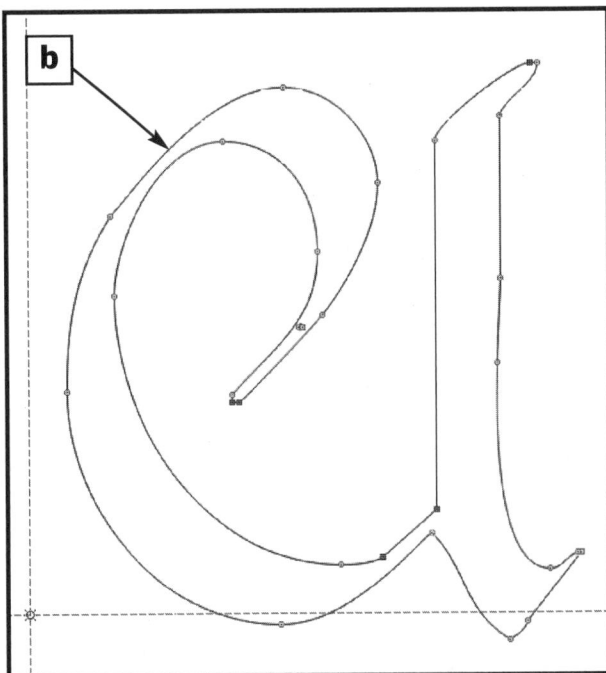

Many would stop here, consider the characters done, and move on to spacing and kerning. But autotracing, even at its best, rarely produces adequate point placement and lettershapes. When we are working from scans of old logos and fonts, or from hand lettering found in old books or magazines, remember that such examples—for all their spontaneous flair—are typically sloppy and imprecise in execution. Compared with lettering, high-quality, modern fonts require precision. And stroke widths, angles and proportions must usually be more regimented and consistent in order to achieve an even "color" when typeset. At **c**, right, my improvements to the autotraced contour involved removing redundant points and aligning almost-straight lines, sharpening corners by removing bezier handles from corner nodes, equalizing widths and angles where strokes become thin, improving interior and exterior curves, and so on. See pages 46, 50–53 for more.

Creating glyphs with a digital pen tablet

Frankly Speaking...

"**F**riends, if you've ever tried to draw with a mouse or track-ball, you know just how clumsy and imprecise that can be. Take it from me, a seasoned professional: A digital tablet is a wise addition to any graphic arts computer set-up. It doesn't have to be large. A modest 6 x 8-inch model has long served me well. Some designers—perhaps even you yourself—eschew the mouse entirely for the digital pen. And if you are experiencing nagging carpal tunnels, you can 'toggle' between pen and mouse to offset repetitive motion problems."

There are several reasons you might want to input character drawings into FontLab with a digital pen tablet (such as a Wacom tablet): **1.** *To use the* Brush *tool to create script, casual, handwriting or funky fonts;* **2.** *To trace your own sketches with the* Pen *tool, especially if they were drawn too loosely or lightly to scan well.* **3.** *To "input" a single letter sketch quickly, rather than scanning it; and* **4.** *To capture an elusive curving letter shape with the ease of hand movement when you just can't seem to make the bezier curves do what you want. We'll explore these procedures in the following pages.*

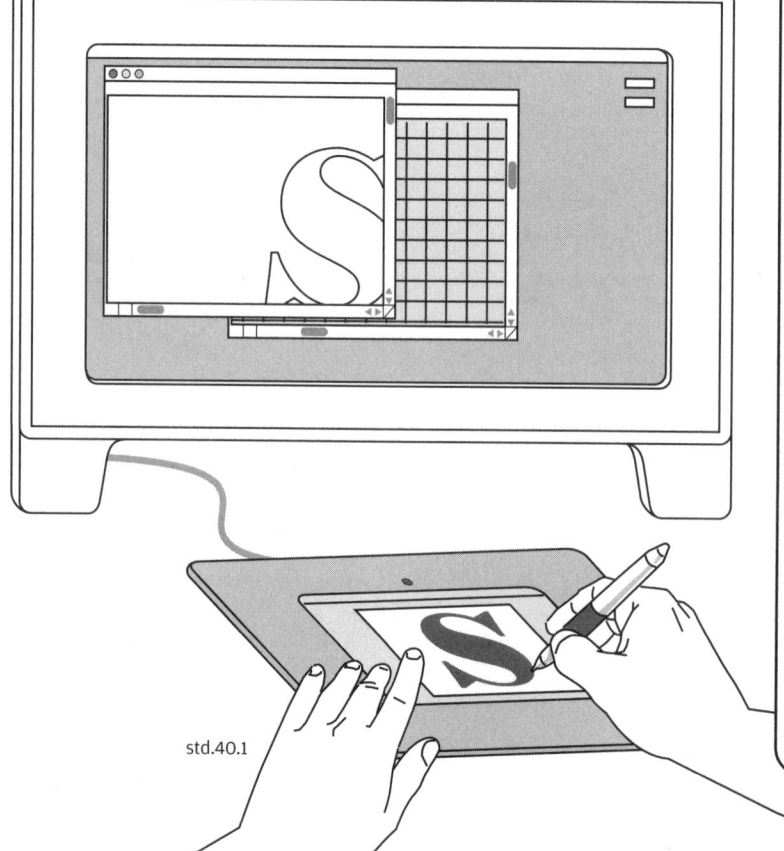

std.40.1

Before using your digital tablet, open its Control Panel and select either the Proportional or One To One aspect mode.

Position your printed image or sketch on the tablet straight. Before choosing FontLab's Pen, Brush or Drawing tools, use the digital pen to touch the extreme edges of the sketch to make sure all points fall within the open Glyph window's limits (as seen in the standard technical diagram at left).

Otherwise, you will have to stop drawing in mid-sketch when the Pen goes off the window edge. Reposition your sketch so that the entire drawing can be done within the window's limits (you can also open the Glyph window to its fullest extent for more room to draw).

Brush tool and digital pen tablet

Aside from dipping a real brush into ink, the second best way to achieve the look of brush lettering is to use the Brush tool found in the Vector Paint toolbar (VIEW>Toolbars>Vector Paint). Sure, you can use the vector paint tools without a digital tablet, but by using a mouse to draw, you'll probably get shakier strokes, which just means more curve editing later.

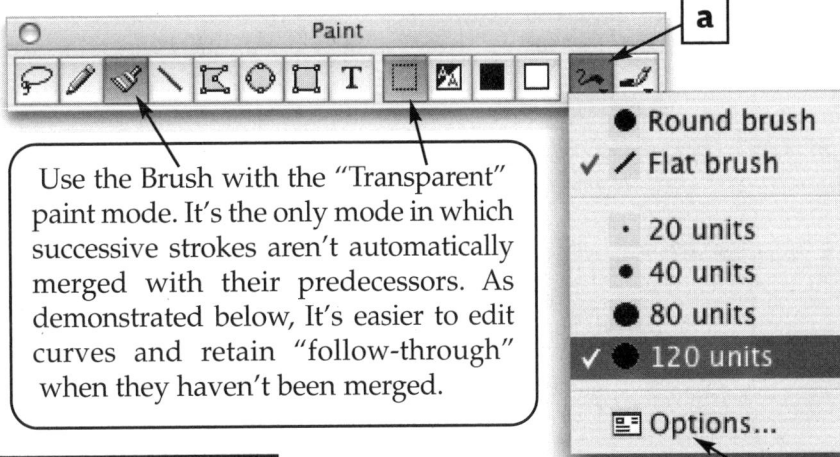

Use the Brush with the "Transparent" paint mode. It's the only mode in which successive strokes aren't automatically merged with their predecessors. As demonstrated below, It's easier to edit curves and retain "follow-through" when they haven't been merged.

Click the Brush Options tool, above, **a**, to choose a brush shape and width or scroll down to Options, **b**, to open the Paint Options dialogue box, left, containing all the paint settings. To create the script below, I used the Brush tool with the calligraphic "flat brush" setting and an angle of 60°. It was, of course, done on a digital tablet. Experiment with the settings in the Paint Options box to see which ones suit your specific needs.

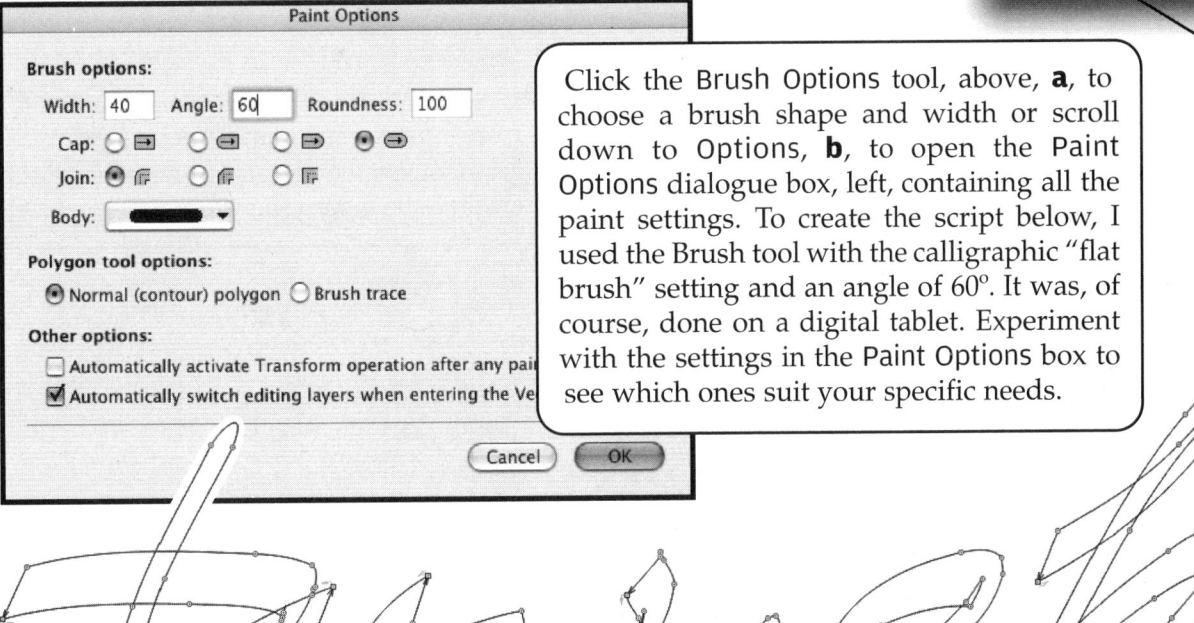

The Transparent paint mode I chose in creating this lettering (written across a single, wide-open Glyph window) shows all my overlapped strokes. Since freehand work never comes exactly right, I'll tweak the contours, merge strokes and eventually remove overlaps (*see next page*).

One nice thing about using Vector Paint tools is you don't have to manually place nodes; it's done automatically, though not always adequately. So the first thing I did—after using the Edit tool to make a few initial tweaks—was to use FontLab's marvelous Optimize feature (TOOLS>Outline>Optimize or Cmd- or Ctrl-E—not offered in TypeTool). Optimize moves nodes into extrema while generally maintain-

ing existing contour shapes or even improving them (this seems to occur naturally when nodes are put in proper extrema positions). But Optimize doesn't want to mess with your intention by removing **too** many points. And it can't know when you'd prefer a sharp corner to be rounded or that some excess points are causing bumps in a curve that should be smooth. Fixing these is **your** job.

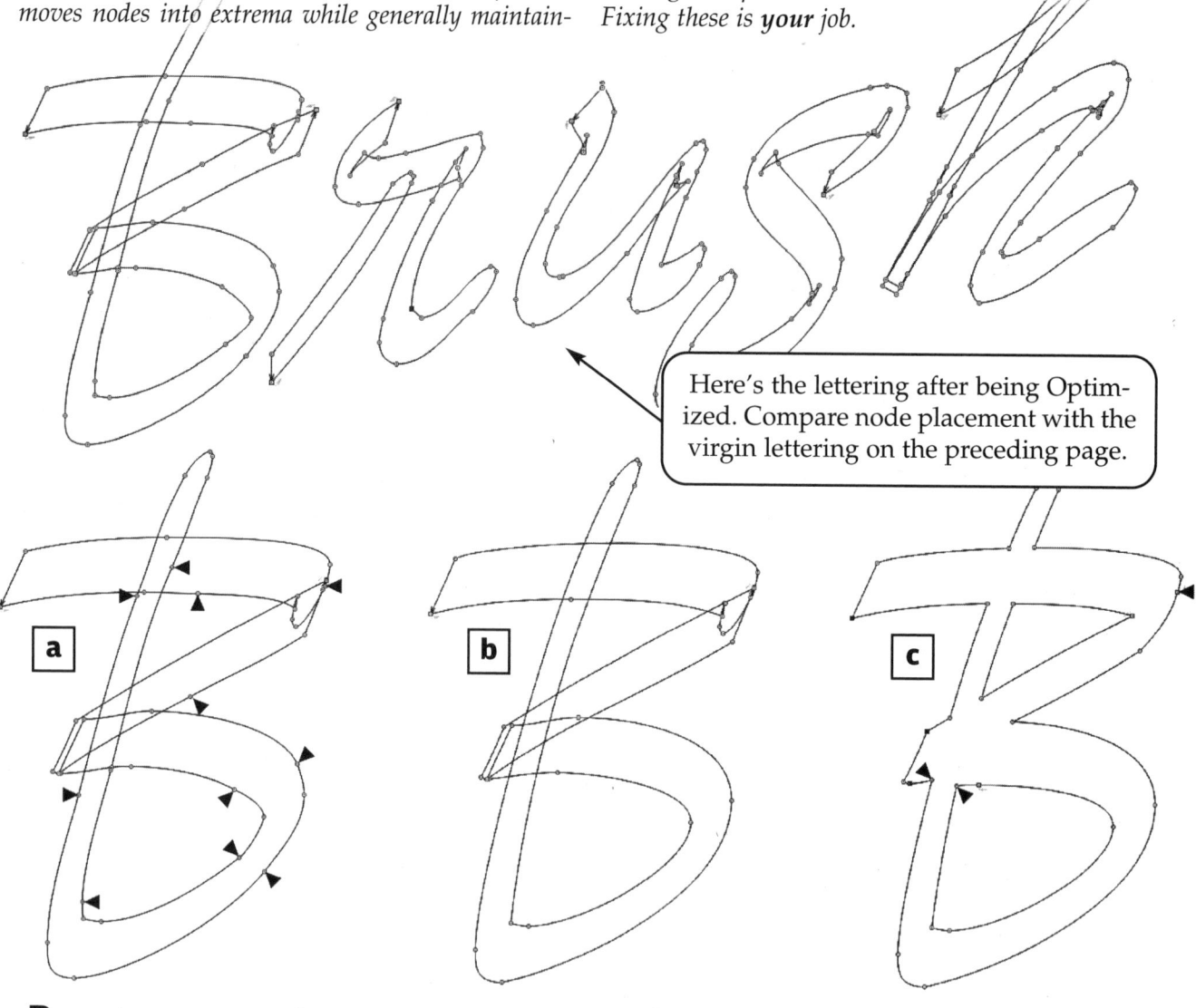

Here's the lettering after being Optimized. Compare node placement with the virgin lettering on the preceding page.

Removing excess nodes generally results in smoother curves. Notice above at **a**, how when all the nodes with arrows were removed by deleting them (go to TOOLS>Preferences>Glyph Window; leave Edit/Delete command breaks contour *unchecked*), the remaining nodes, **b**, were allowed to express their curves smoothly. Finally, all brush-

strokes were merged (TOOLS>Outline>Merge Contours), **c**, and final edits, like deleting the extra point (top arrow), were done. By editing nodes and contour shapes before merging, you can better avoid "follow-through" errors (lower arrows) where a brush stroke does not seem to line up properly as it crosses a stem or other stroke.

Vector Paint tools

Let's look at a few more of the Vector Paint tools, and consider when they might be useful, either in conjunction with a digital pen tablet or with deft mouse manipulation. Note that most of the Paint tools are also available in the vertical Edit tool palette, far left.

The **Pen** tool (looks like a pencil) is for freehand contour drawing

The **Polygon**, **Ellipse** and **Rectangle** tools are most commonly used in conjunction with the Drawing (pen) tool, not for freehand and digital tablet drawing.

The **Line** tool.

The **Drawing** tool (looks like a pen) is for placing nodes manually (see pages 50–53).

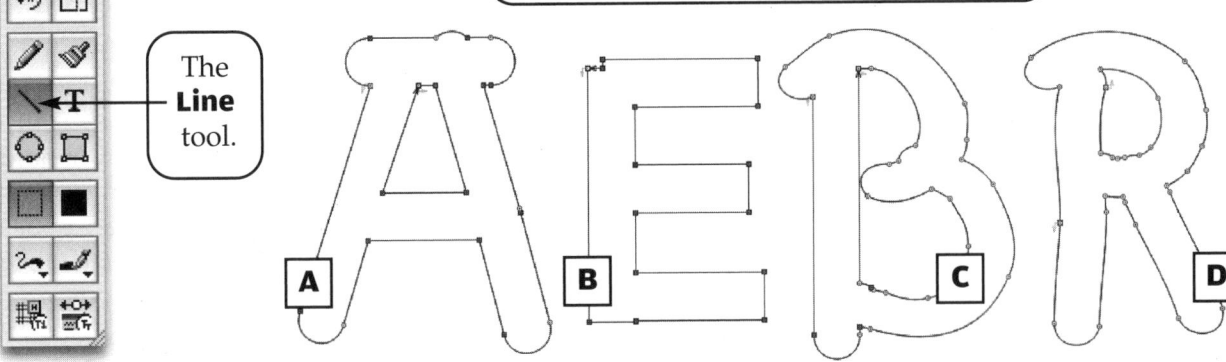

A: The **Line** tool used with Round cap stroke ends and *black* color *(which means strokes auto-merge with previous ones)*. **B**: Press the Shift key to force the **Line** tool to make straight horizontal or vertical lines (square cap ends used this time). **C**: The **Line** tool (with Shift key) was used for the vertical stem, but I had to switch to the **Brush** tool for the curved bowls of B. Notice how difficult it is to draw nice, accurate curves by hand! **D**: The *R* was drawn freehand with the **Brush** tool and digital tablet. Although there are already thousands of such fonts, you could use this technique to make yet another funky, handwriting or "school-daze" font.

The **Select** lasso tool is like an eraser that can be used to encircle, **a**, and then Delete errors such as an unwanted bump *(double-click to stop lassoing and close the lassoed selection, **b**)*. But even with the added accuracy of the digital pen, it is difficult with this tool to achieve a clean result *(enlarged area shown at **c**)*.

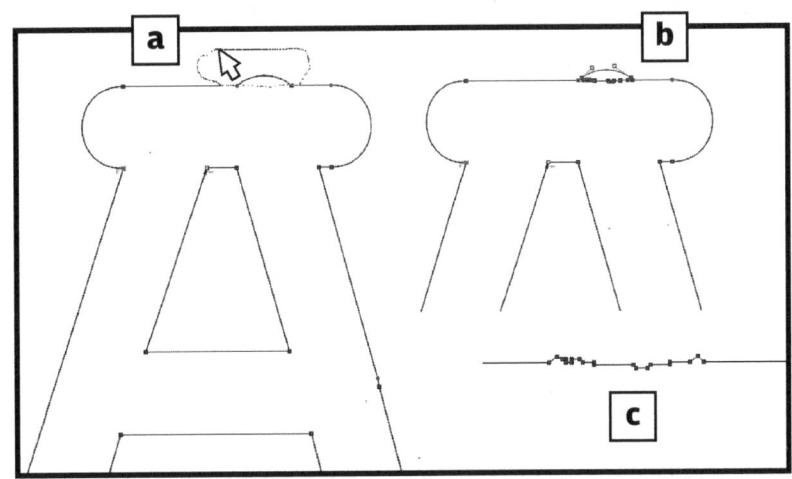

Problem above resolved on top of next page

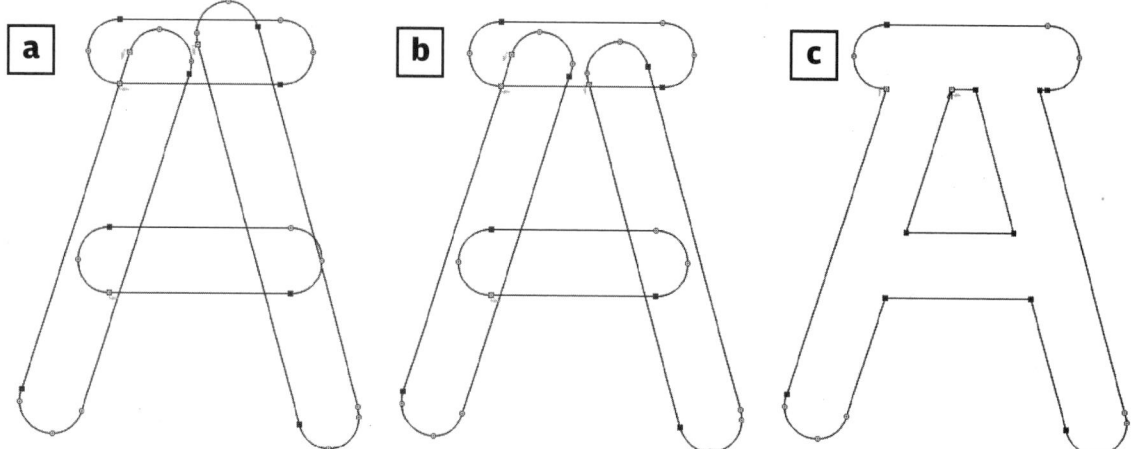

What you should have done: If you select the Transparent paint setting—*not* Black paint—each stroke remains an individual, **a**. Then you can select stroke-ends to lengthen, shorten or adjust any under- or over-reaching strokes, **b**. Finally, you'll select and merge all strokes (TOOLS>Outline>Merge Contours), **c**, because final glyphs can't contain overlapping contours.

As you'll recall, the *A* above was created with the **Line** tool. To draw a letter in this style, where accuracy is important (notice that the two slanting sides of *A* are not symmetrical as they should be), it would be better to use the **Drawing** tool to draw single paths with precisely placed nodes and bezier points (see page 50), and then to Make Parallel Paths (see page 60) to fill them out.

Using the Brush "Body" Options

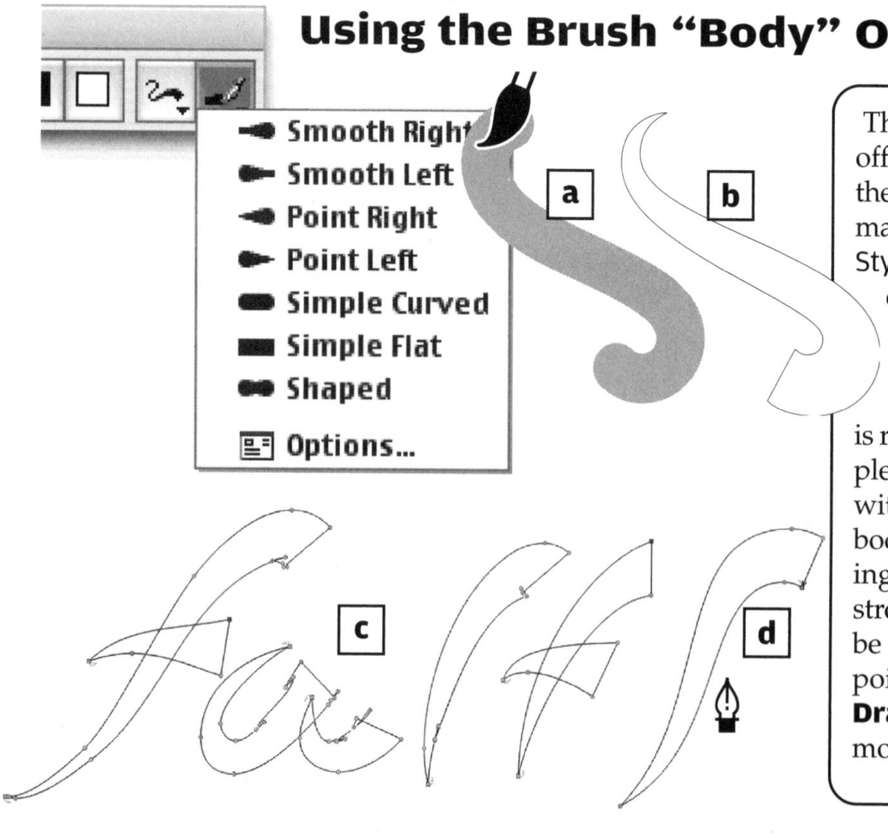

- Smooth Right
- Smooth Left
- Point Right
- Point Left
- Simple Curved
- Simple Flat
- Shaped
- Options...

The Brush Style tool menu, left, offers various shape options for the **Brush** tool. These Body shapes may also be found in the Paint Style dialogue box (click mouse on Options). When the **Brush** tool is in use, the in-progress stroke appears disconcertingly fat and gray, **a**. The final stroke is revealed when the stroke is completed, **b**. At **c**, a sample created with digital tablet and Point Right body style reveals that major editing must be done before such strokes are acceptable. So it may be better to compose such shapes point by point with the contour **Drawing** Tool, **d**. Are paint tools more trouble than they're worth?

Tracing with Pen tool and digital tablet

We have seen how FontLab's **Brush** tool (like Illustrator's Brush tool) creates a weighted stroke, which then automatically becomes a closed contour. The **Pen** tool allows us to create single paths that we may close (by dragging the final path node on top of the first one) or leave open and use Expand Strokes to fill out.

We'll use the **Pen** tool to trace a printed image or sketch that we've placed upon the digital tablet. This is a way to get it into the computer without taking the time to scan (making a scan takes longer, but an actual scanned image is, of course, superior to any tracing you can do with the Pen tool or the mouse).

FIGURE 80

1. Start with original printed images or your own sketches, right. If tracing from a book, Xerox the page and place the copy on the digital tablet. Be sure to position your image *straight* on the tablet's platen, either under the plastic cover, or taped on top of it (*drawing with the digital pen touching paper, rather than the plastic cover, provides more friction to slow down the action of the hand and may help produce a tracing of greater accuracy*).

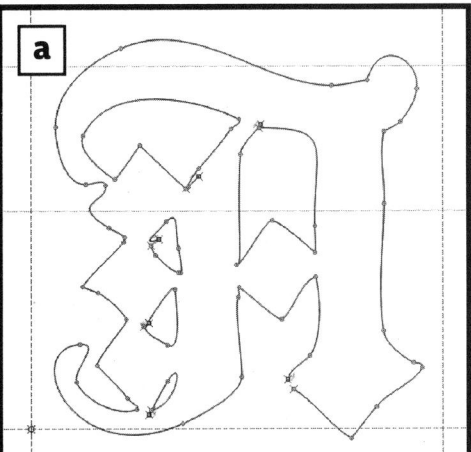

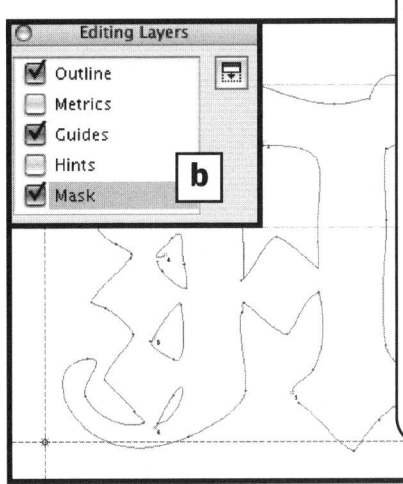

2. With the digital pen and FontLab's **Pen** tool, trace around the perimeter of the image, **a**, into an open Glyph window. Try to edit as you trace to improve the contour, if necessary. You'll probably have to Transform (Cmd- or Ctrl-9) by scaling, rotating and/or slanting the tracing to get it into proper position at cap height.

3. To proceed, here are two approaches: 1. With the Edit tool, begin tweaking the traced contour to place nodes and curves as they should be; adding/subtracting points as you go. 2. Copy the traced contour, click the Mask layer, **b** (*Mask not available in TypeTool*), and Paste into it. Then go back to Outline layer and use the **Drawing** tool (see pages 50–53) to redraw contours neatly, from scratch.

How to trace a scan

Before leaving the subject of scans and tracing characters with digital tablets, here are the best tips I've found for working from scans to create high-quality contours.

Most letters can be broken down into series of parts. The Rectangle tool makes a stem, **a**, which can then be copied and pasted to become a sheared stem, **b**, which maintains consistent stem width. Hold Shift to make a perfectly square rectangle, then Rotate it 45° to make **c**. For any shape even remotely elliptical, **d**, Ellipse tool will conjure perfect ones, segments of which may be used to create well-curved contours: Shift-click the two paths on each side of node **e** then hit Cut (Cmd- or Ctrl-X) to delete top segments. Some glyph contours must be drawn with the Drawing tool, **f**. The top arrows point to where the intrinsic wisdom of the bezier curve cures the defects of the scan image.

(Wow--really long arrow. Isn't it?!)

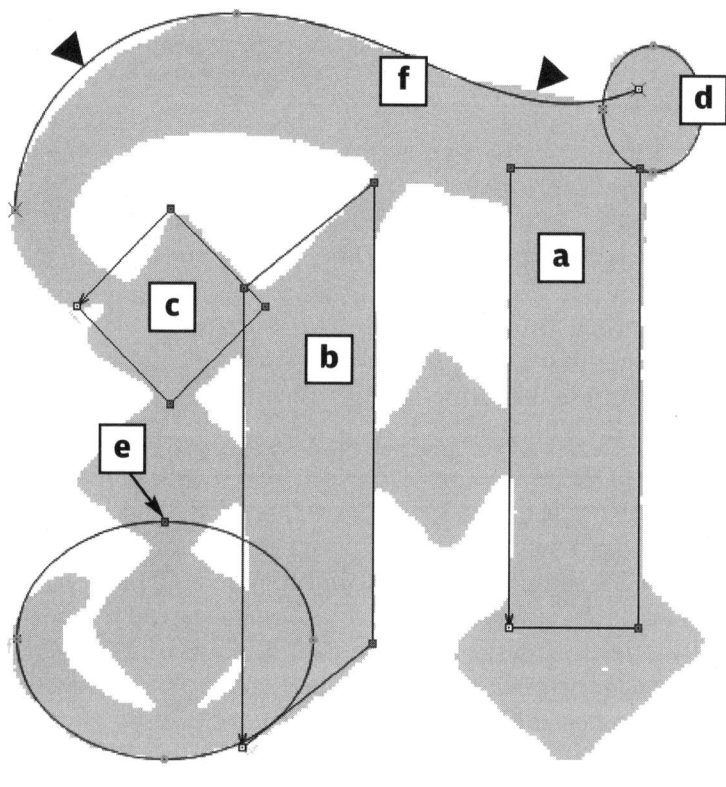

Note: Windows users must access the Rectangle and Ellipse tools through the Vector Paint toolbar.

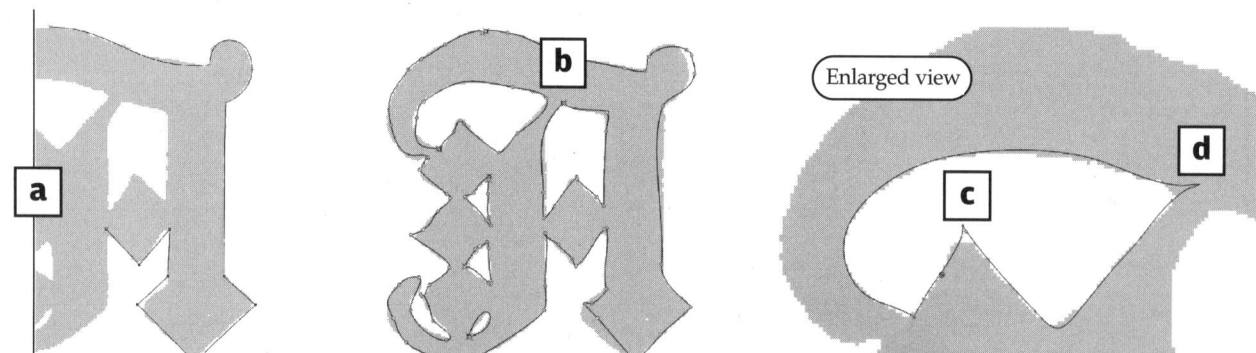

Enlarged view

Background layer scans may be traced with the Drawing tool starting from a point and working your way around, **a**, and back to the start. This straight-ahead approach is usually less accurate than using the parts method shown above. When you trace a Background scan with the Pen tool and a digital tablet, the results will always require lots of work to repair, and tight corners (like the corner just below **b**) are often rounded over and lost. But you can capture tight turns by exaggerating your pen's path by drawing too far beyond a corner, **c**, or into a corner, **d**, and later push the nodes back.

DRAWING A FONT

Page **48** *Glyph Window details*

49 *Alignment Zones*

50 *Making points with the Drawing tool*

52 *Making and Breaking connections*

54 *How to select points and paths*

55 *Selecting, Deselecting; the Magic Wand*

56 *Working with nodes and paths*

58 *Drawing Glyphs*

61 *How to Preview your drawing*

65 *Pop-up Menus*

67 *Transform, Transforming, Transformation*

71 *Letter spacing 101*

72 *Check progress in the Metrics Window*

73 *Working suggestions*

74 *Optional drawing tools: Sketch mode*

75 *Working in Sketch mode*

76 *Drawing with TrueType curves*

77 *The Grid and off-curve points*

78 *Meter mode*

Glyph window details

Let's prepare to draw glyphs–that's the point of all this, after all! First we must open a Glyph window.

(If you're impatient and want to get to the Drawing part, go to page 50.)

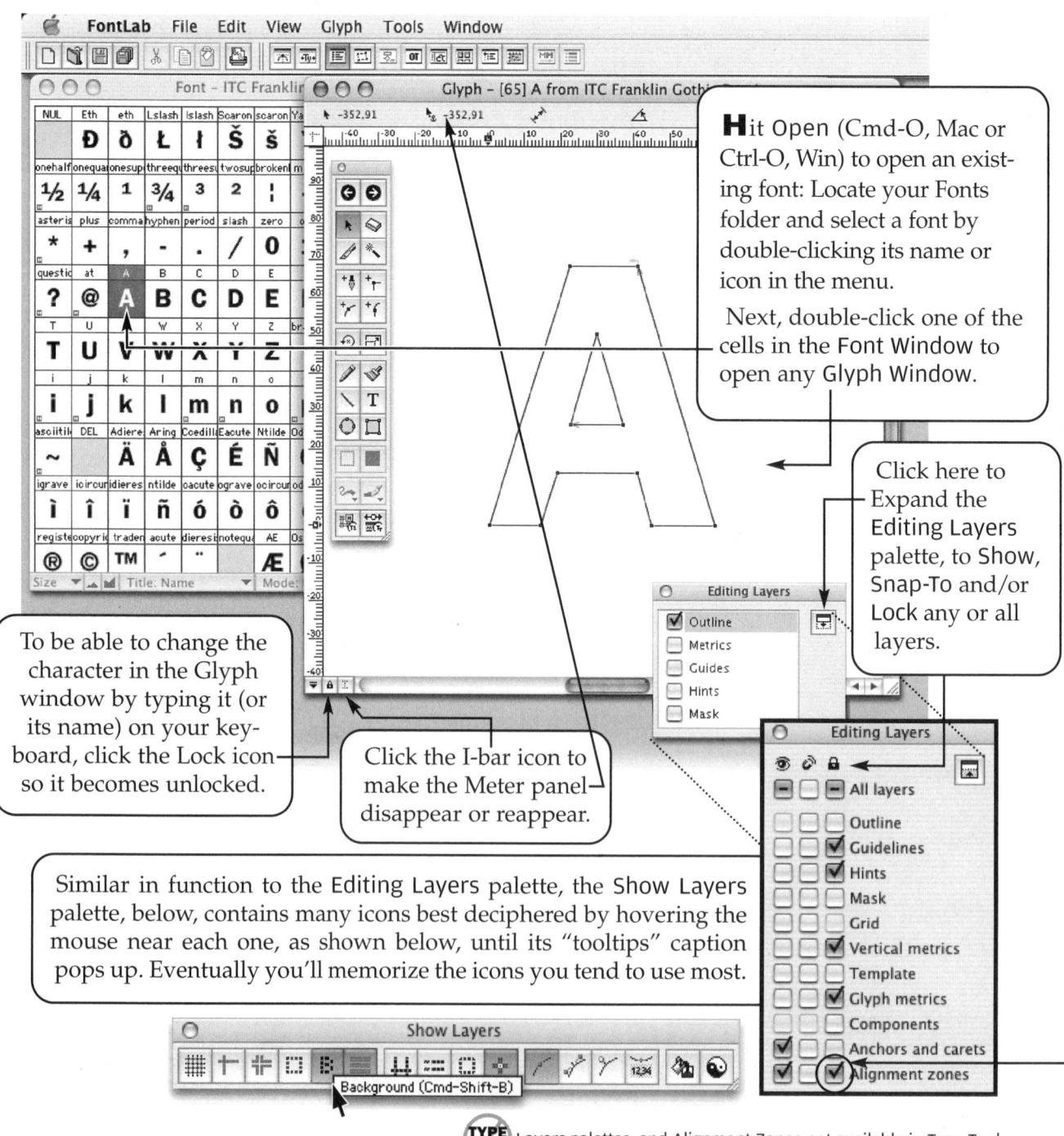

Hit Open (Cmd-O, Mac or Ctrl-O, Win) to open an existing font: Locate your Fonts folder and select a font by double-clicking its name or icon in the menu.

Next, double-click one of the cells in the Font Window to open any Glyph Window.

Click here to Expand the Editing Layers palette, to Show, Snap-To and/or Lock any or all layers.

To be able to change the character in the Glyph window by typing it (or its name) on your keyboard, click the Lock icon so it becomes unlocked.

Click the I-bar icon to make the Meter panel disappear or reappear.

Similar in function to the Editing Layers palette, the Show Layers palette, below, contains many icons best deciphered by hovering the mouse near each one, as shown below, until its "tooltips" caption pops up. Eventually you'll memorize the icons you tend to use most.

Editing Layers
- ☑ Outline
- ☐ Metrics
- ☐ Guides
- ☐ Hints
- ☐ Mask

Editing Layers
- All layers
- Outline
- ☑ Guidelines
- ☑ Hints
- ☐ Mask
- ☐ Grid
- ☑ Vertical metrics
- ☐ Template
- ☑ Glyph metrics
- ☐ Components
- ☑ Anchors and carets
- ☑ Alignment zones

Show Layers

Background (Cmd-Shift-B)

TYPE TOOL Layers palettes and Alignment Zones not available in Type Tool.

Alignment Zones

Understanding Alignment Zones is important because when you open an existing font, you may see strange, lavender horizontal bars running through the characters and ask yourself, "Hey, what th—?"

In a font, rounded or pointy-ended characters like *G, o, V* and *v* should slightly "overshoot" the baseline, x-height and cap-height. Otherwise, such characters will appear smaller than flat-top/-bottom characters such as *E* or *x*. Amount of overshoot is established in Alignment Zones.

FontLab can automatically calculate Alignment Zones based on the average overshoot values of the character drawings. If we draw our own fonts, we can, early on, specify the Alignment Zones, which will aid us in making all overshoots consistent.

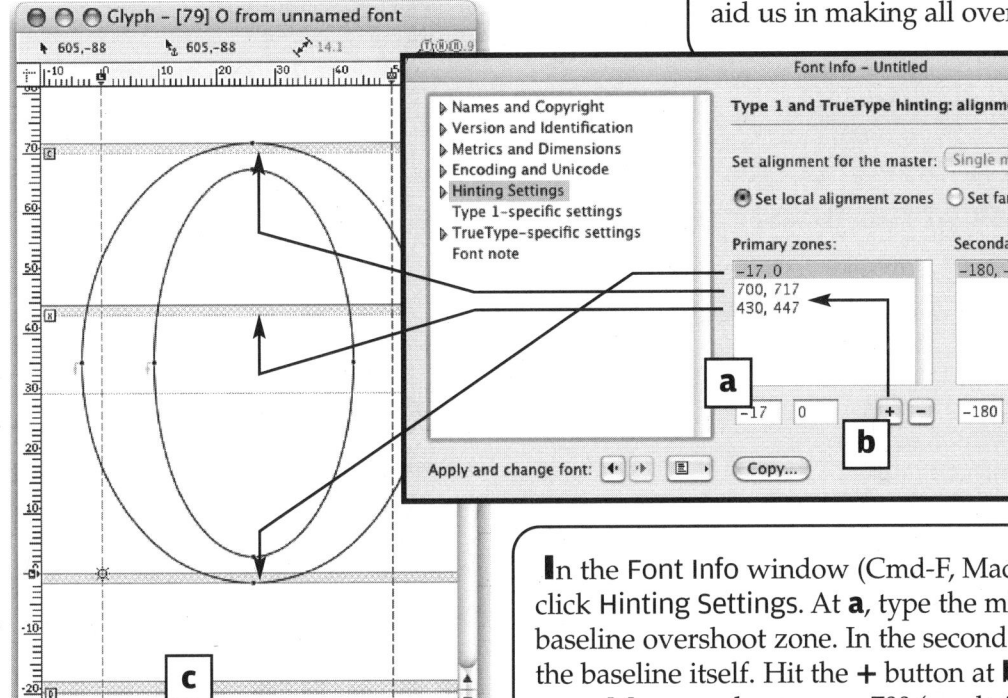

Note: Alignment Zones can also be changed by hand. Just uncheck the Lock button (circled, opposite page) in the Editing Layers palette, place cursor near top or bottom line of any zone and drag it to where you want it.

In the Font Info window (Cmd-F, Mac or Ctrl-F, Win), click Hinting Settings. At **a**, type the minus value for the baseline overshoot zone. In the second field, 0 represents the baseline itself. Hit the **+** button at **b** to add your next zone. My second zone was 700 (cap height), 717 (the same 17 points of overshoot as from the baseline down). My third zone provided overshoot parameters for x-height of lower case characters, and for additional zones I used the Secondary Zones field, **c**, to put in an Alignment Zone for descenders. To check the placement of Zones as you work, hit the Apply button, **d**. Click OK when finished.

+✒ Making points with the Drawing tool

Select the Drawing Tool *to create straight paths and curves. As you draw, the tool intuits the proper style of node by the way you draw your lines. FontLab classifies nodes in two ways: by curve or path type and by connection type.*

An exercise in drawing various kinds of Postscript Type 1 points.

1. Create the first point or "node" with the Drawing tool by clicking the mouse button anywhere within an open Glyph window.

2. Click again. Now we have a second node forming a straight path between two points.

3. Click to make node 3. Now hold Option (or Alt, Win), and click node 3 again but keep mouse button pressed down and drag upwards. A bezier control handle, **a**, will emerge.

4. Click node 4, but keep mouse button down, hold Shift key and drag towards the right. Bezier control handles emerge equally on both sides of the node and they're straight horizontal because you held Shift.

Keep reading straight across →

An in-depth look at the point connections that were created above.

1.
Start point is a blue square with a large X through it and a hanging arrow* that reveals the direction in which the path was created. (*Don't want arrows? Go to TOOLS> Preferences>Glyph Window *then* uncheck Show Contour Direction.)

2.
Corner point is a red* square. Unfortunately, holding the Shift key when you draw a point does *not* constrain the next point to absolute vertical or horizontal. (*Don't want color nodes? Go to TOOLS> Preferences> Glyph Window *then check* Black/white node icons.)

Bezier handles also called "Bezier Control Points" or BCPs.

3.
Corner point with one bezier handle emerging in the outgoing direction.

4.
Curve Point looks like a green circle, has two handles emerging from either side of the point. Both handles are connected so, like a teeter-totter, lowering one side will raise the other. This is a Smooth Connection.

Keep reading straight across →

Click for node 6, but keep the mouse button down. Hold Shift key and drag out a bezier control handle towards the right. Let up mouse. Hold Option (or Alt, Win) and click node 6 to make the right handle disappear (the left handle, **b**, remains).

> **Tip: Make a more perfect arc:** If you press Shift-Option (or Shift-Alt, Win) while clicking on a curve, its adjacent bezier handles will snap to equal lengths. And technically, that's how they should be.

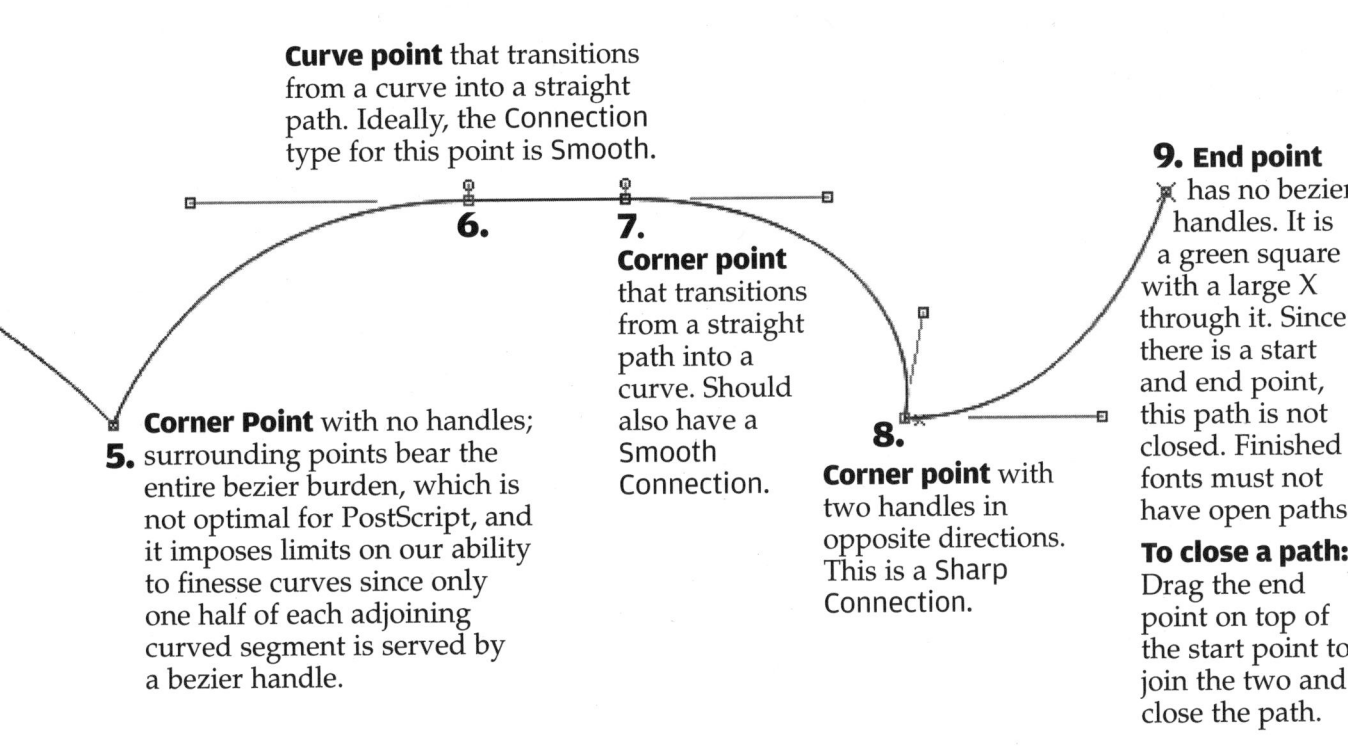

5. Click to create node 5. Immediately release mouse button, don't drag out any handles.

7. Click node 7, release mouse. Hold Option (Alt), click the point again and drag out a handle. Hold Shift too to constrain the handle straight. This time we added the right-side handle, **c**, *after* the node had been made.

8. Click node 8, hold button down and drag a handle downward. Release mouse. Click the node again while pressing Option (Alt) to delete the outgoing handle. Press-hold Option once again, click node 8 and drag a new outgoing handle, **d**, to the right.

9. Click to make final point.

Curve point that transitions from a curve into a straight path. Ideally, the Connection type for this point is Smooth.

Corner Point with no handles; surrounding points bear the entire bezier burden, which is not optimal for PostScript, and it imposes limits on our ability to finesse curves since only one half of each adjoining curved segment is served by a bezier handle.

Corner point that transitions from a straight path into a curve. Should also have a Smooth Connection.

Corner point with two handles in opposite directions. This is a Sharp Connection.

9. End point has no bezier handles. It is a green square with a large X through it. Since there is a start and end point, this path is not closed. Finished fonts must not have open paths.

To close a path: Drag the end point on top of the start point to join the two and close the path.

On the next pages we'll alter these point connections.

Making and breaking connections

As in social life, making proper connections is very important. Sharp connections that should be smooth, and smooth connections with BCPs on corners that should be sharp, will usually produce unattractive contours.

Adjusting paths and changing point connection types.

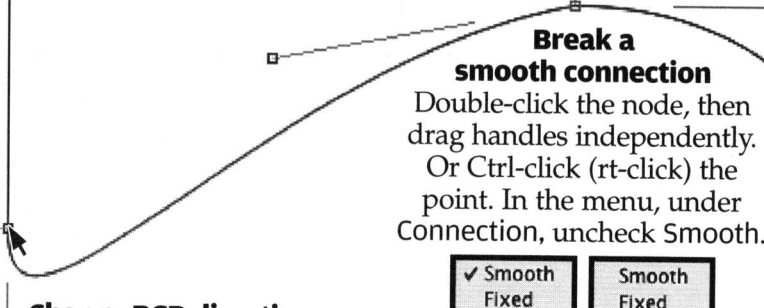

Straighten a path When you drag any point, you'll see a crosshair centered on the point enabling you to visually align it with any other point. (To hide the crosshair, go to Tools>Preferences>Glyph Window and check the Do not show a crosshair box.)

Straighten a path .2 Marquee or Shift-click two or more points to select them. Control-click (Right-click, Win) the selected path to open the menu shown below. Scroll to Align points. Done!

Break a smooth connection
Double-click the node, then drag handles independently. Or Ctrl-click (rt-click) the point. In the menu, under Connection, uncheck Smooth.

✓ Smooth	Smooth
Fixed	Fixed
Before	After

Change BCP direction
Double-click the node. Or Control-click this point (Right-click, Win) to open the menu shown below. Scroll to Connection>Smooth. The outgoing BCP handle will jump into alignment with the preceding straight path, becoming, in effect, a "transition point."

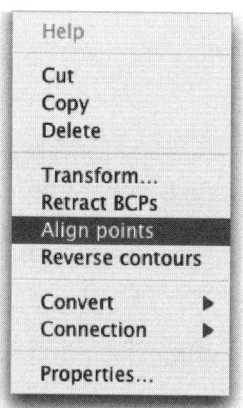

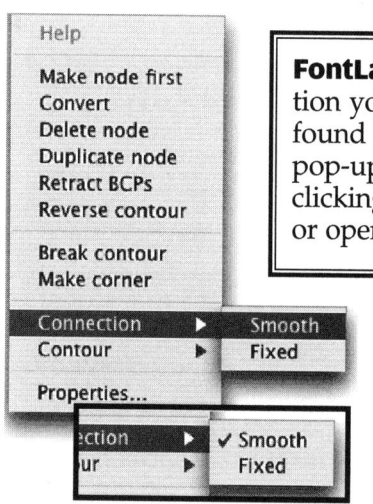

FontLab Tip: Virtually every operation you want to accomplish will be found listed in the many contextual pop-up menus accessed by Control-clicking (Rt-click, Win) a node, path or open area. See page 65 for more.

Keep reading straight across →

FontLab Tip: To toggle to the Edit (arrow) tool, while in another tool, give the Command key (Ctrl, Win) a good swift tap. No need to keep pressing the key. Tap Cmd again to return to your original tool.

(After you let your mouse up on Smooth, you would find that it has become checked, above, were you to go back to the menu and look.)

Node Code: A small circle or cross near a point indicates its connection mode. To hide/show these, click the Connection Mode icon in the Show Layers Palette (VIEW>Toolbars>Show Layers).

Sharp corner • Sharp curve • Smooth curve • Sharp Transition • Smooth Transition • plain Corner

Make a smooth connection sharp

Double-click the node. Or Control-click (Rt.-click, Win) the node to open the pop-up menu, go down to Connection. Smooth will be checked. Release mouse to uncheck it. Handle will become unconstrained and can be bent in any direction. as shown above.

Make a sharp connection smooth

Click on the left side of the point above, hold Option (Alt, Win) and drag out a handle, as shown below. Again hold Option, click and pull out the right side handle. Ctrl-click (Rt-click, Win) the point, scroll to Connection >Smooth (or double-click the node). Both handles now twist together as though connected.

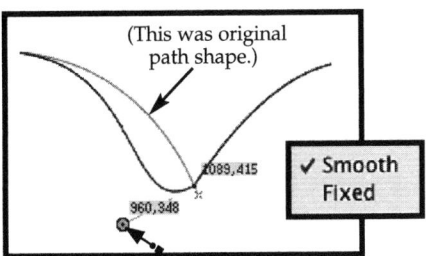

Notice the numbers in the screenshot above? If you don't want to see digital readouts of every selected point's exact position, go to Preferences>Glyph Window then disable Show node's position.

Why the numbers? If one point at cap height reads *116, 700* and the next point reads *422, 702*, then you'd know that the path defining the top of your glyph is crooked. You could fix it by dragging the second point down 2 units until it read *422, 700*.

Make a sharp connection by removing handles

Control-click or Right-click this point to open the menu, go down to Retract BCPs and click. Both handles from this point will be gone so that the final path segment will no longer be curved.

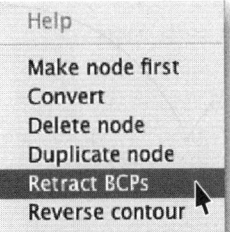

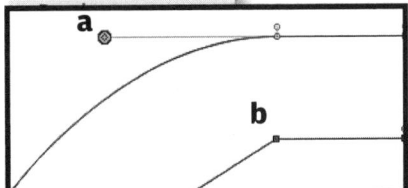

Or click on *one* handle to select the handle point itself, **a**, then hit Delete. The result is shown at **b**.

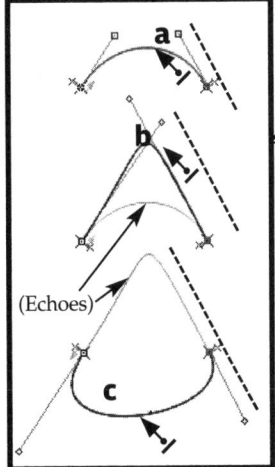

What is 'Fixed'? It's relevant only when you edit a curve by dragging the path between two nodes, not the node itself. Go to Preferences>Glyph Window and enable All BCPs are fixed. Then, if you drag a curved path, **a**, adjacent handles are constrained to their original angles, **b**, even if you drag the curve inside out, **c**. (*A curved path can of course be edited without Fixed handles.*) If All BCPs are fixed is *not* enabled, Ctrl- or Rt.-click a node for the pop-up menu, go to Connection> Fixed, to assign this state on an "as-needed" basis.

How to select points and paths

In some ways, FontLab handles the selecting of nodes (or "points"), paths and contours differently than other font and illustration programs. This can be confusing until you learn the logic of it. Becoming familiar with how to make specific selections is important because you will be doing lots of it, in the process of drawing fonts.

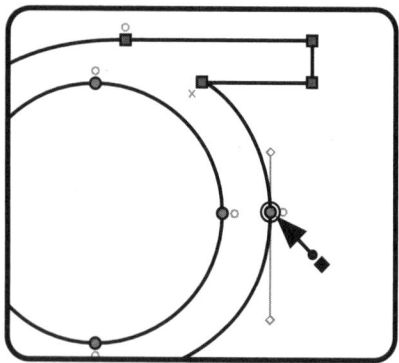

Select/move a point

Click the point with the Edit tool. The BCPs are revealed and a bigger circle surrounds the point. Now you could Ctrl-click (Rt-click) the point to open the point options menu, drag the point, or use Arrow keys to move it.

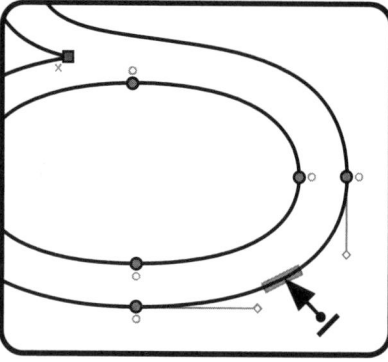

Select a path, show BCPs

Click a path to show the surrounding points' bezier handles. Then you can pull them in or out to edit them. See how the point at the tail of the Edit tool changes to a tiny line as it approaches a path segment?

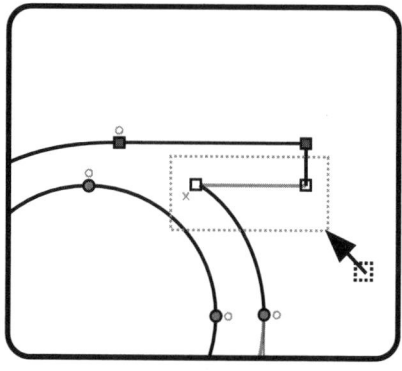

Select multiple points

Hold down the mouse button and drag a rectangular marquee around one or more points to select them. Selected paths will become red and selected points will lose their fill colors to appear hollow. Bottom of Edit tool gains a little marquee.

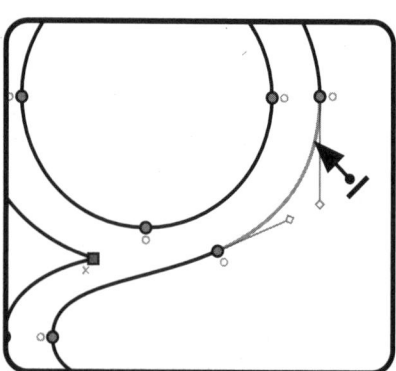

Shift select a path

Press the Shift key as you click a path or contour segment between two points. It will turn red and, as shown in the next picture, can be dragged without affecting the BCPs.

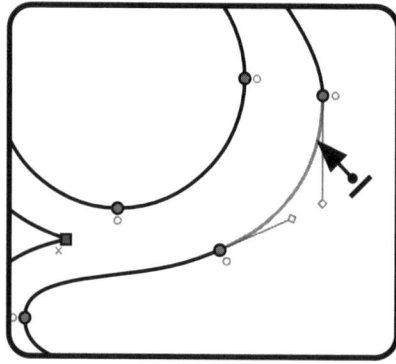

How to drag a path

Once the path is Shift-selected, the points move as though locked together; Bezier Control Points (I call them "handles") don't change. Multiple nodes can be selected this way.

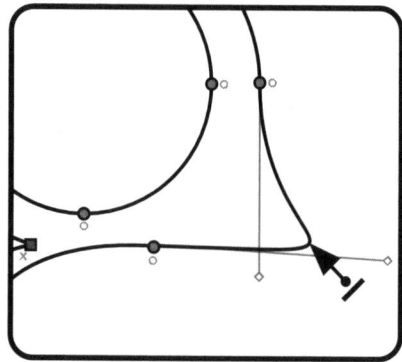

How not to drag a path

If you click a path without holding Shift, then try to drag it, the above will happen. A curved path *can* be tweaked this way, by purposely dragging it—though less extremely.

Selecting, Deselecting; the Magic Wand

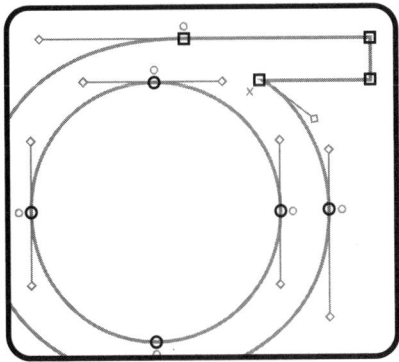

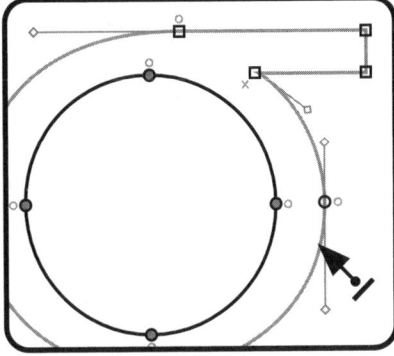

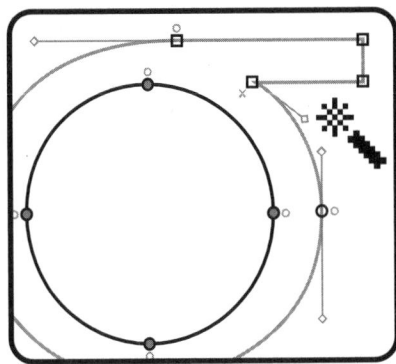

Select all
Hit Command-A (Ctrl-A, Win) to select every point and path in the Glyph window. Now the entire glyph can be moved or Transformed as a unit. A slower method of selecting all is to go to EDIT> Select All in the top menu bar.

Select All .2
With the Edit tool, double click any path or contour segment—not on a node—and the entire path or contour will become selected. Hold Shift and double click again to completely select an additional path like the counter in *g*.

Magic Wand select
While in the Edit tool, you can hold the Command (Ctrl, Win) key and the Edit tool temporarily becomes the Magic Wand tool, which, with but a single click, selects any nearby open path or closed contour.

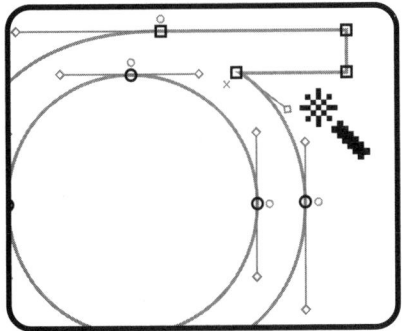

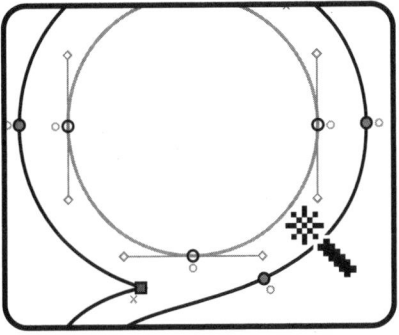

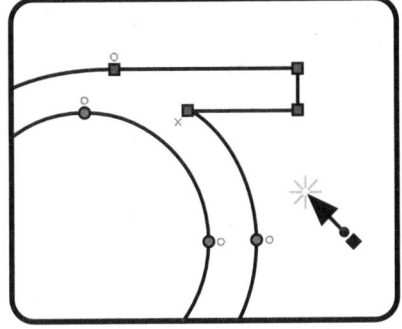

Magic Wand Select All
If you've accessed the Wand thru the Edit tool with the Cmd key (or Ctrl, Win), then also press Opt (Alt) to Select All. If you get the actual Magic Wand tool from the toolbar (I try to avoid switching tools because it wastes time), hold Option (Alt, Win) as you click the Wand to select all a glyph's contours at once.

Deselect, add Selection
Whether with Edit tool or Magic Wand tool, clicking while holding the Shift key reverses the selection state (just as in virtually every other draw program). So, a selected path becomes unselected and vice versa. And if a node or path is selected, hold Shift and click more nodes or paths to add to the selection.

Deselect All
To deselect everything that's selected, click with the Edit tool anywhere that's not a point, path or contour. You may also (if you have a lot of extra time on your hands) go to EDIT>Deselect.

Working with nodes and paths

Here are more details on using nodes, especially how they are affected by keyboard shortcuts. Remember that FontLab usually allows more than one method of doing a task, and it's up to you to discover your preferences.

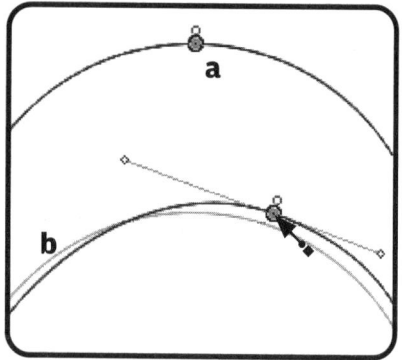

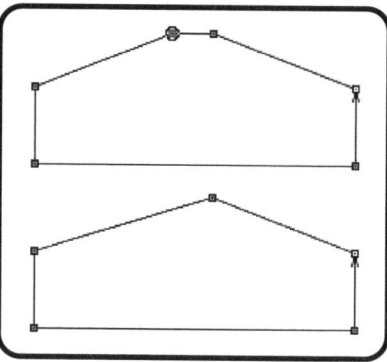

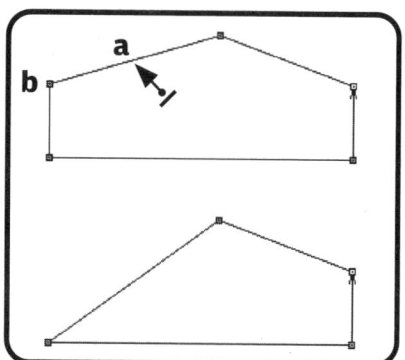

Move a node along a curved path

Press Option (or Alt, Win), select a node, **a**, with the Edit tool and drag it along a curving path. The original curve remains basically preserved (gray line, **b** above), though nodes may go out of extrema.

Remove a node, leave path intact

If Edit/Delete command breaks contour is **unchecked** in Preferences>Glyph window, then selecting and deleting a node removes the node and leaves the path intact, hence the contour remains closed.

Remove a path, leave contour closed

With Edit/Delete command breaks... **unchecked,** clicking and deleting one or more path segments, **a**, will remove the path and the next point away from the click, **b**, But the contour will stay closed.

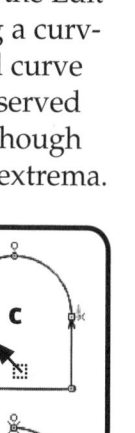

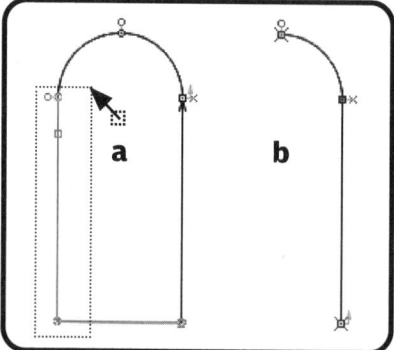

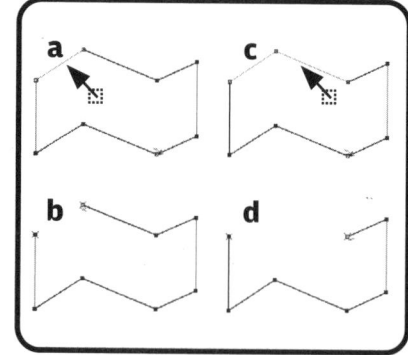

Delete a node, open the contour

If Edit/Delete command breaks contour is **checked**, click a node, **a**, hit delete, node's gone, but contour remains closed, **b**. But if you *marquee* the node, **c**, then hit delete, you'll remove the node and break the contour, **d**.

Delete a path, open the contour

With Edit/Delete command breaks contour **checked** (enabled), marquee one or more nodes, **a**, hit Delete and those nodes and paths will be gone. Also, Shift-click any number of paths and hit Delete to vanquish them, **b**.

Shortcut: Break contour

To break open a contour, whether or not Edit/Delete command breaks... is checked, Shift-click a path, **a**, and Cut it (Cmd- or Ctrl-X), **b**. Or Shift-click two paths bordering a node, **c**, Cut and the paths are gone along with the node, **d**.

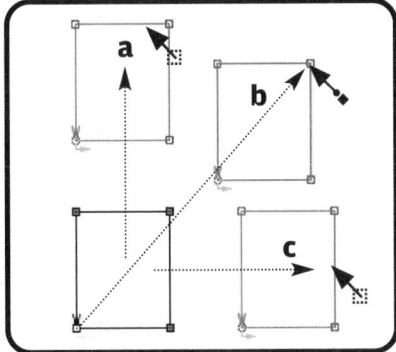

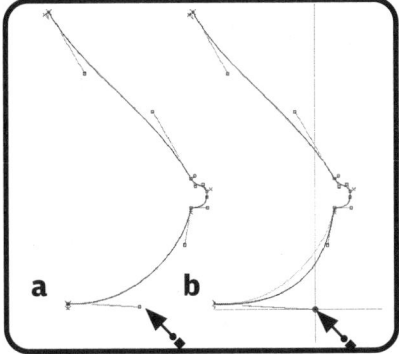

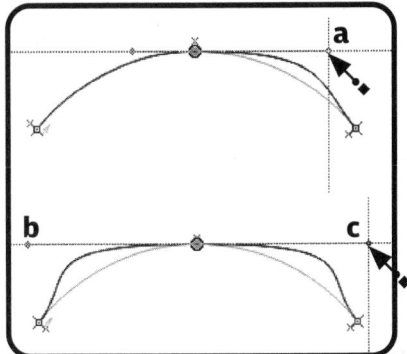

Constrain drag direction

Hold Shift while dragging a node, a path, an object or many nodes, paths and objects to constrain their movement to vertical, **a**; 45°, **b**; or horizontal, **c**. Items will snap to these preset angles as you Shift-drag them.

Constrain BCP handles

Hold Shift, then begin to drag a bezier control handle, **a**, and its direction of movement will be constrained to its original angle, **b**. This is helpful when minutely tweaking a curve the angle of whose handle we like, but not the length.

Drag BCP handles symmetrically

Drag one BCP, **a**, and only that handle will move. But Option- or Alt-drag one bezier handle of a curve point and the adjacent handle will move symmetrically, **b–c**. (*But if tried on a corner point, both handles snap to colinearity.*)

The Node Properties palette

This palette pops up when you Cmd or Ctrl-click a node, and then it hangs around, morphing into the Glyph Properties and other applicable palettes, until you close it. Its purpose is to provide digital readouts and shortcuts for performing actions that may also be done with the Edit tool and through other means.

Node Properties

Control- or Rt.-click a node for the sub-menu, below. Scroll to Properties to open this palette.

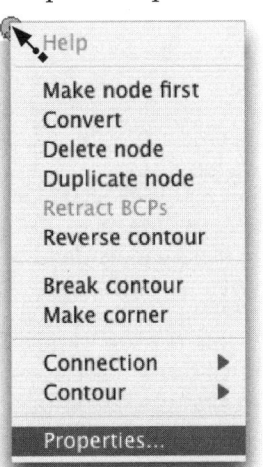

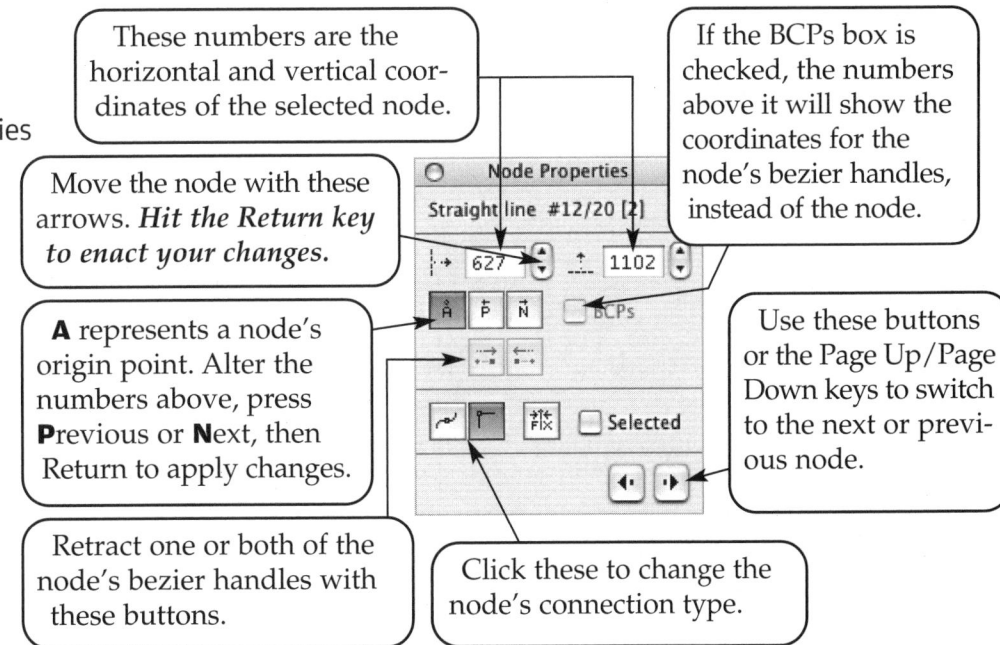

These numbers are the horizontal and vertical coordinates of the selected node.

If the BCPs box is checked, the numbers above it will show the coordinates for the node's bezier handles, instead of the node.

Move the node with these arrows. *Hit the Return key to enact your changes.*

A represents a node's origin point. Alter the numbers above, press **P**revious or **N**ext, then Return to apply changes.

Retract one or both of the node's bezier handles with these buttons.

Use these buttons or the Page Up/Page Down keys to switch to the next or previous node.

Click these to change the node's connection type.

Drawing Glyphs

Perhaps the best way to explain how to draw a font is to do it and demonstrate in context many of the tools and procedures that you'll be most likely to utilize.

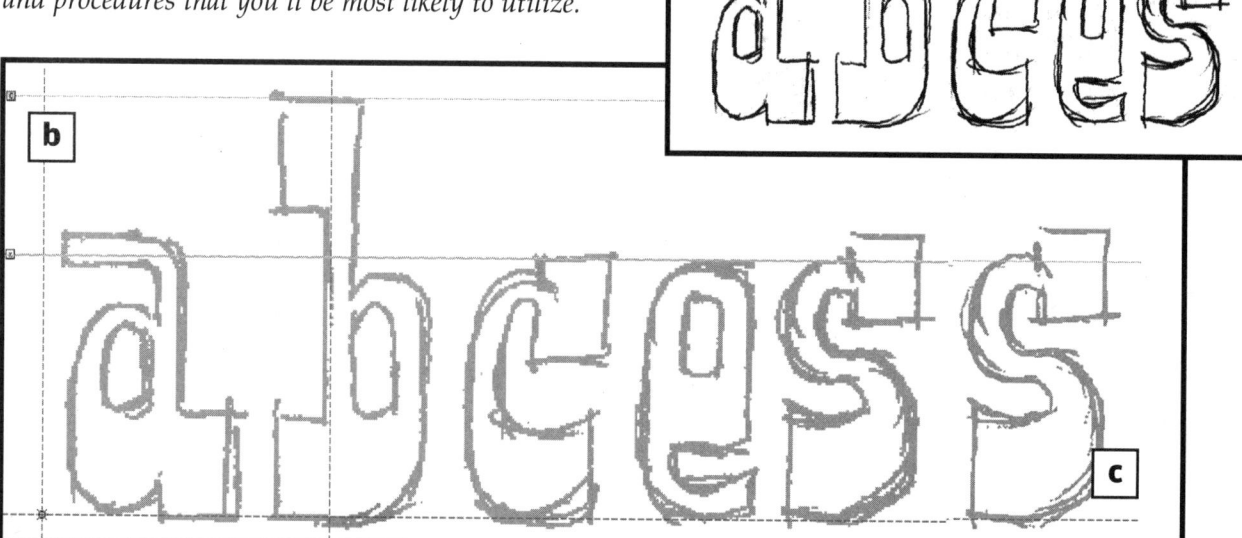

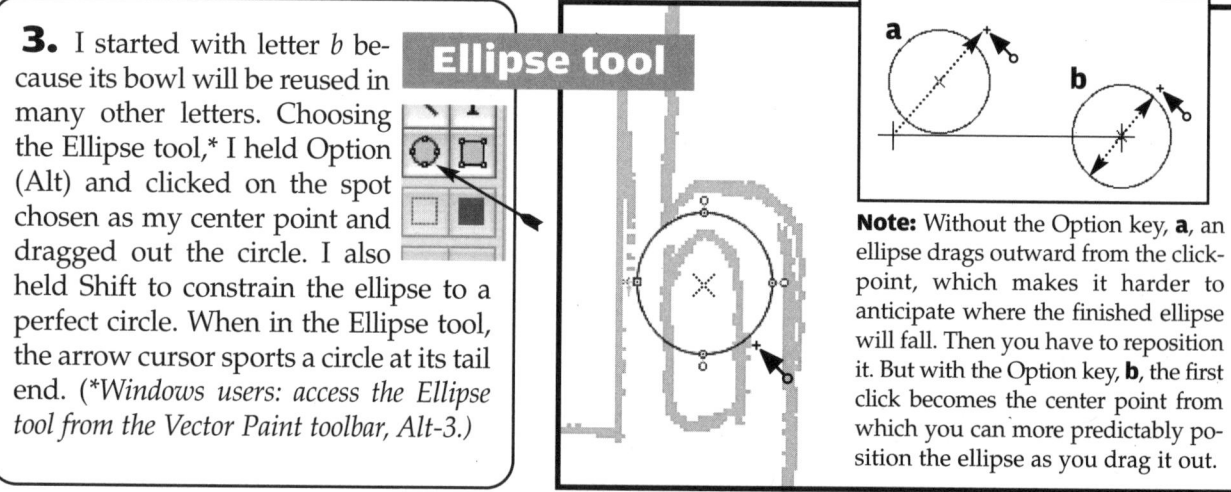

1. I started with a sketch, above at **a**, of a string of random letters. It's a loose sketch with lots of ambiguity that'll be resolved in the drawing process as I proceed. The Photoshop scan was selected and pasted into the Glyph window for lowercase letter *a*, where FontLab automatically placed it into the Background layer, **b**. (See scans on page 30.) As these five letters are drawn, they will be pasted into their own slots.

2. For the sake of comparison, I used SCANFONT to import the duplicate *s*, above at **c**. What you see is ScanFont's autotracing of the sketch, that was exported as vectors into FontLab. I hit Select All (Cmd/Ctrl-A) and then Create Background (Cmd/Ctrl-B) to make the contours into a background.

3. I started with letter *b* because its bowl will be reused in many other letters. Choosing the Ellipse tool,* I held Option (Alt) and clicked on the spot chosen as my center point and dragged out the circle. I also held Shift to constrain the ellipse to a perfect circle. When in the Ellipse tool, the arrow cursor sports a circle at its tail end. (*Windows users: access the Ellipse tool from the Vector Paint toolbar, Alt-3.)

Note: Without the Option key, **a**, an ellipse drags outward from the click-point, which makes it harder to anticipate where the finished ellipse will fall. Then you have to reposition it. But with the Option key, **b**, the first click becomes the center point from which you can more predictably position the ellipse as you drag it out.

4. The circle (ellipse) needed to be split up into two parts to create a lozenge shape. With the **Break Contour** Edit tool, I clicked the "9 o'clock" point to select it, held the Ctrl (Right-click, Win) key to open the contextual point menu and scrolled down to Break Contour. I then did the same thing by clicking the 3 o'clock point and breaking that contour. This means that I'd created two open crescent-shaped paths from one closed ellipse.

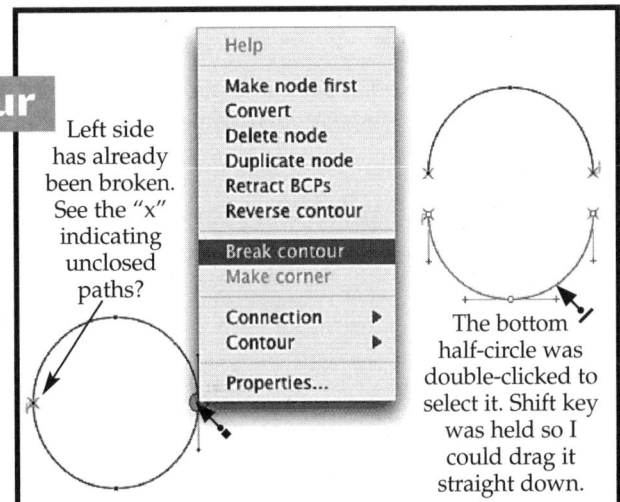

Left side has already been broken. See the "x" indicating unclosed paths?

The bottom half-circle was double-clicked to select it. Shift key was held so I could drag it straight down.

5. I dragged the lower crescent to a temporary position (final position isn't known yet), selected the point at **a**, got the **Add Tangent tool** and clicked a point, which extended the path to **b**. I then dragged the **b** point on top of **c** where the two merged into one.

Why not just select point **a**, then use the Drawing tool to click directly on **c** to close the path? If we do that, the BCPs in the merged **c** point will mutate, as shown at **e**.

Connecting paths/Closing Contours

I used the Add Tangent tool, though it's no different than the Add Corner tool, because the **c** point is one that transitions from a straight to curved path. The Add Tangent is actually a sort of ersatz point tool.

6. If you've been wondering why I drew this lozenge shape as **Expand Strokes** a centerline through the bowl of b, it's so it can be expanded to a specific stroke width that can be applied to all subsequent narrow stems so *they all will be perfectly matching*. Select the lozenge and go to TOOLS>Outline>Expand Strokes. My settings were as shown at right (try playing with the settings yourself, to learn what this feature can do). As you can see, my results are poor: nodes have been moved to weird places, paths are lumpy. Expand Strokes may not be the best way to go.

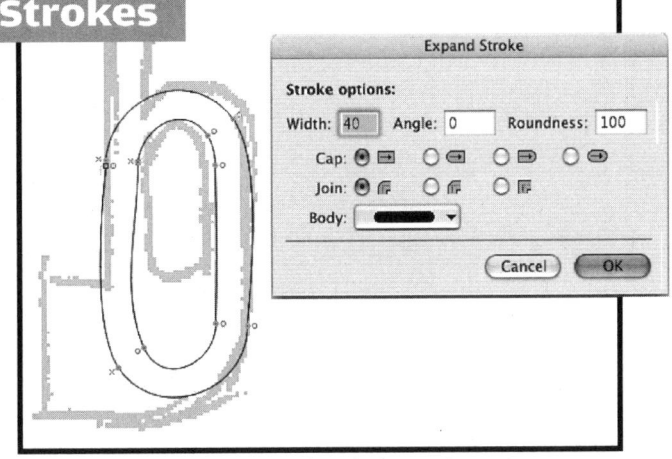

Expand Stroke

Stroke options:

Width: 40   Angle: 0   Roundness: 100

Cap:

Join:

Body:

Cancel   OK

Drawing glyphs continues on next page

7. Let's try an alternative to Expand Strokes. Go to TOOLS>Outline>Make Parallel Path. This setting produced a satisfactory result, right, with proper point placement and perfect parallelism. In the Parallel Contour dialogue box, far right, I chose to expand the contour by 20 units on Both sides of my original contour. By example, **a**, **b** and **c** show the effect upon a simple right angle path when it has been expanded Left, Right, or Both. If I had checked Remove the original, the original center line would have been eliminated.

Make Parallel Path

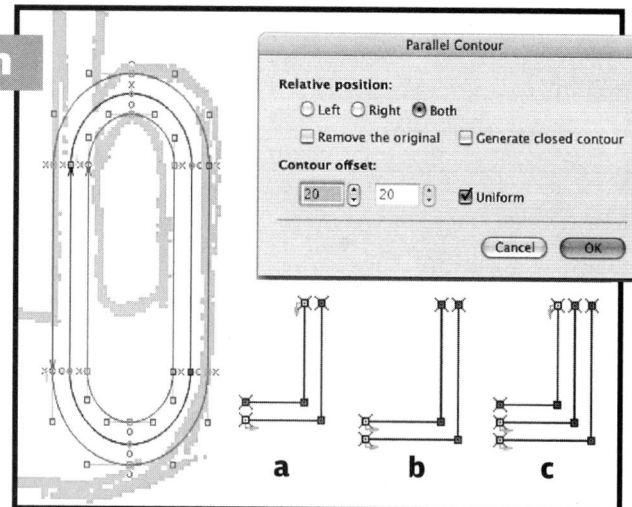

8. With the Edit tool, I marqueed all the bottom nodes of the compound contour (now expanded to 40-units, which is to be the standard thin stem width). Then I hit the Down Arrow key several times until the lowest node touched the baseline. You'll know it's touching when the lowest bezier handles become, in effect, invisible, **a**. (If an Arrow key's incremental steps fall·shy of, or overshoot your destination point, then manually drag the point to the desired position.) At **b**, I selected the bottom three nodes of the inner lozenge and Arrow keyed them upwards.

Arrow keys to move

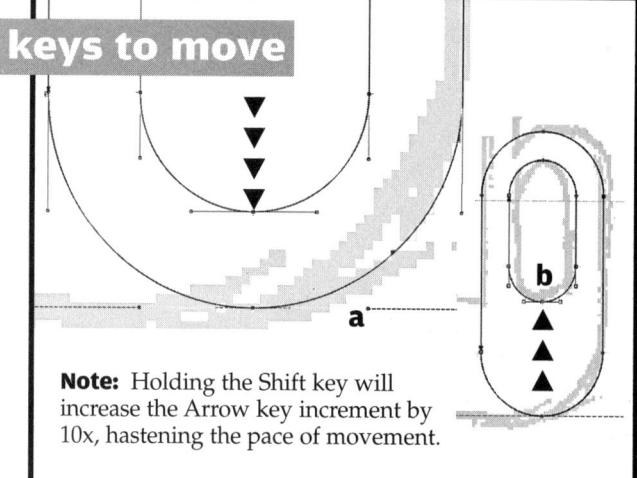

Note: Holding the Shift key will increase the Arrow key increment by 10x, hastening the pace of movement.

9. I chose the Rectangle tool from the toolbar and dragged a rectangle, **a**, downward from the cap-height line to make the top serif. (Notice that I'm not following the scan exactly—I'm revising as I go.) The selected rectangle was Copied (Cmd/Ctrl-C) and Pasted (Cmd/Ctrl-V) and then (with the Shift key held) the new Copy was dragged straight downward to become the bottom serif, **b**. With the Edit tool again, I Shift-clicked the right side path of this bottom serif and used the Left Arrow key to narrow its width.

Rectangle tool

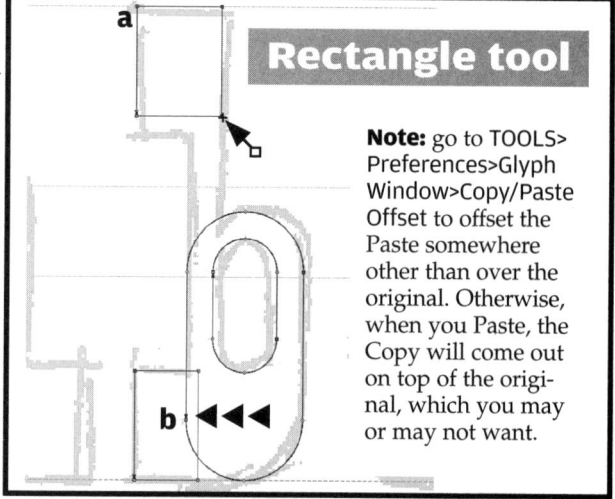

Note: go to TOOLS> Preferences>Glyph Window>Copy/Paste Offset to offset the Paste somewhere other than over the original. Otherwise, when you Paste, the Copy will come out on top of the original, which you may or may not want.

Drawing glyphs continues on page 62

How to Preview your drawing in progress

We now interrupt the drawing instructions to show a few methods for checking your work as you proceed.

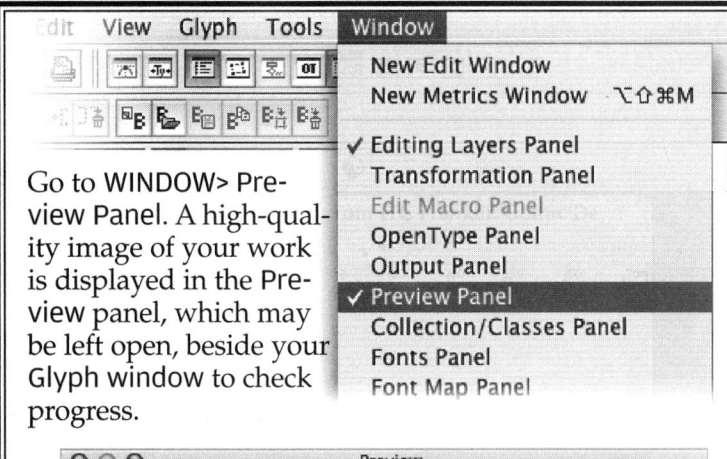

Go to WINDOW> Preview Panel. A high-quality image of your work is displayed in the Preview panel, which may be left open, beside your Glyph window to check progress.

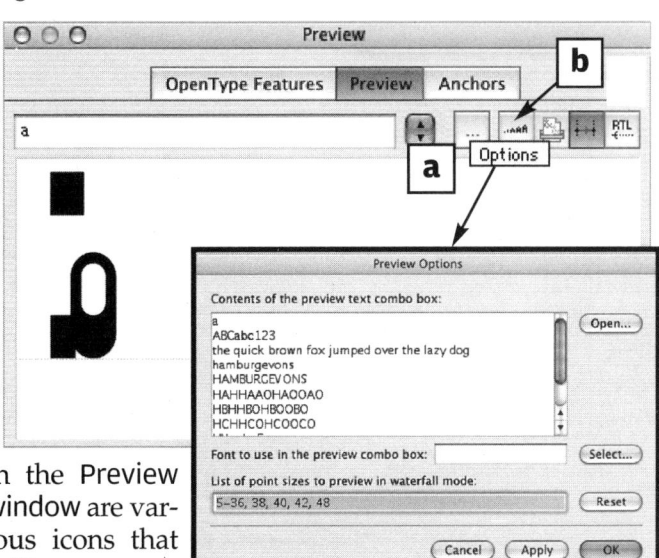

In the Preview window are various icons that will announce their functions if you hover the cursor over them so their captions come up, **a**. The Preview Options window, above, provides ready-made previewing options, like the alphabet or useful character strings like *HAHHAAO.*You can also click to specify a "waterfall" preview, **b**, so you can inspect your glyphs at different sizes. A waterfall will look something like thisssSSSS.

Work in Preview Mode: *go to* VIEW>Show Layers> Preview Mode, *or Shift-Cmd-P (Sh-Ctrl-P, Win) to see your drawings filled black as you work in the Glyph window.*

And, *For a black-filled preview in the open glyph window itself, press the tilde (~) key (Ö key on German keyboards).*

Or, go to WINDOW>New Metrics Window to see, not only a high-quality rendition of your glyph, but to be able to preliminarily adjust your spacing as well as kerning (click the K box).

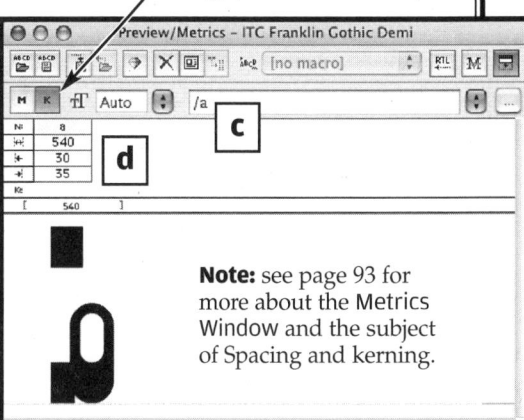

Note: see page 93 for more about the Metrics Window and the subject of Spacing and kerning.

By default, the Metrics window, seen above, opens to show the currently open Glyph window character preceded by a slash, **c**. If you try to type additional characters, they won't appear in the window unless you delete the first slash.

Why the slash? Any glyph *name* must be preceded with a slash and followed with a space (see page 97). So type a space after "/a" and you can continue typing other characters. Without the slash, the Unicode character 0026 typed into the Metrics window would appear as "0-0-2-6," rather than "&."

At **d**, the values for slot width, and left and right sidebearings are given for each character. If you've clicked the M, the kern value will appear below the other values. There's no kern value here because only our in-progress *letter b* is showing, so there's nothing kerned to it yet.

10. Checking Preview mode, I realized that the bottom of the bowl, **a**, needed to overshoot the baseline to make it appear level with the bottom of the serif, not higher than it. The bottom part of the counter (the "hole"), **b**, also needed to be lowered so it would appear to be in line with the top of the serif. So the inner and outer contours were marquee-selected then lowered with the Down Arrow key. (Since the marquee encompassed the right-side corner nodes of the lower serif, they each had to be Shift-clicked to deselect them before the bowl could be lowered.)

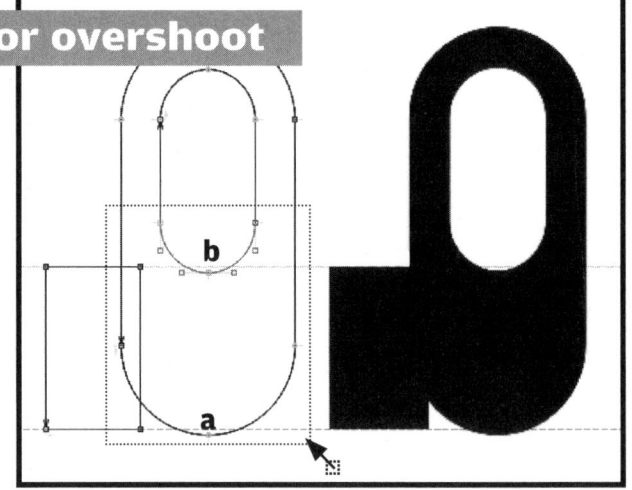

Allow for overshoot

11. I drew a single path down the middle of *b* for the vertical stem. Using either the Drawing tool or the Add Corner tool next to it, I drew a line from **a** to **b**. Since Drawing tools are not constrained by the Shift key, if a path we've drawn isn't absolutely straight, we can Shift-click the line, then click it holding Ctrl (Right-click, Win) to open the menu shown at right. Click on Align Points, **c**. Note: This feature always aligns to the left- or bottom-most point(s), and it works with any amount of selected points.

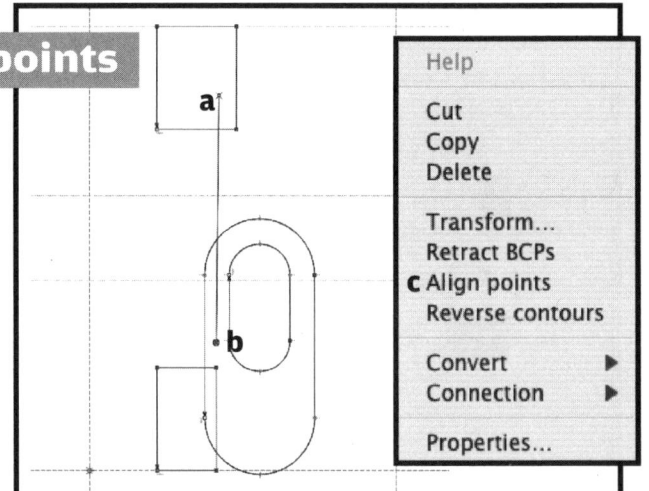

Align points

12. With the straightened vertical stem shown above selected, I went to TOOLS>Outline>Make Parallel Path (see step 7). Since this process yielded three paths, totaling 40-units wide, I needed to connect them into a closed contour. Here's one way: Drag bottom point of middle stroke, **a**, to top point of left stroke, **b**. Drag top point of middle stroke to top point of right stroke, **c**. (*Placing the point of an open path on top of another open path point automatically merges them.*) Click-select bottom point of right path. Draw a point anywhere, **d**, then drag it closed, **e**.

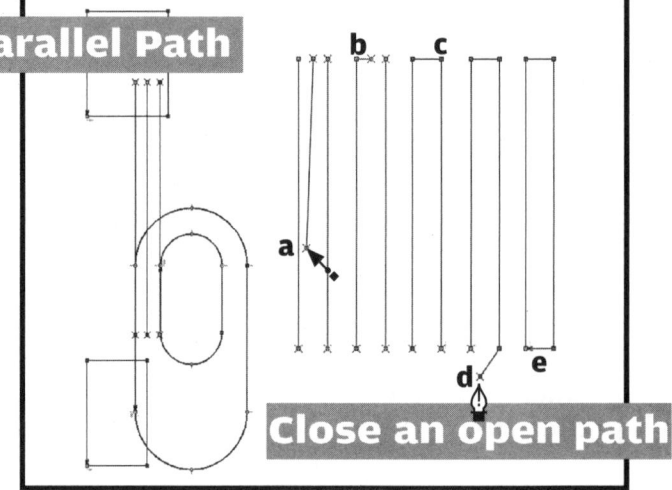

Make Parallel Path

Close an open path

Q & A:

In step 12., Why were two different methods used to join the top and bottom of the vertical stem?

In FontLab, there are usually many ways to accomplish any given task. It's up to you to figure out the most efficient strategy for getting a job done. For example, at **a**, the Add Corner tool was used to insert a new point onto the right-side path (the tool takes on the appearance of a knife). The bottom right corner point was dragged on top of the left corner point, **b**, which merged them into one, thereby closing the contour. Then the bottom of the stem was straightened, **c**, with Align Points

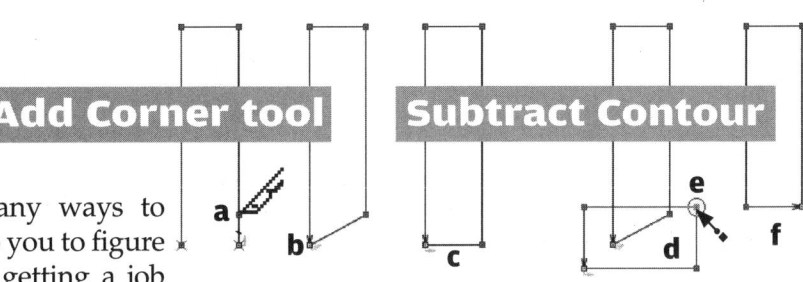

(see step 11.). Here's another approach to straightening a crooked path: chop it off. Draw a rectangle like **d**, that overlaps the crooked stem end and select one of the rectangle's nodes, **e**. Control-click (right-click, Win) that node to pop up the menu. Scroll to Contour>Subtract contour. This knocks out the rectangle and whatever lies within it, **f**.

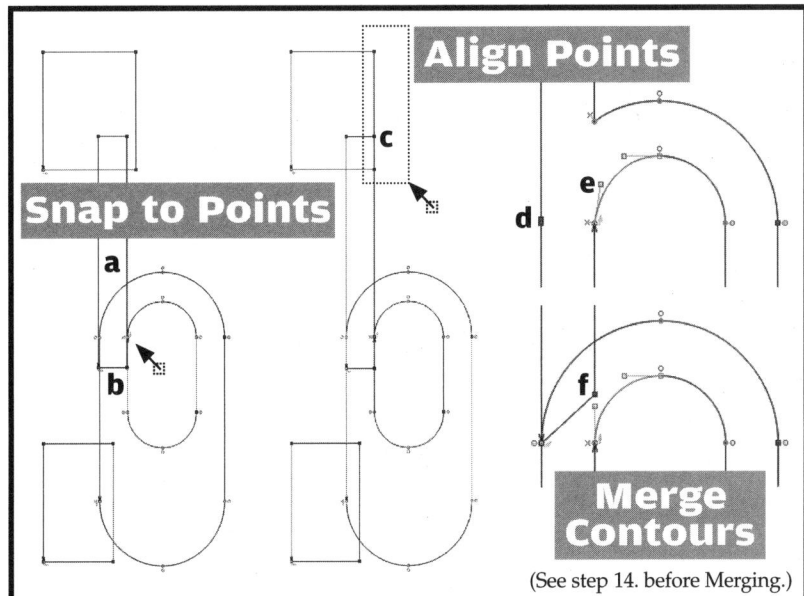

(See step 14. before Merging.)

13. Now it's time to start putting it all together. With the Edit tool I double-clicked the vertical stem, **a**, and dragged it over to Snap to perfect alignment with the thin left stem of the bowl, **b**. (In the expanded Editing Layers palette, Snap to Points is *on* by program default.)

Next, to drag the right side of the upper serif into line with the vertical stem, I marqueed the right side of the serif, **c**, which also selected the upper right corner point of the vertical stem. Normally, we would not want that stem point selected, but in this case we'll use it: Remember that Align Points always aligns to the left-most point, so that by applying Align Points (see step 11.), the right side of the serif that stuck out too far is drawn into alignment with the vertical stem.

The next step is to merge (TOOLS>Outline>Merge Contours) the assembled parts. At **d**, two excess nodes have resulted from merging the overlapped stems, which also caused the curve and its BCP handle to distort, **e**. The nodes can be deleted, but I hit Undo (Cmd/Ctrl-Z) and moved the point at **f** off the curve and then re-Merged.

You may have noticed that much of what I've drawn so far has been roughed-in. For example, the position of the "lozenge" I first drew, the widths of serifs, and the length of the line that I just expanded into a vertical stem were all drawn to rough sizes with the intention of repositioning them later when their proper positions could be determined. I call this *"putting in the knowns."* I *know* my stem width will be 40 units wide, I just don't know yet how tall the stem will need to be until I assemble all the other parts.

14. In step 13., I Merged all character parts, but before that, I saved them to the Mask layer to later be reused or even revised in the same glyph. To get drawings into the Mask layer, go to TOOLS>Templates>Copy to Mask. You can hide or show the Mask by clicking its box in Editing Layers or Show Layers palettes, left, And you can Clear Mask (**a**, right), or Copy to Template, **b**, so the same grayed image will appear globally in *all* Glyph Windows.

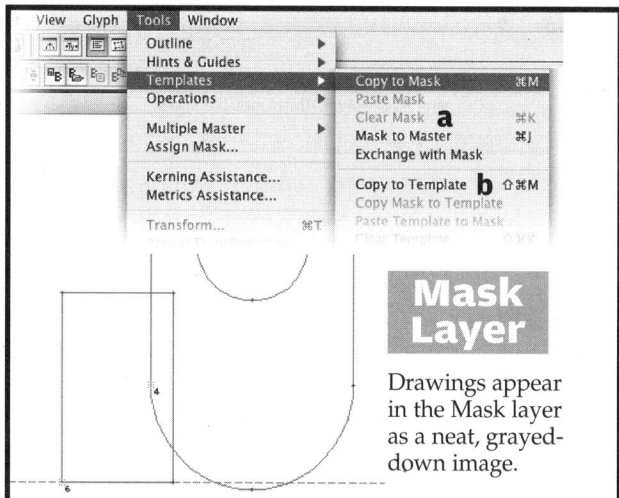

Mask Layer

Drawings appear in the Mask layer as a neat, grayed-down image.

15. After merging the parts to make the letter *b*, I cut/pasted it into its own character slot: the Glyph Window for lower case *b*. Now I can preliminarily adjust the metrics by clicking on the *word* "Metrics" in the Editing Layers palette to take me to that layer itself. Here I can slide the right sidebearing closer to the *b*, leaving about the same visual space as between the letter and the left sidebearing. Final spacing must be done in the Metrics window with other characters to compare.

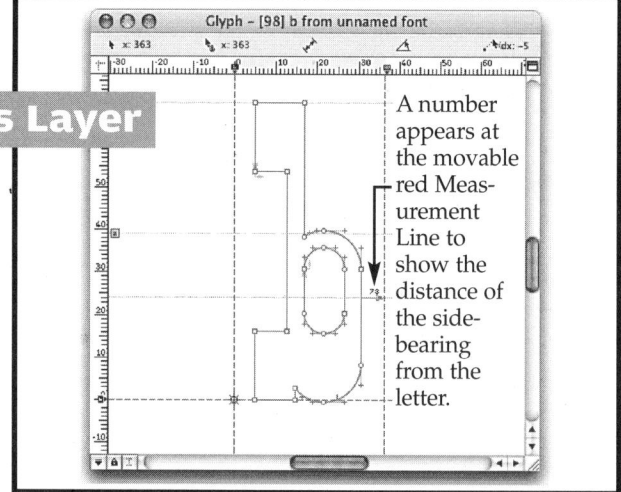

Metrics Layer

A number appears at the movable red Measurement Line to show the distance of the side-bearing from the letter.

16. I'll now draw more characters. In the *b* Glyph window I went to TOOLS>Templates>Paste Mask, to place a copy of the unmerged *b* parts from the Mask layer into the Outline layer. I Cut (Cmd-X or Ctrl-X) the parts, which were still selected from the paste, opened the Glyph window for *a*, and Pasted (Cmd-V or Ctrl-V). I then went to TOOLS>Outline>H Mirror to reflect (also called flopping) the *b* parts, and as you can see, right, the mirrored *b* already looks something like *a* (and like *d*, too). (The Ctrl-/Rt-click pop-up menu also gives access to Mirror.)

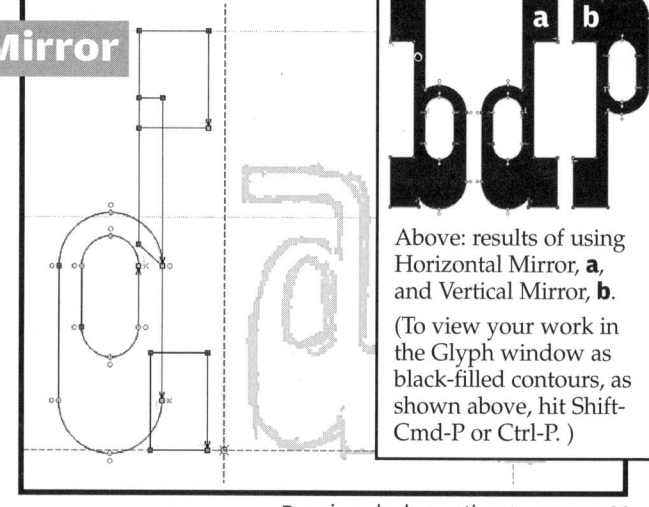

Horizontal Mirror

Above: results of using Horizontal Mirror, **a**, and Vertical Mirror, **b**.

(To view your work in the Glyph window as black-filled contours, as shown above, hit Shift-Cmd-P or Ctrl-P.)

Drawing glyphs continues on page 66

Pop-up menus

As briefly discussed on page 50, FontLab contains dozens of contextual pop-up menus that serve as a short cut to many of the most useful commands. Depending upon where you Ctrl-click (Right-click, Win), the pertinent menu changes. If you can't get the correct menu to pop up, it may be that you're not clicking on the right spot.

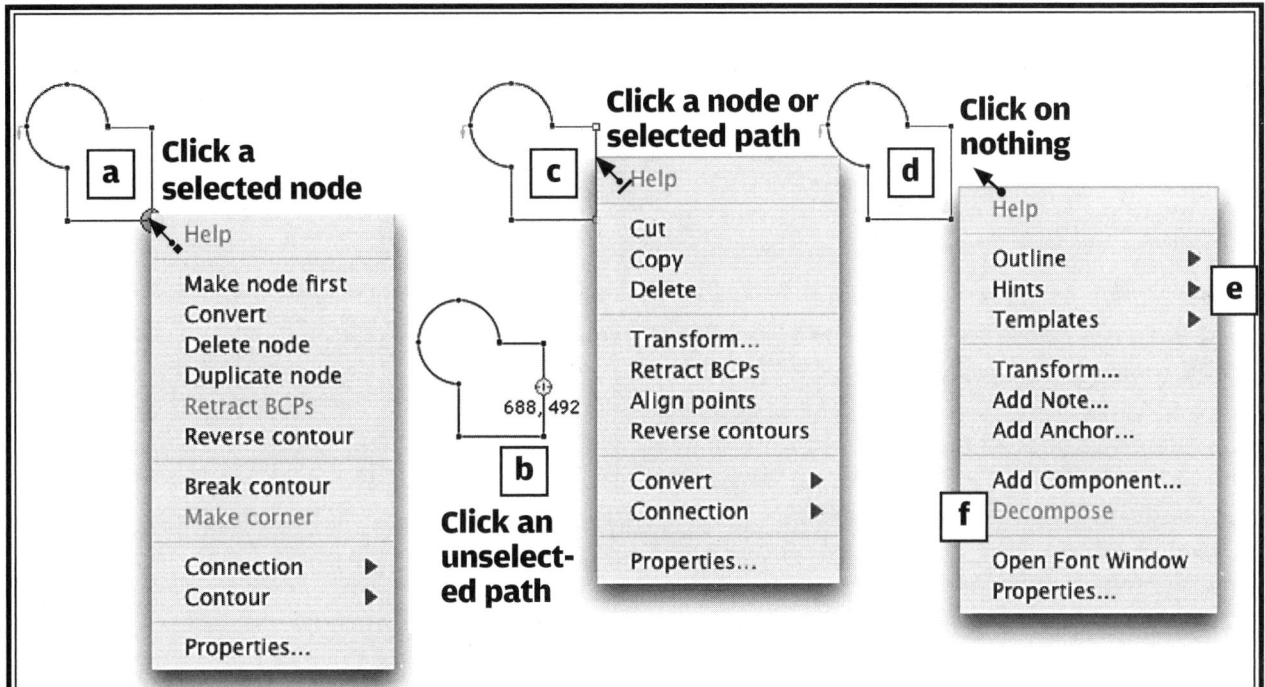

Above is what you'll get when you Ctrl-click: **a:** a node; **b:** a line that isn't selected (all you see is a read-out of the exact position you clicked; **c:** a selected path; **d:** anywhere that's nowhere, i.e., not a path or point. When you

see arrows in the menu, such as at **e**, that indicates there are further available options when you roll the mouse over them. When a menu item is grayed-out, **f**, that indicates an operation that cannot be performed with the present selection status.

These pop-up menus are available for most operations. The pop-up at left, comes up when you Ctrl-click on a Mask layer.

Again, If you can't get the desired menu to pop-up, you're not clicking the right spot or the relevant condition does not exist. For example, if you want to Align points, but that option isn't available in the pop-up menu, it may be because you haven't selected two or more points to be aligned.

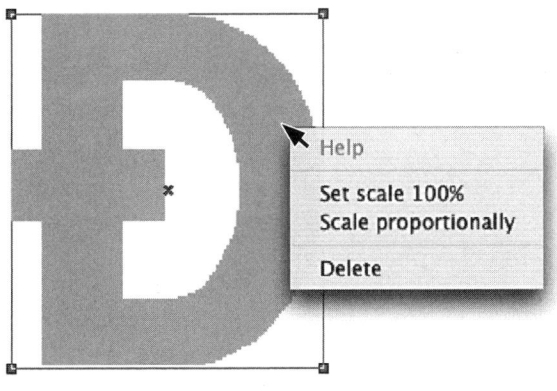

17. I deleted the top parts of the *b*, leaving the bottom bowl and serif, far right, from which to build the *a*. With the Ellipse tool, I held Shift to drag out a perfect circle and then selected the node at **a**. Ctrl-clicking that node opened the pop-up menu and I selected Break Contour. That created two unconnected endpath nodes, **b**, where one had been. I marqueed and deleted the nodes shown and then chose the Drawing tool to extend a horizontal and a vertical line from the remaining points of the ellipse, **c** and **d**. I put the path in place at **e**.

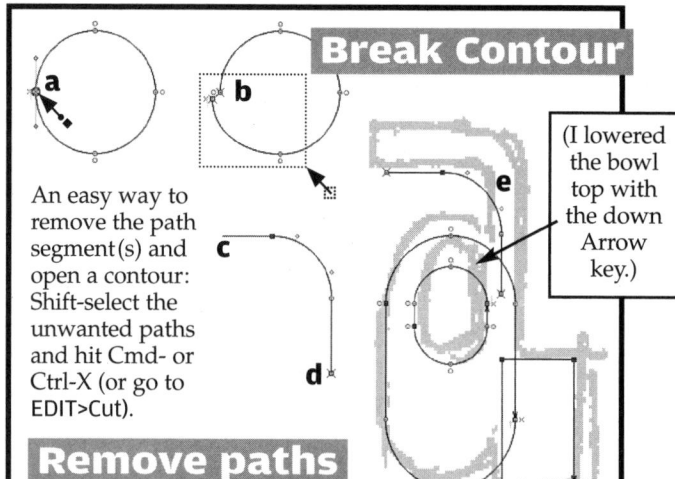

Break Contour

An easy way to remove the path segment(s) and open a contour: Shift-select the unwanted paths and hit Cmd- or Ctrl-X (or go to EDIT>Cut).

(I lowered the bowl top with the down Arrow key.)

Remove paths

18. Make Parallel Path (see step 7.) was used to expand the new path to our standard thin stem width of 40 units, **a**. But I don't like the radius of the curve: it's too large. Why not just scale the two paths smaller? Because then the width, **b**, becomes less than 40 units. So hit Cmd/Ctrl-Z or EDIT>Undo to revert to a single line. Ctrl-click on a node or selected path and choose Transform from the pop-up menu, **c**. Hold Shift to constrain proportion and drag handle, **d**, up to reduce the curve. Choose Make Parallel Path again. Width will be 40 units, but the curve radius, **e**, is less.

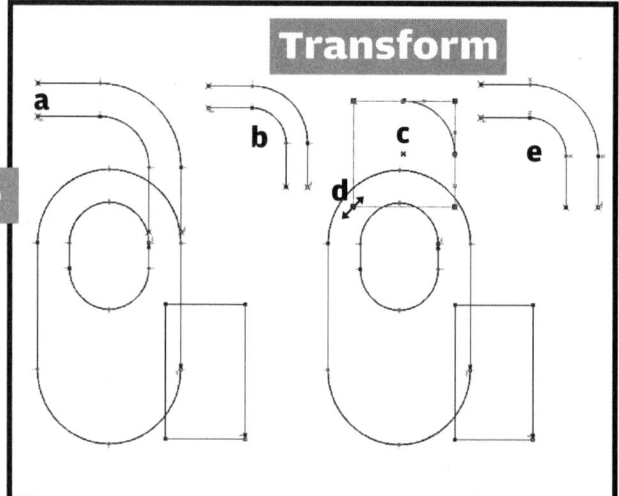

Transform

Undo

19. The curving stem path that I made into two unconnected paths, **a**, must now be joined at both ends to become one closed contour. I'll do this, as I did in step 12., by selecting an end node, clicking a new point with the Drawing tool, **b**, then doing the same at the other end, **c**. Then I'll drag both new points on top of their adjacent endpath points to close the contour, **d**. Notice that I raised point **e** of the contour to clear the bowl's counter so when the just-made curving stem is merged with the bowl, the BCP handle won't go awry (see step 13.).

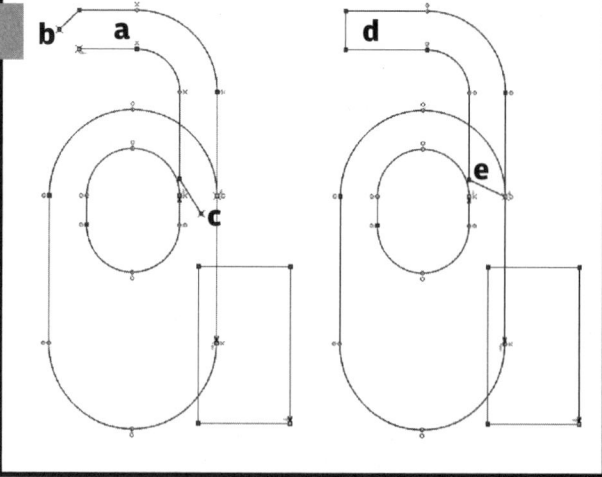

Close paths

Drawing glyphs continues on page 68

Transform, Transforming, Transformation

There are several different ways to transform (alter the shape of) a selected drawing, a selected portion of a drawing or every glyph in a font. Each method is accessed differently, and has slightly different capabilities.

The single-function Rotate and Scale tools located in the toolbar, **a**, are transforming tools, but you'll have to leave the Edit or Drawing tool to get one of them, and that's a bother.

Instead you can Ctrl-click (Rt-click, Win) a node or any selected contour(s) to choose Transform, **b** (called "Free Transform" in Studio 5). This will cause a six-handled bounding box to form around the selected drawings, as shown far right, **c**.

Drag one of the four corner handles on the Transform tool to Scale (enlarge or reduce)

the selection. The slanted center-top handle is for "slanting" (also called shearing or skewing), and the round handle at center-right side is for rotating the selection.

To transform from any spot—not just the center point —drag the center axis, **d**, to any desired location. This versatile Transform tool may even obviate use of the Rotate and Scale tools.

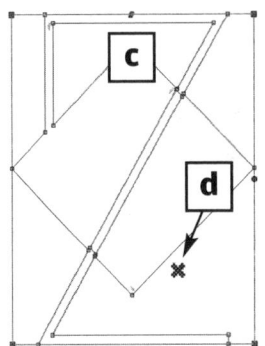

Fastest way *to get the Transform tool: Double-click on a path or contour that is selected.*

The Transform tool described above allows manual transforming to the eye's standard only, which is fine 97% of the time. But if you want to set specific values—such as *12°*—to alter either a part of a contour or one complete glyph, go to WINDOW>Transformation panel *(this panel not pictured).*

But to transform an entire glyph, or many glyphs at once (eg: to make a font italic), use the Transformation dialog window, right (go to TOOLS> Transform (or Cmd-/Ctrl-T). Among other actions, like special Effects available in this window, you can Scale, Rotate, Mirror or Slant, **e**, to your exact numerical specifications.

Check the Apply to whole font box, to transform every glyph in the font, **f**. A warning will pop up that this action is undoable. You *can* undo, though. Close the font (Cmd-/Ctrl-W), but don't Save. Then reopen it.

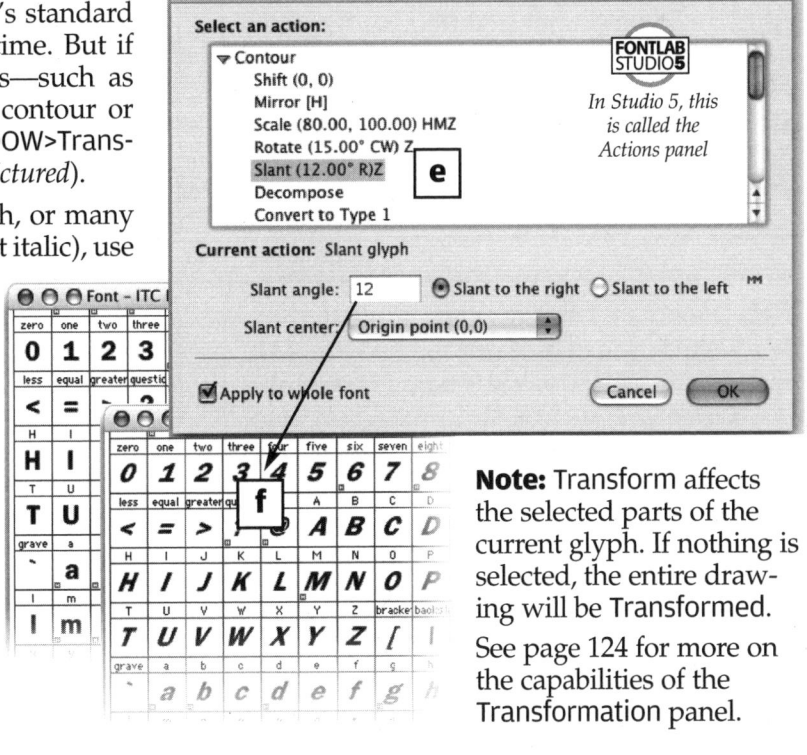

Note: Transform affects the selected parts of the current glyph. If nothing is selected, the entire drawing will be Transformed.

See page 124 for more on the capabilities of the Transformation panel.

20. When I checked the *a* glyph in Preview mode (Shift-Cmd- or Ctrl-P) I discovered that the direction of the curving stem contour, **a**, was reversed. Every contour has a direction—either clockwise or counter clockwise—based upon the direction we first created the nodes. The little arrows at the start and end points of every contour, **b**, reveal their direction. At **c**, both circles run counter-clockwise. At **d**, the inner circle was selected and Ctrl-clicked to pop up the menu so Reverse Contour could be chosen to turn it clockwise. The curving stem, **e**, was also fixed this way.

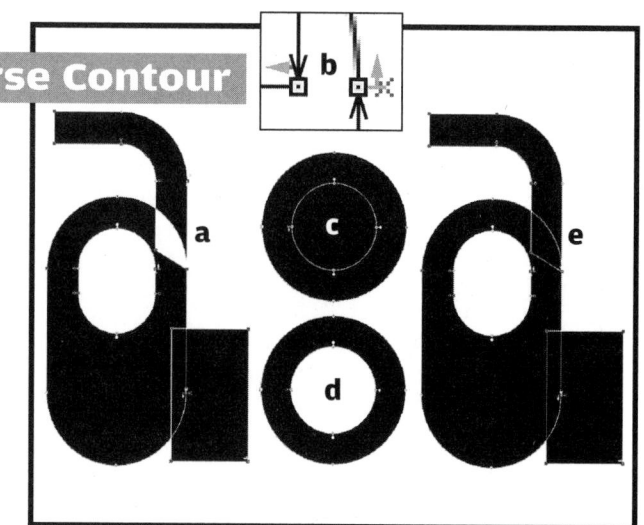

21. Moving on to lower case *s*, I made a copy of the *a* bowl and deleted its left side by Shift-clicking each path segment then hitting Cut (Cmd- or Ctrl-X), which easily breaks the contour regardless of whether Edit/Delete command breaks contour is enabled in the Preferences>Glyph window. Instead of using the *a* bowl, I could have started from scratch with a single circle and again expanded it with Make parallel path. There are usually many approaches to any task and though one may be no more difficult than another, it behooves us to strategize the simplest way.

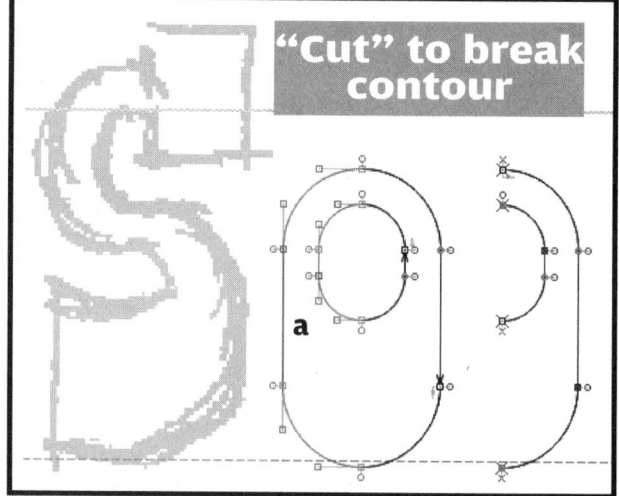

22. I marqueed then dragged down the top of my shape until node **a** was on top of node **b**. Overlapping nodes is not OK, but Optimize (Cmd-/Ctrl-E) removed one of the nodes. With the Edit tool I clicked node **c**, then drew node **d** and so on until I'd closed the contour at **e**. This letter needn't overshoot the baseline, so I marqueed points **e** and **f** and dragged them both up until **e** touched the baseline. If I had only moved **e** up to the baseline, but not **f**, the perfect quarter-circle corner would have become elliptical, not circular, and I'd have broken style.

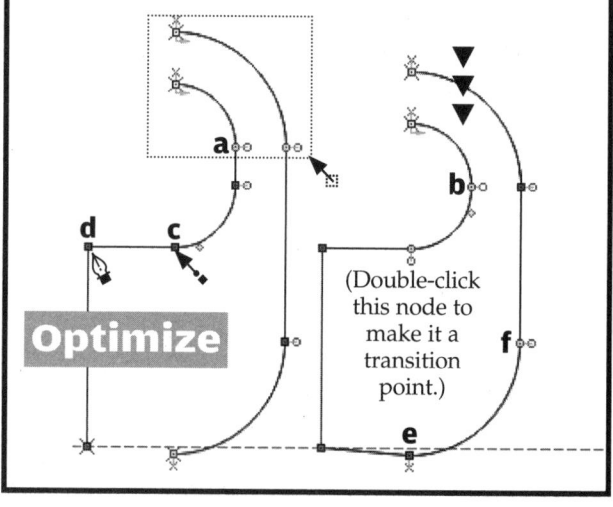

(Double-click this node to make it a transition point.)

23. I marqueed the four nodes shown, **a**. I copied, pasted and dragged the result, **b**, to the side. With the Rotate tool, I clicked and held on an arbitrary center point and rotated both open quarter-circle paths to position **c** (*as I rotated, I also held down Shift to snap the rotating shape to straight horizontal*). Shape **c** was dragged up to position **d**. Then I selected, copied and pasted **d**, and rotated this new pasted copy to the **e** position and merged the two quarter circles into a half circle by dragging the lower two nodes of **e** onto the upper two of **d**. Then the combined shape was merged at **f**.

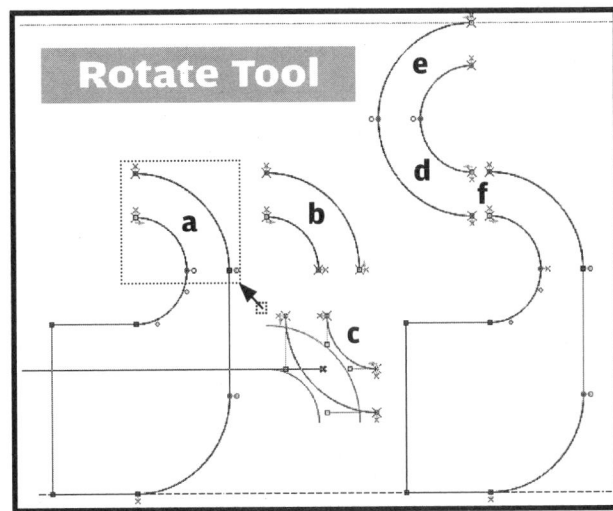

24. Before merging a serif with the body of *s*, the contour must be closed. I click-selected node **a**, then drew node **b**. If I'd drawn node **b** right on top of node **c**, to close the path, the node's connection type would have changed, as in **d**, and the curve would have been ruined. Instead, I dragged the outgoing BCP handle into the point, **e**, and dragged the new node **b** on top of the top-most one, which closed the contour. (*Open contours won't be visible in Preview mode unless you go to* Preferences>Glyph Window *and uncheck* Do Not Fill Open Contours).

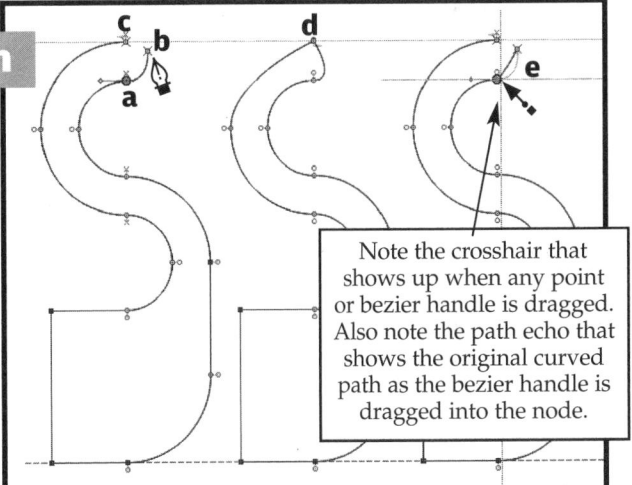

Note the crosshair that shows up when any point or bezier handle is dragged. Also note the path echo that shows the original curved path as the bezier handle is dragged into the node.

25. I dragged my standard serif (first created for the *b*) into position on the *s*. Notice that I changed the design of *s* from my initial rough sketch as reality intervened upon theory. Selecting both *s* and serif, I tried to Merge but could not, **b**, because the contour direction of the *s* was counter-clockwise, inset **c**, and the serif's direction was clockwise, **d**. As in step 20., I Reversed Contour direction of the serif and then pressed Ctrl/Rt-click to open the pop-up menu. I chose Outline>Merge Contours, **e**, to join serif to letter and finalize this character (until I start tweaking it, that is).

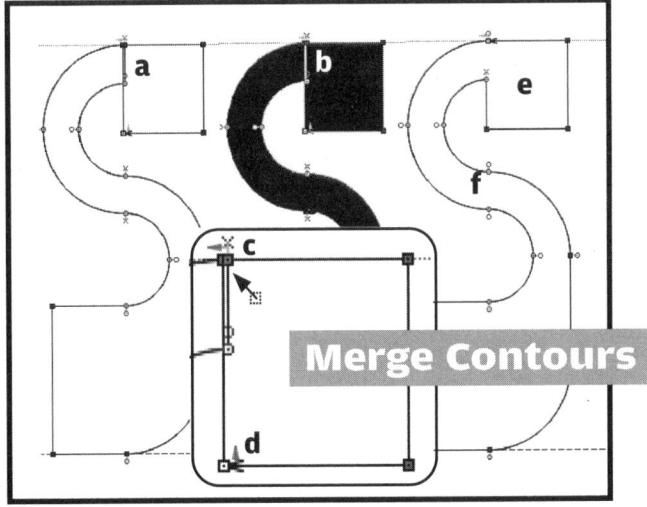

26. Right, I copied letter *s* and pasted it into the Glyph window for *c*. Holding the Shift key, I click-selected four path segments (arrows) and hit Cmd-/Ctrl-X to Cut them, thereby breaking the contour open. I selected the bottom half of *s* at **a**, hit Ctrl/Rt-click to open the pop-up menu and went to Outline>H Mirror to reflect it over backwards. To align the top and bottom pieces along their left edges, I dragged the selected bottom piece by the node, **b**. When the vertical crosshair snapped to node **c**, I knew the two were aligned. (If you still don't like the crosshair, go to Preferences>Glyph Window> Don't Show Crosshair.) With the Drawing tool, I then connected the upper and lower parts, as previously demonstrated in steps 12. and 24.

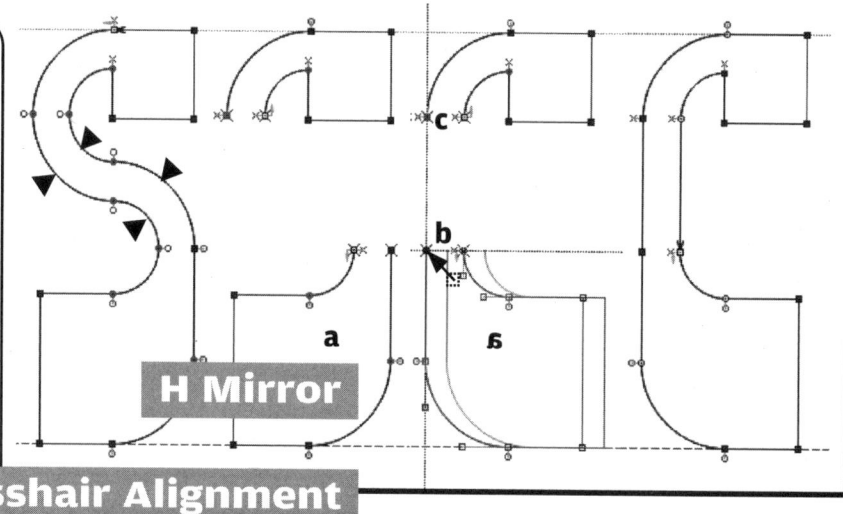

H Mirror

Crosshair Alignment

27. Below, here are the steps I took to make letter *c* into *e*. I pasted both the lower part of *c*, **a**, and then the stem, **b**, and bowl, **c**, from the letter *b* into the *e* Glyph window. Stem **b** was rotated (and then dragged narrower) to become the crossbar of *e*. The lower right side of bowl **c** was Cut out, **d**, but I purposely didn't delete node **e** so I could drag it atop node **f** to close the contour on that side. Next, I dragged nodes **f** and **g** up so they wouldn't stick out below the crossbar. At **h** the crossbar is in place and the **a** and **c** parts have been connected. Finally, at **i**, I Merged Contours to complete letter *e*.

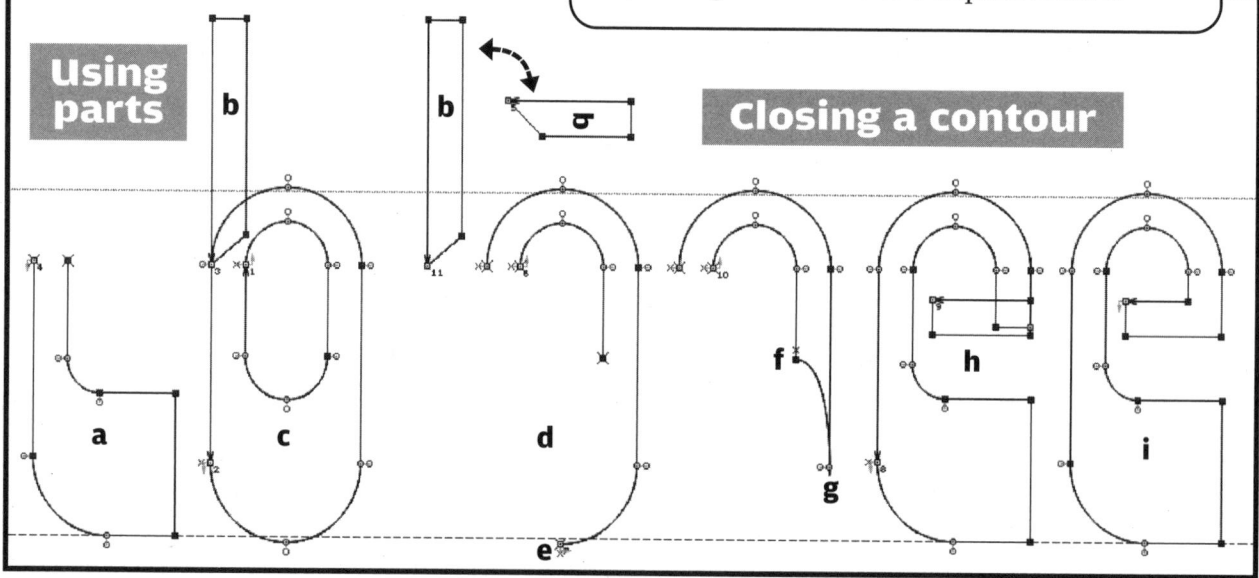

Using parts

Closing a contour

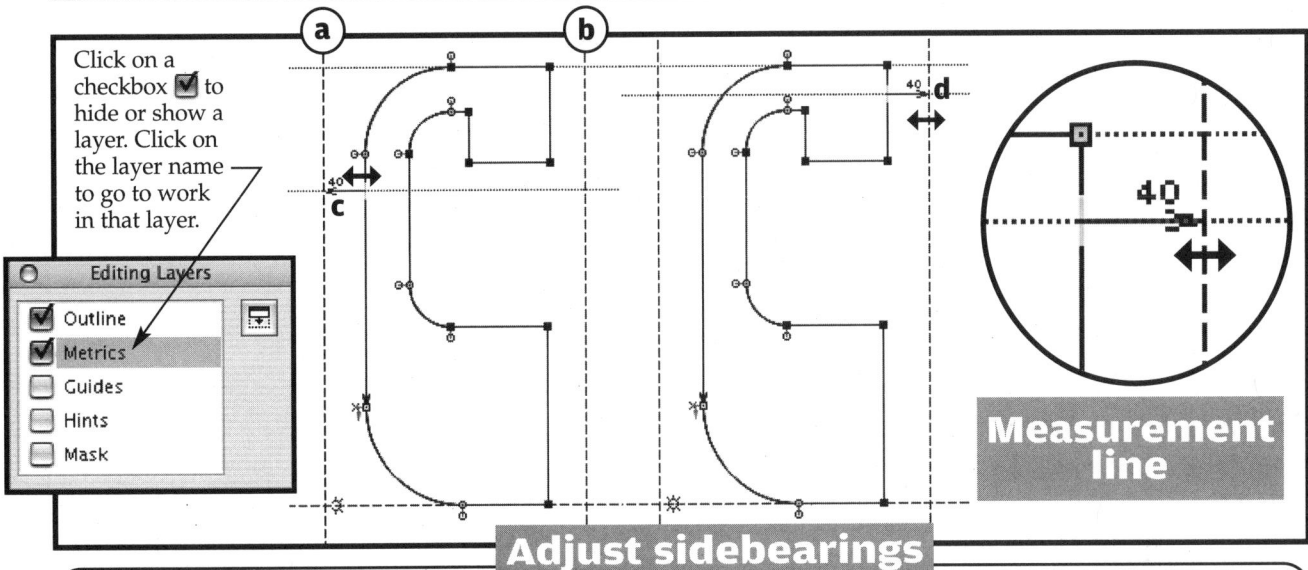

Click on a checkbox ☑ to hide or show a layer. Click on the layer name to go to work in that layer.

Editing Layers
- ☑ Outline
- ☑ Metrics
- ☐ Guides
- ☐ Hints
- ☐ Mask

Measurement line

Adjust sidebearings

28. Above, as I work, I like to roughly space characters in their Glyph windows. In the Editing Layers palette, click the word Metrics to go to that layer. Now you'll find that the vertical left and right sidebearings, **a** and **b**, may be dragged to any position in relation to the character. I dragged the red Measurement line to cross at the letter's vertical left stem. As I dragged the left sidebearing, a digital readout, **c**, told me the distance from sidebearing to letter. I then dragged the red Measurement line to the right edge of the top serif (I can't measure thru the bowl) to measure the distance between it and the right sidebearing. As you drag a sidebearing, the cursor becomes a double arrow (see detail).

Letter spacing 101 *Let your eyes be the final judge of spacing.*

Leave a wider space, **a**, between two characters (like *I-H*) whose straight sides will create a claustrophobic effect. Make a narrower space, maybe fifty-percent less than at **a**, between protruding bowls of curved characters like *b-d, p-e, O-O or D-G*, **b**. Once established, use the same values for the sidebearings of all similar-sided letters. If 80-units looks right between two straight-sided letters, assign 40-units per side.

At **c** below, a bit tighter spacing was required than at **a** because the round-cornered left side of letter *c* lets in some air. Two round-cornered sides at **d** meant still tighter spacing. Where serifs meet, **e**, the space must be narrow to close up the gap above, between vertical stems, **g**.

The near impossibility of decently spacing the letters below indicates to me, as the designer, that I ought to rethink some of the lettershapes and reduce those wide serifs to avoid huge gaps like **f, g,** and **h**. Is it surprising that a "secondary" consideration like letter spacing should impact upon character design? Not when you realize that a font's functionality can be impeded by poor legibility that may result from bad spacing.

Check progress in the Metrics window

up until now, in the "Drawing Glyphs" section that began on page 58, I've been working on individual letters, unable really, to judge them as a group. In the spacing exercise on the previous page, I discovered that I would have to tweak some of the letters. The whole point of a font is to make all the characters work together as a matched set. In the Preview/Metrics Window I'll now check my existing glyphs so far. The decisions and changes I make at this early stage will lead to the adoption of a set of standards that will help me to avoid having to go back and redraw entire characters or make major revisions on the subsequent characters I create based on these first ones. You can also use WINDOW> Preview Panel to preview strings of characters.

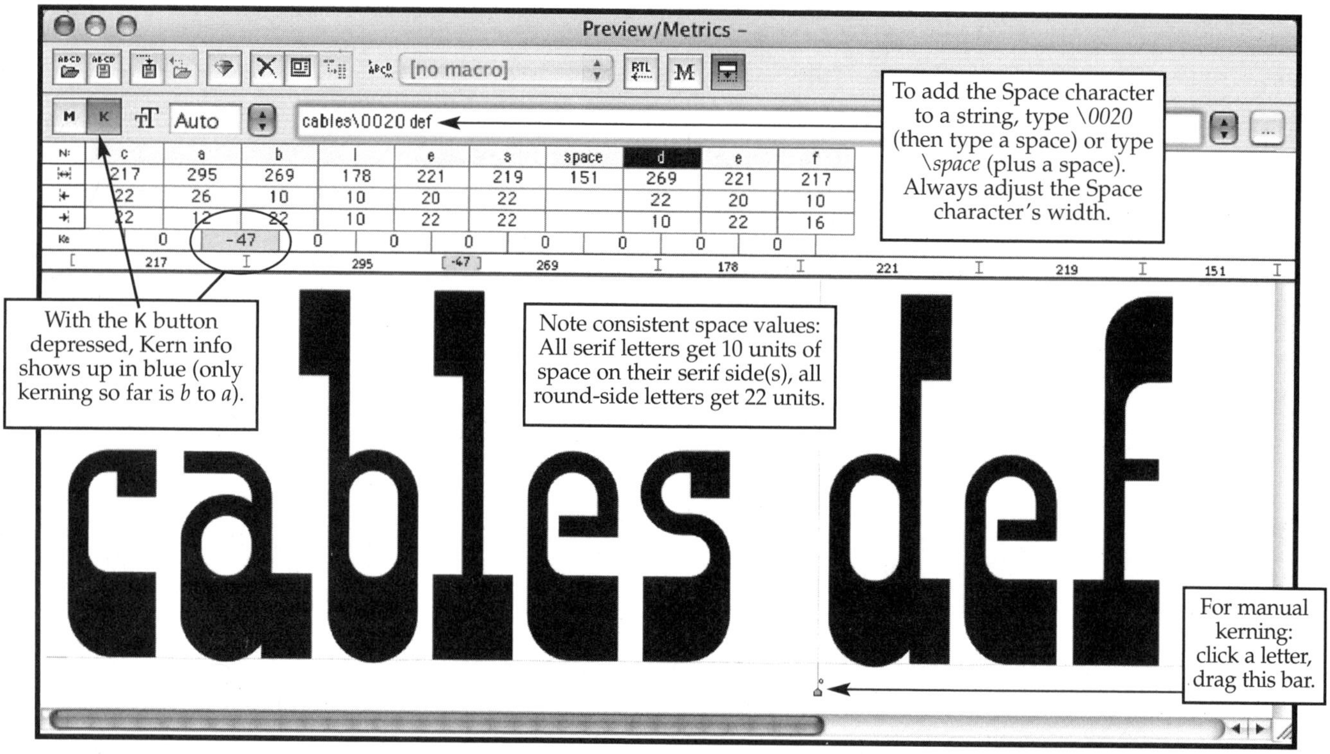

The window shows the Preview/Metrics title bar with toolbar buttons, the string field "cables\0020 def", and a metrics table:

N:	c	a	b	l	e	s	space	d	e	f
↔	217	295	269	178	221	219	151	269	221	217
⊢	22	26	10	10	20	22		22	20	10
⊣	22	12	22	10	22	22		10	22	16
Ke	0		-47	0	0	0	0	0	0	0
[	217	I	295	[-47]	269	I	178	I	221	I	219	I	151	I

To add the Space character to a string, type \0020 (then type a space) or type \space (plus a space). Always adjust the Space character's width.

With the K button depressed, Kern info shows up in blue (only kerning so far is b to a).

Note consistent space values: All serif letters get 10 units of space on their serif side(s), all round-side letters get 22 units.

cables def

For manual kerning: click a letter, drag this bar.

Open Preview/Metrics

Just go to WINDOW>New Metrics Window (Shift-Op-Cmd-M, Mac or Shift-Alt-Ctrl-M, Win) and the window above opens showing any selected glyphs in the Font window or the currently open character in the Glyph Window. You can also type any string of characters, as I have done. Most agree that it's better to judge letters when composed into words, rather than as random letters.

Character changes

Because of the spacing problems I noted on page 71, I removed the bottom serif from b and decreased all the other serifs by 20 units by selecting each of their right- and/or left-most points and hitting the Right (or Left) Arrow key two times (10 units per Arrow key hit) toward the center of each letter. Oops, I forgot to decrease letter a's right serif; it's still wider than the other serifs.

FONTLAB STUDIO5

See Page 103 for a more complete explanation of spacing/kerning and the FontLab Studio 5.0 Metrics Window, which differs from the version 4.6 Metrics Window shown above.

Working Suggestions

How you arrange the palettes and windows on your monitor can affect efficiency. If you can afford two monitors (one for palettes only), that's ideal. Open the Metrics window on one side of your monitor as you work to check progress and see contour changes updated instantly. Here are some other navigation tips to consider.

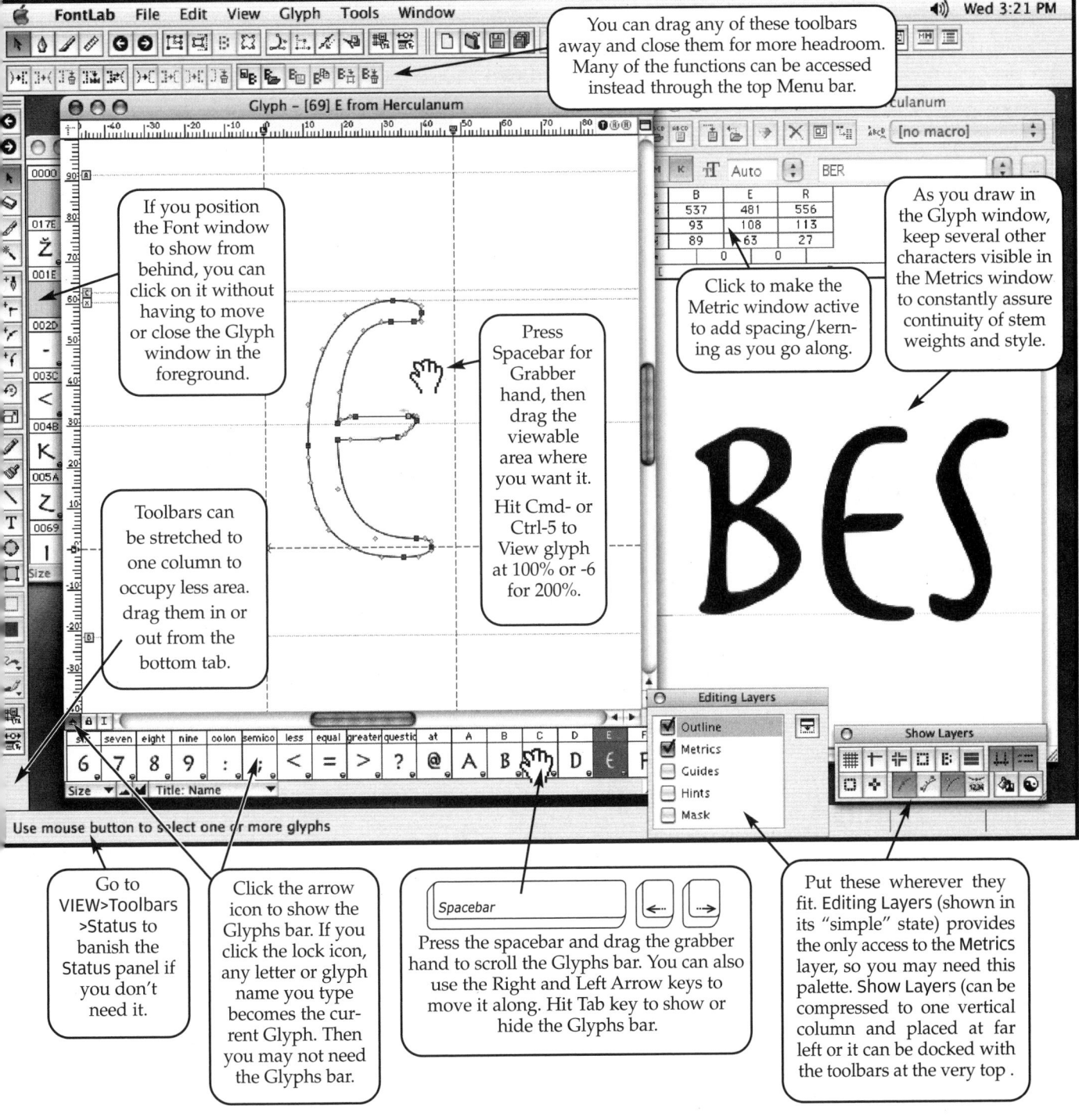

You can drag any of these toolbars away and close them for more headroom. Many of the functions can be accessed instead through the top Menu bar.

If you position the Font window to show from behind, you can click on it without having to move or close the Glyph window in the foreground.

Press Spacebar for Grabber hand, then drag the viewable area where you want it. Hit Cmd- or Ctrl-5 to View glyph at 100% or -6 for 200%.

Click to make the Metric window active to add spacing/kerning as you go along.

As you draw in the Glyph window, keep several other characters visible in the Metrics window to constantly assure continuity of stem weights and style.

Toolbars can be stretched to one column to occupy less area. drag them in or out from the bottom tab.

Go to VIEW>Toolbars>Status to banish the Status panel if you don't need it.

Click the arrow icon to show the Glyphs bar. If you click the lock icon, any letter or glyph name you type becomes the current Glyph. Then you may not need the Glyphs bar.

Press the spacebar and drag the grabber hand to scroll the Glyphs bar. You can also use the Right and Left Arrow keys to move it along. Hit Tab key to show or hide the Glyphs bar.

Put these wherever they fit. Editing Layers (shown in its "simple" state) provides the only access to the Metrics layer, so you may need this palette. Show Layers (can be compressed to one vertical column and placed at far left or it can be docked with the toolbars at the very top .

Optional Drawing tools: Sketch Mode

Sometimes, you just can't seem to make a bezier curve take the shape you want. In that case, Sketch mode may be the solution. While this feature is temporarily enabled, you can make minute shape tweaks to character contours. When you're done, you must switch back to regular drawing mode: either Type 1 or TrueType curves.

Enter Sketch mode: Click the pen icon in the Tools palette, right. If this palette is not open, go to VIEW>Toolbars>Tools.

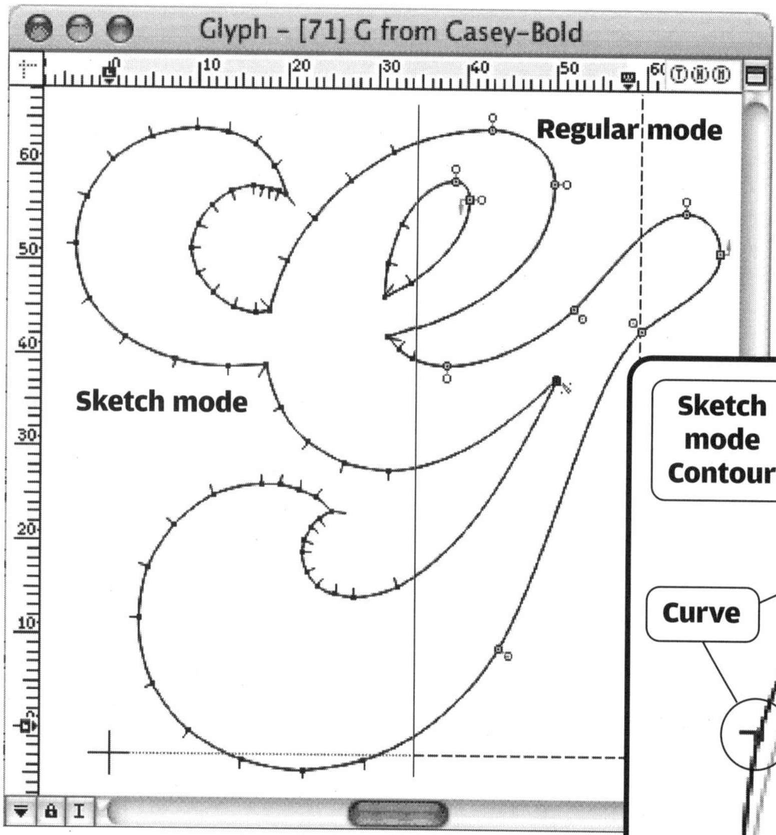

In Sketch mode, left, regular nodes are replaced by dozens of points, any of which may be individually nudged to make minor adjustments to a contour. A grayed-down reference copy of the original contour appears also in the Outline layer under the Sketch-mode glyph. You can't see it until you move a few points, as shown below.

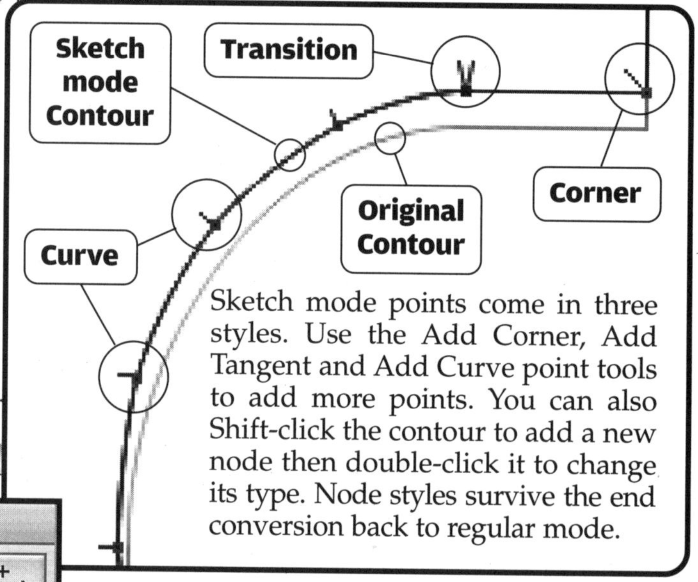

Glyph – [71] G from Casey–Bold

Regular mode

Sketch mode

Sketch mode Contour

Transition

Curve

Original Contour

Corner

Sketch mode points come in three styles. Use the Add Corner, Add Tangent and Add Curve point tools to add more points. You can also Shift-click the contour to add a new node then double-click it to change its type. Node styles survive the end conversion back to regular mode.

The Sketch palette appears when you enter Sketch mode.

Sketch

Show Outline	Show Marks	New Sketch	Import Sketch	Replace Outline	Add to Outline
Click here to hide or show the underlying original contour.	*Hide or show the Sketch mode point types. Instead you'll see dots for points.*	*Delete the present Sketch mode contour. Use the point tools to draw a new sketch.*	*Lets FontLab make a new Sketch if you regret deleting the first one.*	*Replaces original contour with the changed one you've made in Sketch mode.*	*Adds your edited Sketch to the underlying original contour.*

Working in Sketch mode

In *Type 1 glyph construction, the fewer nodes you have, the smoother your contours will be. In Sketch mode, having more points is the point. Get further details about Sketch mode in FontLab's free .pdf manual.*

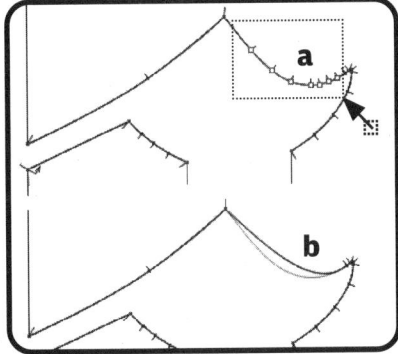

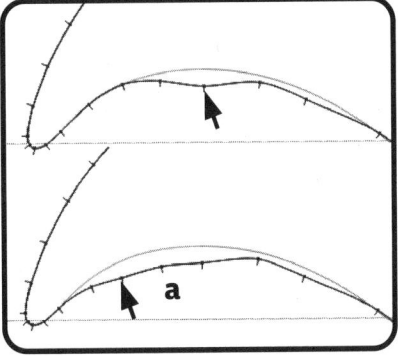

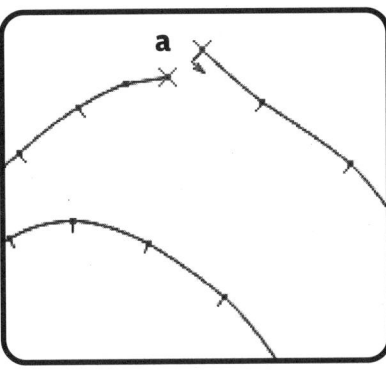

Delete points
Use the Eraser tool or marquee any points, **a**, to Delete them. In Sketch mode, you can't drag the contour itself, so you may just need all those points. See, without the points there's no way to get the curve, **b**, to dip down again.

Move points
Drag points one by one or marquee a bunch and drag all at once. Single points may also be dragged sideways along the path. Because points are all entwined, to avoid a ripple effect, **a**, you must move many points when tweaking a curve.

Break/Open the contour
Option- or Alt-click a node to break open the contour, **a**. Drag an end point on top of another to merge them and close the contour. Personally, I'd do all my major surgery in regular mode and use Sketch mode just to nudge the occasional curve.

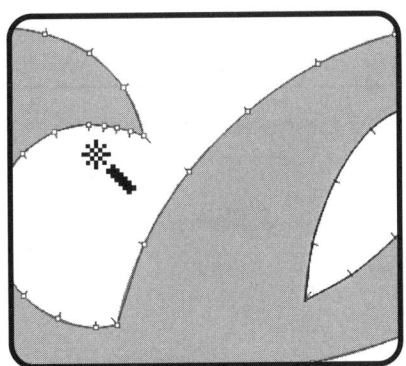

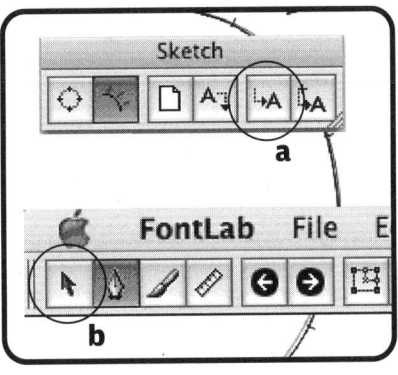

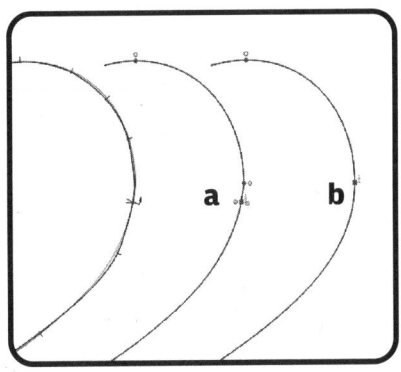

Previewing
The Magic Wand and many other functions work just as in regular editing mode. Use Preview mode (Shift-Cmd- or Ctrl-P to see the original contour as a grayed-out background image, or hit the ~ tilde key for a sneak preview.

Leaving Sketch mode
Hit the Replace Outline button, **a**, to apply the changes you've made in Sketch mode. If you don't do this before hitting the Arrow button, **b**, to go back to regular mode, your Sketch mode changes to the original outline won't take effect.

Optimize
The last step after using Sketch mode is to Optimize (Cmd- or Ctrl-E) the contour for output. Notice that after switching to Type 1 mode, **a**, some excess, ill-positioned nodes have occurred. Optimize will usually get rid of them, **b**, or do it yourself.

Drawing with TrueType Curves

TrueType (TT) curves with their "off-curve points" are an alternative-to-beziers drawing method that feels some-what similar to Sketch mode. If you don't like bezier handles, try using TT curves. Of course, while working on a glyph, you can switch back and forth between drawing modes. It's not necessary to use TT curves when making a TT font. FontLab will convert your contours when you generate a font as TrueType. However, since slight alterations to contours can occur, you may want to convert Type 1 glyphs to TT yourself and check for problems.

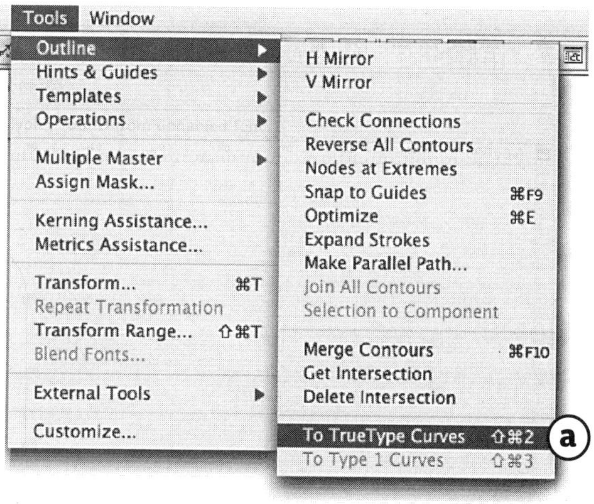

Converting

Naturally, there are several ways to "Convert" a drawing from the default bezier, or Type 1 Curves mode, to TrueType Curves:

- Go to TOOLS>Outline>To TrueType Curves, **a**.
- Hit Shift-Cmd-2 (Mac) or Shift-Ctrl-2 (Win).
- Control- or Rt-click a path, scroll to Convert, **b**.
- Control- or Rt-click a node, scroll to Convert, **c**.
- Option- or Alt-click a node to convert only the curve segment downstream from the node.

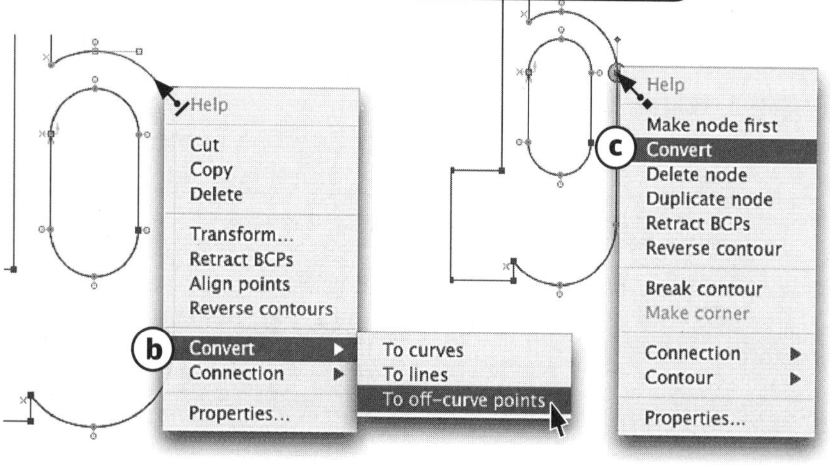

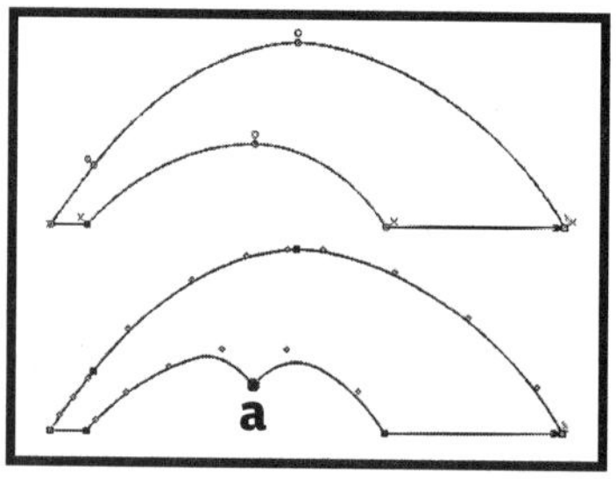

Many nodes to travel

Convert to TrueType curves and a few nodes become hundreds. Drag a TT anchor node, **a**, and look what happens.

Comparison: Type 1 curves vs. TrueType curves Create a circle. With bezier curves you'll have two handles bordering a curve segment, **a**. Drag the curve itself ("off-point editing"), **b** or edit one handle, **c**, and the entire curve segment responds. Convert to TrueType curves, **d**. Drag one of the four off-curve points (arrows) and only that part of the curve moves, **e**. So you'll have to adjust four points, rather than two, to get a smooth curve. Drag the anchor node, **f**, and things get worse.

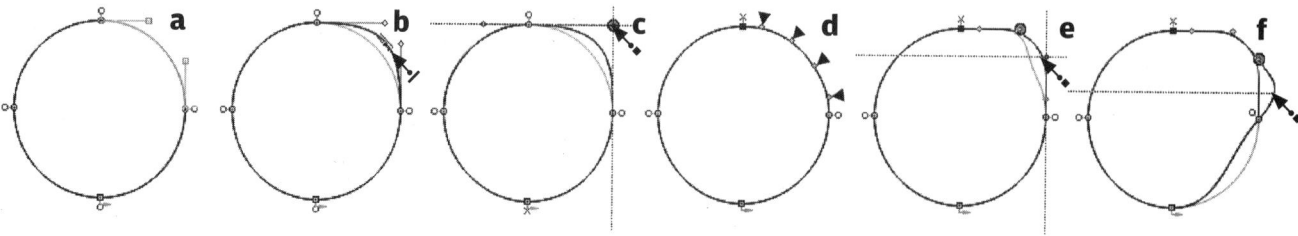

The Grid and Off-curve points

Turn on the Grid layer in the Glyph window and you'll see a faint network of grid lines that can help with the accuracy of your drawing, especially when making simpler, geometrically-constructed fonts. The grid's customizable intervals can be set to your stem width. And with Snap to Guides enabled (as is it by default), any node drawn or dragged near a grid line will snap to it.

Turn on the Grid:
1. Click the expansion button, **a**, on the Editing Layers palette then check Grid. Be sure to check the center column also, so objects will snap to the grid.

2. Or hit the Grid icon, **b**, in the Show Layers palette.

Set Grid dimensions in Preferences>Glyph window> Grid step, **c** (both dimensions need not be the same). In FontLab Studio 5.0, Grid color is specified here, too.

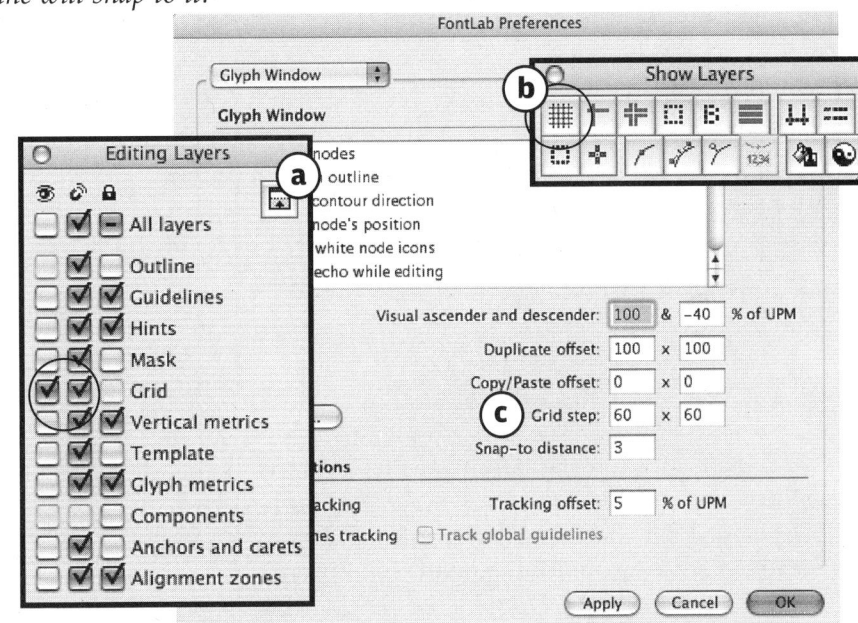

You can plan the grid to include a standard width of sidebearing that would apply to many (though not all) characters.

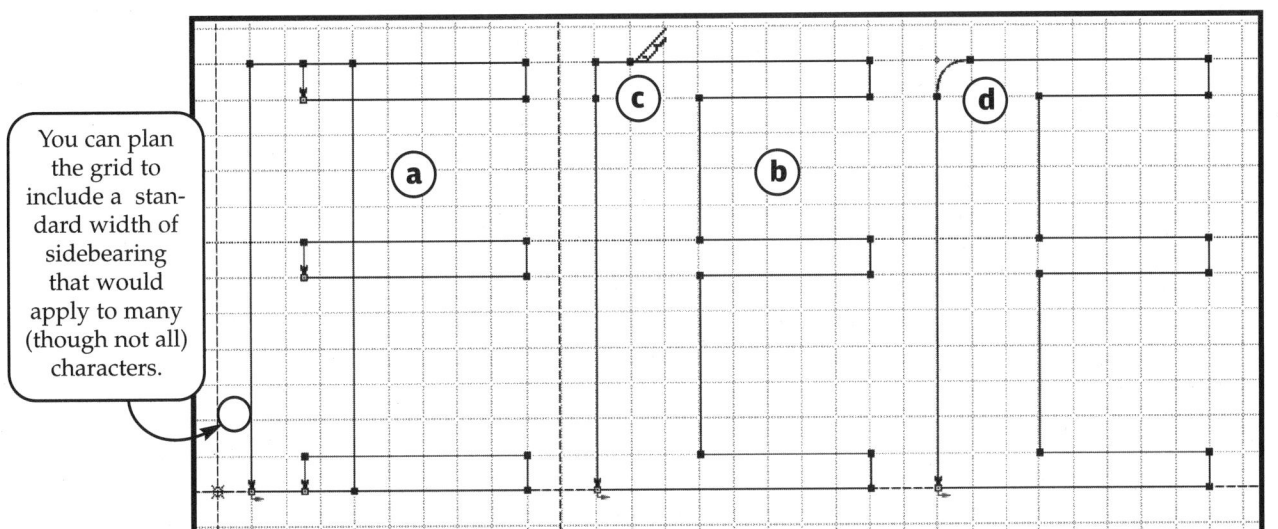

Perfect rounded corners with the Grid and TrueType curves The grid above was set so three grid squares would be my vertical stem width and one square would be the height of horizontal stems. Letter *E* was composed of three rectangles, **a**, which were then merged, **b**. The Add Corner tool (it resembles a knife) was used to add two nodes at the corner, **c**, positioned according to the grid. The three nodes in that corner were selected and converted to TrueType curves, which created a rounded corner. Next we'd round the lower corner. (*Thanks to Ray Larabie for this technique.*)

Meter mode

Meter mode is not a drawing mode, it's a measuring mode. Enter Meter mode by clicking the ruler icon in the **Tools** toolbar. The cursor now becomes a measuring tool for ascertaining character width, serif projection and whatever else. You can, for example, use it to check that all your vertical stems are the same width.

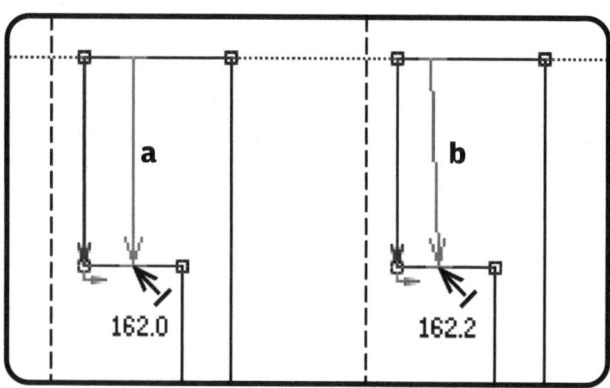

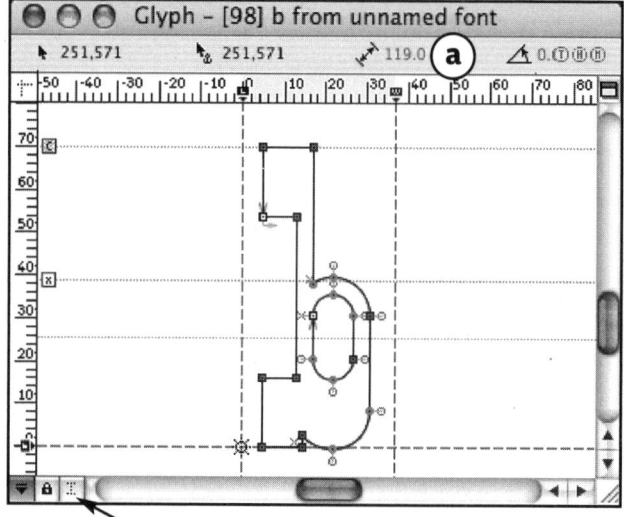

In Meter mode, click anywhere as a start point, drag the cursor and note how the number increases the farther away you drag. For an accurate reading, hold the Shift key to constrain the cursor to vertical or horizontal. Above, with Shift held and the cursor pulled straight down, **a**, a more accurate reading was obtained than at **b**, where Shift wasn't held and the cursor was dragged crooked.

Click the I-bar at the bottom of a Glyph window to view the Meter panel at top. The numbers displayed relate to cursor position, distance and angle. Value **a**, will be the same number as the Meter mode tool shows.

To Meter or not to Meter

Aside from the numerical values we assign to cap height and sidebearings, it is usually unnecessary to measure drawings. If we construct our characters in a methodical and consistent way from the start, by copying and mirroring serifs, bowls, angled stems and so on, the computer does the measuring for us.

In letter design, there are no mathematical standards for things like widths of thick to thin stems in a latin-style letter or "proper" x-height compared to cap height. If there were, all alphabets would look the same. Proportions are the font designer's decision.

Therefore, in my opinion, if you feel you have to measure parts of your glyph drawings, it is...

1. an indication that you haven't constructed your drawings logically and correctly in the first place;

2. a waste of time, because you'll have to remember that the serif you measured was 26.9 units wide, or jot down that a stem was 12.4 units high;

3. an attempt to substitute accuracy for creativity. As one highly-respected font designer recently told me, "It is characteristic of inexperienced designers to rely on numbers rather than the eyeball."

However, when I go back to tweak contours—as I invariably do—I often find things to have gone awry; e.g a path may accidentally get moved. In such cases, the solution might be to use Meter mode to recheck your measurements. Or not. The methods shown next page are more WYSIWYG and don't involve numbers.

The old way

What if the ruler says your stem is $9/16$ of an inch or 39.69999 cm or "almost, but not quite" a pica wide? It's annoying! To avoid rulers and measurement in the pen and pencil days, we would scribe the stem and counter widths we wanted onto a scrap of paper, then tick off each measure onto tracing paper as we moved the scrap along the baseline of our letters. Accuracy depended upon how carefully we copied off the marks with our pencils.

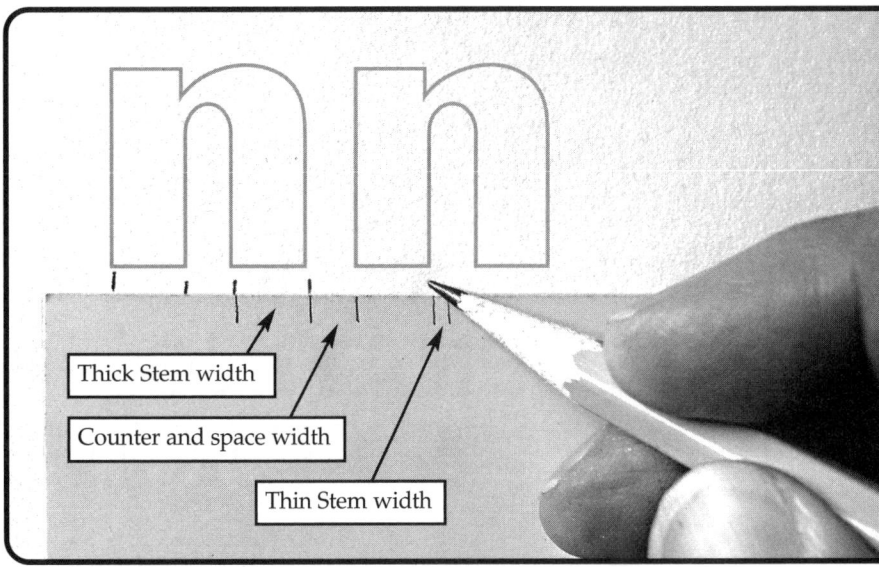

Thick Stem width

Counter and space width

Thin Stem width

Make a Gauge Ball Circles—or "gauge balls"—can be used to ensure that all stems are of equal width. Circles, unlike squares, will gauge diagonal stems as well as horizontal and vertical ones. I usually make two or three per font, corresponding to my thick stem, thin stem and counter widths. I "store" them in the Template layer or in the cap *A* Glyph window, to be pasted into any glyph window where they're needed. Right, with the Ellipse tool, click on one side of a stem, **a**, hold Shift to constrain the ellipse to a perfect circle, and drag 45° down to the opposite side of the stem, **b**. You'll know your ellipse is precisely the width of the stem when its extreme edges seem to disappear at the overlap, **c-d**. The finished circle, **e**, can be dragged onto any horizontal, vertical, curved or diagonal stem. (Gauge balls may be deleted after finishing the font.)

Template method Place your most favored version of any letter part, like this italic terminal stroke, **a**, into the Template layer (open its toolbar by going to VIEW>Toolbars>Templates). Hit the Copy to Template icon, **b**. The letter or selected letter portion will appear globally, in the template layer of every Glyph window, until removed. Now you can adjust all applicable stems according to the template model. *Note: It is not always practical or desirable that every similar part be drawn exactly alike. Subtle differences, made consciously, for aesthetic reasons, are admirable in a font!*

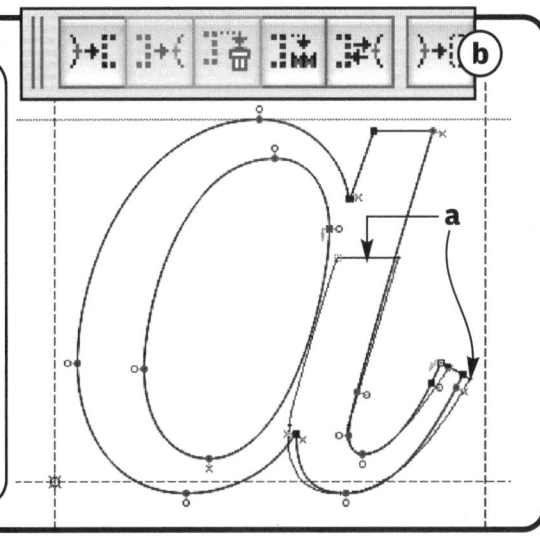

GENERATING, INSTALLING & PRINTING a FONT

Page **81** *Making a usable font; Comparing font formats*

83 *Generate a Mac Type 1 font*

84 *Generate a Mac Type 1 font and install it into Mac OS X.3*

85 *Generate a Mac or PC TrueType font*

87 *Install TrueType, OpenType or Type 1 fonts for Mac into Macintosh OS 8.x or 9.x*

88 *Install TrueType, OpenType or Type 1 fonts for PC into Windows XP or 2000*

89 *Printing test documents in FontLab*

90 *Test print-outs from installed fonts*

91 *FontLab Studio 5's expanded printing*

Making a usable font

If you've begun drawing a font as described in the previous chapter, you still have the completion of the character set, spacing, kerning, and perhaps hinting ahead of you (see page 92). But at any time—or many times, even before completion—you may wish to generate your font-in-progress. FontLab calls it "exporting," when you generate a font for installation into a computer fonts folder. The classic term is "generating a font."

Several font formats have been developed over the past years, but at present, no one technology has overtaken another. That is changing. OpenType now holds the promise of becoming the universal format, or it may become relegated to virtual ignominy like the once-heralded MultipleMaster format. "Not likely," says Adobe's Thomas Phinney. "Only about 30–40 MM font families were ever released. There are already about 4500 OpenType fonts shipping, from a wide range of vendors." Nonetheless, we who make fonts for distribution, should be able to generate them in all available formats to satisfy our various customers' requirements.

What are the differences in font formats? Let's compare them:

PC TrueType / OpenType TT

(Also known as: Data-fork TrueType, Windows TrueType, TrueType-flavored OpenType, TTF)

Pros: Works on Windows, Linux and Mac OS X. May contain up to 65,535 characters, supports Unicode and can contain OpenType layout features, making the format suitable for multilingual fonts, non-latin fonts and advanced typographic features (such as automatic ligatures, small caps). TrueType hinting allows precise control in small screen sizes, can also contain bitmaps. Can include embedding rights information defining whether or not the font may be attached to electronic documents.

Cons: Does not work on Mac OS 8/9; not completely cross-platform. May cause output problems on ten-year-old PostScript output and printing devices. The designer usually needs to convert the outlines from beziers which may introduce slight changes in the shape. When converted back to beziers (e.g. in Illustrator), the resulting curves have superfluous points. Manual TrueType hinting is laborious to create. The multilingual and advanced typography features only work with new OpenType-savvy applications, otherwise just the basic character set is available. For font families, requires two versions of the family name within each font: the first may contain any number of styles; the second "mini-family" may contain only four styles.

OpenType PS

(Also known as: OpenType-CFF, PostScript-flavored OpenType, OTF)

Pros: Works on Windows, Linux, Mac OS 8.6, 9, and OS X. Uses the bezier curve system preferred by designers and used in drawing apps such as Illustrator and Freehand so letterforms can be drawn precisely and outlines need not be converted. May contain up to 65,535 characters, supports Unicode and can contain OpenType layout features, making the format suitable for multilingual fonts, non-Latin fonts and advanced typography (automatic ligatures, small caps). Type 1 hinting is comparatively easy to create. Can include embedding rights information.

Cons: Type 1 hinting does not allow precise control in small screen sizes. Can theoretically contain bitmaps, but they are not displayed. Since this is a relatively new format, there are problems with some applications (some styles are not displayed in menus, kerning for non-Western characters does not work.) The multilingual and advanced typography features only work with new OpenType-savvy applications, otherwise just the basic character set is available. Two alternative family namings within each font must be devised: one where a family contains an arbitrary number of styles, and second where one family does not contain more than four styles. Does not work on Mac OS 8.

Mac Type 1

(Also known as: Mac PostScript)

Pros: Works in all PostScript commercial output and printing devices. Uses the bezier curve system preferred by designers and used in drawing applications such as Illustrator and Freehand so letterforms can be drawn precisely and outlines need not be converted. Type 1 hinting is fairly easy to create. May contain bitmaps for small screen sizes. One family can contain an unlimited number of styles.

Cons: Works on Mac OS only, not cross-platform. Contains two parts, the screen font (the suitcase) and the printer font, both of which must be loaded into the Fonts folder. Sometimes one or the other becomes corrupt or is misplaced. Difficult to move to other systems, or to send via e-mail. Type 1 hinting does not allow precise control in small screen sizes. Glyph set cannot include more than 256 encoded characters and lacks advanced layout features such as ligatures, making the format unsuitable for multilingual or non-latin fonts. Can't include embedding rights information. Type 1 may soon become obsolete.

PC Type 1

(Also known as: Windows PostScript)

Pros: Works in all PostScript commercial output and printing devices. Uses the same curve system (bezier) as drawing applications such as Illustrator and Corel DRAW!, so letterforms are easy to edit when converted to curves. Type 1hinting is comparatively easy to create.

Cons: Works on Windows and Linux, not cross-platform. Contains two parts, the outline file

(.pfb) and the metrics font (.pfm), both of which must be in the same folder. Type 1 hinting does not allow precise control for very small screen sizes. Cannot include more than 256 encoded characters and lacks advanced layout features such as ligatures, making the format unsuitable for multilingual or non-Latin fonts. Cannot contain bitmaps for small screen sizes. Does not contain embedding rights information. One family cannot contain more than four styles.

Mac TrueType

(Also known as: Resource-fork TrueType)

Pros: May contain up to 65,535 characters and supports Unicode, making the format suitable for multilingual or non-Latin fonts. TrueType hinting allows precise control in small screen sizes, can also contain bitmaps. Can contain embedding rights information defining if the font can attached to electronic documents. One family can contain an arbitrary number of styles.

Cons: Works on Mac OS only, not cross-platform. Difficult to move to other systems or send via e-mail. Older PostScript commercial output and printing devices are occasionally intolerant of TrueType fonts. Few designers like drawing in its curve system so they usually need to convert the outlines from bezier which may introduce slight changes in the shape. When converted back to beziers (e.g. in Illustrator), the resulting curves have superfluous points. Manual TrueType hinting is laborious to create. This format is now considered somewhat obsolete.

Recommendation: *Draw fonts with beziers as Type 1. When complete, make a duplicate FontLab master .vfb file and make TT conversions to it. Generate either a PC-TT / OT-TT or an OT-PS font for the newest systems (Windows and Mac OS X), and in addition, perhaps a Mac Type 1 font for Mac customers running a pre-8.6 Mac OS.*

—Adam Twardoch

Generate a Mac Type 1 font

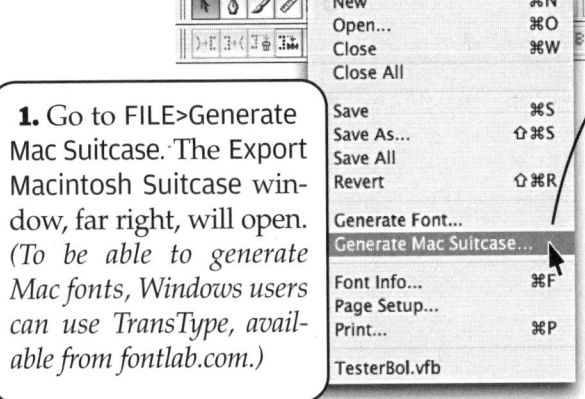

1. Go to FILE>Generate Mac Suitcase. The Export Macintosh Suitcase window, far right, will open. *(To be able to generate Mac fonts, Windows users can use TransType, available from fontlab.com.)*

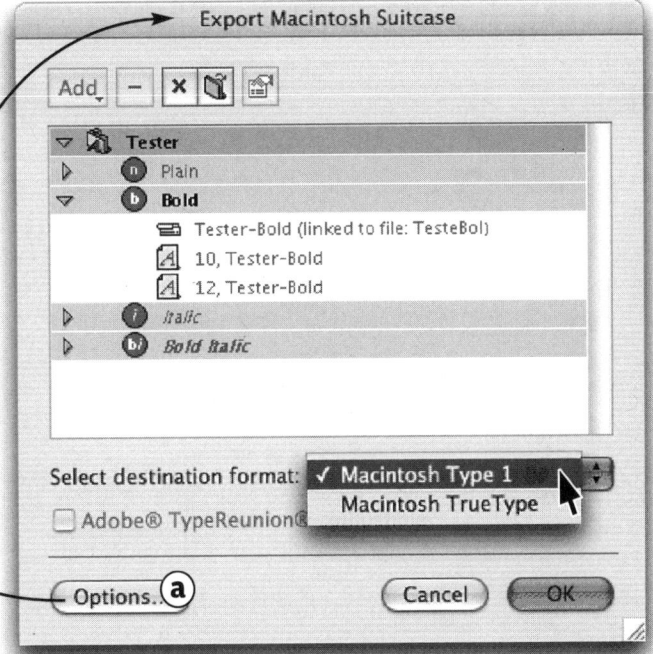

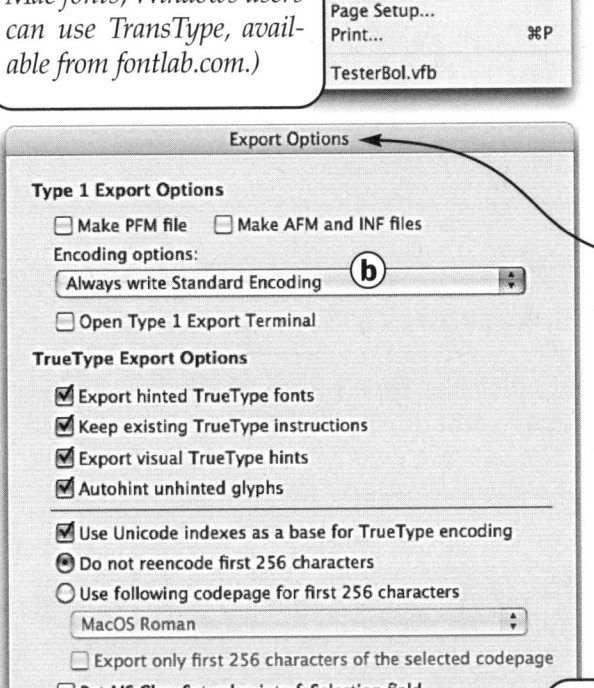

2. In the window above, the Suitcase set-up is shown. I'd previously checked Bold in the Font Info window (see page 128-130), to tell FontLab that this font was the *Bold* weight of the potentially four allowable weights that may occupy any one FontLab Suitcase. In the Select destination format menu, choose Macintosh Type 1.

3. Hit the Options button, **a**, to open the Export Options window, above left. For now, we'll only work with the top of the panel that relates to Type 1 Export Options. Don't Make PFM, AFM and INF files because those are for Windows fonts, which we are not generating at this time. Do choose Always write Standard Encoding, **b**, if you're making a Western font, otherwise choose Write custom encoding. Click OK. *Warning message:* I hadn't defined the plain style in what is assumed to be a family of four fonts, so this message, left, came up. I just clicked OK.

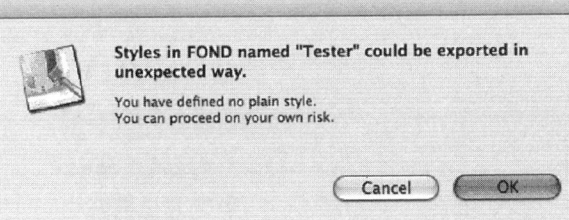

Generate a Mac Type 1 font and install it into Mac OS X.3

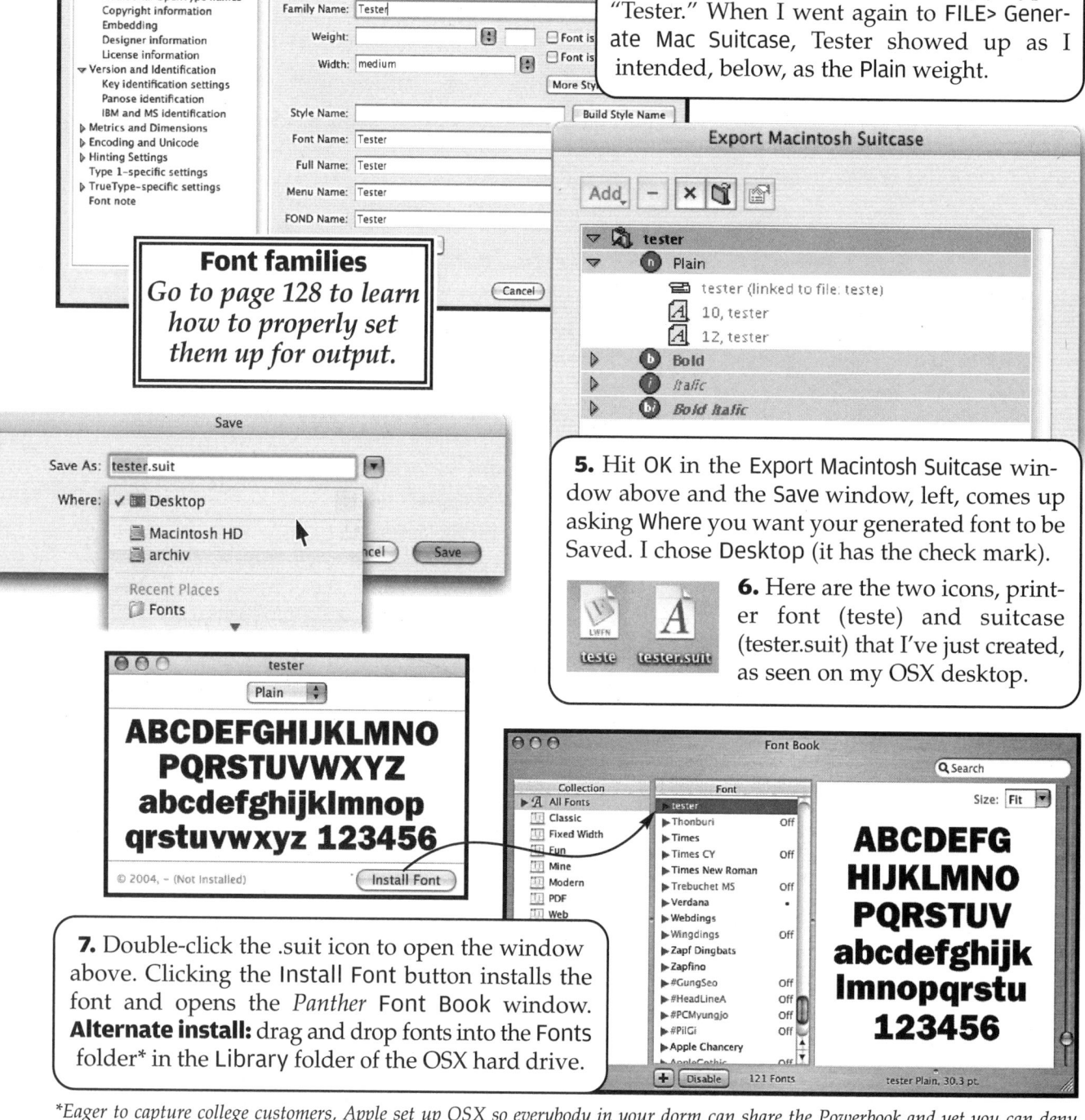

4. As an experiment, I stopped generating TesterBold to instead make a plain, or single-style font, not to be part of a family. In Font Info (Cmd- or Ctrl-F), left, I simply typed "Tester." When I went again to FILE> Generate Mac Suitcase, Tester showed up as I intended, below, as the Plain weight.

Font families
Go to page 128 to learn how to properly set them up for output.

5. Hit OK in the Export Macintosh Suitcase window above and the Save window, left, comes up asking Where you want your generated font to be Saved. I chose Desktop (it has the check mark).

6. Here are the two icons, printer font (teste) and suitcase (tester.suit) that I've just created, as seen on my OSX desktop.

7. Double-click the .suit icon to open the window above. Clicking the Install Font button installs the font and opens the *Panther* Font Book window. **Alternate install:** drag and drop fonts into the Fonts folder* in the Library folder of the OSX hard drive.

Eager to capture college customers, Apple set up OSX so everybody in your dorm can share the Powerbook and yet you can deny other users access to your personal font collection (thereby forcing passwords and redundant Fonts folders upon professional users who don't share their Macs). So when installing a font into OSX, check which of the half-dozen Fonts folders it's going in to!

Generate a Mac or PC TrueType font

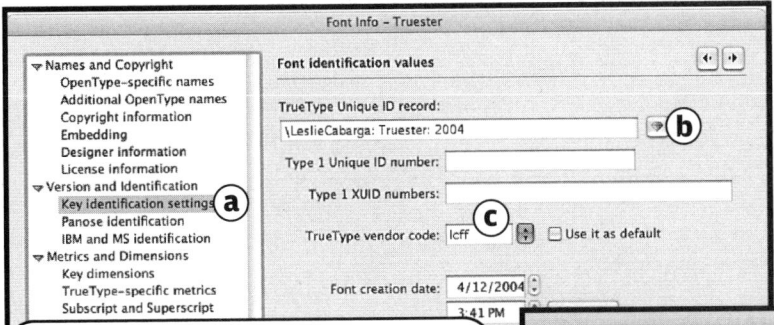

Before you generate the font, go into the Font Info *window (Cmd- or Ctrl-F) and correctly fill in some of the parameters specifically relating to TrueType (Mac or Win) fonts. Presumably you've already filled out basic info such as* Names *and* Copyright, *as described on pages 19-23.*

1. In Font Info, go to Key Identification, **a**. Click the magic emerald, **b**, to fill the TrueType Unique ID record with info from earlier sections of this window. You can apply for an official Type Vendor code, **c**, or make an unofficial one: type four letters in lowercase only. TrueType specific metrics, **d**, can be the same as Type 1 metrics unless you alter them here or as you work in the Metrics layer of the Glyph window.

There are a few other sections of the Font Info *window dealing with TrueType issues such as hinting. Find out more about them in the free, FontLab .pdf manual available from fontlab.com*

2. *For a Macintosh TrueType font*, open the FILE menu and choose Generate Mac Suitcase, as shown on page 83 and 84. Then, in the Export Macintosh Suitcase window click Macintosh TrueType.

To make a Windows TrueType font, choose Generate Font and the window below will open. You'll usually leave the name of the font (with the .ttf suffix) alone, but open the Where menu to scroll to the location where you want the font to be saved.

Generate a TrueType font continues on next page

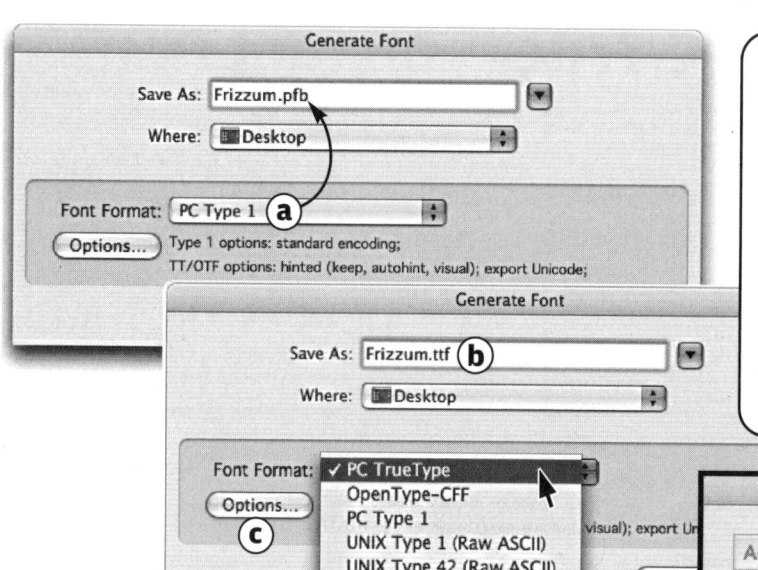

3. Left, in the Generate Font window (for making PC fonts) you can select from several font formats, such as PC Type 1, **a**, or PC TrueType. The suffix (*.pfb, .otf* or *.ttf*) in the Save As field will change automatically, according to the font format you choose, **b**. Notice that a summary of the current Export Options settings is shown to the right of the Options button, **c**. Click it if you want to change your current options.

4. When you want to generate a Macintosh font (PC users can get TransType for making Mac fonts), instead of opening the Generate Font window, you must go to FILE>Generate Mac Suitcase to open the Export Macintosh Suitcase window, right. In the pull-down menu, choose TrueType (or Type 1) for Mac, **d**. The Options button will show you the current settings, some of which you may already have specified in either the Font Info window or in Preferences>TrueType>TrueType Export.

5. If you created your glyphs using the Names mode in the Glyph window—in a latin font it makes sense: you can see each character name— you may get the error message at right. Since TrueType Fonts are arranged in Unicode, it is best to click No in this window. The font will still be generated. If generated as a Windows TrueType font, it will have the .ttf suffix (icon shown as it appears in OSX), **a**, and OS 9 menu listing, **b**. TrueType fonts for Mac are generated as a suitcase and the name contains no suffix, **c**. *See page 88 for how to load Windows fonts.*

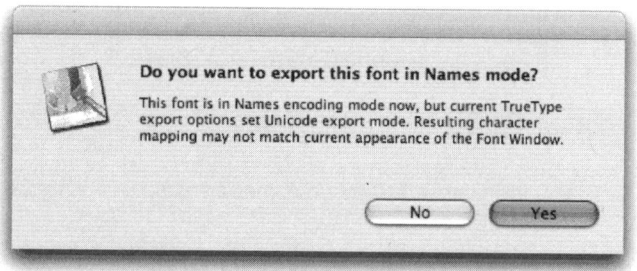

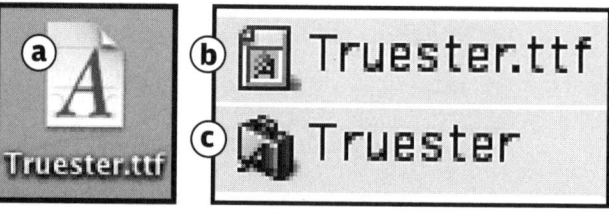

For more specific info about generating OpenType fonts, see pages 129 and 130

Install TrueType, OpenType or Type 1 fonts for Mac into Macintosh OS 8.x or 9.x

1. Close FontLab and any other open programs. Double-click your hard drive to open it (type "sys" to jump right to the System *folder*), **a**.

2. Locate your Fonts folder within the System folder* and drag the font(s) you want to load either on to the System folder or Fonts folder icon, **b**, or into the open folder as at **c**.

3. If you still have applications running, you'll get this error message, **d**. You must quit all open applications first, load the font then reopen the apps. Otherwise, the new font won't show in your apps' font lists.

Or... Choose your Fonts folder as the Save destination when generating a font, but it won't become available until you've quit all apps, as said above.

*By creating System folder and/or Fonts folder aliases (Cmd-M), **e**. and placing them on the Desktop or in an aliases folder, you can quickly get to and open them.*

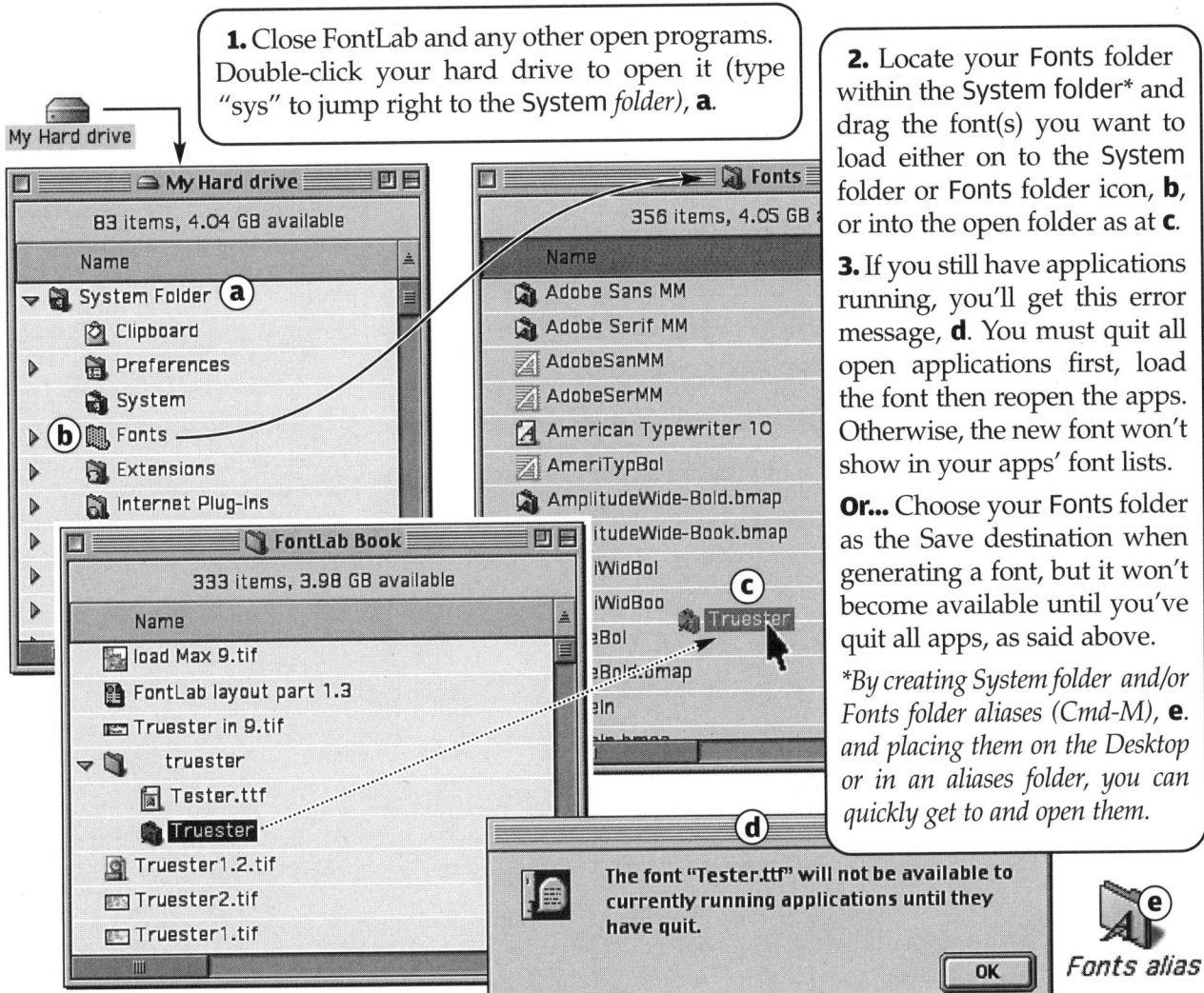

Fonts alias

Some font-loading pointers: *It's often best to open the* Fonts *folder and check for and delete old versions of a font that might have a slightly different suffix (and therefore wouldn't be automatically replaced by the newer version you're installing). Don't have both a TrueType and Type 1 version of the same font in the* Fonts *folder at once. Unless you are using a font-management program that categorizes fonts, (into what are sometimes confusingly called "Suitcases"), Mac OS 8 and 9 can handle a maximum number of 128 and 512, respectively. If your newly-loaded fonts start not appearing in your apps, you may have to remove less-used fonts. If you are using PostScript Type 1 fonts, you should have Adobe Type Manager installed. ATM Deluxe may be purchased, but the Lite version (which is quite sufficient) may be downloaded free from Adobe.com.*

Install TrueType, OpenType or Type 1 fonts for PC into Windows 98, XP or 2000

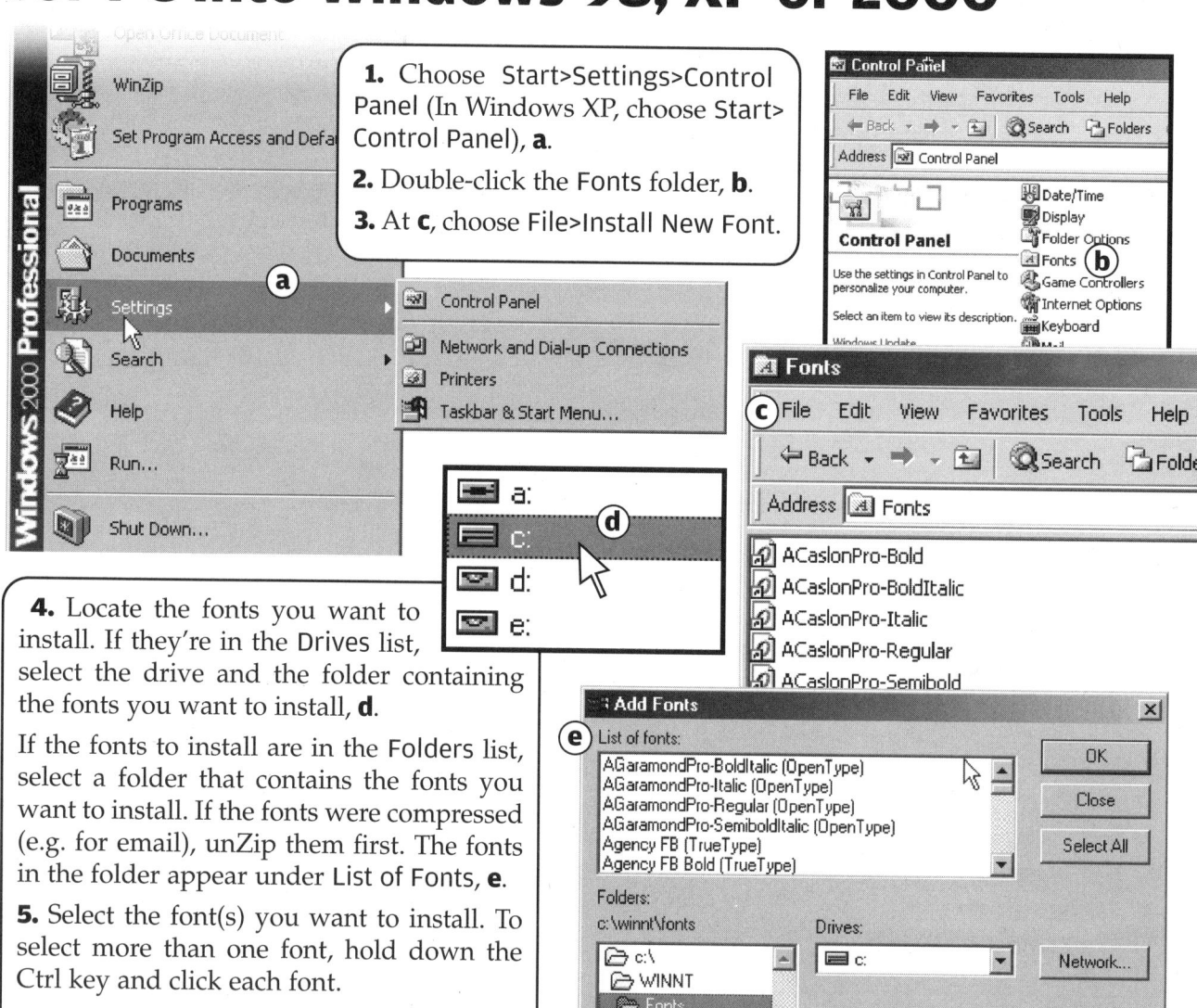

1. Choose Start>Settings>Control Panel (In Windows XP, choose Start>Control Panel), **a**.

2. Double-click the Fonts folder, **b**.

3. At **c**, choose File>Install New Font.

4. Locate the fonts you want to install. If they're in the Drives list, select the drive and the folder containing the fonts you want to install, **d**.

If the fonts to install are in the Folders list, select a folder that contains the fonts you want to install. If the fonts were compressed (e.g. for email), unZip them first. The fonts in the folder appear under List of Fonts, **e**.

5. Select the font(s) you want to install. To select more than one font, hold down the Ctrl key and click each font.

6. To copy fonts to the Fonts folder, make sure the Copy fonts to Fonts folder check box is selected, **f**. If you are installing fonts from a floppy disk or a CD-ROM, this check box should also be selected. Otherwise, to use the fonts in your applications, you'd have to keep the disk in the disk drive.

7. Click OK to install the fonts.

PC font installation pointers: *Don't install two different fonts with the same menu name or PostScript FontName, regardless of format. To use Type 1 fonts, you'll need Adobe Type Manager (ATM) unless you are running Windows XP or 2000 in which ATM is included in the operating system. After installing fonts, you may need to restart an application or reselect the printer in the application to make the fonts appear in the font list.*

Printing test documents in FontLab

Making print-outs of our fonts is a vital way of checking on their progress. It is surprising how a "hard copy" can provide objective insights far different than viewing the font on screen only. There are three ways to create print-outs of your fonts: The first two involve FontLab's own printing options. The third way is to generate and install the font onto your computer, then set some type and print it out in a text document using a program like Quark, InDesign, or MSWord.

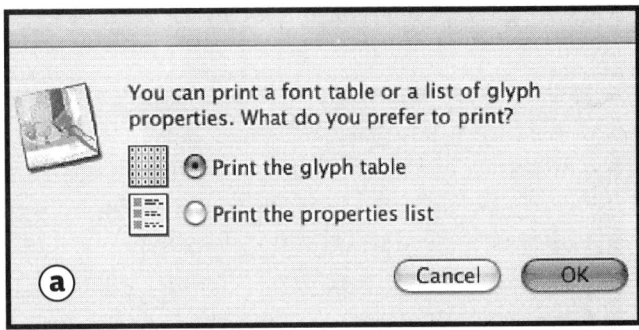

(a) You can print a font table or a list of glyph properties. What do you prefer to print?
- ● Print the glyph table
- ○ Print the properties list

Cancel OK

When you hit FILE>Print (Cmd- or Ctrl-P), the first dialogue box you'll see will be **a**, above right, asking you whether to print a glyph table, such as **b**, or a properties list, such as **c** (shown below in Preview mode, not actually printed). Hit OK to get the Print window, **d**. Select a printer and go to print.

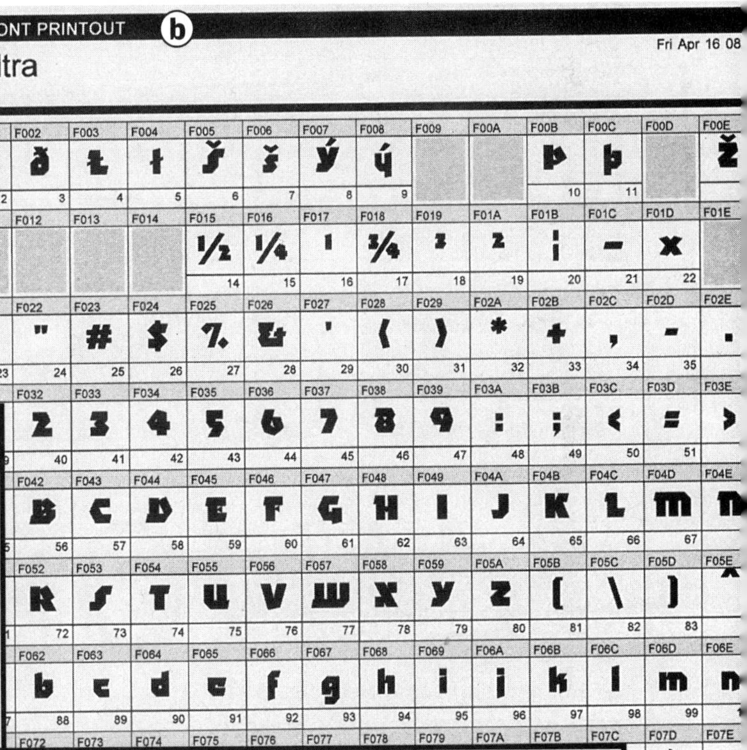

(b) FONTLAB FONT PRINTOUT
AngleUltra Fri Apr 16 08

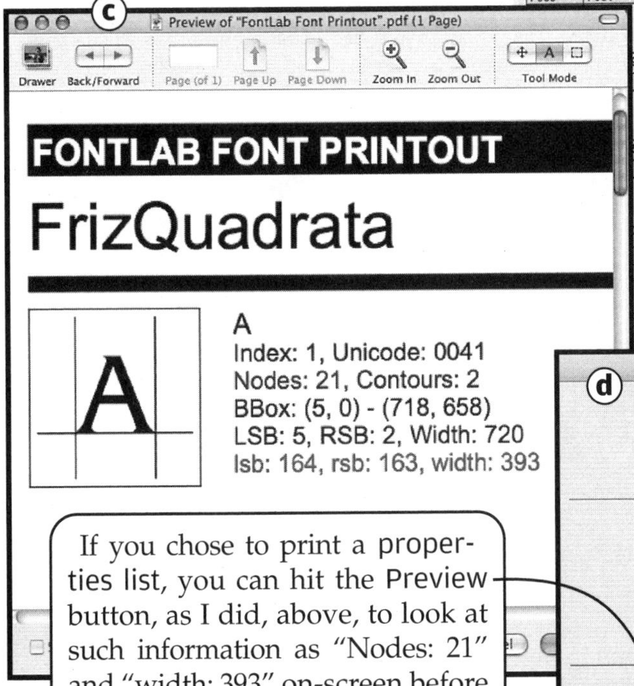

(c) Preview of "FontLab Font Printout".pdf (1 Page)

Drawer Back/Forward Page (of 1) Page Up Page Down Zoom In Zoom Out Tool Mode

FONTLAB FONT PRINTOUT

FrizQuadrata

A

A
Index: 1, Unicode: 0041
Nodes: 21, Contours: 2
BBox: (5, 0) - (718, 658)
LSB: 5, RSB: 2, Width: 720
lsb: 164, rsb: 163, width: 393

If you chose to print a properties list, you can hit the Preview button, as I did, above, to look at such information as "Nodes: 21" and "width: 393" on-screen before you print, or in lieu of printing.

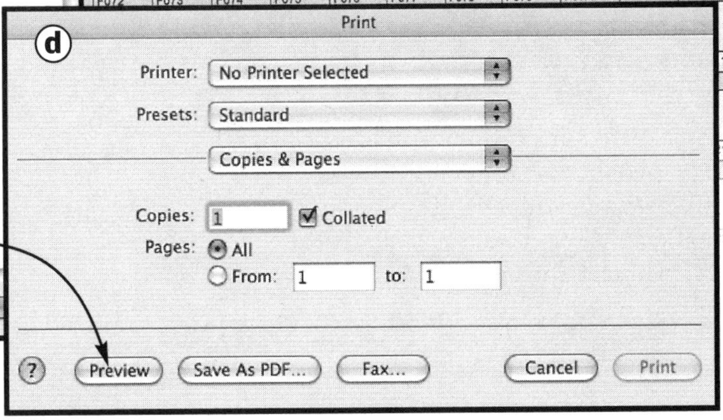

(d) Print

Printer: No Printer Selected
Presets: Standard

Copies & Pages

Copies: 1 ☑ Collated
Pages: ● All
○ From: 1 to: 1

(?) Preview Save As PDF... Fax... Cancel Print

Test print-outs from installed fonts

Here is a list of just some of the typical kinds of tests font designers will print-out—not directly from Font-Lab, but in a word-processing app, after having generated and loaded the font—in order to check our work:

1. All characters (or perhaps just upper and lower case alphabets, to start) in large pt.-sizes for scrutinizing letterforms and comparing one to another.

2. All characters set between Hs to check spacing.

3. AA-AB-AC-AD-AE, etc.; BA-BB-BC-BD, etc.

4. Waterfalls showing letters in successively graduated point sizes to check out what happens to curves and counters at different sizes.

5. "Zwei boxkämpfer jagen Eva quer durch Sylt" and other *pangrams* (sentences that contain every letter in the alphabet) because letterforms and spacing are best judged as words set in sentences, rather than as random letter strings. Visit my website www.logofontandlettering.com and click "Kern King" to copy a paragraph of words containing every (English alphabet) kerning pair.

Below, early test prints by Christian Schwartz of the medium-weight font in his Popular family.

HAHBHCHDHEHFHGHHHIHJHKHLHMH
HNHOHPHQHRHSHTHUHVHWHXHYHZH

ABCDEFGHIJK
LMNOPQRSTU
VWXYZ.,;:" "''
abcdef

We font designers all seem to develop our own shorthand notational systems for marking up printed proofs. Above, Schwartz reconsiders: his "too boxy" *B*; the shape of *G*; the lower leg angle of *J*, the inner right serif of *K*; the top, right-side curves of the counters in *a* and *c*, and many, many other aspects as he works on fine-tuning all his letterforms.

FontLab Studio 5's expanded printing

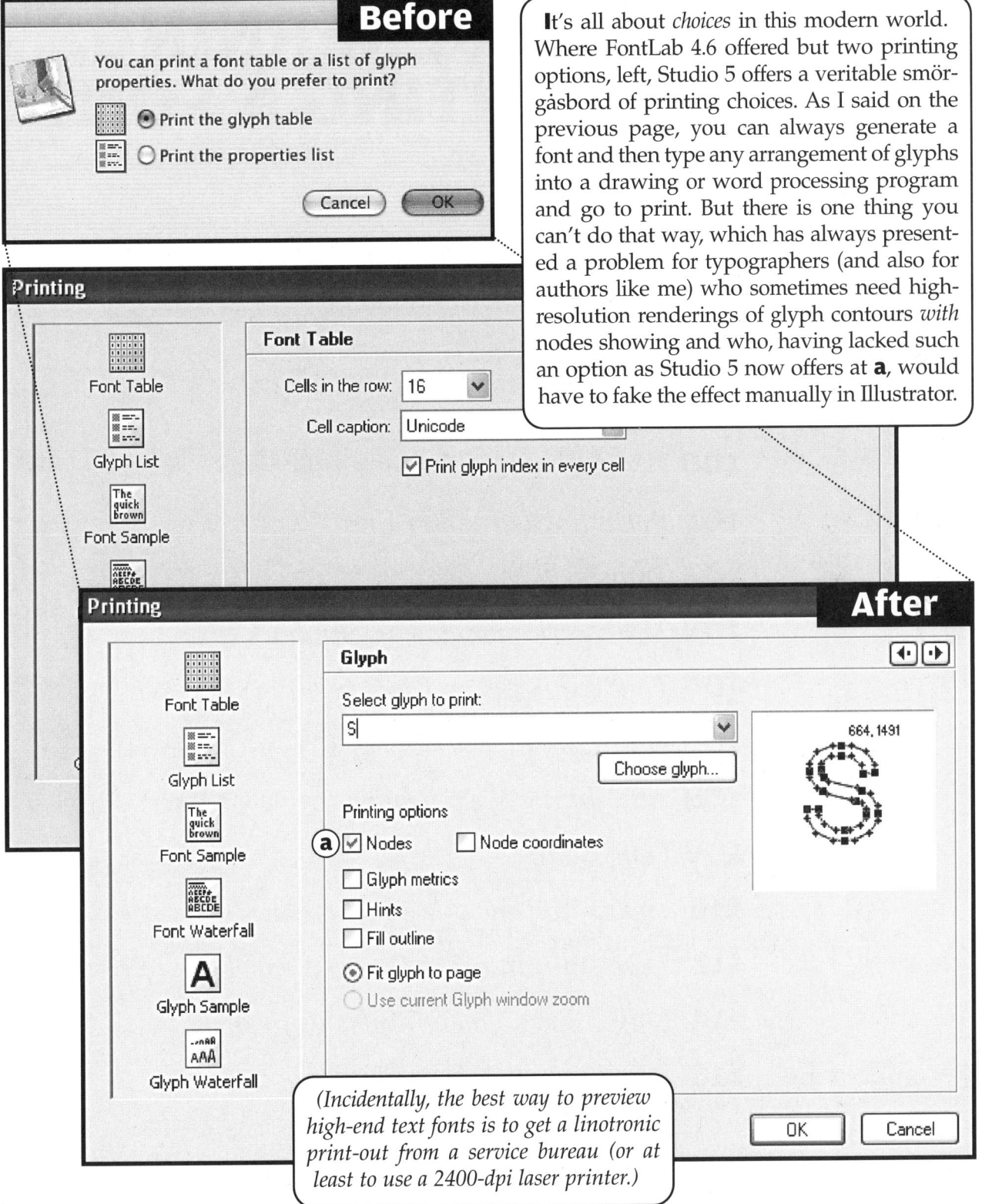

Before

You can print a font table or a list of glyph properties. What do you prefer to print?

● Print the glyph table
○ Print the properties list

Cancel   OK

It's all about *choices* in this modern world. Where FontLab 4.6 offered but two printing options, left, Studio 5 offers a veritable smörgåsbord of printing choices. As I said on the previous page, you can always generate a font and then type any arrangement of glyphs into a drawing or word processing program and go to print. But there is one thing you can't do that way, which has always presented a problem for typographers (and also for authors like me) who sometimes need high-resolution renderings of glyph contours *with* nodes showing and who, having lacked such an option as Studio 5 now offers at **a**, would have to fake the effect manually in Illustrator.

Printing

Font Table

Font Table

Cells in the row: 16

Cell caption: Unicode

☑ Print glyph index in every cell

Glyph List

Font Sample

Printing   **After**

Font Table

Glyph

Select glyph to print:

S

Choose glyph...

664, 1491

Glyph List

Printing options

Font Sample

(a) ☑ Nodes   ☐ Node coordinates

Font Waterfall

☐ Glyph metrics
☐ Hints
☐ Fill outline
● Fit glyph to page
○ Use current Glyph window zoom

Glyph Sample

Glyph Waterfall

(Incidentally, the best way to preview high-end text fonts is to get a linotronic print-out from a service bureau (or at least to use a 2400-dpi laser printer.)

OK   Cancel

SPACING, KERNING, and HINTING a FONT

Page **93** *The Metrics window*

96 *Spacing and Kerning concepts*

97 *Using the Metrics window*

98 *Auto Metrics*

99 *Kerning*

100 *Kerning and the Kerning Info panel*

101 *Remove existing Kerning*

102 *Transform Metrics*

103 *The Metrics window in Studio 5*

104 *Time-saving class-based kerning*

106 *Hinting*

108 *Auto-hint a Type 1 font*

109 *Font Audit*

110 *Type 1 hinting; Alignment Zones*

112 *Type 1 hinting; The Preview panel*

114 *Links, Replacement hints, Auto stems*

116 *Beginning TrueType hinting*

The Metrics window

The white spaces that separate letters are as integral a part of a font as the characters themselves. The goal is to create even spacing between letters for visual balance and legibility. Good Metrics, or letterspacing, doesn't just happen. We designers must decide how much spacing is appropriate given the particular style of a font.

Glyph-window spacing As you draw a glyph, you can do preliminary spacing while working in the Glyph window. Click on the *word* Metrics in the Editing Layers palette, **a**, to go into the Metrics layer. While in this layer, contours can't be changed; nodes can't be selected or edited. However, you are now able to drag the left and right sidebearings, **b** and **c**, nearer or farther to define how much space there will be on either side of the letter. Notice that when you drag a sidebearing, the red Measurment line (which can be dragged up or down, as you need it) gains a red arrow and shows you how far the sidebearing is from any part of the letter's edge. This allows you to visually ascertain that both sides have the same value.

The Metrics window is where spacing/kerning is mostly done. Go to WINDOW>New Metrics Window, below, or click the Metrics Window icon, **d**.

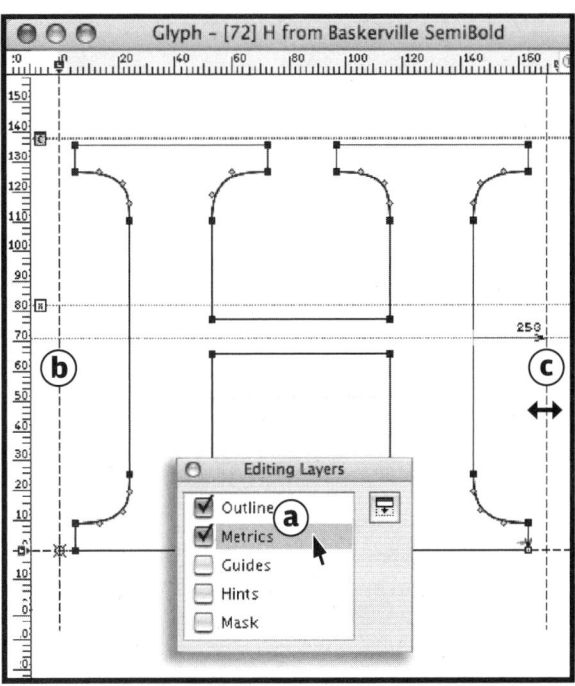

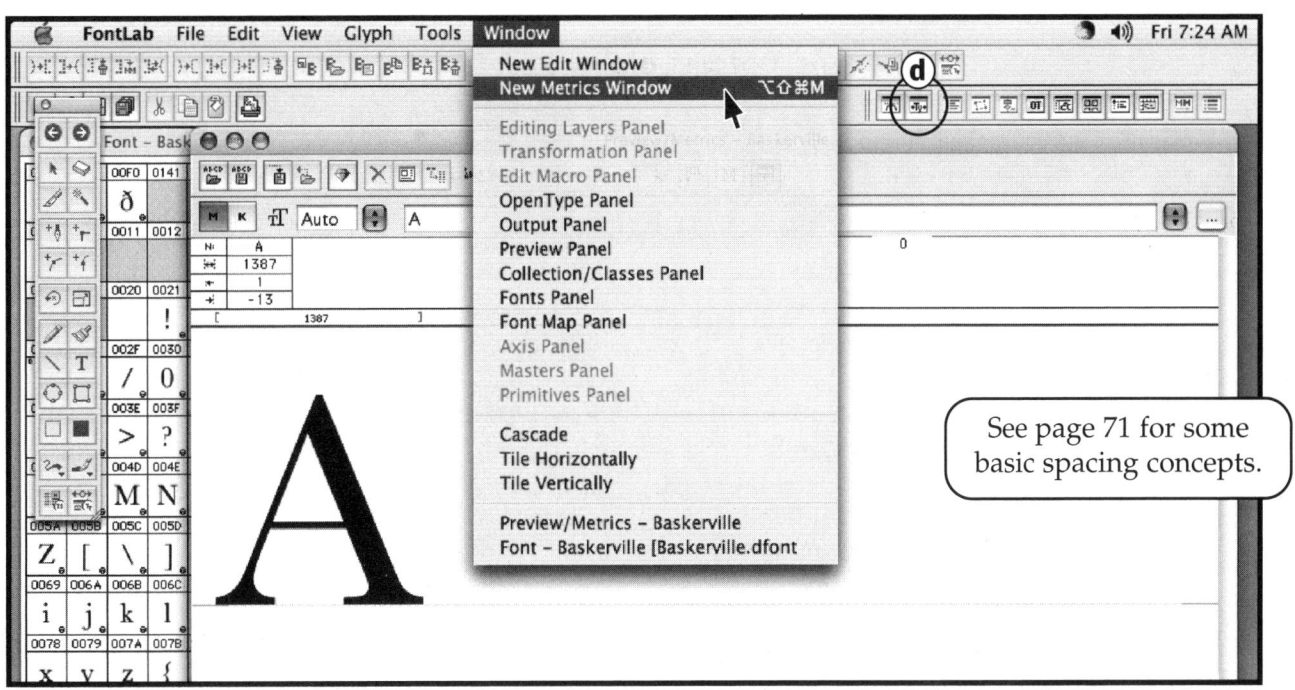

See page 71 for some basic spacing concepts.

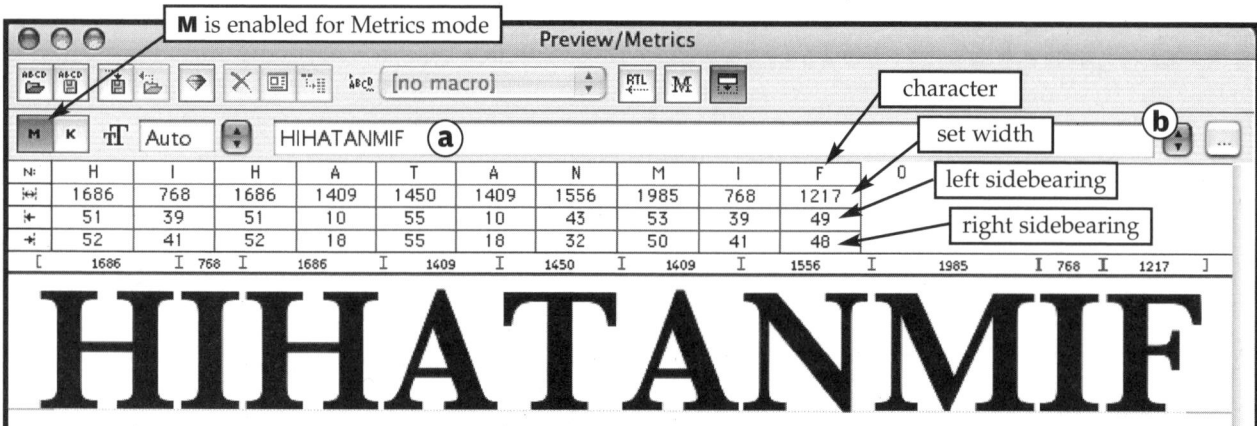

Set up for spacing Type a string of characters into the Metrics window, **a**. Or click the button, **b**, for a choice of ready-to-go strings. Below this, each letter, its width, its left sidebearing (henceforth: LSB) value and its RSB value is displayed.

Haphazard spacing The font above wasn't spaced well. Letters like *H* and *I*, whose serifs are exactly alike, and whose right and left sides mirror one another, should therefore have identical RSB and LSB values. *N, M,* and the left side of *F*, should also have the same SB value as *H* and *I*. Instead, each value for each side of each letter is different. That is *so* not right.

The LSB of letter *A* measures 10 units, yet the RSB of this symmetrically-shaped letter is 18 units. Both values should be the same. The rule is: ***Use the same sidebearing value for every alike side of every alike character.***

Better spacing The LSBs and RSBs for all similar, straight-sided letters above are the same, as they should be. Both SBs of *T* are identical and the same is true of *A*, which has negative SBs of -12 units to nestle it closer to straight-sided letters. Taking into account its right-side openings, *E* got a narrower RSB so it would set tighter.

Kerning Above, clicking the **K** button, **a**, places us in Kerning mode and adds a fifth row with existing kerning pairs highlighted in blue and yellow, **b**. Assigning a -113 kern value to *T* will allow it to snuggle up past *A*'s RSB and close the spacing gap that otherwise occurs. But notice that the second *A* was only kerned -82 to the *T* so it appears slightly farther away from *T* than the first *A*. Without kerning, combinations of letters like *A* and *T* will look strangely spaced-out, as they do in the screenshot at the top of this page.

How much spacing or how little?

When you edit Metrics in the Preview/Metrics window you are usually working at a large scale and the spacing you assign may turn out too open or too tight when the font is set at smaller text sizes. On this page are some approaches to consider, but it is always wise to open some existing fonts and study how the Metrics were handled, just as we are doing here.

Spacing matches counters

This is one rule of thumb, although it may not always be applicable to every letter style. Below, here are lower-case letters from the bold-style font shown on the previous page. The first thing to notice is that the standard spacing of straight-sided letters such as *l*, *u*, *m*, *n* and *i* is only 70 units, less than the 85 units used for upper case. The total space width between most letters, 140 units, is about the same width as the counters in letters like *u*, *m*, *a* and *n*. Because of the open break in *a*'s left side, its LSB was decreased from the standard—same with *t*.

N:	l	u	l	u	space	m	a	n	t	i	n	i
↔	556	1071	556	1071	361	1580	1025	1072	630	556	1072	556
⊢	70	70	70	70		70	44	70	0	70	70	70
⊣	70	70	70	70		70	70	70	12	70	70	70

lulu mantini

N:	A	V	A	I	L	space	h	a	n	d	l	e
↔	805	799	805	321	482	259	580	531	580	583	287	510
⊢	0	1	0	44	44		41	14	41	24	41	24
⊣	0	1	0	44	7		39	40	39	41	41	6
Ke	-276	-276	-38	0	-68	0	0	0	0	0	0	

AVAIL handle

Another boldface

The spacing between characters in my font Kobalt Bold generally match the counter widths.

A–V–A were kerned –276, to match the space between letters like I–L.

Spaces may need kerning, too. To compensate for *L*'s wide-open right side, I kerned the Space character –68 to the *L*. (*You always kern from the glyph on the right to the one on the left.*)

straight-sided lower case letters such as *l* have sidebearings 3 units less than the uppercase, such as *H*. The humped right sides of *h* and *n* necessitated still less spacing.

LSBs of *d* and *e* are the same since both letters' left sides are the same shape.

There's no rule regarding spacing of odd letter shapes. Just move *a*'s LSB in closer until it looks evenly spaced with the rest.

			Auto		AHIOOHulio				
N:	A	H	I	O	O	H	u	I	I	o
↔	783	830	335	784	784	830	603	292	292	546
⊢	21	21	21	21	21	21	18	21	21	32
⊣	21	21	21	21	21	21	22	21	21	32

AHIOOHulio

Serif spacing Sidebearings are measured at the outermost edges of the letter. In serif fonts, the serifs stick out farthest and in the font above, 21 units was used as the standard sidebearing distance between serifs, even for the letter *A*, so its serifs would space consistently with most of the other serif letters. Rounded letters, such as *O*, are always spaced closer to straight-stem letters (but here, I think *O* looks too tight). The lower case letters *l* and *i*, above, also have sidebearings of 21 units, though the LSB of *u* is only 10 units to compensate for its receding, rounded bottom.

How to edit spacing With the **M** button active, just click a character and two sidebearing lines appear, above, that you can drag. You can also select a field and type in a new SB value or copy and paste a value from another field. And, say you want *H* to have the same RSB as *N*, type "=N" into *H*'s RSB field, instead of a number.

			Auto		Bassoprofundo				
N:	B	a	s	s	o	p	r	o	f	u	n
↔	889	444	333	333	444	444	333	444	222	444	444
⊢	98	0	-34	-34	12	-261	-58	12	-566	-16	-62
⊣	-75	-129	-126	-126	-125	-132	-127	-125	-362	-129	-127

Note the negative sidebearing values (especially for *f*'s swashes) needed to make all connecting ligatures overlap.

Bassoprofundo

Scripts Successful script spacing requires a system of connecting ligatures that is fairly consistent so every letter can join up with the next one. Properly spaced, a script font will need only minimal kerning.

All the right-side connecting strokes of Snell Roundhand were designed to join at similar height…

…and to automatically create equal spacing between letters. The crossbar of *f* had to be long enough to reach *o*, yet not stick out past the left stem of *u*.

Using the Metrics window

Click **M** to work on spacing (Metrics).

Click **K** to work on kerning. Or let neither button be enabled to view the window in nonediting Preview mode. But why do that? It's better to have editability at the ready.

Click the arrows to specify a point size in which to display your font, or Auto will allow characters to resize when the window is resized.

RTL is for fonts like Hebrew and Arabic that need to be displayed right-to-left, as shown below.

Play with these buttons and see what happens.

ASCII characters, such as *ABC*, can be typed into the string directly. Enter Unicode codes preceded by a back-slash: *\0635\0637*. For characters that can't be typed on your keyboard, use glyph names preceded by a slash: */Aogonek. /Ccedilla.* Mixed characters can be entered separated by a space: */Aogonek\0634.* (see also page 61.)

How to get character strings into the window
Any highlighted glyphs in the Font Window or open glyph in the Glyph window will be displayed when the Metrics window is opened. You can also type or paste characters, glyph names or Unicodes into the string field, above **a**; drag a glyph to the Metrics window from the font window, **b**; or open some sample strings here, **c**. Click **d** to open Preview Options, right, and then edit and/or add to the sample strings, **e**. If you want a non-editable lower, second string for comparison, **f**, Type or paste one in at **g**.

Using the Metrics window continues on next page

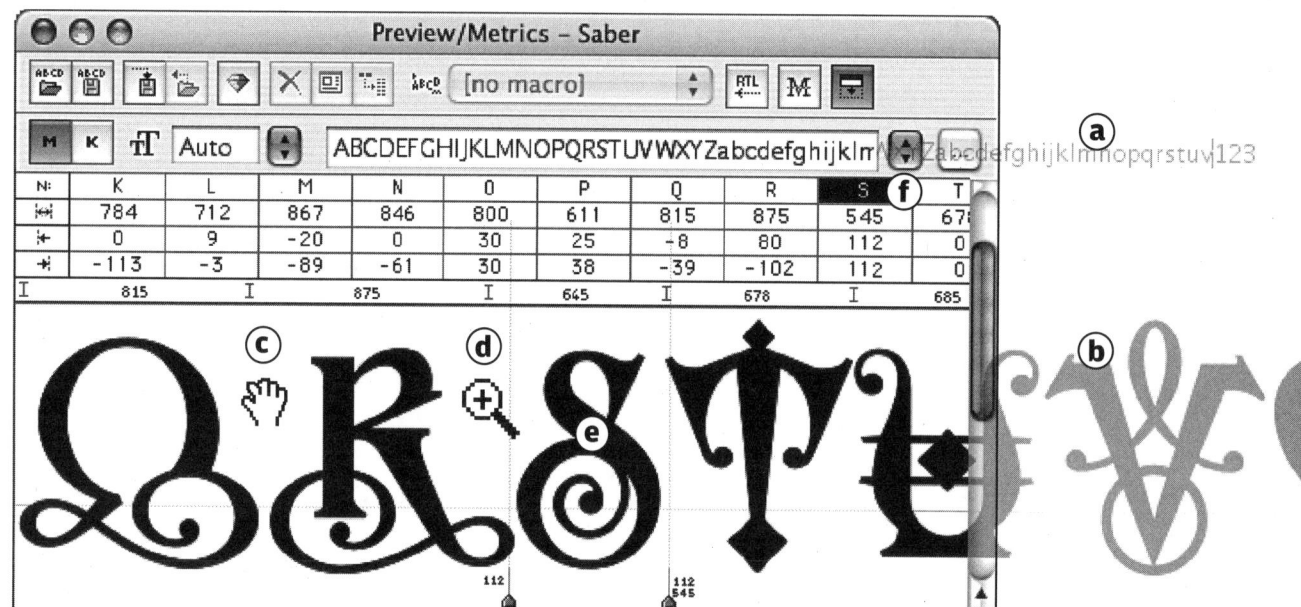

Working in the fields A glyph string may be much longer than is visible in the field, above **a** and **b**. Use the Right and Left Arrow keys to move the string along. Scroll the editing field with the grabber hand (hold down the Spacebar while dragging mouse), **c**. Enlarge glyphs in the editing field with the magnifying glass (hold Cmd- or Ctrl-Spacebar; add Option or Alt keys to reduce), **d**.

Changes to the string Click a glyph to select it, **e**. Holding the Shift key allows you to drag the character vertically up or down. Hitting Cmd-] or [in Mac (Ctrl-] or [in Win) will change the selected glyph to the next or previous character,. alphabetically. Typing any character, **f**, will replace the currently selected one with the new one you typed.

Auto Metrics

Click the magic emerald and let FontLab do your Metrics!

First, choose to generate new metrics for, **a** , only the currently selected character, for the character string in the Metrics window, or for the whole darn font (the latter two choices are not undoable; save a copy of your font). Then try this: Choose Custom and set RSB and LSB at 0 to cancel out existing metrics. Click OK. Open this panel again. Now in the pulldown, **b**, choose a degree of spacing. Medium might be a good choice, but experiment on the string, before doing the entire font. Hit OK. You will probably find that Auto Metrics, as with any auto-operation, always requires manual tweaking.

Kerning

Where spacing leaves off, kerning picks up. First you space each character as carefully as possible to avoid excess kerning. After checking spacing (generating and installing the font and using it to set a few paragraphs of type is one way to do it), make notes as to where kerning is needed to fill up visual holes between letters. As an aid to locating spacing/kerning problems, I've produced a list of words comprising every possible (latin-based) letter combination. You can copy "Kern King" from my web site, www.logofontandlettering.com, paste it into a word processing or layout program document, look at the words in lowercase, then as all caps, see how they set, then go back into FontLab and adjust spacing/kerning accordingly.

HIGH MacTav "Arthur L"

A'F.K-P}T,V:W;Y- rtfhgjky

RS Break P. T, ▽: "△p¢hup L"

Kerning considerations If spaced well, certain character shapes, such as **a**, may never need kerning. There are many unexpected kern pairs, like cT, **b**. Don't forget that quotes and punctuation, **c**, and **d**, need to be kerned, too. Some kern pairs, such as *rt*, *fh* (as in *sulfhydryl*), *gj* (*logjam* or *gjellerup*), and *ky* are almost always difficult to deal with, **e**. Eccentric fonts, such as Delorita from bvfonts.com, **f**, may contain virtually no common sidebearing standards and will therefore require that every letter be individually spaced and kerned by eye. Some characters in an oddball font like this author's Cymbal, **g**, may present typical kerning issues, but other characters require a unique treatment.

Common letter pairs needing kerning

As demonstrated above, the number of kerning pairs a font requires is based on its style. Some of the following commonly called-for kerning pairs may not pertain at all to our fonts. And other pairs, not included in this brief listing, may present themselves as eyesores to be corrected.

The market for fonts is an international one, and many kerning pairs, representing non-English accent characters, and character combinations, such as Hr, Nd, Mg, and Qa, may also need to be included in our kerned fonts.

AC AG AO AQ AS AT AU AV AW AY A' A" Ac Ad Ae Ag Ao Aq As At Au Av Aw Ay BV BW BY

CT CV CW CY DA DJ DV DW DY FA FG FJ FO FT FV FW FY Fa Fc Fb Fe Fo Fr Fs Ff Fu Fy GY Hr KO Ka Ko Ku Ky LO LT LV LW LY L' L" Lo Lv Lw Ly OA OT OV OW OX OY PA PT PV PW PY Pa Pc Pd Pe Po Ps P. P, Qa Qu RA RT RV RW RY Ra Rc Rd Re Ro Rs Ry SS ST SY SV SW Sy Sv Sw TA TO TT Ta Te Ti To Tr Ts Tu Tw Ty T. T, T: T; T- VA VO Va Ve Vi Vm Vn Vo Vp Vr Vs Vu Vy V. V, V: V; V- WA WO Wa We Wi Wo Wr Wu Wy W. W, W: W; W- YA YC YG YO Ya Ye Yi Yo Yp Yr Yu Yv Y. Y, Y: Y; Y- XO xo ew ey ev ff fg f' f ij 's 't of ot ov ow oy ox qu qa ra rc rd re rf rh ro rq rr rt ru rv rw rx ry rz r. r, r- ve vo v. v, w. w, y. y,

*(This list has been reprinted from the author's book **Logo, Font and Lettering Bible**.)*

Kerning and the Kerning Info panel

Open an existing font to examine its kerning. Go to WINDOW>New Metrics Window to open the Metrics Window. Make sure the **K** button, **a**, is enabled, click on any letter, and move the kern bar, **b**, to see how it works. A font can, of course, be kerned just by individually tweaking the kern bars on every necessary kerning pair, but for this exercise, let's get scientific: Hit the button, **c**, to open the Kerning Information window.

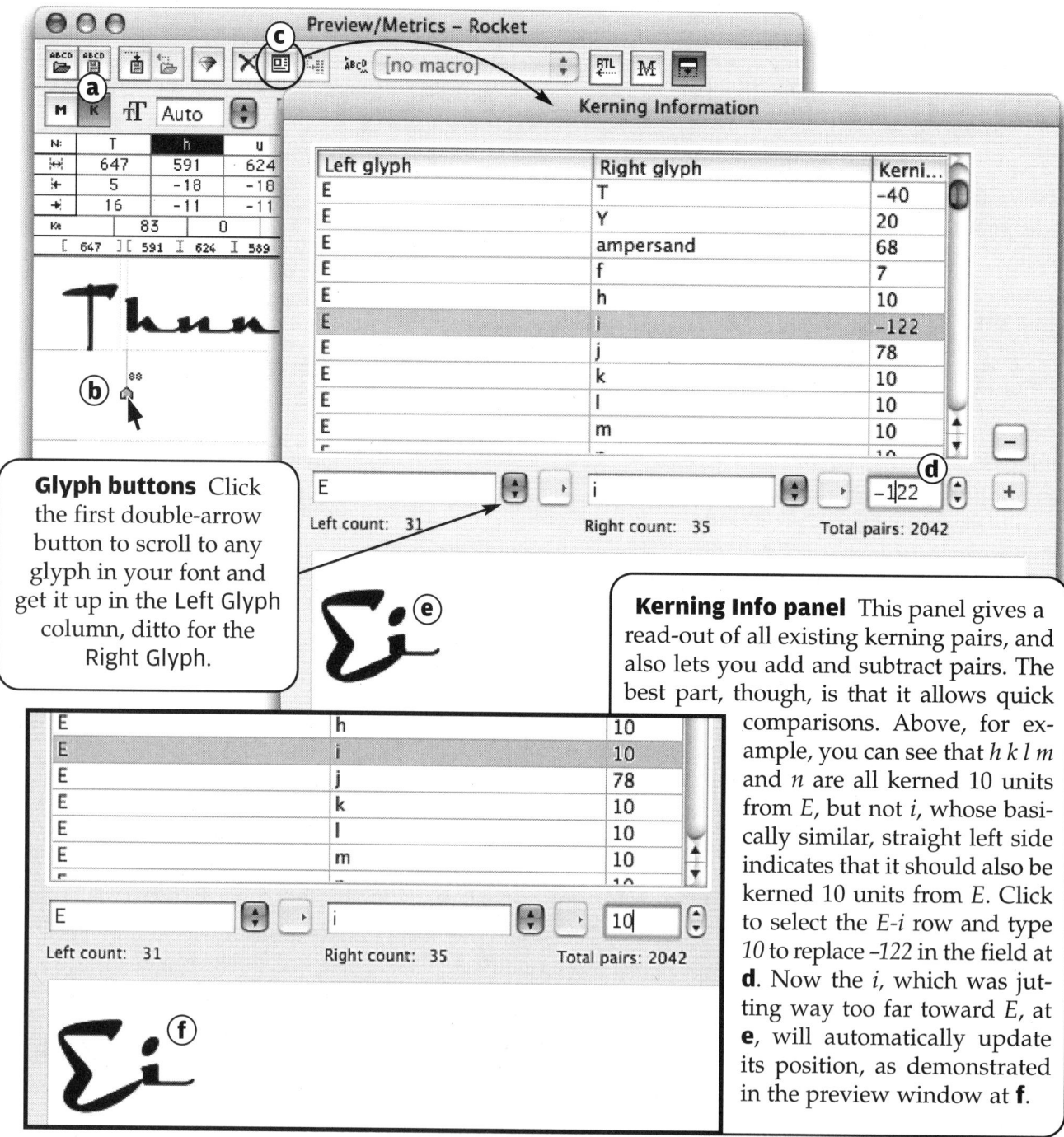

Glyph buttons Click the first double-arrow button to scroll to any glyph in your font and get it up in the Left Glyph column, ditto for the Right Glyph.

Kerning Info panel This panel gives a read-out of all existing kerning pairs, and also lets you add and subtract pairs. The best part, though, is that it allows quick comparisons. Above, for example, you can see that *h k l m* and *n* are all kerned 10 units from *E*, but not *i*, whose basically similar, straight left side indicates that it should also be kerned 10 units from *E*. Click to select the *E-i* row and type *10* to replace *–122* in the field at **d**. Now the *i*, which was jutting way too far toward *E*, at **e**, will automatically update its position, as demonstrated in the preview window at **f**.

Remove existing kerning

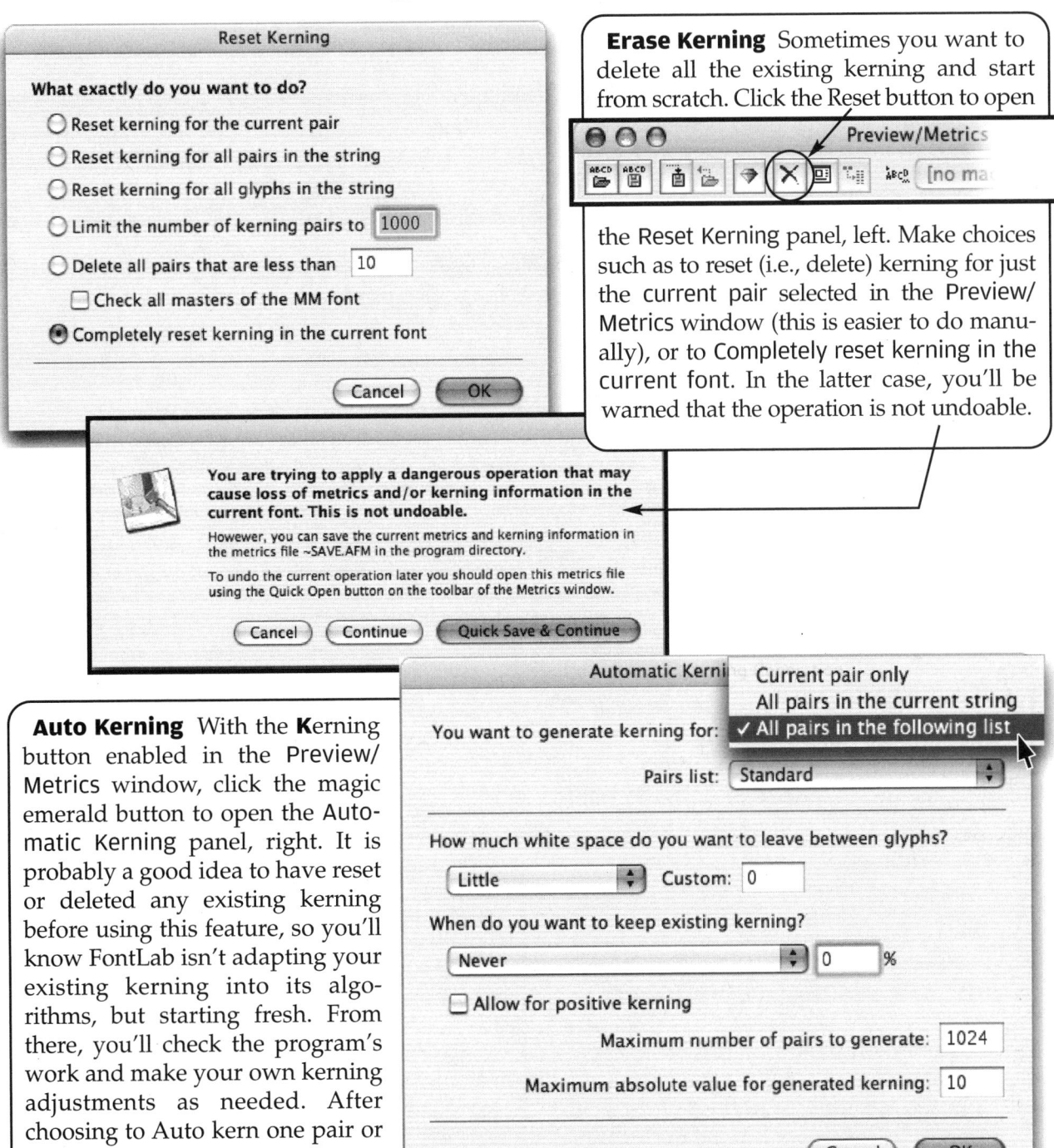

Reset Kerning

What exactly do you want to do?

○ Reset kerning for the current pair

○ Reset kerning for all pairs in the string

○ Reset kerning for all glyphs in the string

○ Limit the number of kerning pairs to [1000]

○ Delete all pairs that are less than [10]

　　☐ Check all masters of the MM font

◉ Completely reset kerning in the current font

(Cancel)　(OK)

Erase Kerning Sometimes you want to delete all the existing kerning and start from scratch. Click the Reset button to open

Preview/Metrics

[no ma]

the Reset Kerning panel, left. Make choices such as to reset (i.e., delete) kerning for just the current pair selected in the Preview/Metrics window (this is easier to do manually), or to Completely reset kerning in the current font. In the latter case, you'll be warned that the operation is not undoable.

You are trying to apply a dangerous operation that may cause loss of metrics and/or kerning information in the current font. This is not undoable.

Howewer, you can save the current metrics and kerning information in the metrics file ~SAVE.AFM in the program directory.

To undo the current operation later you should open this metrics file using the Quick Open button on the toolbar of the Metrics window.

(Cancel)　(Continue)　(Quick Save & Continue)

Auto Kerning With the **K**erning button enabled in the Preview/Metrics window, click the magic emerald button to open the Automatic Kerning panel, right. It is probably a good idea to have reset or deleted any existing kerning before using this feature, so you'll know FontLab isn't adapting your existing kerning into its algorithms, but starting fresh. From there, you'll check the program's work and make your own kerning adjustments as needed. After choosing to Auto kern one pair or the entire font, the next most important section is How much white space.... Experiment on the string first, with all these various settings.

Automatic Kerni

Current pair only

All pairs in the current string

✓ All pairs in the following list

You want to generate kerning for:

Pairs list: [Standard]

How much white space do you want to leave between glyphs?

[Little]　Custom: [0]

When do you want to keep existing kerning?

[Never]　[0] %

☐ Allow for positive kerning

Maximum number of pairs to generate: [1024]

Maximum absolute value for generated kerning: [10]

(Cancel)　(OK)

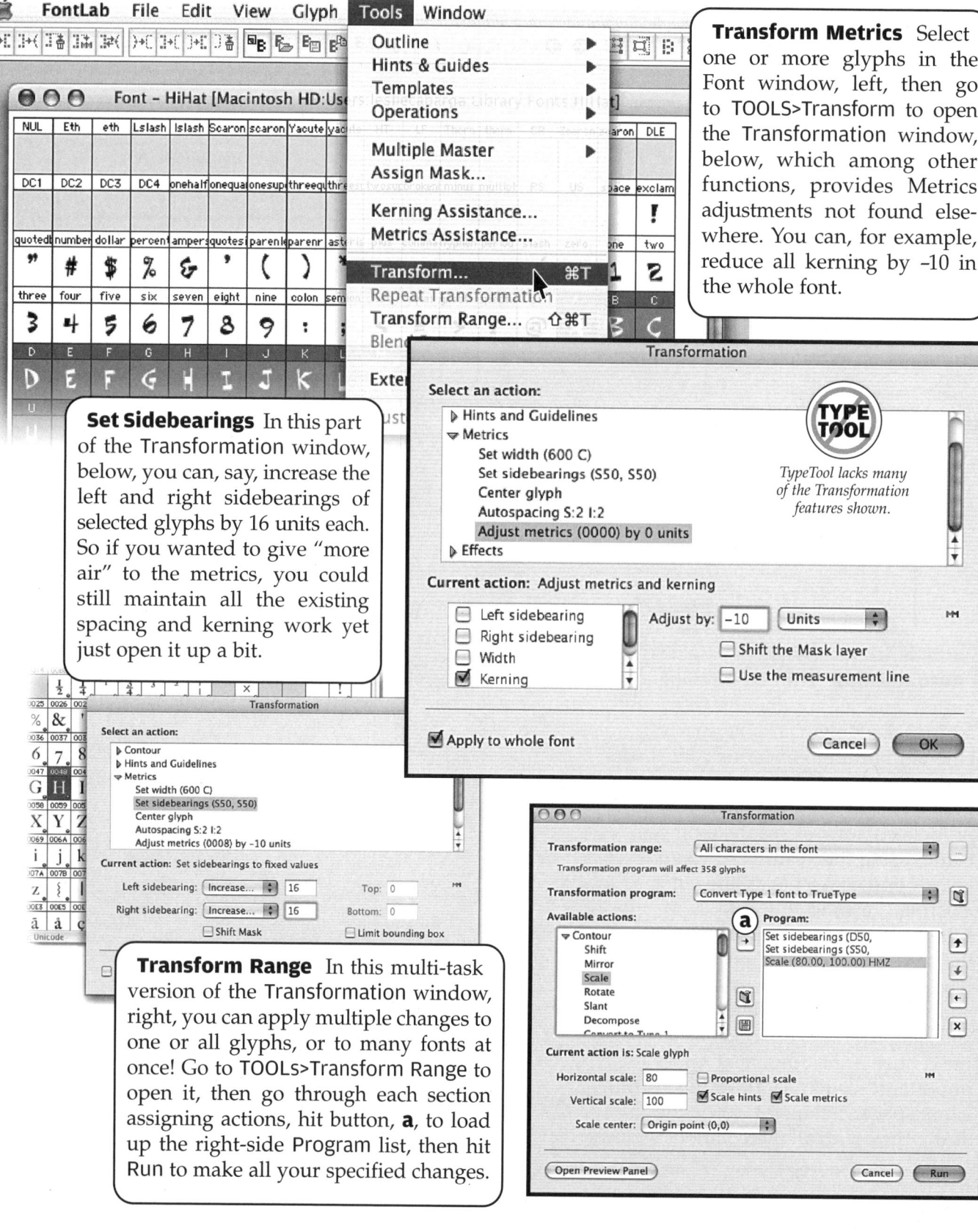

Transform Metrics Select one or more glyphs in the Font window, left, then go to TOOLS>Transform to open the Transformation window, below, which among other functions, provides Metrics adjustments not found elsewhere. You can, for example, reduce all kerning by –10 in the whole font.

TypeTool lacks many of the Transformation features shown.

Set Sidebearings In this part of the Transformation window, below, you can, say, increase the left and right sidebearings of selected glyphs by 16 units each. So if you wanted to give "more air" to the metrics, you could still maintain all the existing spacing and kerning work yet just open it up a bit.

Transform Range In this multi-task version of the Transformation window, right, you can apply multiple changes to one or all glyphs, or to many fonts at once! Go to TOOLS>Transform Range to open it, then go through each section assigning actions, hit button, **a**, to load up the right-side Program list, then hit Run to make all your specified changes.

The Metrics window in Studio 5

The major change in this window is that we now can assess our metrics as a multi-line column, the way type is typically set. Three other major changes:
1. By selecting the I-bar tool, detail **a**, you now can type/select text, **b**/copy/paste into the display area.
2. The Metrics/Kerning table is now dockable on the right side, **c**, providing a handy permanent overview of the metrics and kerning pairs in the font.
3. Handling of Class-based metrics and kerning has been seriously-improved, so that the same metrics and kerning can be immediately applied to any class of similar glyphs, **d**.

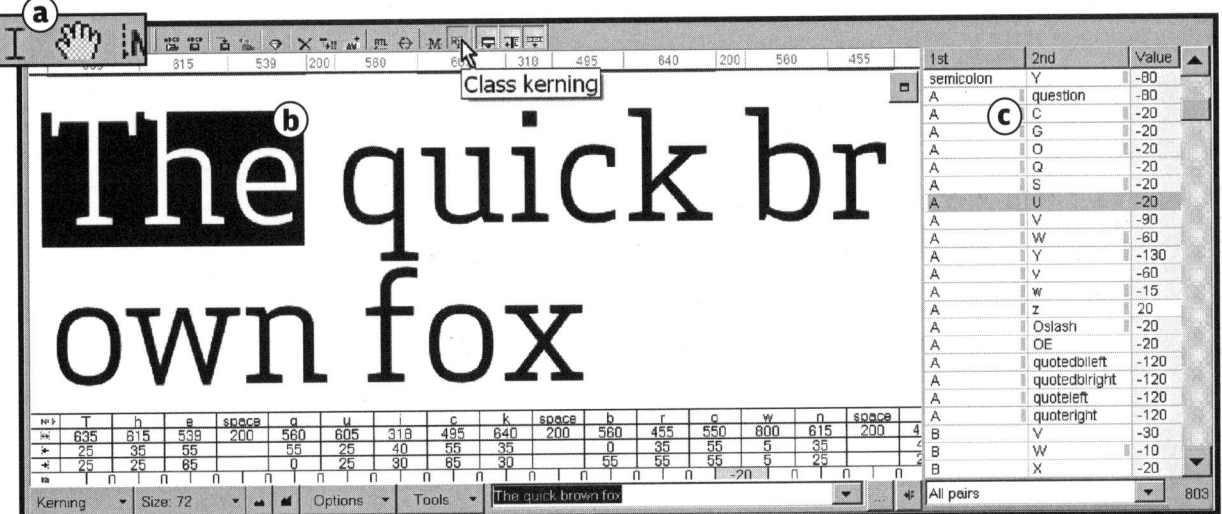

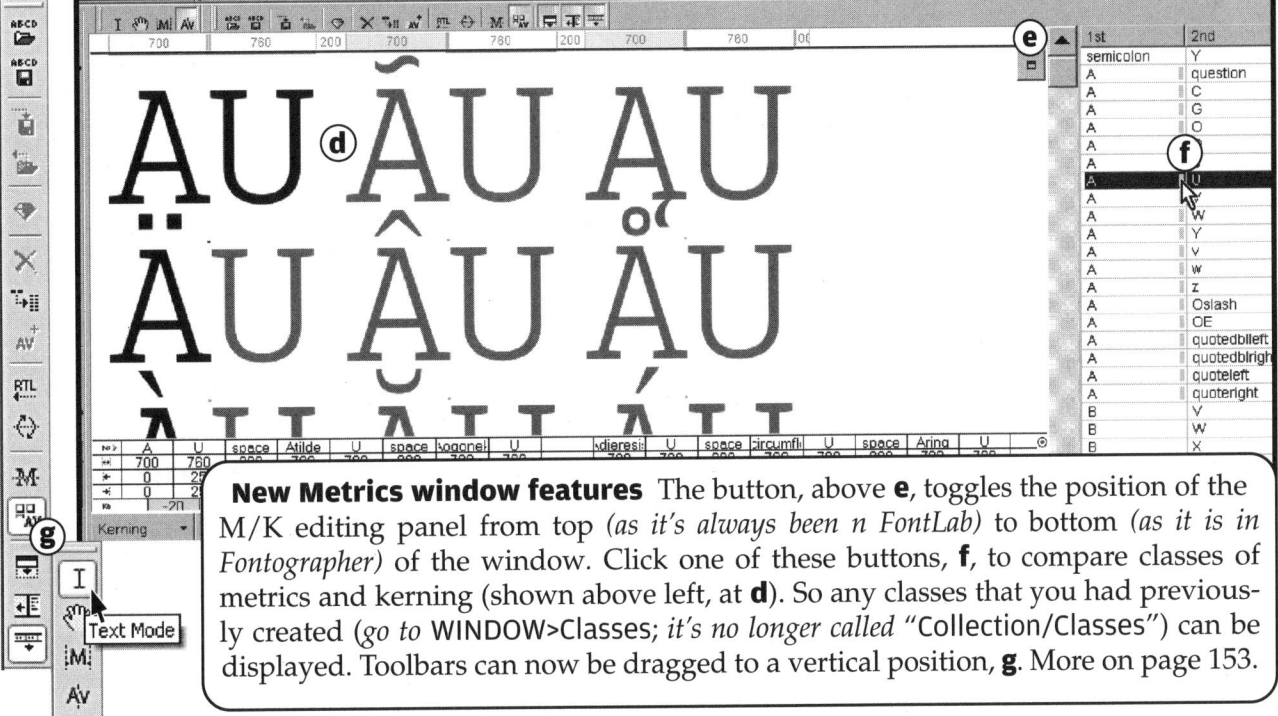

New Metrics window features The button, above **e**, toggles the position of the M/K editing panel from top *(as it's always been n FontLab)* to bottom *(as it is in Fontographer)* of the window. Click one of these buttons, **f**, to compare classes of metrics and kerning (shown above left, at **d**). So any classes that you had previously created *(go to WINDOW>Classes; it's no longer called "Collection/Classes")* can be displayed. Toolbars can now be dragged to a vertical position, **g**. More on page 153.

Time-saving Class-based kerning

FontLab makes it easy to kern composited accented characters* by simply applying the same kerning you did for "master" characters to their accented "dependents," instead of having to kern accent characters individually. And whatever metrics or kerning changes you may make to the master are applied to the class.

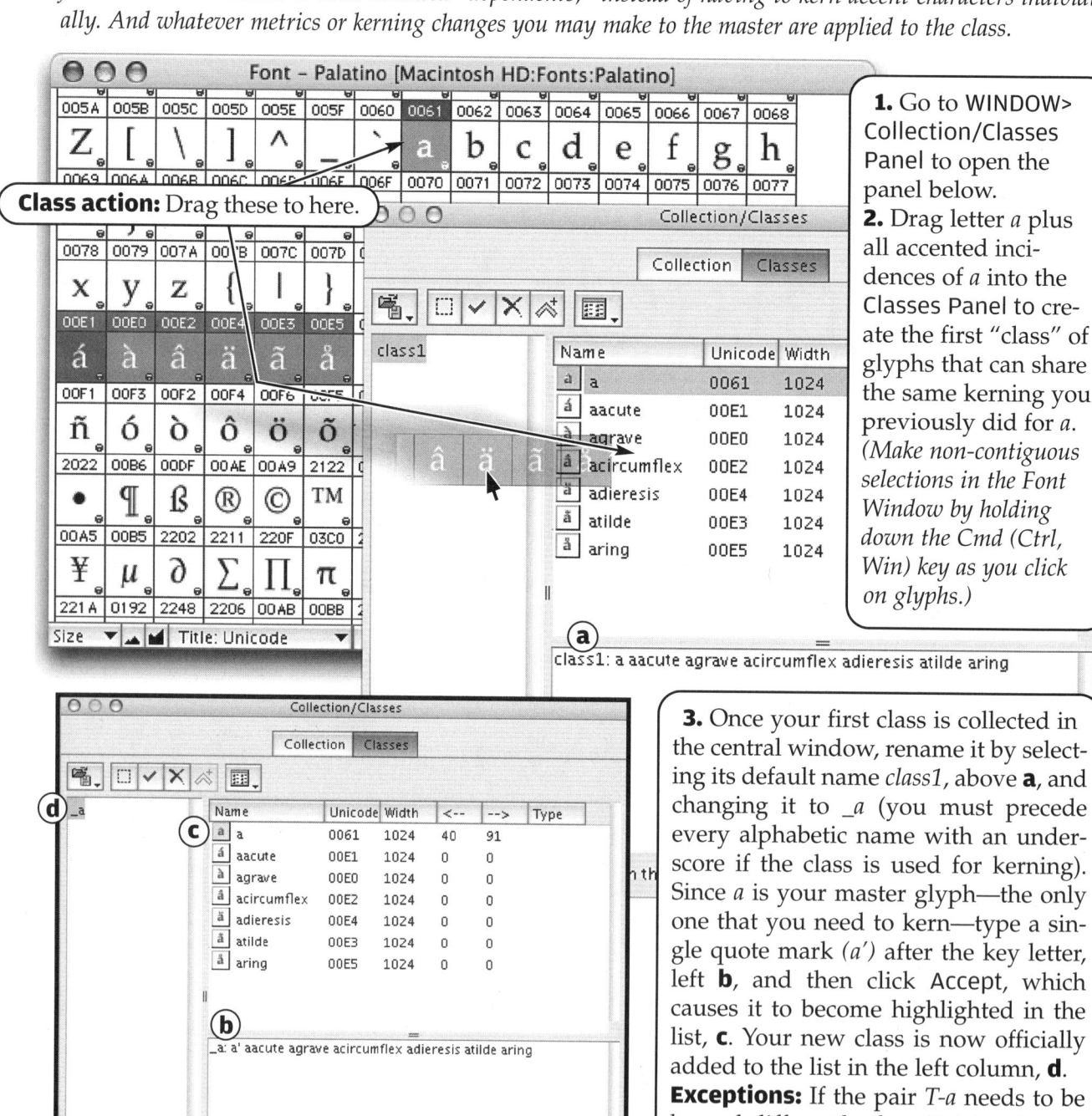

Class action: Drag these to here.

1. Go to WINDOW> Collection/Classes Panel to open the panel below.

2. Drag letter *a* plus all accented incidences of *a* into the Classes Panel to create the first "class" of glyphs that can share the same kerning you previously did for *a*. (*Make non-contiguous selections in the Font Window by holding down the Cmd (Ctrl, Win) key as you click on glyphs.*)

3. Once your first class is collected in the central window, rename it by selecting its default name *class1*, above **a**, and changing it to _*a* (you must precede every alphabetic name with an underscore if the class is used for kerning). Since *a* is your master glyph—the only one that you need to kern—type a single quote mark (*a'*) after the key letter, left **b**, and then click Accept, which causes it to become highlighted in the list, **c**. Your new class is now officially added to the list in the left column, **d**.

Exceptions: If the pair *T-a* needs to be kerned differently than *T-ä*, just kern *ä* to *T* separately from the class.

(**Go to page 119 to find out how to make composited accent characters.*)

TypeTool lacks Class-based Kerning feature.

4. Complete your classes: Click the **+** button, right **a**, to add another class and repeat steps 1–3 until classes for all applicable letters have been entered. Following are the characters for which classes are most likely to be needed: *AC DEILNOSUYZaceilnosuyz.*

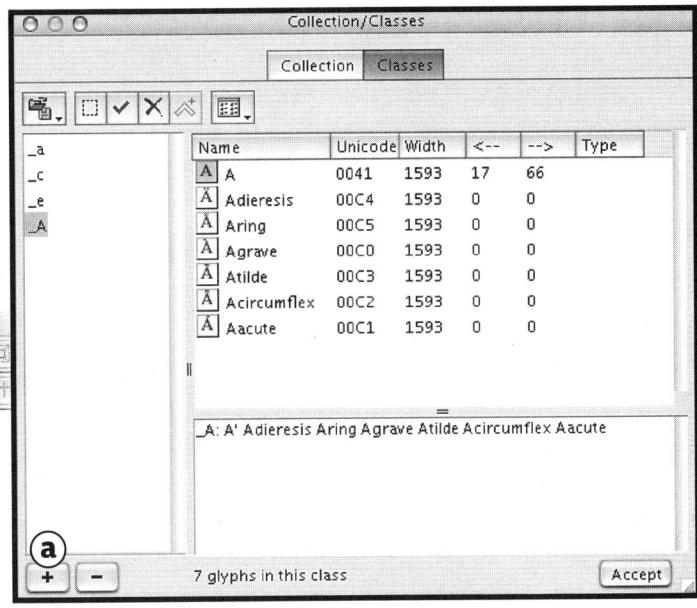

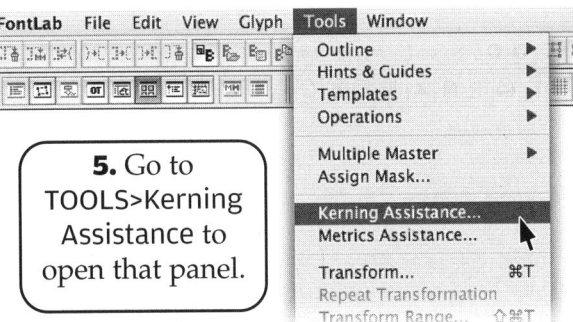

5. Go to TOOLS>Kerning Assistance to open that panel.

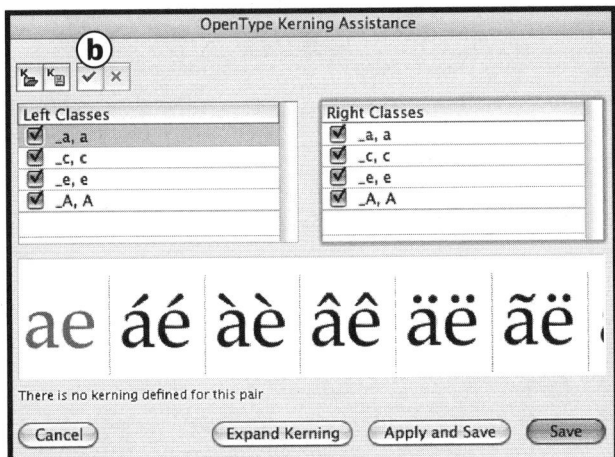

6. The Kerning Assistance panel, below, has several functions, such as the ability to compare class-to-class kerning, but we are mainly concerned here with the two buttons that tell FontLab to go ahead and apply the kerning you did on your master glyphs to all dependent glyphs in all the enabled classes. Click in each of the two Classes windows and hit the Select All button, **b**, once for each side. Click the Apply and Save button for .otf and .ttf fonts, then reopen the panel and this time hit the Expand Kerning button for Type 1 fonts.

The Metrics Assistance panel, right, is not exactly related to this kerning discussion, but it should be mentioned. It is great for making metrics adjustments to all the glyphs in a given class in one step, rather than having to adjust each accent pair individually. For example, if you decided *a* had been spaced too tightly (or loosely), you could add (or subtract) 15 units of space to the **L**eft, **R**ight or total **W**idth, which could then be applied to all instances of *a* in the class. The preview area, **c**, provides a perfect rendition of your changes.

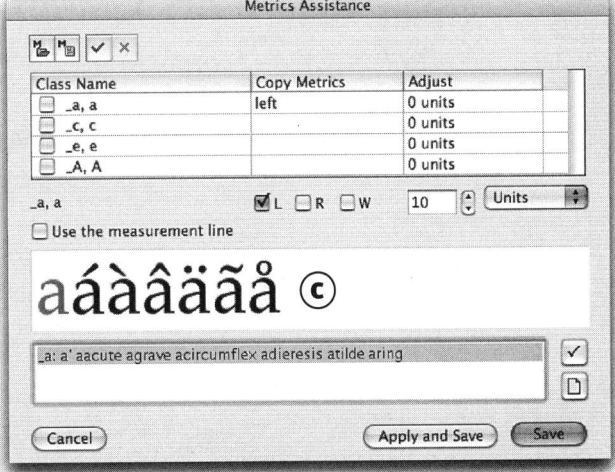

Hinting

After the interesting, creative aspects of designing a font have been completed, the less-fun, technical parts begin. We've already talked about the Joy of Kerning. Hinting a font may be the least fun of all. But first, let's ask…

Why should we hint?

Unhinted type, like the above blown up from 9- and 8-point, will look bad and be hard to read in low-resolution situations such as 72–96 dpi computer monitors and 300 dpi printers.

Hinting is irrelevant in commercial printing. Its primary purpose is to make fonts more legible on-screen at 9- to 14-point. Hints also help to maintain a clear difference between serif and sans styles, and more usefully, between regular and bold font weights.

In time, as screen resolutions increase, causing pixel grids to become finer, the innate absurdity of hinting may become a thing of the past.

Can we avoid hinting?

Text fonts are the most important to hint. You can often avoid hinting display fonts (headline fonts) that are complex or fancy because they will most likely never be used at smaller point sizes. At 12 pixels high—regardless of whether such a display font has been expertly hinted or not—its complexity or boldness would probably make it impossible to read. An exception: At smaller sizes, the hinting detail of Augsburger Initials, right, gets progressively simpler, an idea with practical application in Asian fonts.

To avoid hinting a font that really should be hinted, just let FontLab do it with Auto-hinting and either leave the results as-is or selectively tweak just a few glyphs.

Left, the top line of text was set in Verdana at a high resolution. The lower four lines were set in Verdana at 14-, 12-, 10-, and 8-point in a 72 dpi Photoshop file alongside a photograph, all of which are shown vastly enlarged. It is obvious that at the smaller point sizes, the font's hints, corresponding to the photo's pixel grid, bear no resemblance to Verdana's true contours. Yet we can see that at 10, 8 and 7 pixels high, the nicely-designed hints improve legibility (it all seems to fall apart, though, at 8 point).

Good hinting has simple forms

Set at 9-point on the web, you can abandon all hope of retaining any of your font's unique contours (or of it even being identifiable). So your next hope would be to achieve order and symmetry in the way the hints are arranged in the pixel grid. Comparing the hinted fonts below, you notice there are only small differences between them. It is just a pity that hinting information can't be cut and pasted from one font into another and then just tweaked slightly.

ABCDE abcde Verdana
ABCDE abcde Helvetica
ABCDE abcde Eurostile
ABCDE abcde Myriad

ABCDE abcdeTimes
ABCDE abcdef New Cent

Why is Verdana such a successfully-hinted font?

Legend has it that Verdana was designed backwards. That is, carefully planned stair-step bitmap patterns were created first, for every letter, at three text sizes. Then, against these, the final glyph contour drawings were traced, or as Matthew Carter himself puts it, "I wrapped the outline around the bitmaps." He adds, "Tom Rickner, who hinted it, contributed a lot, and we revised a few of the outlines to help the resulting bitmaps." So instead of allowing hints to fall where they may in afterthought, Verdana's preplanning gained it the rep as one of the world's best-hinted fonts.

Idea: Design your contours so all stems will fall in alignment with the pixel grid. Set a 20 pixel per em grid in the Background layer, draw the font to fall on those lines. Then, at least at 20, 40, and 10 ppm, the bitmap can be perfect without hints.

Flash and Photoshop

In order to see your beautifully-hinted font on the web, visitors to your website would have to have your font installed in their systems. So unless you invented Times, Courier, Helvetica, Arial or Verdana, you might as well forget about your font needing to look good on the web. Fonts may be embedded in Flash files, but small type can look bad in Flash (unless you use well-made pixelfonts or purchase FontFlasher, from www.fontlab.com).

However, gifs with small text *are* used on the web. Therefore, hinting is helpful for use in Photoshop and Fireworks. As shown below, the position, relative to the pixel grid, in which you place type in Photoshop, **a** or **b**, may affect its appearance. And this is a good lesson in how the screen forces our stems to jump into alignment with the pixel grid. Because its metrics are hinted, Verdana, **c**, doesn't jump around. in this way.

a Stonehearth
b Stonehearth
c Stonehearth

Two kinds of hinting

FontLab offers two kinds of hinting. Type 1 hinting is easy, but limited in its results. TrueType hinting is laborious but the results can be much more comprehensive. A labor-saving approach would be to Autohint a font, overall, as Type 1, then solve a few problem areas using TrueType hinting on selected glyphs. Yes, both kinds of hinting can coexist within the same font, but if you output a font as Type 1, any TT hints will not be present. However, Type 1 hinting *is* automatically converted to TT hints in TT and OT fonts.

Auto-hint a Type 1 font

1. Open a font Hit Cmd- or Ctrl-O to Open an existing font on which to practice hinting. If you select, say, Georgia (the lack of a suffix indicates this is a Mac TT font), or any font suitcase, you will have to click the arrow, **a**, to open the suitcase's contents. Then double-click on a font to open it (or select one or more and hit OK).

2. Save a copy Go to FILE>Save As and save the font you've opened as a new Fontlab "master" .vfb document to a different folder than where the original was located. That is, don't save your test version into your Fonts folder.

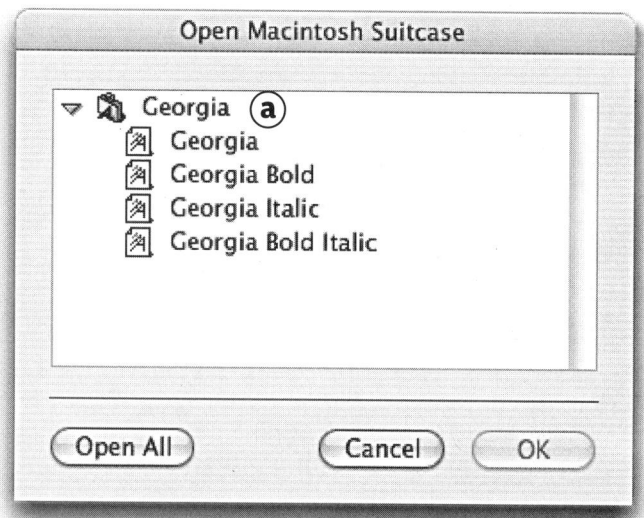

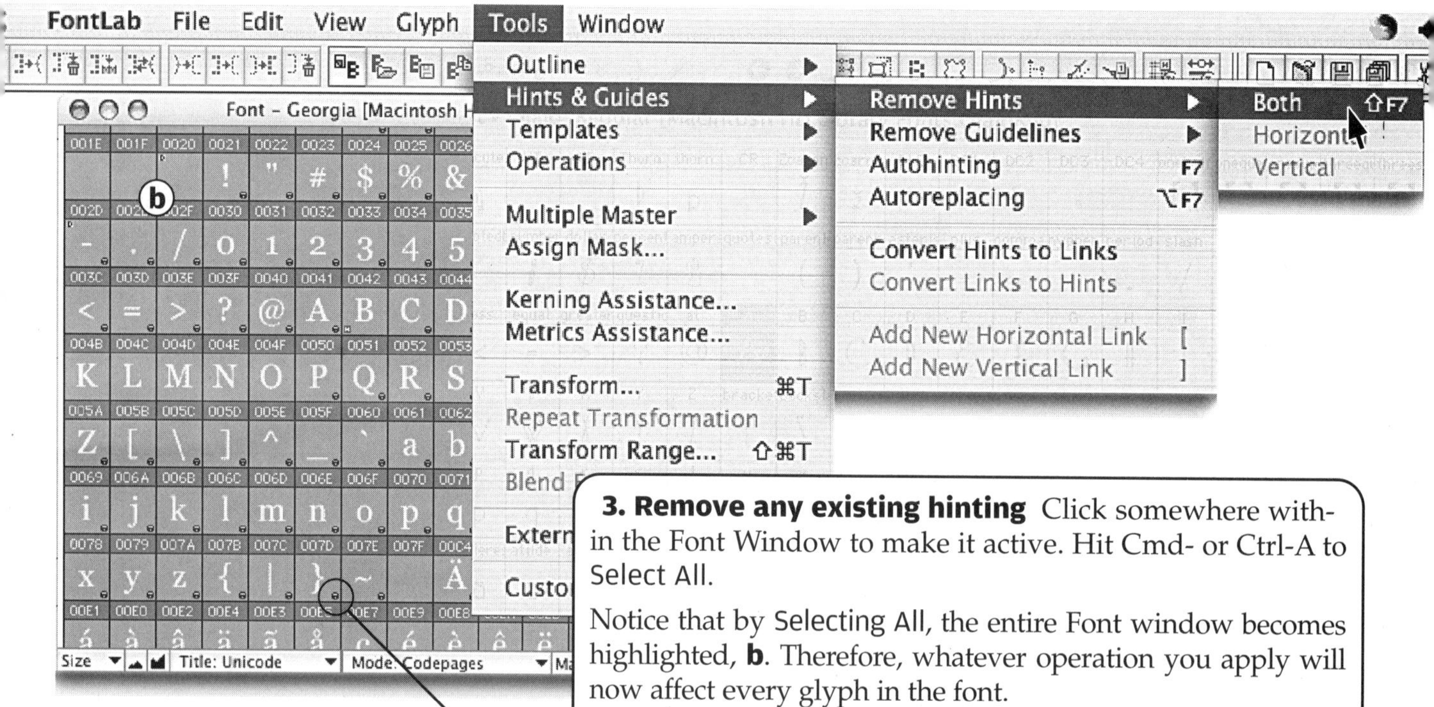

3. Remove any existing hinting Click somewhere within the Font Window to make it active. Hit Cmd- or Ctrl-A to Select All.

Notice that by Selecting All, the entire Font window becomes highlighted, **b**. Therefore, whatever operation you apply will now affect every glyph in the font.

The "**T**" Control mark symbols in the corner of each glyph cell, **c**, are your indication that those glyphs already have TrueType hints. (some hinted fonts may not display Control marks).

As shown above, go to TOOLS>Hints & Guides> Remove Hints>Both. Of course, the font you've selected to work on may not have been originally hinted.

TypeTool lacks hinting capabilities.

4. Prepare a TrueType font for Type 1 Autohinting If you are working from an existing TrueType font, or a new font that you've designed, you can perform the following operations to make sure that everything will be correct prior to hinting:

a. Change to Type 1 curves If the font has TrueType curves, Select All in the Font window, then go to TOOLS>Transform>Contour>Convert to Type 1>Apply to whole font.

b. Reverse contours Type 1 outlines must go in the counter-clockwise direction (the opposite of TT curves). Go to TOOLS>Transform>Contour>Reverse All>Set counter-clockwise (counters will automatically be changed to clockwise direction). *Hinting instructions continue on following page.*

FontAudit

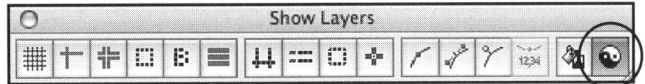

Before commencing with hinting, we recommend using FontAudit as an easy way to check for errors in contours. FontAudit is great; it's like a built-in Norton Utilities for fonts, and it will give your font a professionally-drawn edge. Click the yin-yang button in the Show Layers palette, above, to activate FontAudit.

Using FontAudit Flip through all the glyphs in your font *(use Cmd-/Ctrl-] or the "Next" arrow at the top of the Edit toolbar)* and watch out for the red arrows, **a**, **b** and **c**, right, indicating contour problems. Click a red arrow to open the explanation panel. *(I love this error message! "Not exactly vertical" and horizontal lines are a very common problem.)* Click Fix or Fix All to solve the errors or hit Cancel to fix them yourself.

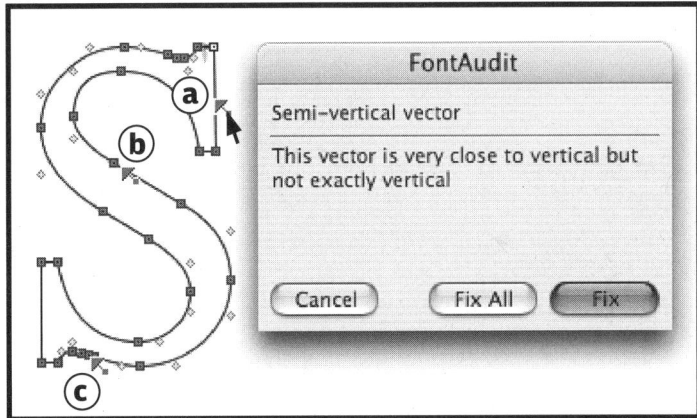

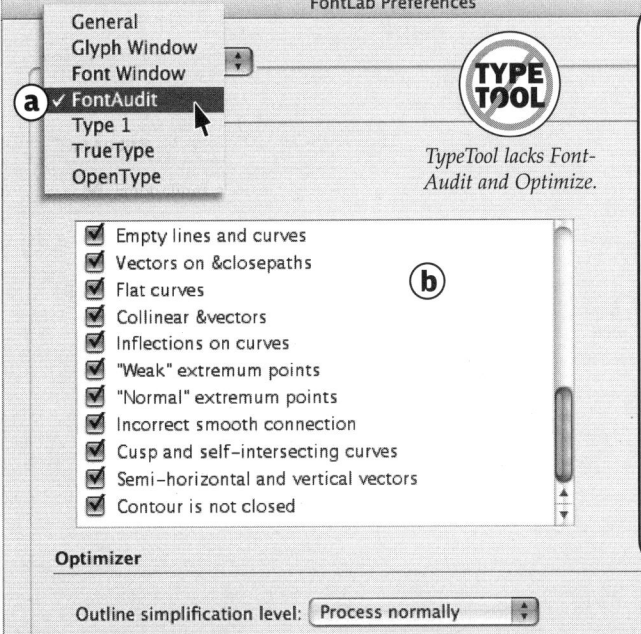

TypeTool lacks Font-Audit and Optimize.

FontAudit Open the Preferences window and go to the FontAudit page, **a**. Click to enable or disable any of the features, **b**, that you don't want. Download the free .pdf manual from fontlab.com for a full explanation of what these FontAudit features do.

Optimize This is another contour-improving feature that can be done on individual glyphs or globally *(go to TOOLS>Outline>Optimize or Cmd-/Ctrl-E)*. **Warning:** Both FontAudit and Optimize can cause subtle alterations to curves, so it may be advisable to paste copies of each glyph into the Background layer. And compare, letter by letter, the results of auto-correction against your original contours.

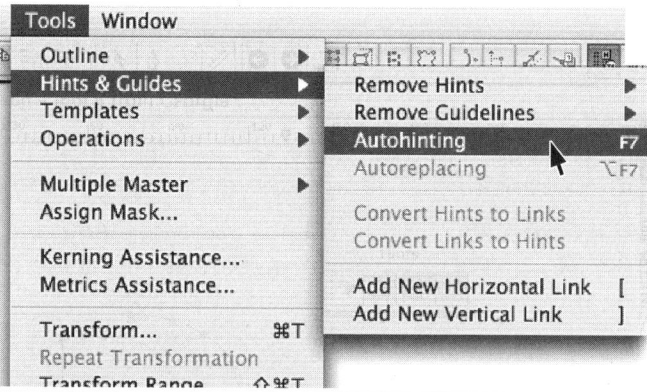

5. Apply Autohinting Go to TOOLS>Hints & Guides>Autohinting. It's always best to start by letting FontLab hint for us and later make adjustments if we disagree with the program's decisions.

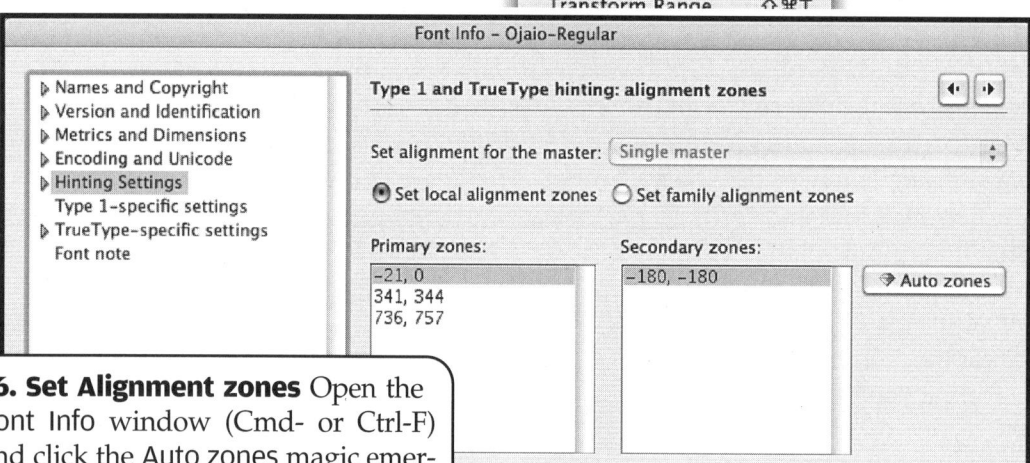

6. Set Alignment zones Open the Font Info window (Cmd- or Ctrl-F) and click the Auto zones magic emerald button. FontLab will instantly check all glyphs and place average values in the Primary and Secondary zones fields. Which zones get placed in which field is fairly arbitrary and up to you. (*See page 49 to learn how to manually set Alignment zones.*)

Overshoot suppression Alignment zones not only serves to guide us in applying overshoot consistently as we draw letters, but it also suppresses overshoot during hinting. Before adding Alignment zones, you might notice in the hints Preview window (below), that the tops and bottoms of rounded or pointy letters such as *a, e, v* and *o* tend to get bumped up to the next pixel causing a bouncy result.

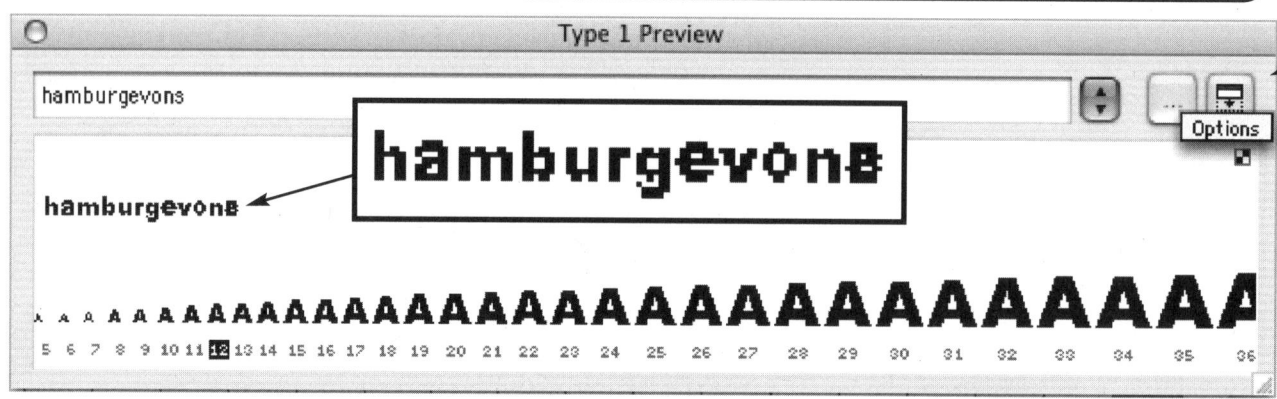

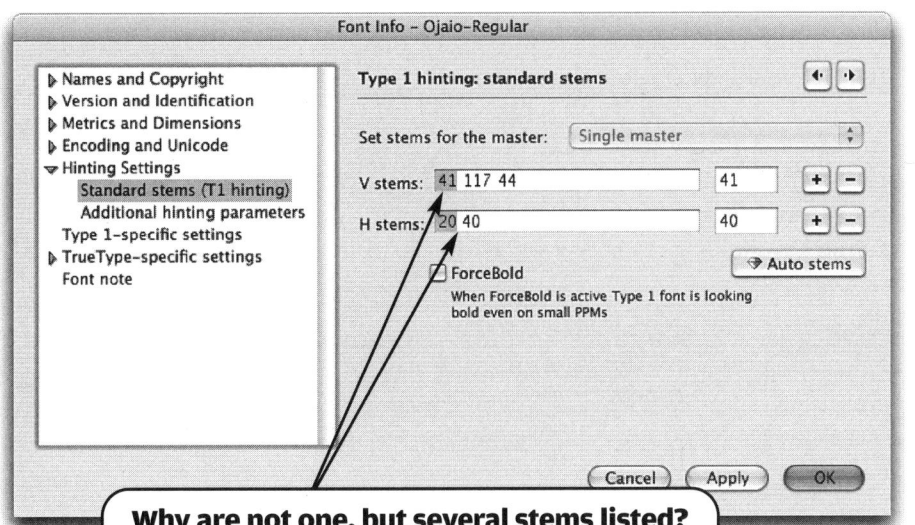

7. Set Standard stems

Click on the next page in the Hinting Settings section of the Font Info window. click the Auto stems magic emerald button. FontLab will check all glyphs and place some average values in the V stems and H stems fields. These stem widths tell the program where to place the hints.

Why are not one, but several stems listed?

FontLab takes into account, not only a standard vertical stem width, such as that of *I* or *H*, **a**, but of errant stems like **b**, that should have been the same as **a**, and lower case stem widths, like *l*, **c**, that are often designed to be narrower than the capital stem. And, for the purposes of hinting, FontLab considers the broadest parts of rounded letters like *o*, **d**, as stems to be measured.

8. Go into Hinting mode

You must have a glyph window open, then you'll be able to begin the actual hinting process by going to TOOLS> Operations>Type 1 Hinting, right. Doing this opens the hinting tool palette and the Type 1 Preview window (that we first visited, opposite).

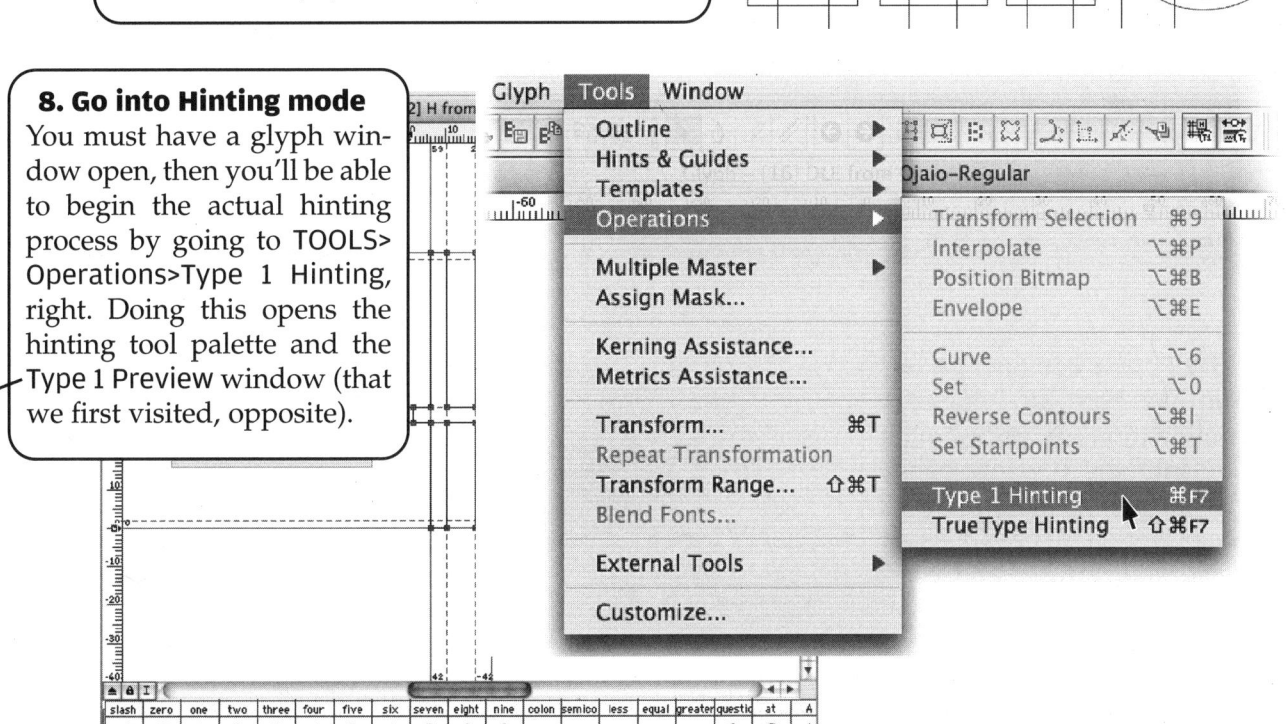

Type 1 hinting mode   Below is what you'll see when you enter this mode: The Hints palette opens along with the Type 1 Preview window. Notice the intersecting vertical and horizontal green lines, **a** and **b**, that define the stems. These bands show where the hints will be. All contours have directional arrows, **c**, which—for Type 1 purposes—will run counter-clockwise for the main contour and clockwise for the counter(s). The prominent numbers, 1 and 2 at **d**, tell how many contours there are in the glyph and the starting points of each contour. To make the green hint lines visible, make the Hints layer active by clicking on the word Hints, **e**, in the Edit Layers palette.

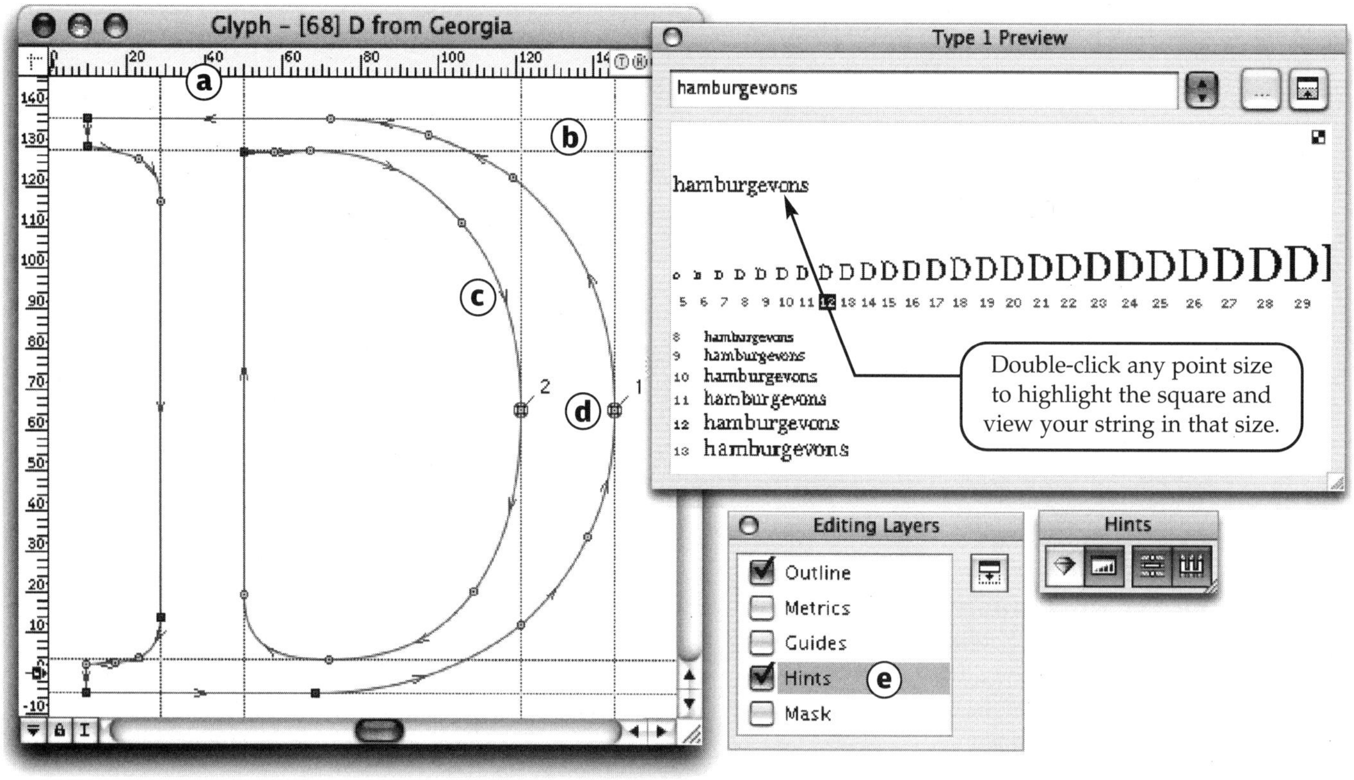

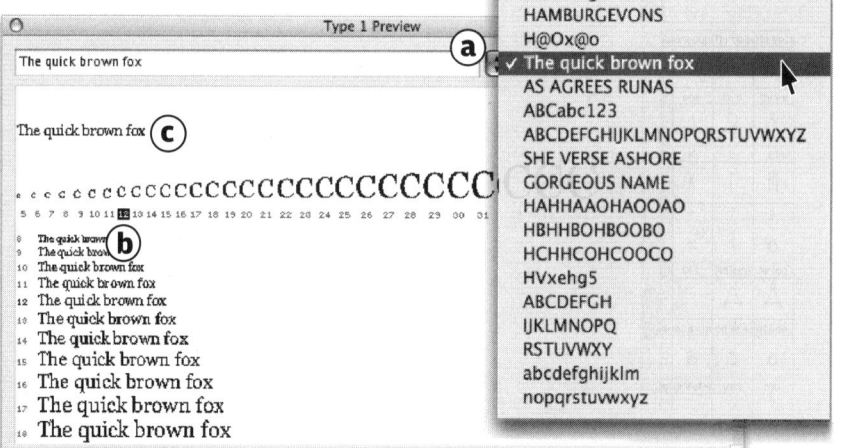

Double-click any point size to highlight the square and view your string in that size.

The Type 1 Preview panel

You can type any character combination or phrase you like into the Preview panel, right, but you can also click the button, **a**, to open a list of suggested phrases and combinations. Double-click on any of the point sizes beneath the waterfall display, **b**, to have the phrase rendered above, **c**, in that point size.

hamburgevons
HAMBURGEVONS
H@Ox@o
✓ The quick brown fox
AS AGREES RUNAS
ABCabc123
ABCDEFGHIJKLMNOPQRSTUVWXYZ
SHE VERSE ASHORE
GORGEOUS NAME
HAHHAAOHAOOAO
HBHHBOHBOOBO
HCHHCOHCOOCO
HVxehg5
ABCDEFGH
IJKLMNOPQ
RSTUVWXY
abcdefghijklm
nopqrstuvwxyz

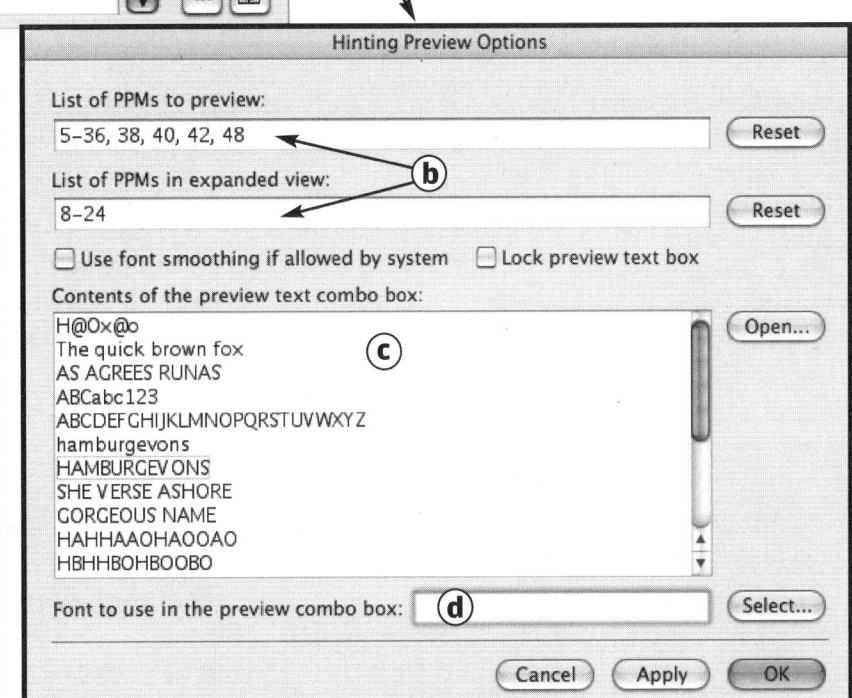

Hinting Preview Options

Usually, you can skip this window, right, but as you gain experience with hinting, there may be details you want to tweak. Click the button, **a**, above, to open the Options window. Change the point sizes (PPMs) in the Type 1 Preview window at **b**, type in your own text string, **c**, which will show up in the Preview window pulldown (*or hit* Open *to grab a text string somewhere on your hard drive*). If hinting a non-latin font, select a non-latin font to display in the preview box, **d**.

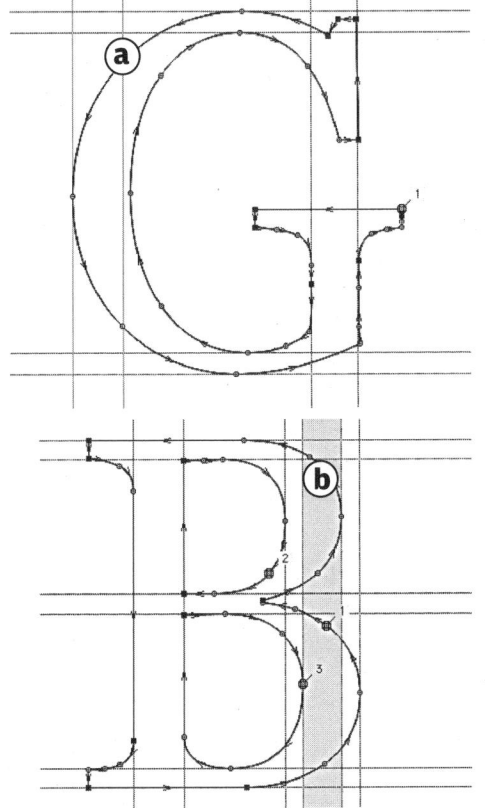

9. Double-check Autohinting Flip through all your glyphs and check for stems that Autohinting may not have correctly judged, such as **a** (the right side line doesn't align with the widest part of *G*'s stem), or overlapped hints, such as **b**, that show up as yellow bands (shown here as a gray band). Overlaps aren't allowed. Remember, in Type 1 hinting, all that we have control over are horizontal and vertical stems. FontLab itself deals with curving and diagonal stems and junctures and we just let it do its thing.

Slow-down lowdown If you notice a slow-down in reaction time during operations such as a delayed response in bringing up the Font Info window, do not panic. In order to keep up with your hinting changes, FontLab has to continually generate actual fonts on-the-fly reflecting the current state. This slows down program functioning.

10. Editing hints When in hinting mode, you can click on one of the two green lines defining a stem hint and the cursor becomes a double arrow. You can drag the two lines, in unison, anywhere, **a**. *But to move just one line at a time, hold the Shift key and drag it.* Or you can go to TOOLS>Hints & Guides>Convert Hints to Links, as shown below.

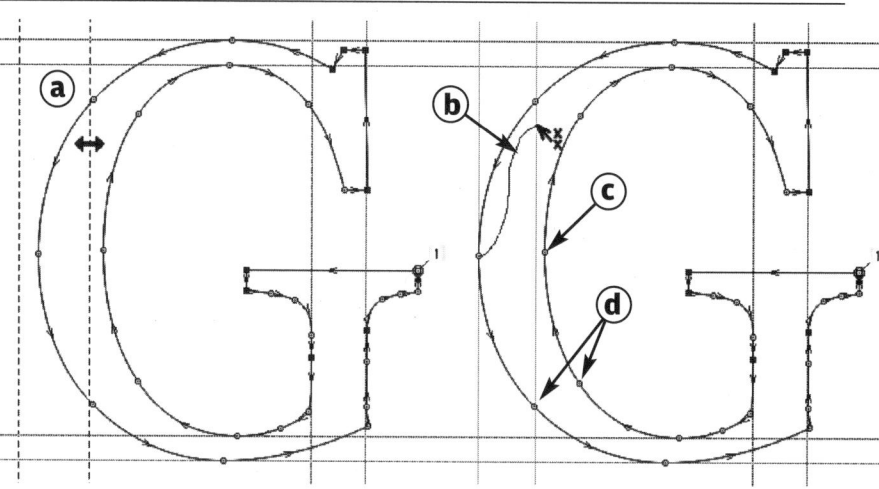

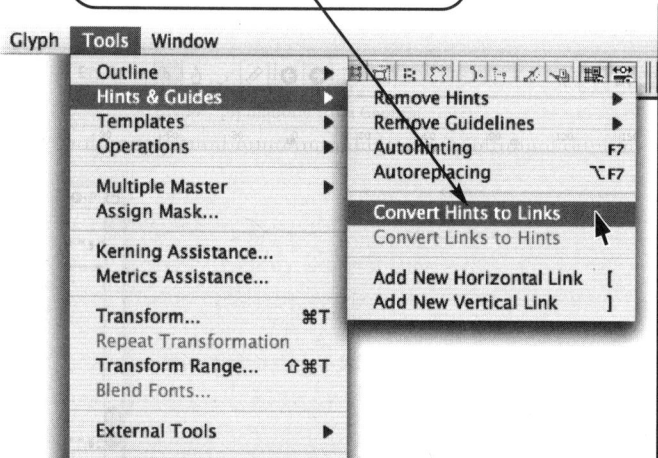

What is Links? It's not a separate operation from hinting. Links sort of describes the funny link line, above **b**, that pops up after you Convert Hints to Links and begin to drag a single green line to another position, **a**. *You'll notice that the hint line will only stay where you put it if you link it to a node* such as **c**, which would be the proper position to align the right side of this hint. Note that because we converted this glyph contour from TrueType, there were many extraneous, out-of-extrema nodes, such as **d**, that may have fooled Autohinting into misplacing its hint. *(This is why you should use Optimize and FontAudit before applying hinting.)* To get out of Links mode, go to TOOLS>Hints & Guides> Convert Links to Hints.

11. Fixing overlapping hints with Replacement hints When two or more stems, such as in letters *B* and *g*, sit atop one another, but aren't aligned, you get an overlap problem that can result in some weird bitmaps as seen at **a**, in the 11- and 14-point sizes (blown up from the Preview window). The arrows from **b** and **c** define the top and bottom stems. Letter *g* has three vertical, and two horizontal stem overlaps. The enlarged bitmaps for *g*, at **d**, show the weird effects this causes (*also note the hard-to-avoid proportional changes that hinted bitmap letters endure at different point sizes*).

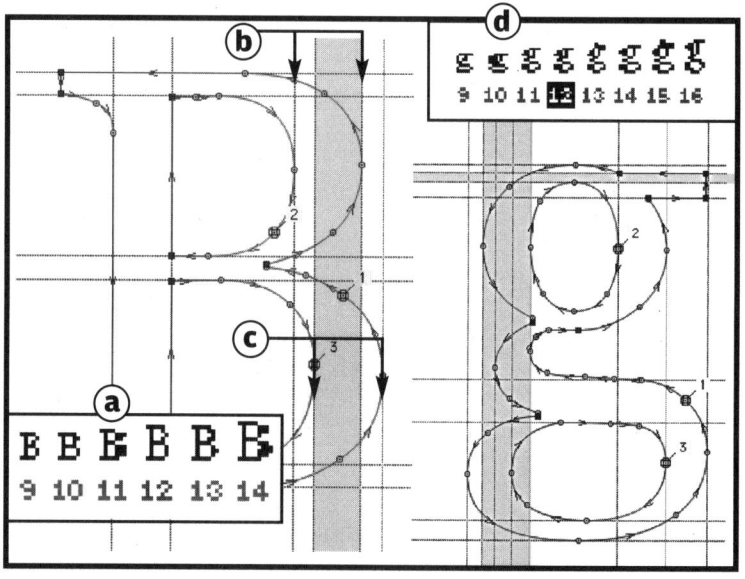

One approach to overlaps: Avoid them by compromising the contour. As shown in step 10, click on one hint and drag it, this time away from the letter. Then hit Control-click (or Rt-click, Win) to open the pop-up menu, **a**, and choose Delete (*the hint slated for termination—almost as a plaintive cry for help—will develop diagonal lines, **b***). Next you'll choose a position for the single remaining hint, **c**, and check the Preview window, detail at **d**, until you like the result, which as you see here, is still not exactly great hinting.

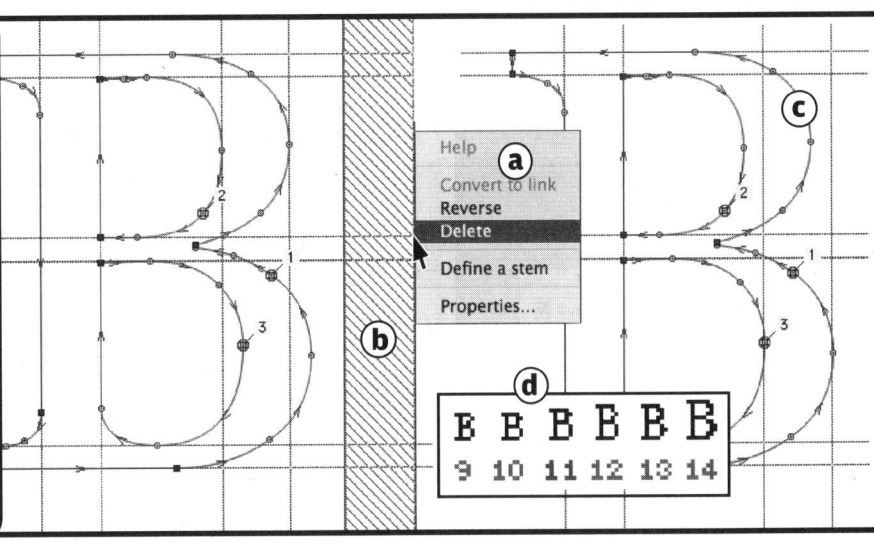

12. Removing the overlap with Replacement hints When the vertical or horizontal bands that comprise Type 1 hints overlap, a Replacement command must be added so the rasterizer can tell which hint applies to, say, the upper bowl, and which to the lower. Your last step in Type 1 hinting is to go to TOOLS>Hints & Guides>Autoreplacing, left **a**, or click the Autoreplace button on the Hints toolbar, **b**, to add these special Replacement commands. You'll still see the yellow areas where the hints overlap, but you'll also notice **HR** (Hint Replacement) icons, below left at **c**. As you check the result, **d**, if still not acceptable to you, some TrueType hinting may be required.

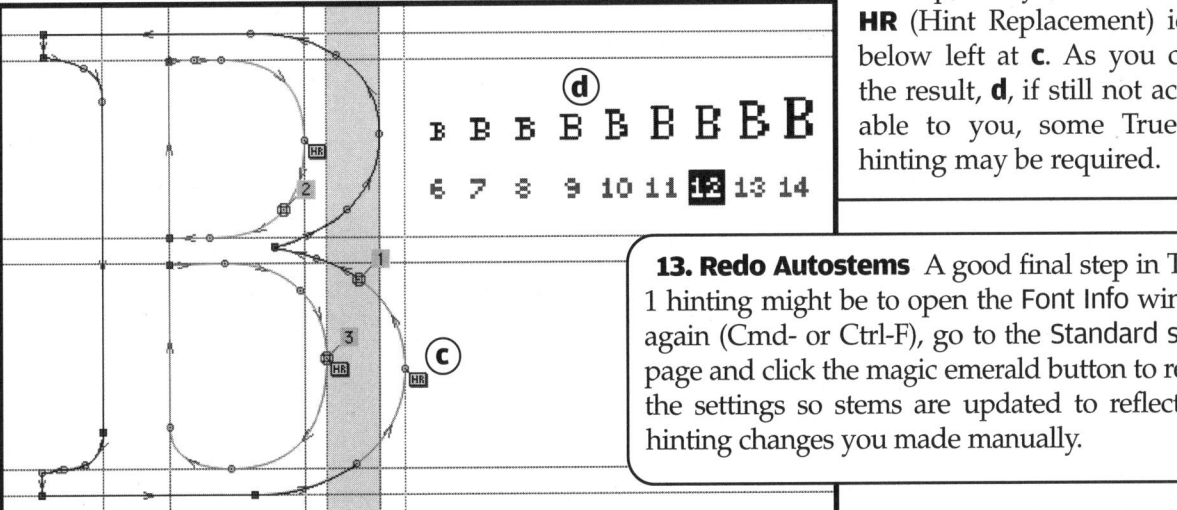

13. Redo Autostems A good final step in Type 1 hinting might be to open the Font Info window again (Cmd- or Ctrl-F), go to the Standard stems page and click the magic emerald button to renew the settings so stems are updated to reflect any hinting changes you made manually.

Beginning TrueType hinting

After you have completed Type 1 hinting, and thus solved many of the more simplistic hinting issues, you can go further into the fearsome world of TrueType hinting. Unfortunately, the process of TrueType hinting is too complex to be fully explained here. The following introductory steps merely show you how to start the process by getting into the correct areas. Refer to the FontLab user manual from www.fontlab.com for further details.

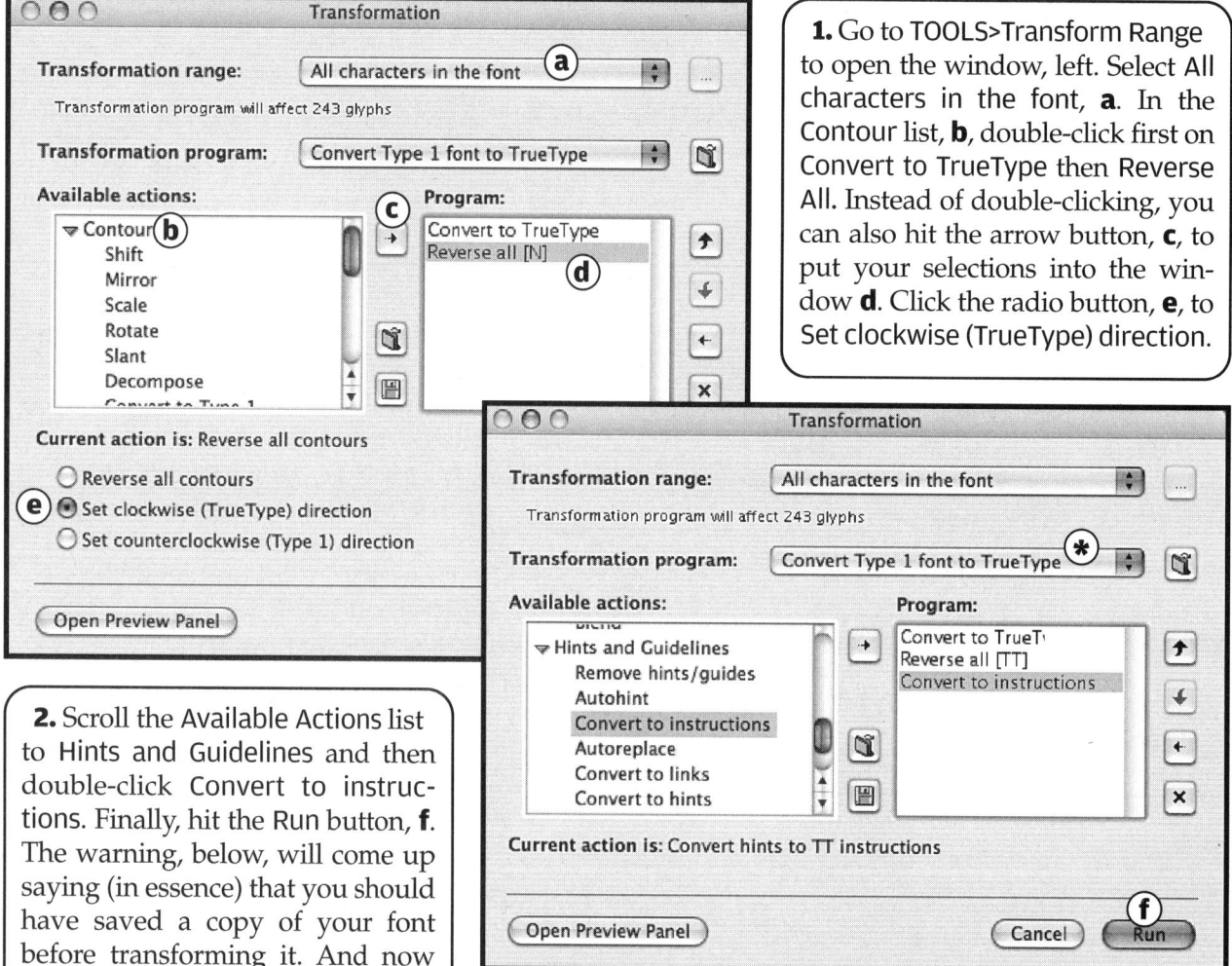

1. Go to TOOLS>Transform Range to open the window, left. Select All characters in the font, **a**. In the Contour list, **b**, double-click first on Convert to TrueType then Reverse All. Instead of double-clicking, you can also hit the arrow button, **c**, to put your selections into the window **d**. Click the radio button, **e**, to Set clockwise (TrueType) direction.

2. Scroll the Available Actions list to Hints and Guidelines and then double-click Convert to instructions. Finally, hit the Run button, **f**. The warning, below, will come up saying (in essence) that you should have saved a copy of your font before transforming it. And now the font is ready (even if it already was TrueType) for you to do True-Type hinting without problems.

3. Double-click in the Font window to open any Glyph window. Enter TrueType hinting mode by going to TOOLS>Operations>TrueType Hinting. Now the panels and toolbars shown at the top of the next page will appear and the hinting grid itself will be seen in the background, with current hints looking like gray balls (*because with squares, you wouldn't see the individual hints*). Note how the hints are at variance with the true outline.

✱ *Unless you click the "combo box" button to the right of* Convert Type 1 font to TrueType, *this pulldown selection won't take effect.*

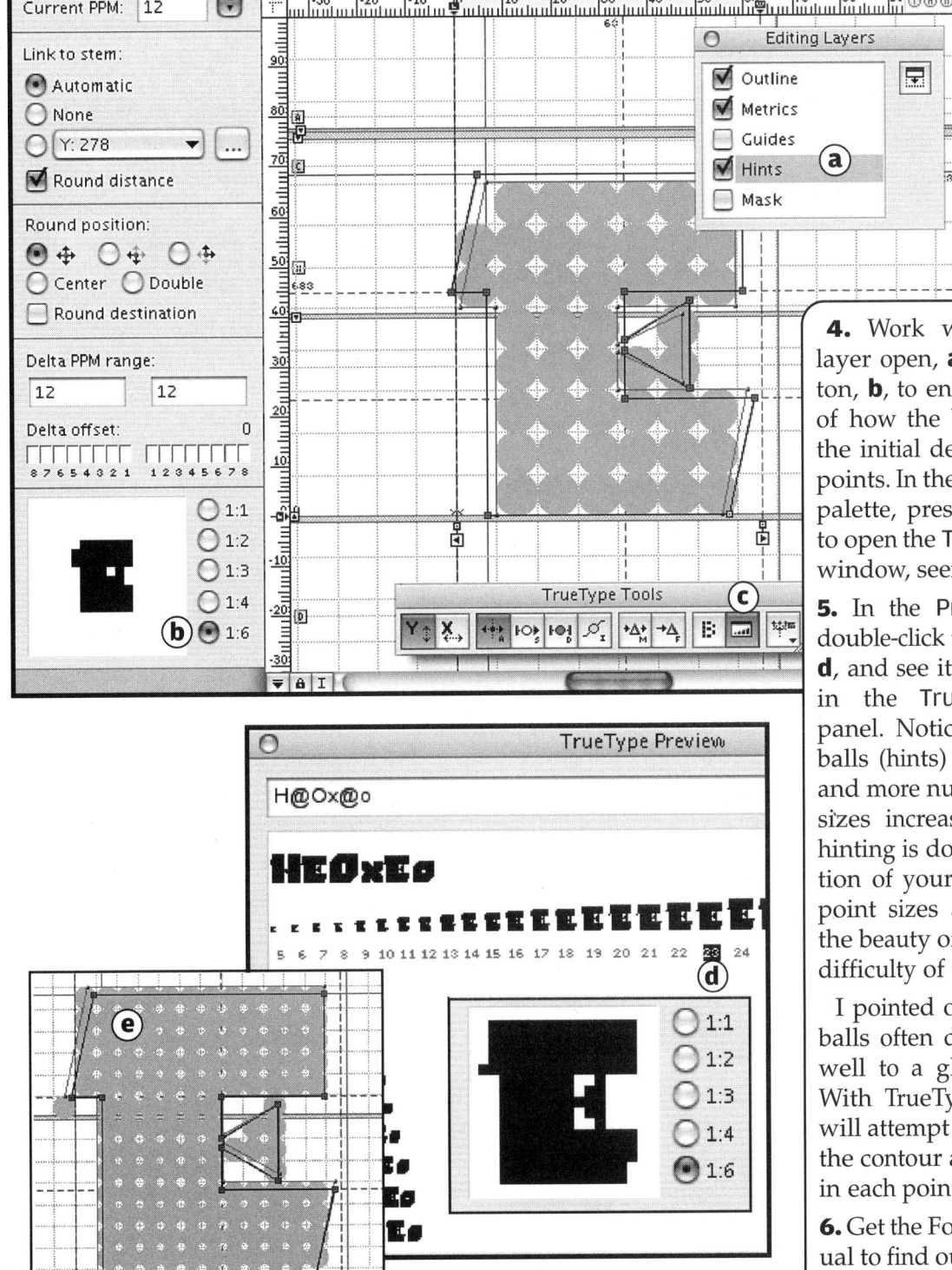

4. Work with the Hints layer open, **a**. Click the button, **b**, to enlarge your view of how the bitmap looks at the initial default size of 12-points. In the TrueType Tools palette, press the button, **c**, to open the TrueType Preview window, seen below.

5. In the Preview window, double-click the 23-point size, **d**, and see it displayed large in the TrueType Options panel. Notice that the gray balls (hints) become smaller and more numerous as point sizes increase, **e**. TrueType hinting is done for optimization of your font at specific point sizes and therein lies the beauty of it as well as the difficulty of the operation.

I pointed out that the gray balls often don't adhere too well to a glyph's contours. With TrueType hinting you will attempt to get as close to the contour as possible within each point size.

6. Get the FontLab user manual to find out how to actually do TrueType hinting.

ACCENTS and COMPOSITE CHARACTERS

Page **119** *Making Accented characters*

120 *Using Anchors to set up composites*

121 *Composite an accent glyph with Components.*

121 *Making composites with Generate Glyphs.*

Making accented characters

Because you could be fêted while appliquéing piñatas on the façade of a Schloß in Köln, you will definitely want to make sure your fonts contain all the required accent characters needed by users around the globe. FontLab offers several very efficient methods of creating accent character glyphs in a basic font.

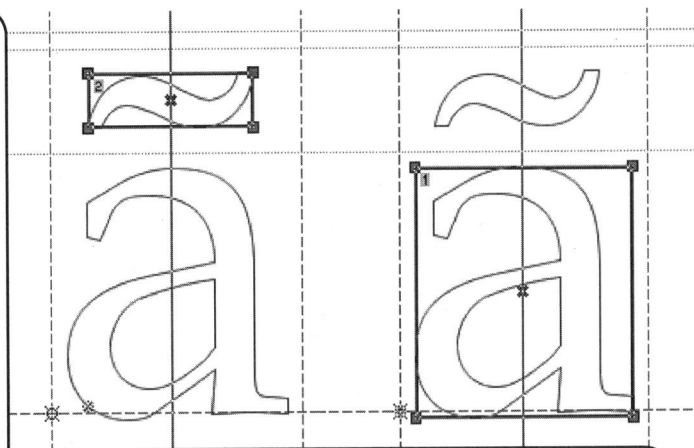

Accented characters are usually created by compositing two or more glyph components. That is, a "referenced copy" of a letter glyph is combined with a copy of an accent glyph. This way, if you edit any of the original "master" glyphs, the changes are automatically updated in the "dependent" components.

Also, as we have seen in class-based kerning (pages 104–105), composited accent characters can share kerning with the glyphs they are linked to without needing to be individually kerned themselves. *Note: Composites are a helpful design tool, but are not mandatory. You can always paste copies of letter and accent contours right into accent-letter glyph slots.*

Some font formats don't like composites. So it is good practice to save an extra copy of your final .vfb file. In the copy, Select All glyphs in the Font window and go to GLYPHS>Decompose to turn all composites into contours prior to generating the font.

Open any existing font and check out one of its accent characters, as above. If the character was composited, you'll notice that it has no nodes. When you click the outline contour of either component you'll see a four-handled bounding box with a centerline going through it. These are the two component parts of a composited accent-character glyph.

If you are unfamiliar with the shapes, or Font window positions, of any of the accent characters, open any basic-style professional font and check it out, **a**. The design of accents should take cues from the font style, but in general, accents tend to vary less in design than fonts themselves. If working on a new font, **b**, be sure that Give empty cells a template glyph image is enabled in Preferences>Font Window, **c**, as a guide to where the accent glyphs go, and what they look like.

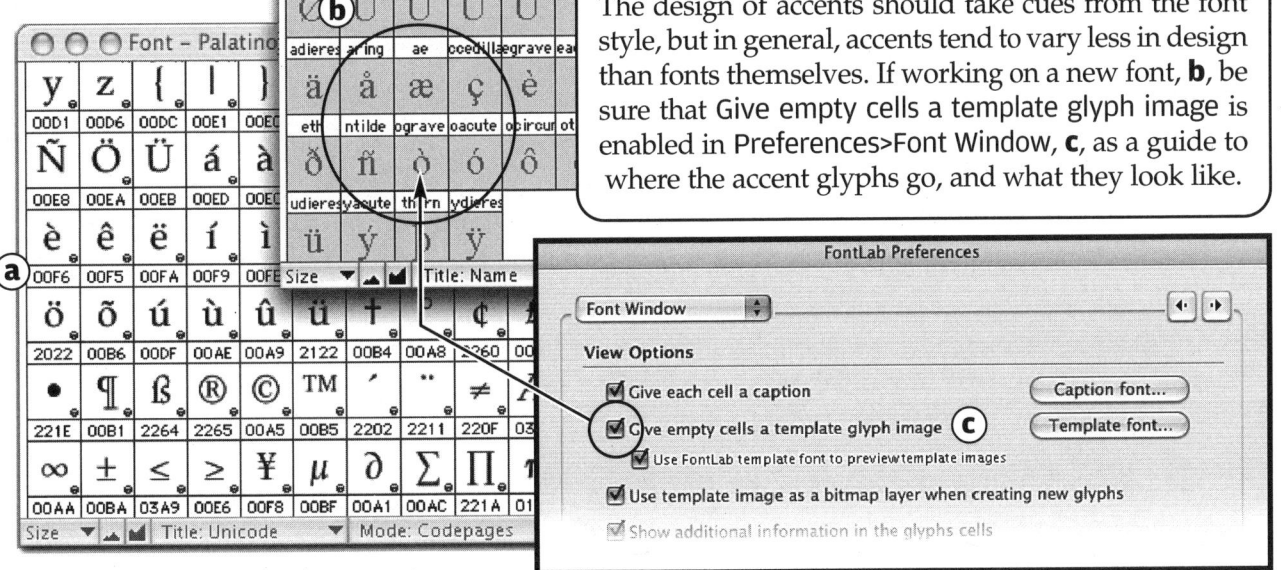

Use Anchors to set up composites

To make composited glyphs, you are not required to use anchors. But anchors do help to automate the placement of accents in relation to the letters. For example, position an anchor in the a glyph and another in the acute glyph. When you Generate Glyphs (previous page) or make composites manually, the two anchors will connect up. Some designers feel that it's just as easy to position accents manually as to place anchors. Also, when fonts are generated, glyph positions that were anchored may become unmoored. Decompose composites first to avoid this.

1. How to place anchors: Press the Shift-Ctrl-Opt keys (Mac), or Alt-Shift-Right click, (Win) to automatically place an anchor called "top" on each of the baselines of the lower-case glyphs (like *aceinosuyz*) that typically get accents, **a**.

2. Now place anchors on the baselines of all accent glyphs, **b**. (*Note that accents are generally positioned in their glyph windows at a proper height to nicely hover above lower-case characters.*) This time, press the Shift-Ctrl-Opt-***Cmd*** keys (Mac), or ***Ctrl***-Alt-Shift-Right click, (Win) to place an anchor called "_top" (*the underscore causes the "top" and "_top" anchors to magnetically link up*).

3. Now place "top" anchors (no _) in upper-case *ACEINOSUYZ*, but place them higher, **c**, to raise the accents above cap heights. Experiment by dragging anchors to get position right.

To view composites, go to WINDOW>Preview panel and click Anchors, **d**. Drag an anchor in a Glyph window and watch the accent's position change, as below **e**.

To Rename, Delete or change the color of an anchor, press the Ctrl key (Rt-click, Win) and click an anchor to open the contextual menu, below left.

Note: glyphs may have more than one anchor (name each one differently) so they can occupy different positions within other glyphs that contain correspondingly-named anchors.

(*This button conveniently adds an anchor in any open Glyph window.*)

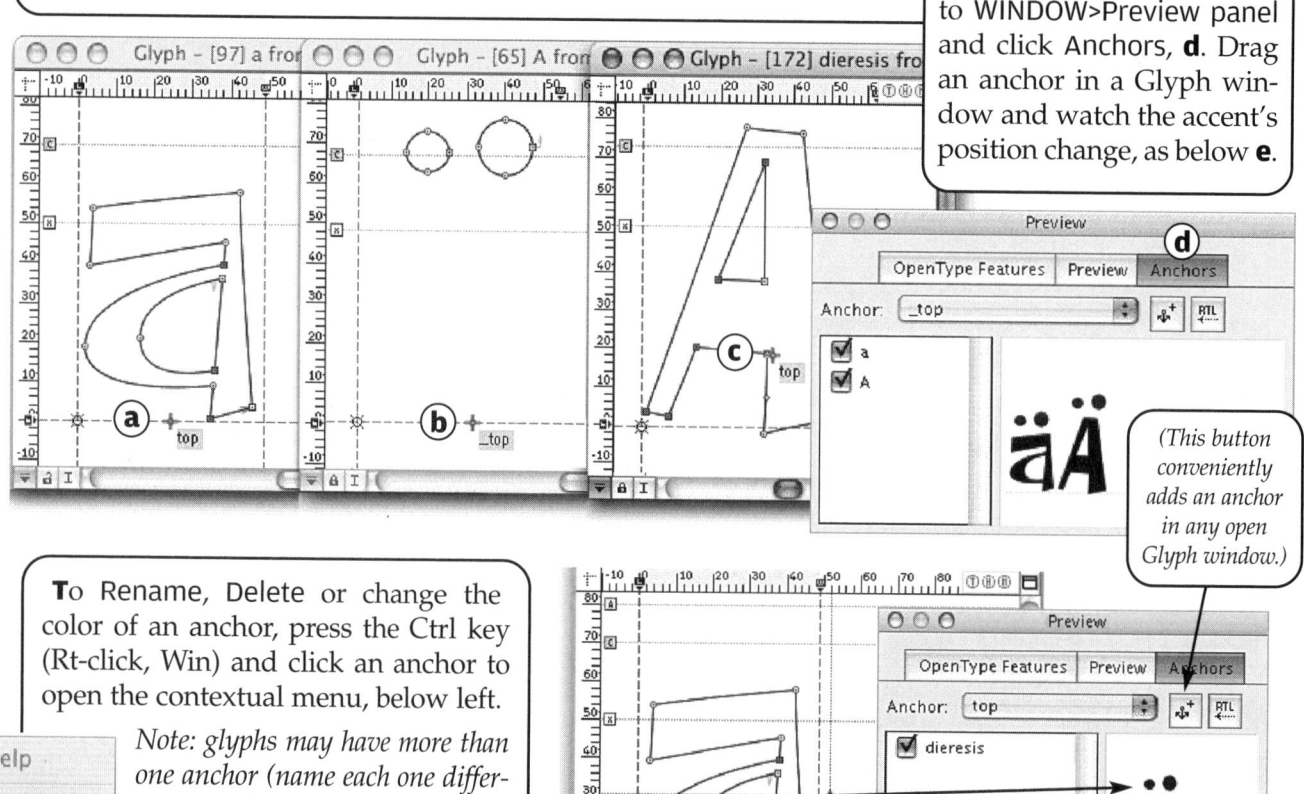

Composite an accent glyph with Components

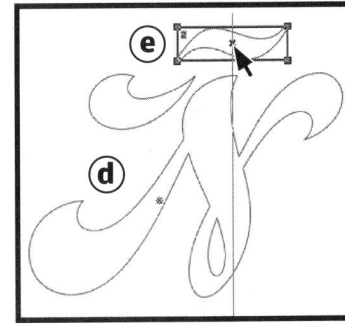

1. Open an empty glyph window, e.g. *N-tilde*. Do Ctrl-/Rt-click to open the contextual menu and choose Add Component. In the Select a Component dialog, **a**, type *N*. Select the *N*, **b**, and click OK to place an *N* component in the glyph window.

2. Repeat first step, but type *ti* for *tilde* at **c**. Click OK. The two components for *N-tilde* are now in place, **d**. Unless you've used Anchors (previous page), you may have to click the accent component and drag it into position, **e**.

Tip: *To turn a component back into an editable contour, choose* Decompose *in the context menu.*

Making composites with Generate Glyphs

This is the simplest way to make composites. Be sure your glyph and accent drawings are all spaced correctly, both horizontally and vertically (for accents). If later you edit a master glyph's contours, your changes will be applied to dependent glyphs. But changes to the master's metrics won't auto-update in dependents. To achieve this, use Classes (page 104) and the Metrics Assistance window (page 105). Also, you should decompose composites (in a duplicate master file) before you generate your final, completed font.

1. Go to GLYPH>Generate Glyphs. To open the panel, right. Type in the names of accent characters, **a**, just as you see them written in the Font window, **b**. If you misspell a name, you'll get a blank space. *Tip: Prepare a text file with all the accent names and paste them instead of typing them in each time.*

2. Check the preview, **c**, for missing, off-centered or vertically misplaced accents. Click OK. All the composite characters you listed are now in place! *Tip: position all accents at about the same optical height in their Glyph windows.*

3. Check each composite glyph, if necessary, to adjust components. *(To align the center lines of components, select one component, drag a guideline over from the ruler, left **d**, on top of the centerline. Now select the accent component, drag it to line up its centerline with the guideline. Of course, not all mechanical centerlines are really centered (check with your eyes, too).*

7
MAKING a FAMILY of FONTS

Page **123** *About font families*

124 *Change weights in the Transform window*

126 *Making families with Effects*

127 *Automate Effects with Transform Range*

128 *Family naming set up for Mac Type 1 and TT*

129 *Family naming for OT, TT, and Win Type 1*

130 *Typical naming plan for an OpenType family*

About font families

The fonts of a family should always be stylistic lookalikes, but each individual must vary enough in weight, width, and sometimes in details of design (as in classic italics) that it warrants a place in the group. In addition to merely providing variety, there are practical reasons for making font families. In writing, italic and bold styles have specific functions. In graphic design, use of font families helps unify the format (though exclusive use of only one family may be boring). Here is a brief examination of several kinds of families, including (of course!) some of mine.

a Practical FAMILY
Practical FAMILY
Practical FAMILY
Practical FAMILY

b Text FAMILY
Text FAMILY
Text FAMILY
Text FAMILY
Text FAMILY
Text FAMILY

c Relative FAMILY
Relative FAMILY
Relative FAMILY

d Weighted FAMILY
Weighted FAMILY
Weighted FAMILY

e DERIVATIVE FAMILY
DERIVATIVE FAMILY
DERIVATIVE FAMILY

f Extended FAMILY
Extended FAMILY
Extended FAMILY
Extended FAMILY

Stempel Garamond, **a**, is a typical four-font family meant for text work. Its classic-style italics have narrower letter widths and are drawn differently than the Roman and Bold. In contrast, *Franklin Gothic*, **b**, gets "italic" function from its Obliques (that are just slanted versions of the regular weights).

The three fonts in my *Angle* family, **c**, would clash if used together in a layout, but are similar enough to comprise a family.

The Light weight of my three-font *Progressiv* family, **d**, was created by auto-lightening-up the Medium and then heavying-up the Medium to make the Bold. With any auto-operation, you'll almost always have to tweak each new weight, especially curves and serifs, which often suffer distortion.

The Solid weight of my family *Love*, **e**, was the first to be drawn followed by Open and Stoned, which were fairly simple variations achieved by adding different outlines. But if "padding" a family in this manner becomes too obvious, users might ask, *"Why buy the whole family? I can create outlines, myself!"*

The *Dispatch* family, **f**, by Cyrus Highsmith for The Font Bureau, carries a theme of intriguing, quirky curves thru to sixteen weights (4 styles: 4 weights each), far more than enough to cover all a publication's needs, from headlines to classifieds.

Extended FAMILY
Extended FAMILY
Extended FAMILY
Extended FAMILY

Extended FAMILY
Extended FAMILY
Extended FAMILY
Extended FAMILY

Extended FAMILY
Extended FAMILY
Extended FAMILY
Extended FAMILY

Change weights in the Transform window

*A*fter you've completed the regular or medium "key" font in your family (finish the kerning/hinting, too), FontLab *can help to automatically create the light, bold, black, extended or condensed weights with the* Transformation *window (go to* TOOLS>Transform*). As with any "auto" operation, you must expect to do some degree of post-operative damage control. Still, using* Transform *is always far superior than redrawing weights entirely by hand.*

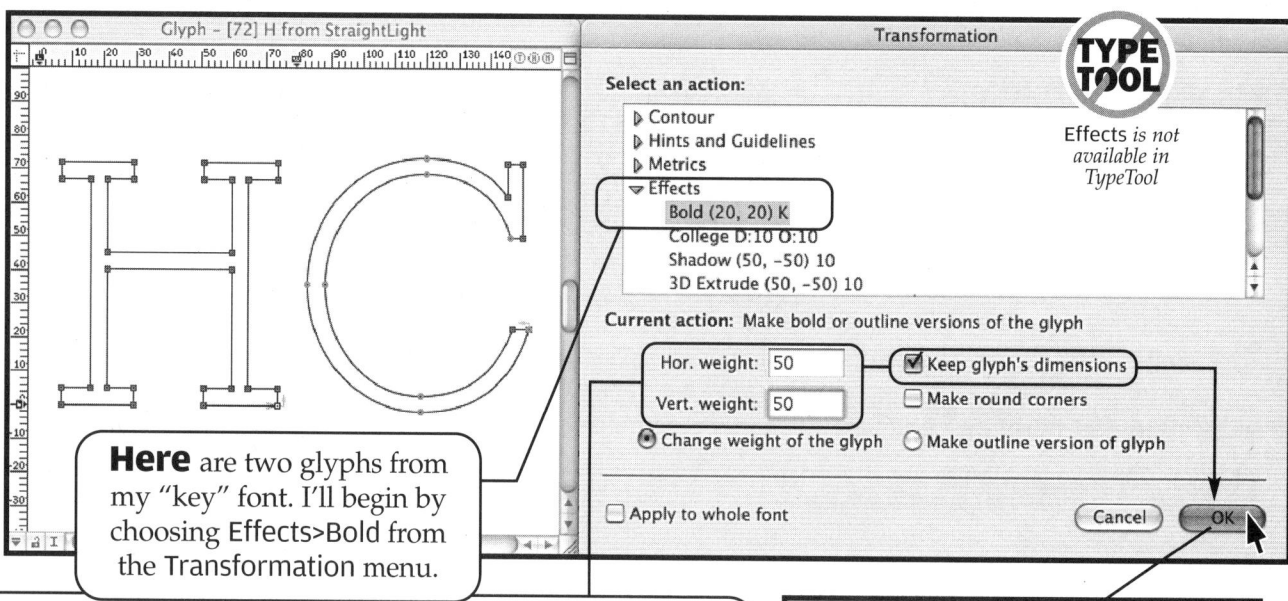

Here are two glyphs from my "key" font. I'll begin by choosing Effects>Bold from the Transformation menu.

Above, I'll increase the weight of the letter both Hor. and Vert. by 50 units, yet I'll Keep glyph's dimensions, which means expansion will occur only from the existing perimeters inward toward the letter's center, without increasing either width or height. At right is the result. See the one flub at **a**?

Right, only the Hor. was increased by 50 units, **b**, making the mono-weight glyphs into roman, thick-thin. This time, Keep glyph's dimensions was left unchecked. The serif, **c**, will need reworking.

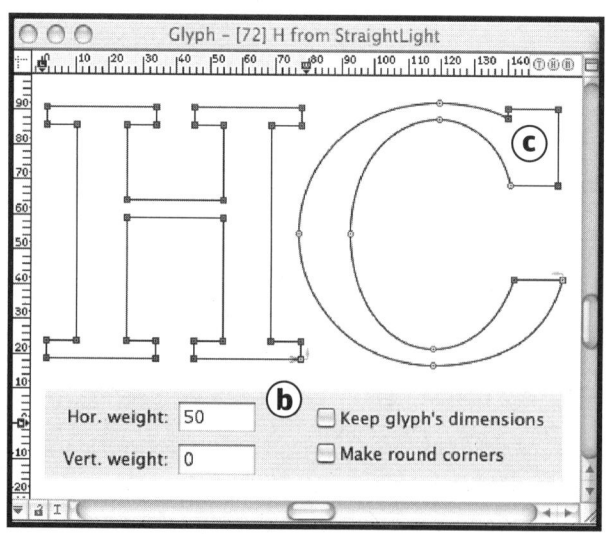

The result of the same settings shown at top, but with Make round corners added. It worked well.

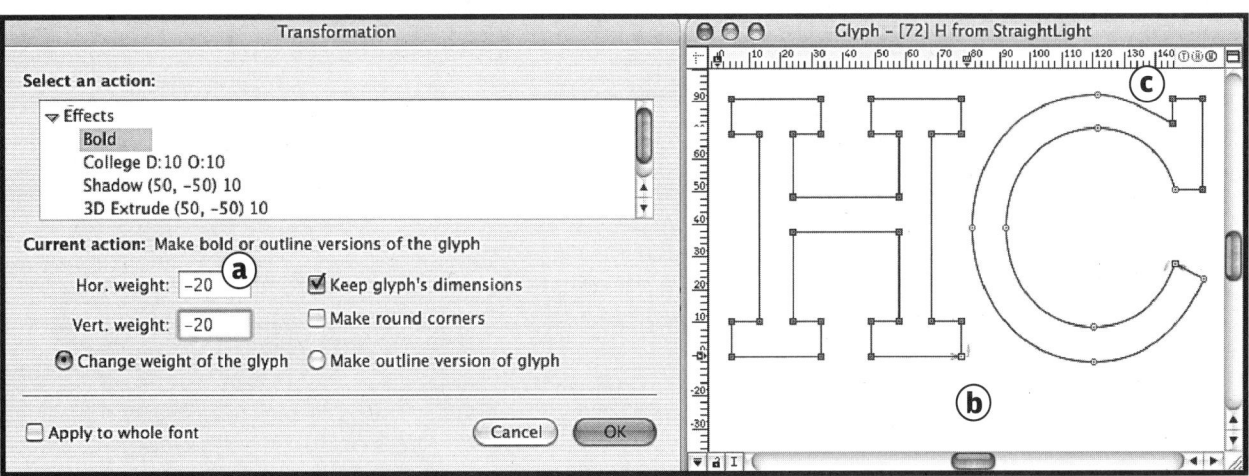

You not only can increase weights, but decrease them by typing minus values, **a**, into the Hor. and Vert. fields. The glyphs at **b** show the result of the above settings, reduced from the 50-unit increase shown on the previous page. Actually, experts recommend that you go from your lightest weight to your heaviest "black" weight in one step, then start decreasing weights with minus values, as I did above, for intermediate-weight family members. You may get less distortion than by weighting-up, say, 20 units and then 20 units again. Notice at **c** that the curve has flattened out.

1. Condense a font Go to Contour>Scale in the Transformation window, below, and click on Scale. Set a Horizontal value, **a**, but leave Vertical at 100 (that means it won't change). Uncheck Proportional scale.

2. Right **b**, letters before Horizontal scaling. After scaling, they are narrower, **c**, but the vertical stems are no longer the same weight as the horizontals. Hit Cmd- or Ctrl-T, go to Effects> Bold, **d**, and add 7 units (*or as required*). Check Keep glyph's dimensions to maintain the overall width, **e**. Strokes are again mono-weight.

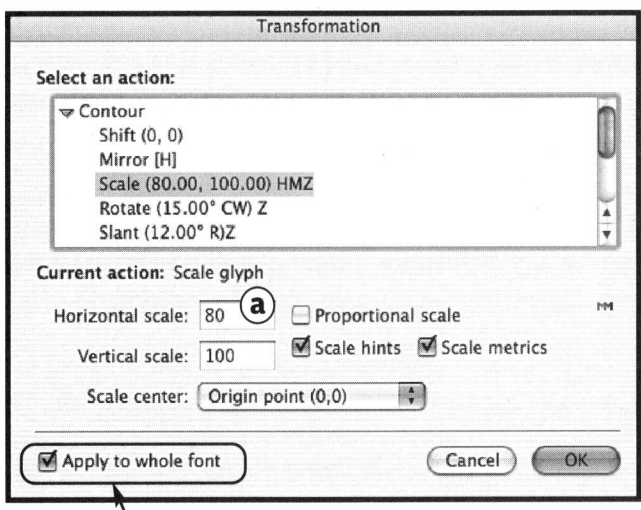

If you check Apply to whole font, *these actions will affect all glyphs, not just open ones. Then you'll have a new family member. But first, always save a copy of your "key" font.*

▽ Effects
    Bold (7, 0) K **d**
    College D:10 O:10
    Shadow (50, –50) 10
    3D Extrude (50, –50) 10

Current action: Make bold or outline versions of the glyph

Hor. weight: 7   ☑ Keep glyph's dimensions

Vert. weight: 0   ☐ Make round corners

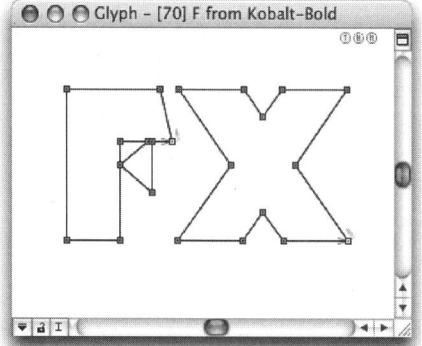

Making families with Effects

As mentioned earlier, using the Effects to Transform your fonts into various snappy family members should be done with caution as some users might regard such fonts as being cheap gimmicks.

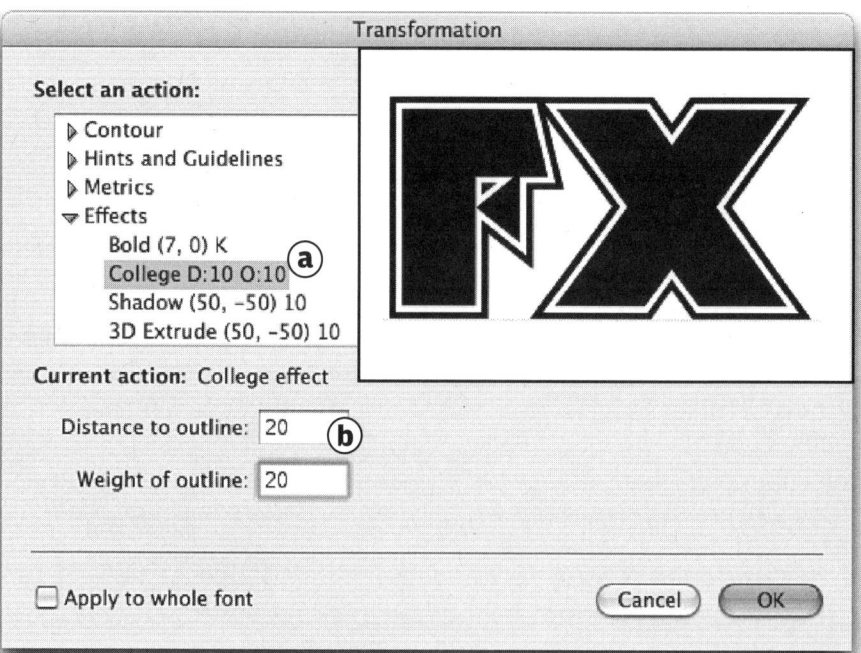

Starting with the letters above, we'll experiment with certain Effects to create variations on our fonts. Right, College produces an outlined letter (as on collegiate sports jerseys). The default setting is 10/10, **a**, but I've made it 20/20, **b**, so the outline will stand farther apart from the letters and they'll be more viable at small point-sizes.

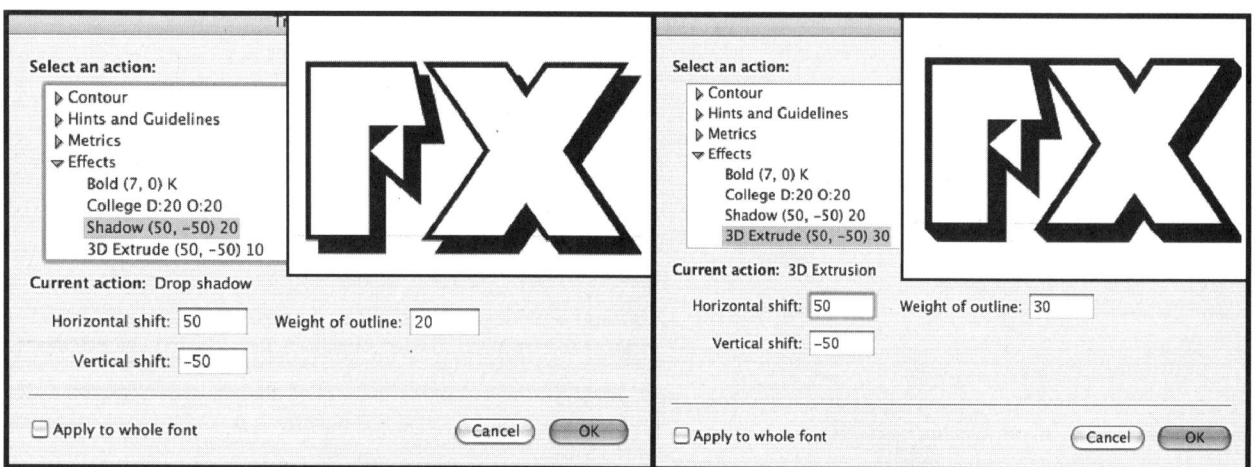

Above, Shadow produces an outline and drop shadow, **b**, To use this effect on all the glyphs in a font would necessitate spacing all letters fairly wide apart so they wouldn't crash. The next fil-ter we tried was 3D Extrude. It produces a great block shadow, but will require some hand work, especially where corners don't always meet at a single point.

Automate Effects with Transform Range

Scale *and* Effects *are also found in* TOOLS>Transform Range. *This souped-up version of the Transform dialog window allows you to perform several operations at once, even multiplying effects like College by specifying them any number of times. Choose from the* Available actions *in column* **a**, *adjust settings then hit button* **b** *to add it to the* Program *column,* **c**. *Note: Don't worry that by hitting* Run *you'll also* Convert Type 1 font to TrueType, **d**. *To activate this pulldown's command, you'd have to click this button on the right.*

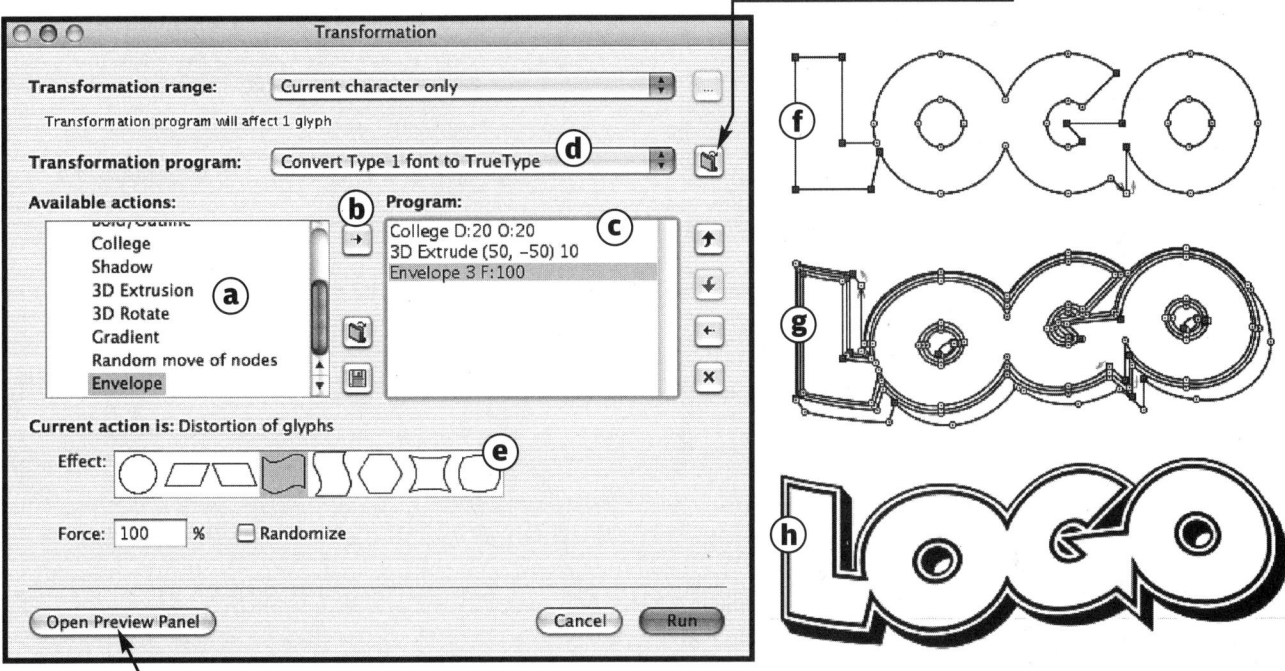

Above, Envelope provides various distortion effects, **e**. Unless applied very carefully, these will mostly produce weird, misshapen letters that are only good for novelty fonts. Of course, you might *want* to make a wacky, novelty font. Perhaps a better application of these effects is in logo work. Sometimes it is effective to create an entire logo in FontLab (or paste vector paths in from elsewhere) just for the ability to add such Effects. I've taken the logo at **f**, and applied the three effects shown in **c**. The somewhat warpy result can be seen at **g** and in preview at **h**.

If you click the Open Preview Panel button, you can see the progressive transformations acting upon your selected glyphs. At right, I tried an Extrusion plus two Colleges. It's really too weird for use, but I was just fooling around.

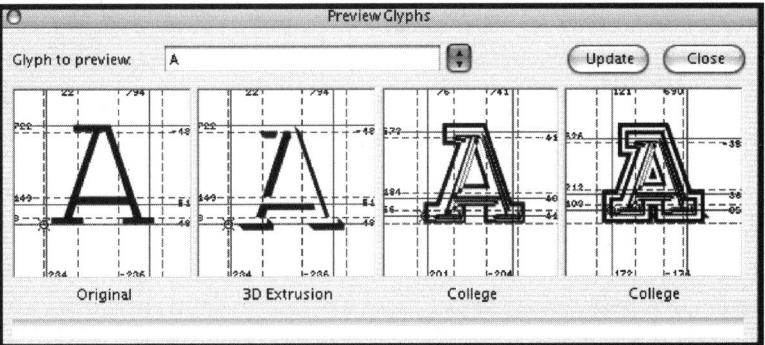

Family naming for Mac Type 1 and TT

Type 1 fonts for Mac are unlimited (within limits, of course!) as to how many fonts may be included in a suitcase. And they are also unfinicky about allowing you to use any Style Name you wish (see bottom of this page).

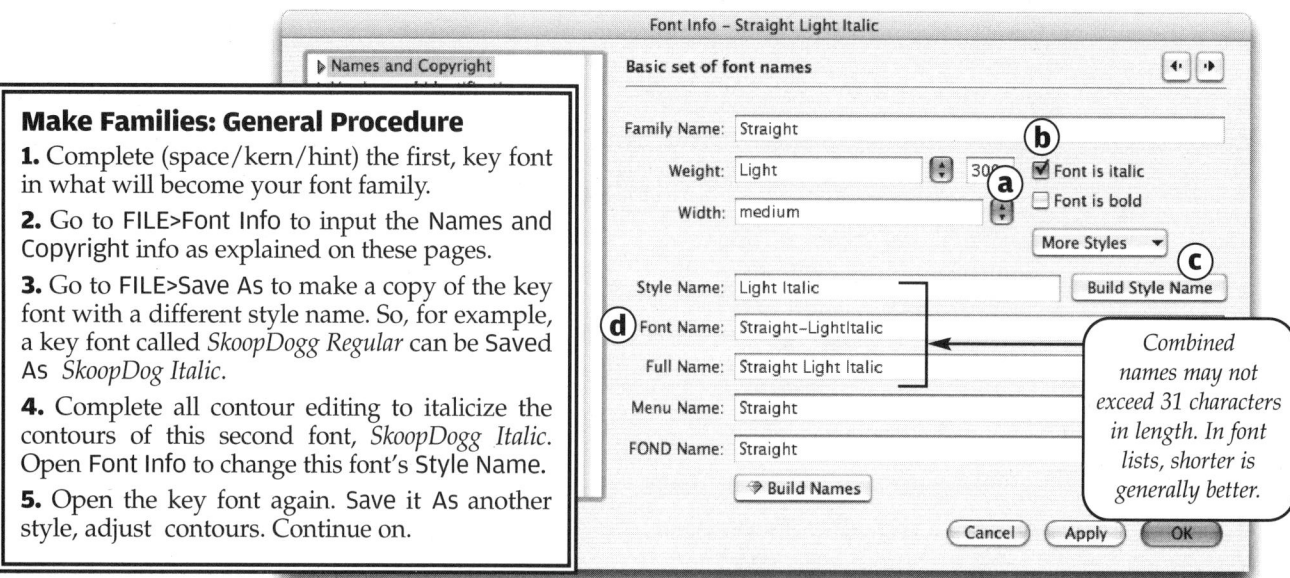

Make Families: General Procedure

1. Complete (space/kern/hint) the first, key font in what will become your font family.

2. Go to FILE>Font Info to input the Names and Copyright info as explained on these pages.

3. Go to FILE>Save As to make a copy of the key font with a different style name. So, for example, a key font called *SkoopDogg Regular* can be Saved As *SkoopDog Italic*.

4. Complete all contour editing to italicize the contours of this second font, *SkoopDogg Italic*. Open Font Info to change this font's Style Name.

5. Open the key font again. Save it As another style, adjust contours. Continue on.

Naming plan for Mac Type 1 font families

1. Fill in the Family Name. Use only English upper- and lowercase letters, numerals and spaces. *Do not use accented letters, hyphens or special characters. Full font names must not exceed 31 characters.* All fonts within a family should share the same family name (in this case, "Straight").

2. Set Weight and Width by selecting the closest, correct-sounding entries from the pulldown, **a**.

3. If the font is Italic, check the Font is italic button, **b**, *unless there will be no corresponding 'Regular' font in the suitcase, then leave the button unchecked.*

4. Check Font is bold only for the one font in your suitcase that is to be named 'Bold' *(but only if a 'Regular" font will also be in that suitcase).*

5. Hit the Build Style Name button, **c**. Each Style Name in a family must be unique. So if two fonts end up as 'Light,' the Style Name of one of them must change. In long style names, abbreviations (*Condensed* as *Cond*; *Black* as *Blk*, etc.) are OK.

6. Finally, hit the Build Names button. *But be sure that the* Font Name *field contains no spaces, only upper- or lowercase letters, numerals, and a hyphen separating the family name from the style name, as in **d**.*

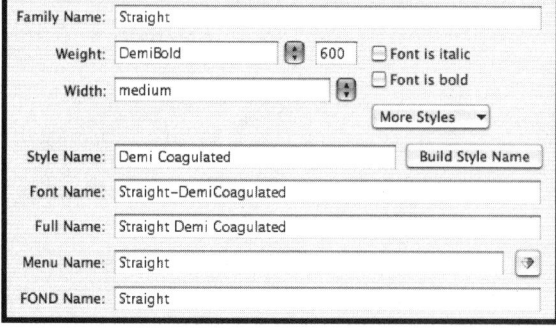

As already mentioned, Mac Type 1 fonts allow us to use any Style Name we like, left, and to have as many fonts as we want in the family suitcase. Even if you plan to generate various other font formats, such as Win Type 1, TrueType, OpenType, always start with devising the family naming as described on this page. Save the fonts. Generate Mac Type 1 fonts if required.

Family naming for OT, TT, and Win Type 1

For these font formats we must create a second, parallel naming plan by organizing our family into "mini-families" of no more than four fonts each. Each mini-family must contain a 'Regular' font, and may also have style-linked Italic, Bold and Bold Italic fonts. Therefore, if you wanted to make a large family of 20 fonts, you'd organize them into five mini-families of four fonts. If you intend 21 fonts, let the sixth mini-family be incomplete, with only one font in it. The family naming as defined on the previous page will be used on Macintosh and in OpenType applications such as Adobe's, while the mini-family naming will be used in Windows applications.

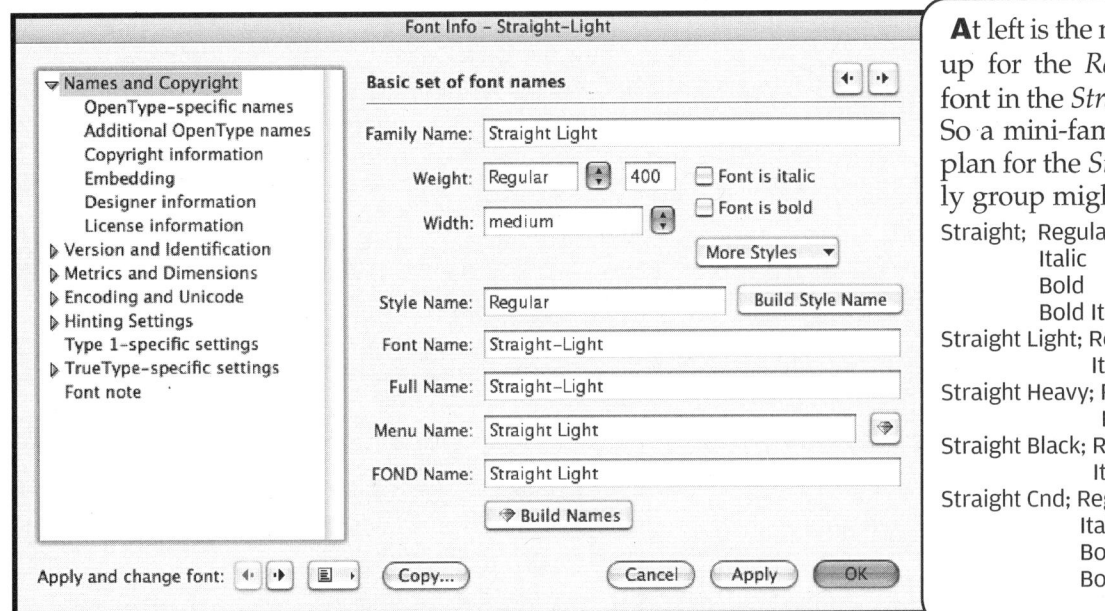

At left is the naming set-up for the *Regular, Light* font in the *Straight* family. So a mini-family naming plan for the *Straight* family group might be:

Straight; Regular
                Italic
                Bold
                Bold Italic
Straight Light; Regular
                        Italic
Straight Heavy; Regular
                          Italic
Straight Black; Regular
                         Italic
Straight Cnd; Regular
                        Italic
                        Bold
                        Bold Italic
                                Etc.

A plan for setting up naming plans

1. Start by creating the Mac Type 1 family naming as on previous page. Save and close all fonts. Copy your .vfb files into a new folder and open these files in FontLab. This second set will be used as masters for the remaining formats (Win Type 1, OpenType, TrueType).

2. Now enter FILE>Font Info>OpenType-specific names. Click on the Build OpenType Names button and repeat that step for all fonts.

3. Go back to the Names and Copyright> Basic set of font names pane. Now, for each font, in the Family Name field, enter the name of your mini-family (e.g. Straight or Straight Light or Straight Cnd, etc.).

Do not exceed 31 characters in length and don't use any special characters, just plain letters, numerals and spaces.

4. In the Style Name, enter one of the following values: *Regular, Italic, Bold, Bold Italic,* exactly as spelled. Set the Font is italic and Font is bold checkboxes according to these names.

(Follow the naming conventions above, substituting your own font names for the ones shown.)

See page 146 for an in-depth treatise on setting up family metrics • More specific examples of OT naming follow on the next page...

Typical naming plan for an OpenType family

Here's how—literally—to set up mini-families of four. The two mini-families, bottom, contain only two styles each. Notice how the Italic/Bold checkboxes are set. These eight fonts will appear in font menus as three items.

One family of four

Insets are from the OpenType specific names page of the Font Info window

Family Name: Myriad Pro
Weight: Normal — 400 — ☐ Font is italic / ☐ Font is bold
Width: medium — More Styles ▾

Style Name: Regular
Font Name: MyriadPro-Regular
Full Name: MyriadPro-Regular
Menu Name: Myriad Pro
FOND Name: Myriad Pro

OpenType-specific font names
Family Name: Myriad Pro
Style Name: Regular
Mac Name:
⚑ Build OpenType Names — ✕ Reset Names

Family Name: Myriad Pro
Weight: Normal — 400 — ☑ Font is italic / ☐ Font is bold
Width: medium — More Styles ▾

Style Name: Italic
Font Name: MyriadPro-It
Full Name: MyriadPro-It
Menu Name: Myriad Pro
FOND Name: Myriad Pro

OpenType-specific font names
Family Name: Myriad Pro
Style Name: Italic
Mac Name:
⚑ Build OpenType Names — ✕ Reset Names

Family Name: Myriad Pro
Weight: Bold — 700 — ☐ Font is italic / ☑ Font is bold
Width: medium — More Styles ▾

Style Name: Bold
Font Name: MyriadPro-Bold
Full Name: MyriadPro-Bold
Menu Name: Myriad Pro
FOND Name: Myriad Pro

OpenType-specific font names
Family Name: Myriad Pro
Style Name: Bold
Mac Name:
⚑ Build OpenType Names — ✕ Reset Names

Family Name: Myriad Pro
Weight: Bold — 700 — ☑ Font is italic / ☑ Font is bold
Width: medium — More Styles ▾

Style Name: Bold Italic
Font Name: MyriadPro-BoldIt
Full Name: MyriadPro-BoldIt
Menu Name: Myriad Pro
FOND Name: Myriad Pro

OpenType-specific font names
Family Name: Myriad Pro
Style Name: Bold Italic
Mac Name:
⚑ Build OpenType Names — ✕ Reset Names

Two mini-families of two

Family Name: Myriad Pro Black
Weight: Heavy — 900 — ☐ Font is italic / ☑ Font is bold
Width: medium — More Styles ▾

Style Name: Bold
Font Name: MyriadPro-Black
Full Name: MyriadPro-Black
Menu Name: Myriad Pro Black
FOND Name: Myriad Pro Black

OpenType-specific font names
Family Name: Myriad Pro
Style Name: Black
Mac Name:
⚑ Build OpenType Names — ✕ Reset Names

Family Name: Myriad Pro Light
Weight: Light — 300 — ☐ Font is italic / ☐ Font is bold
Width: medium — More Styles ▾

Style Name: Regular
Font Name: MyriadPro-Light
Full Name: MyriadPro-Light
Menu Name: Myriad Pro Light
FOND Name: Myriad Pro Light

OpenType-specific font names
Family Name: Myriad Pro
Style Name: Light
Mac Name:
⚑ Build OpenType Names — ✕ Reset Names

Family Name: Myriad Pro Black
Weight: Heavy — 900 — ☑ Font is italic / ☑ Font is bold
Width: medium — More Styles ▾

Style Name: Bold Italic
Font Name: MyriadPro-BlackIt
Full Name: MyriadPro-BlackIt
Menu Name: Myriad Pro Black
FOND Name: Myriad Pro Black

OpenType-specific font names
Family Name: Myriad Pro
Style Name: Black Italic
Mac Name:
⚑ Build OpenType Names — ✕ Reset Names

Family Name: Myriad Pro Light
Weight: Light — 300 — ☑ Font is italic / ☐ Font is bold
Width: medium — More Styles ▾

Style Name: Italic
Font Name: MyriadPro-LightIt
Full Name: MyriadPro-LightIt
Menu Name: Myriad Pro Light
FOND Name: Myriad Pro Light

OpenType-specific font names
Family Name: Myriad Pro
Style Name: Light Italic
Mac Name:
⚑ Build OpenType Names — ✕ Reset Names

Must do before generating TT or OT fonts:

In FontLab 4.6 Preferences:

1. In OpenType>OpenType>Export, *select* Export only OpenType name records *from the pulldown.*

2. *Now open the* Font Info *window, go to* Additional OpenType names, *click the* Import Names *button. Find* 1.1.0.0 [*Family name*] *then below, enter* Macintosh>Roman>English *and the Family Name from the* OpenType-specific names *pane.*

3. *Find entry* 2.1.0.0 [*Subfamily name*], *enter* Mac>Roman>English; *enter* Style Name *from* OpenType-specific names.

4. *Find* 4.3.1.1033 *and put the contents of the* Font Name *field in the Basic set of names pane there.*

In FontLab Studio 5.0 Preferences:

1. *Go to* OpenType and TrueType Export, *enable* Use the OpenType names as menu names on Macintosh, *and select* Append OpenType name record to the names exported by default.

2. *In* Preferences>Export, *under* OpenType PS (.otf), *enable* Use the PostScript Font Name as Full Name.

8 MAKING OPENTYPE FONTS

Page **132** *About OpenType*

132 *Using OpenType in Adobe InDesign CS*

133 *Using OpenType in Adobe Illustrator CS*

134 *Add OpenType features to an existing font*

136 *Add OpenType features using Classes*

138 *Why OpenType failure?*

139 *Some OpenType features*

About OpenType

As discussed on page 81, OpenType holds the great promise of becoming the one universal font format, obviating all others. The three most attractive features of OpenType are: 1. It is cross-platform (a single, one-part font works on both Mac and PC); 2. It offers extended language support; and 3. OpenType can contain a vast number of easy-to-access additional characters, including such things as small caps, ligatures, oldstyle numerals and contextual alternatives.

On the other hand, we all still notice advertising—even classy advertising—in which the designer has failed to replace inch marks with true quotes that I wonder how often OpenType features will be utilized.

Another point seldom mentioned is that ligatures, smallcaps and oldstyle numerals are, well…"old-style." In many cases such typographic features have no place in modern-style advertising. What's the big deal about ffl, anyway? Who cares who Ben Affleck is dating?

But seriously, can you imagine a rave flyer or even an ad for the latest cell phone with ligatures and old-style numerals? However, I have no doubt that—just as the ability to easily create fuzzy drop shadows in Photoshop has led to a proliferation of fuzzy drop shadows—oldstyle features will also be making a comeback. Not because we should be using them, but because we can.

A more important application for ligatures than ffl is in interlocking, calligraphic, and script fonts involving connecting ligatures that have traditionally caused almost insoluble problems for type designers because of certain letter pairs requiring special-case connecting ligatures.

Indeed, such issues had traditionally limited the number of script fonts or simply compromised the design of those that have come into existence. OpenType may well change all that and the possibilities are awesome.

Using OpenType in Adobe InDesign CS

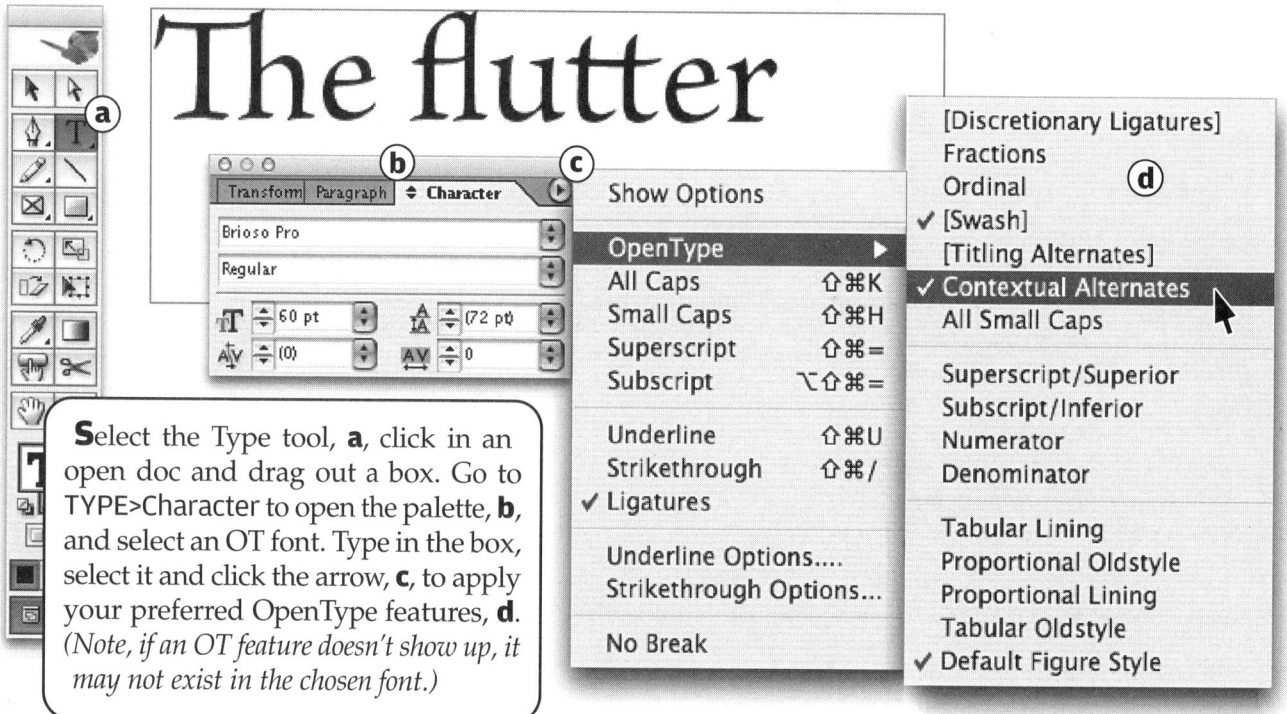

Select the Type tool, **a**, click in an open doc and drag out a box. Go to TYPE>Character to open the palette, **b**, and select an OT font. Type in the box, select it and click the arrow, **c**, to apply your preferred OpenType features, **d**. *(Note, if an OT feature doesn't show up, it may not exist in the chosen font.)*

Using OpenType in Adobe Illustrator CS

Select Illustrator's Type tool, **a**, then go to TYPE>Font and select an OpenType font, hopefully one that is full-featured. Click the Type tool anywhere in an open document and start setting some type. Drag across the type so it is selected. Go to WINDOW>Type>OpenType to open the Character/OpenType palette, **b**. Click the options arrow, **c**, to choose any of the OT features from the menu or just click the buttons, **d**, that enable the very same features in the menu. At **e**, you can see the *Fi*, *Th* and *TT* ligatures in the Adobe font Brioso Pro, along with its oldstyle numerals and fractions. In order to set small caps, however, you must click the Character side of the palette (*nested palettes can be separated by dragging any of the tabs away from the palette*), then open the option menu to select Small Caps, **f**, as seen in **g**, along with the same type as above, sans OT features.

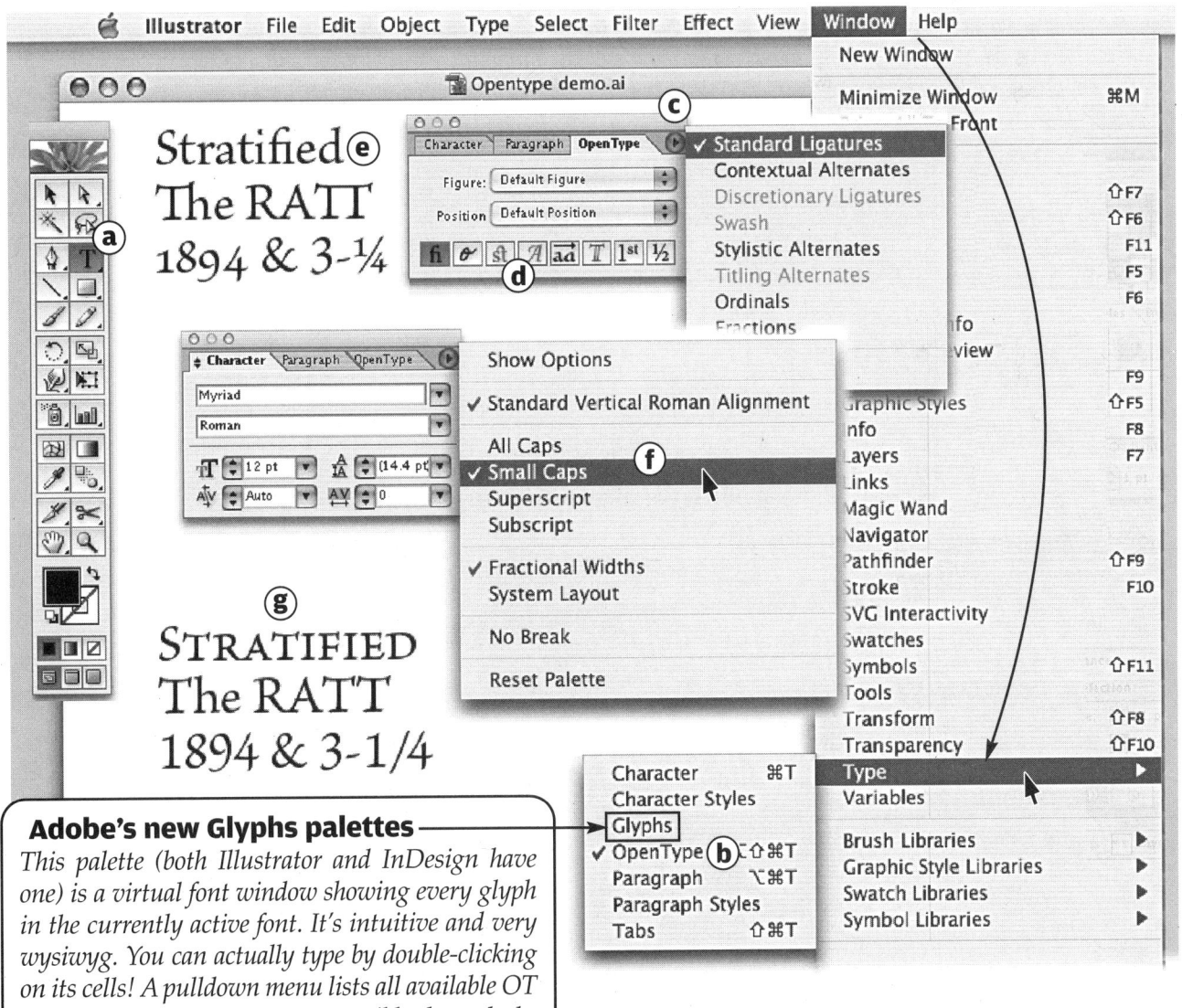

Adobe's new Glyphs palettes
This palette (both Illustrator and InDesign have one) is a virtual font window showing every glyph in the currently active font. It's intuitive and very wysiwyg. You can actually type by double-clicking on its cells! A pulldown menu lists all available OT features, including ones not accessible through the OpenType and Character palettes shown above.

Add OpenType features to an existing font

How do you make an OpenType font? Well, you could start by making a regular font and then…keep on going. So let's assume that you want to expand your 256-character font by including some OpenType features.

1. Add glyph cells Open a font. Go to GLYPH>Generate Glyphs to open the panel, right. Start by typing in the glyph names for oldstyle numerals as shown at **a**. If you create pre-typed text files of various lists, you can paste them in. The numbers that appear in the preview at **b**, are still the "new-style" ones that so far exist in the font. Click OK and you'll see that a new set of numerals has been added at the end of the Font window, **c**.

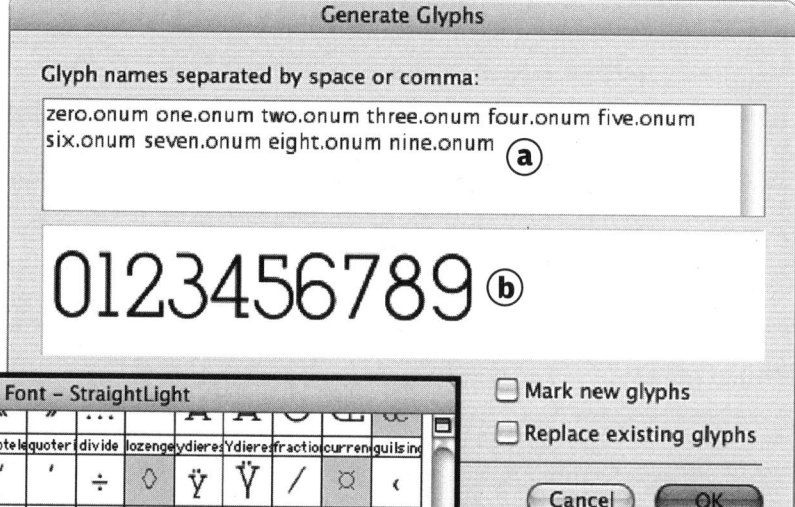

Generate Glyphs

Glyph names separated by space or comma:

zero.onum one.onum two.onum three.onum four.onum five.onum six.onum seven.onum eight.onum nine.onum **a**

0123456789 **b**

☐ Mark new glyphs
☐ Replace existing glyphs

Cancel OK

2. Edit numerals Change the numerals in your new glyph slots to oldstyle ones by editing their contours, below. In some cases you can select the numerals and use the Down-arrow keys to just move them down, **d**, although there are aspects of true oldstyle numerals that are quite different than just lowered regular numbers. Use the Preview panel, left, to check your glyphs as they progress.

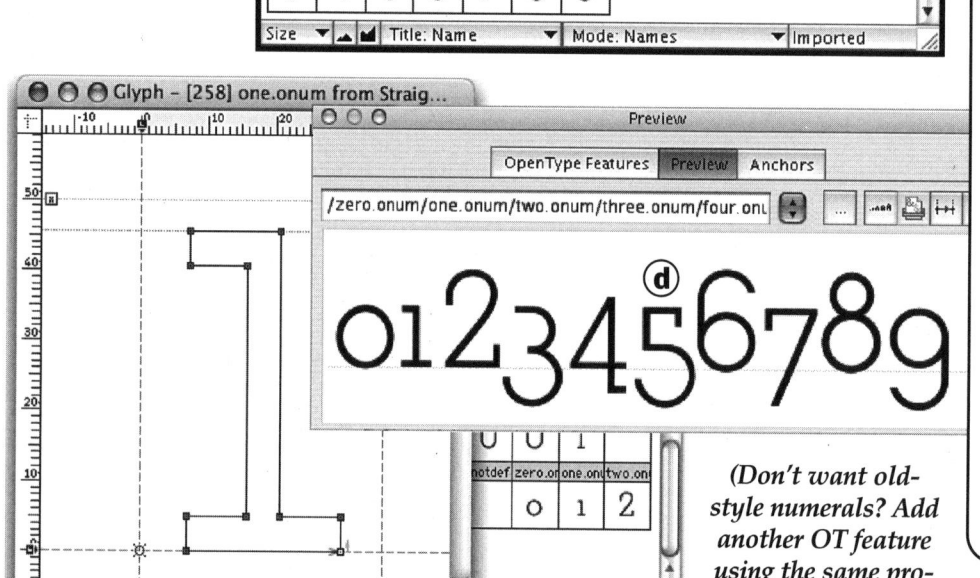

(Don't want oldstyle numerals? Add another OT feature using the same procedure. See page 139 for more features.)

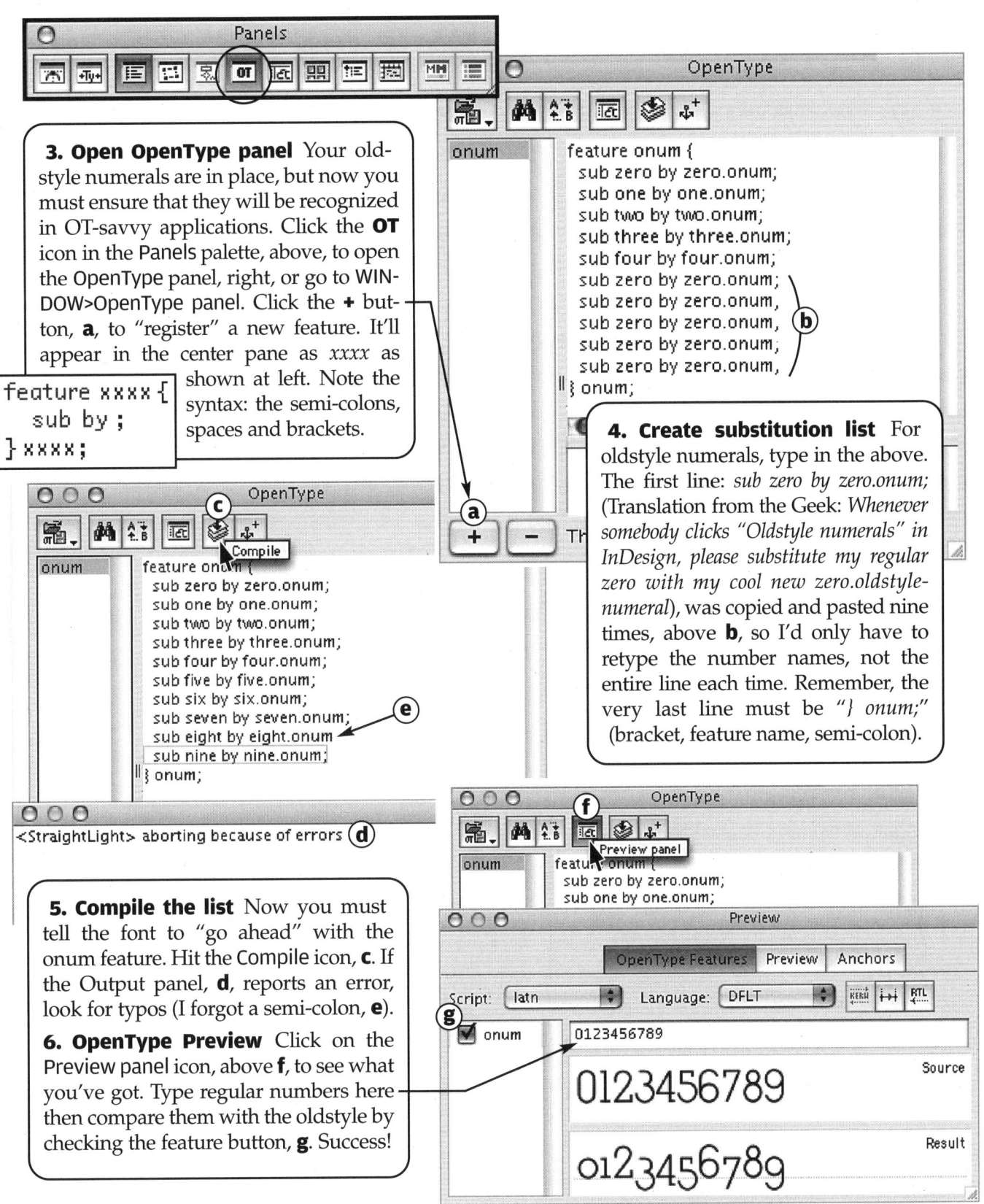

3. Open OpenType panel Your old-style numerals are in place, but now you must ensure that they will be recognized in OT-savvy applications. Click the **OT** icon in the Panels palette, above, to open the OpenType panel, right, or go to WINDOW>OpenType panel. Click the **+** button, **a**, to "register" a new feature. It'll appear in the center pane as *xxxx* as shown at left. Note the syntax: the semi-colons, spaces and brackets.

```
feature xxxx {
  sub  by ;
} xxxx;
```

4. Create substitution list For oldstyle numerals, type in the above. The first line: *sub zero by zero.onum;* (Translation from the Geek: *Whenever somebody clicks "Oldstyle numerals" in InDesign, please substitute my regular zero with my cool new zero.oldstyle-numeral*), was copied and pasted nine times, above **b**, so I'd only have to retype the number names, not the entire line each time. Remember, the very last line must be "*} onum;*" (bracket, feature name, semi-colon).

5. Compile the list Now you must tell the font to "go ahead" with the onum feature. Hit the Compile icon, **c**. If the Output panel, **d**, reports an error, look for typos (I forgot a semi-colon, **e**).

6. OpenType Preview Click on the Preview panel icon, above **f**, to see what you've got. Type regular numbers here then compare them with the oldstyle by checking the feature button, **g**. Success!

Add OpenType features using Classes

The 23-feature OpenType font BriosoPro, below, includes extended language coverage as well as the usual array of ligatures, small caps, etc. But instead of setting them up as we did on the previous page, Adobe's programmers have used classes. Classes replace what would otherwise be too-lengthy lists of individual features.

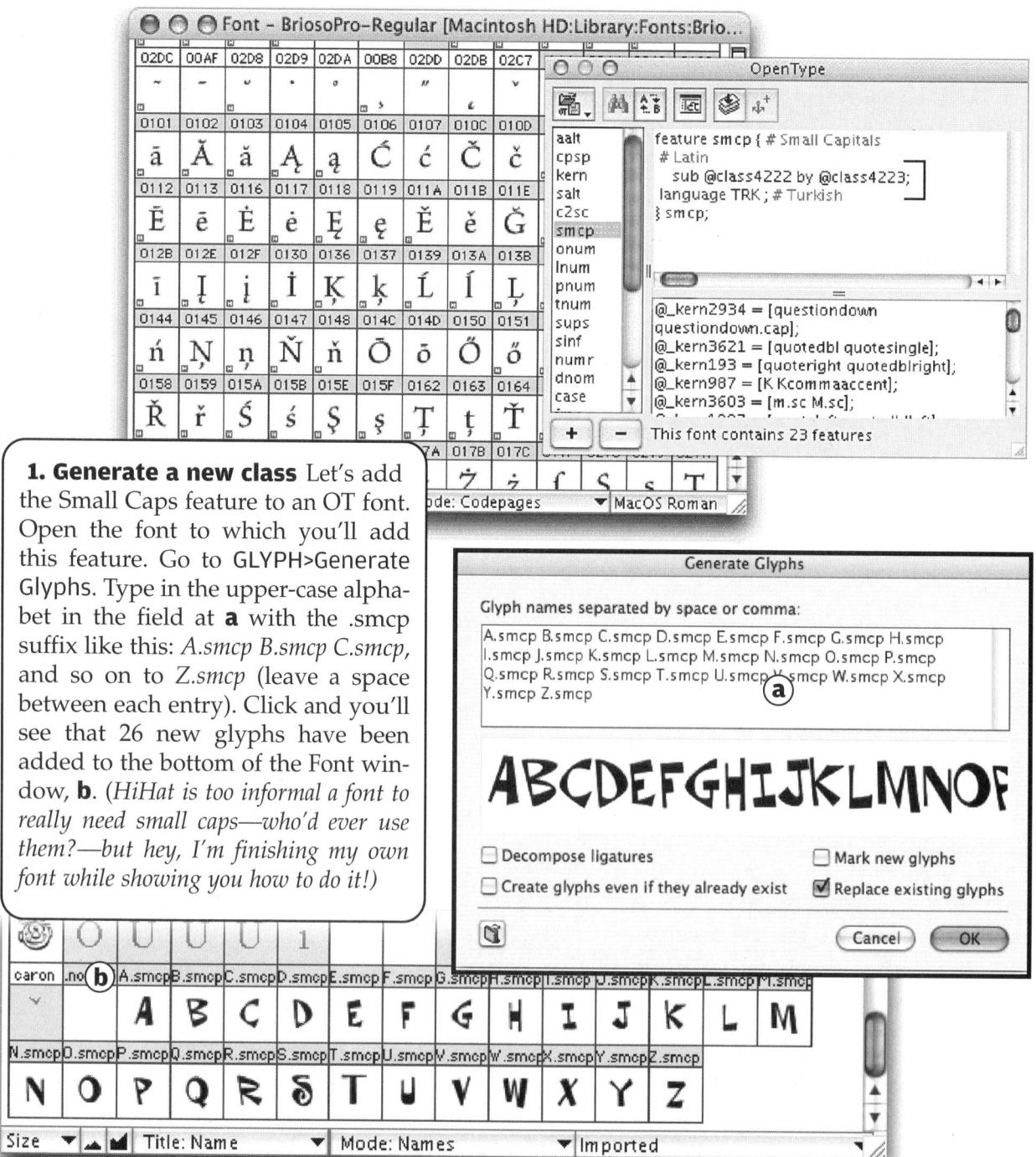

1. Generate a new class Let's add the Small Caps feature to an OT font. Open the font to which you'll add this feature. Go to GLYPH>Generate Glyphs. Type in the upper-case alphabet in the field at **a** with the .smcp suffix like this: *A.smcp B.smcp C.smcp*, and so on to *Z.smcp* (leave a space between each entry). Click and you'll see that 26 new glyphs have been added to the bottom of the Font window, **b**. (*HiHat is too informal a font to really need small caps—who'd ever use them?—but hey, I'm finishing my own font while showing you how to do it!*)

2. Make two classes Go to WINDOW>Collection/Classes panel to open it. In the Font window, select *a* to *z* and drag them into the Classes field, **a**. Rename this class by selecting the default name and typing *lc*. Click Accept, **c**.

3. Click the **+** button, **d** (below left), to add a new class. From the Font window, select and drag the new *A.smcp–Z.smcp* glyphs you made in step 1. into the field, **e**. Rename this class *sc* for "small caps." Now you have two classes to work with.

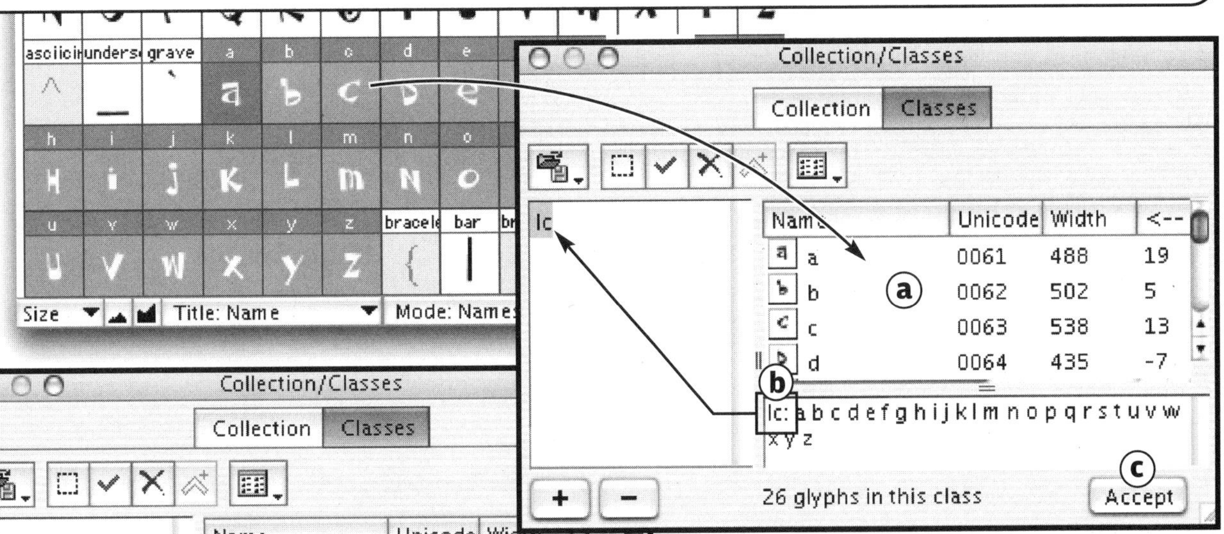

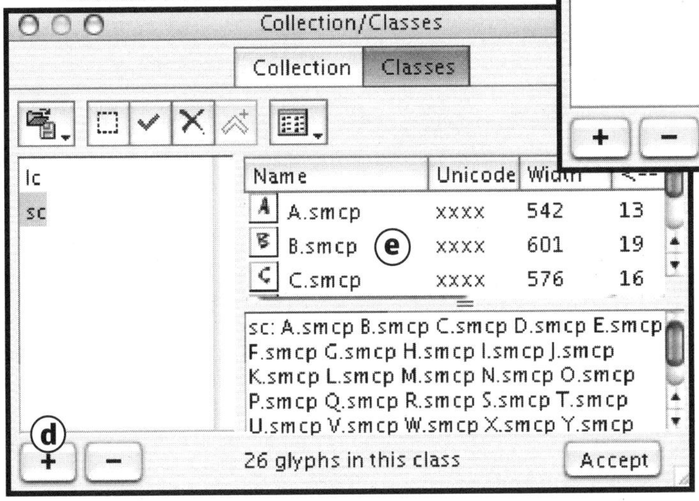

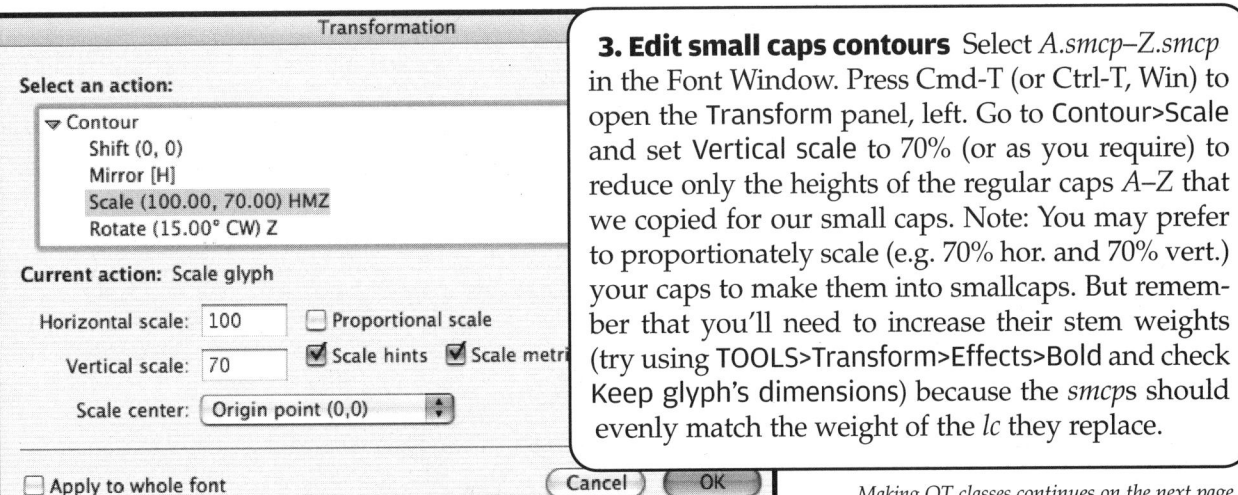

Class name recognition
Open the Preferences (or Options, Win) window and be sure that this feature is

OpenType Editor

☑ Add all glyph classes to OpenType feature definition code

checked. It'll allow class names, such as *lc* and *sc*, to be recognized by OpenType.

3. Edit small caps contours Select *A.smcp–Z.smcp* in the Font Window. Press Cmd-T (or Ctrl-T, Win) to open the Transform panel, left. Go to Contour>Scale and set Vertical scale to 70% (or as you require) to reduce only the heights of the regular caps *A–Z* that we copied for our small caps. Note: You may prefer to proportionately scale (e.g. 70% hor. and 70% vert.) your caps to make them into smallcaps. But remember that you'll need to increase their stem weights (try using TOOLS>Transform>Effects>Bold and check Keep glyph's dimensions) because the *smcp*s should evenly match the weight of the *lc* they replace.

Making OT classes continues on the next page…

4. Enter classes in OT panel
Once again you are admonished to type carefully according to the screenshot, right. Hit the OpenType panel icon and click the **+** button to add a new feature. Replace *xxxx* with *smcp* and insert *@lc* and *@sc* where shown. *(The @ symbol tells OpenType that the name of a class follows.)* Click Compile, **a**, to birth the feature.

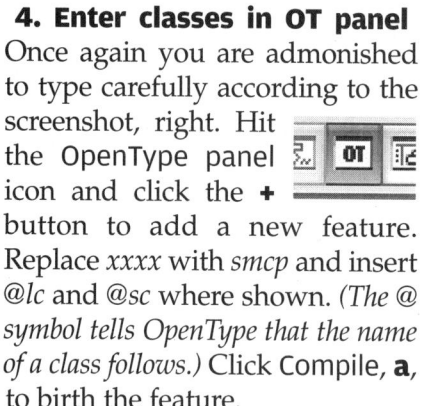

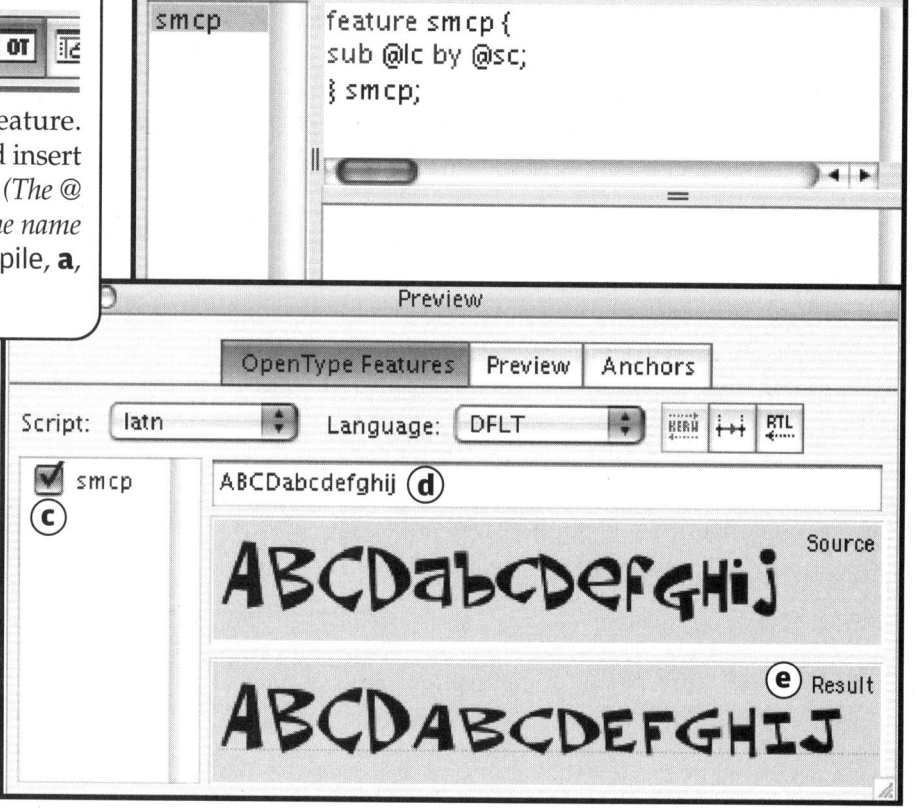

5. Class preview
Hit the Preview panel icon, above **b**, to open the panel, right, and see your small caps in action. Click to enable the *smcp* button, **c**, and (be sure you've got lc letters in the type field, **d**) the small caps will appear in Result, **e**.

Why OT failure?

• *If your feature substitutes one class with another (e.g. @lc with @sc) remember that both classes must have the same number of glyphs.*

• *When you create multiple features for a western font, the application (such as InDesign) will execute them in the order they are set in the font. Therefore, your "liga" feature should be listed in the left pane of the OT panel after the "smcp" feature so small caps will take priority over ligatures. Otherwise, when both features are enabled, your small-caps text will be interrupted by single ligatures sticking out.*

• *Every line after the first must end in a semicolon. Failure to include a semicolon is the most common reason for a feature to fail to compile.*

• *Referring to a glyph name that doesn't exist (or got changed) is the next most common reason.*

• *Unneeded white space (typed spaces) is ignored. You don't need white space before the semi-colon, and extra white space there won't matter. But some white space is required (for instance, in between glyph names).*

• *Hit the Compile button regularly to check that you haven't forgotten anything.*

—Thomas Phinney and Adam Twardoch

Some OpenType features

Here are examples of some popular OpenType features. Note that in addition to the named classes such as @lc, you can also create "ad hoc" classes directly in the OpenType panel, such as in the example shown for case sensitive forms: [*hyphen endash parenleft parenright*] or [*zero-nine*]. For an extensive overview of registered features, see: *http://partners.adobe.com/asn/tech/type/opentype /appendices/feattags.jsp* Also check out the font *Free Font Pro* that you can download for free from the FontLab website.

```
feature smcp { # Small caps
  sub @lc by @sc;
} smcp;
```

Small Ca
SMALL C

```
feature c2sc { # Capitals to small caps
  sub @uc by @sc;
} c2sc;
```

UPPER2
UPPER2

```
feature swsh { # Swashes
  sub K by K.swsh;
  sub Q by Q.swsh;
  sub r by r.swsh;
} swsh;
```

Quik Kar
Quik Kar

```
feature salt { # Stylistic alternates
  sub R by R.salt;
} salt;
```

Rat Kill
Rat Kill

```
feature onum { # Old style numerals
  sub [zero-nine] by [zero.onum-
nine.onum];
} onum;
```

067189
067189

```
feature sups { # Superscript
  sub one by onesuperior;
  sub two by twosuperior;
  sub three by threesuperior;
} sups;
```

H2O123
H^{2}O^{1234}

```
feature case { # Case-sensitive forms
  pos [hyphen endash parenleft
parenright] <0 50 0 0>;
} case;
```

2–30 (E-S)
2–30 (E-S)

```
feature liga { # Standard ligatures
  sub f f i by f_f_i;
  sub f f l by f_f_l;
  sub f i by fi;
  sub f l by fl;
  sub f f by ff;
} liga;
```

ffi ffl
ffi ffl
fi fl ff
fi fl ff

```
feature dlig {#Discretionary ligatures
  sub s t by s_t;
  sub c t by c_t;
} dlig;
```

ct st
ct st

FEATURES, TIPS & TRICKS

Page **141** *Find/Replace; Center Components*

142 *Paste Special; Contiguous selections*

143 *Mark cells; Noncontiguous selections; Annotate cells; Enlarge cells*

144 *Primitives (Smart Shapes) panel: Grid and Star*

145 *Add/Subtract shapes with contour tools*

146 *Envelope; Setting Family Metrics*

In this section *you will find a few random tips and tricks, and mention of certain nifty FontLab features that were neglected in earlier sections. As you use the FontLab apps you'll develop further strategies for increasing productivity. One of the best techniques for doing this involves use of Python scripting, whose complexity, unfortunately, places it beyond the scope of this book.*

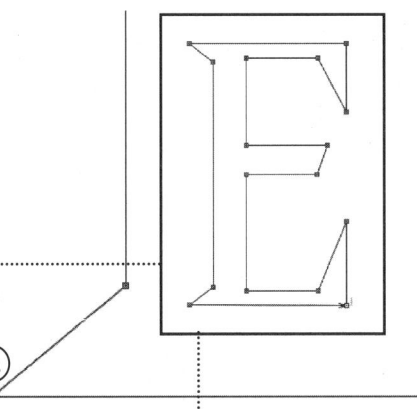

(a)

Find/Replace *Once upon a time I'd completely finished a font called Progressiv whose pointy serifs ended in a single node, left **a**. But I worried that the serif ends might lose density in bad printing so I decided to add second points, **b**, to all serifs to fortify them. Of course, I did it manually, but I'd have saved a lot of work if FontLab and Find/Replace had been around then.*

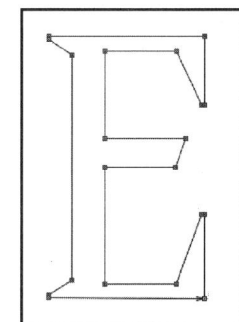

(b)

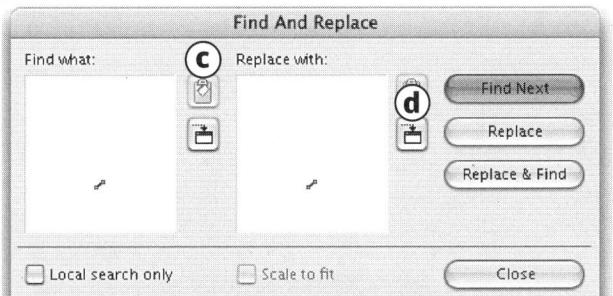

1. *Marquee-select the part you want to change. In this case it's **a**, above left. Go to* EDIT>Copy *(or Cmd-/Ctrl-C).*
2. *Make changes to the same part you just copied and with that part, above **b**, selected, go to* EDIT>Find *to open the* Find And Replace *dialog, left.*
3. *Click the Clipboard icon, **c**, to paste the serif you copied to the left pane. Click the lower button, **d**, in the right pane to load the selected (changed) serif.*
4. *Watch your glyphs as you hit the* Find Next *and* Replace *buttons. If all goes well, use* Replace & Find *to iterate through other applicable glyphs.*

A case for Find/Replace*: insert the edited, rounder hump, **e**, into the h, n, and m.*

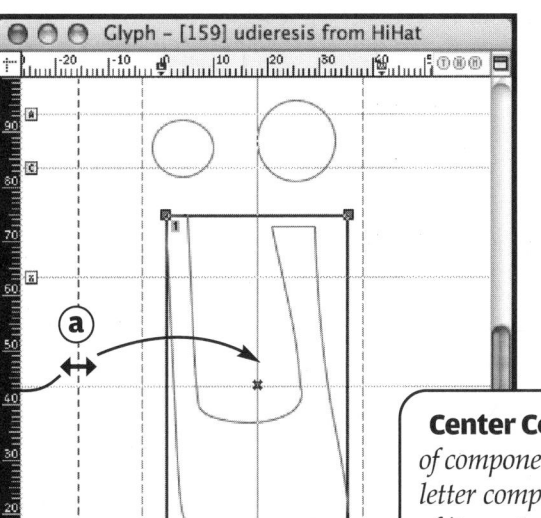

Center Components to one another *To align the center lines of components (See page 121 for how to place components), select the letter component, drag a guideline over from the ruler, left **a**, on top of its centerline. Now select the accent component, drag it to line up its centerline with the guideline. Of course, not all mechanical centerlines are really centered (check with your eyes, too).*

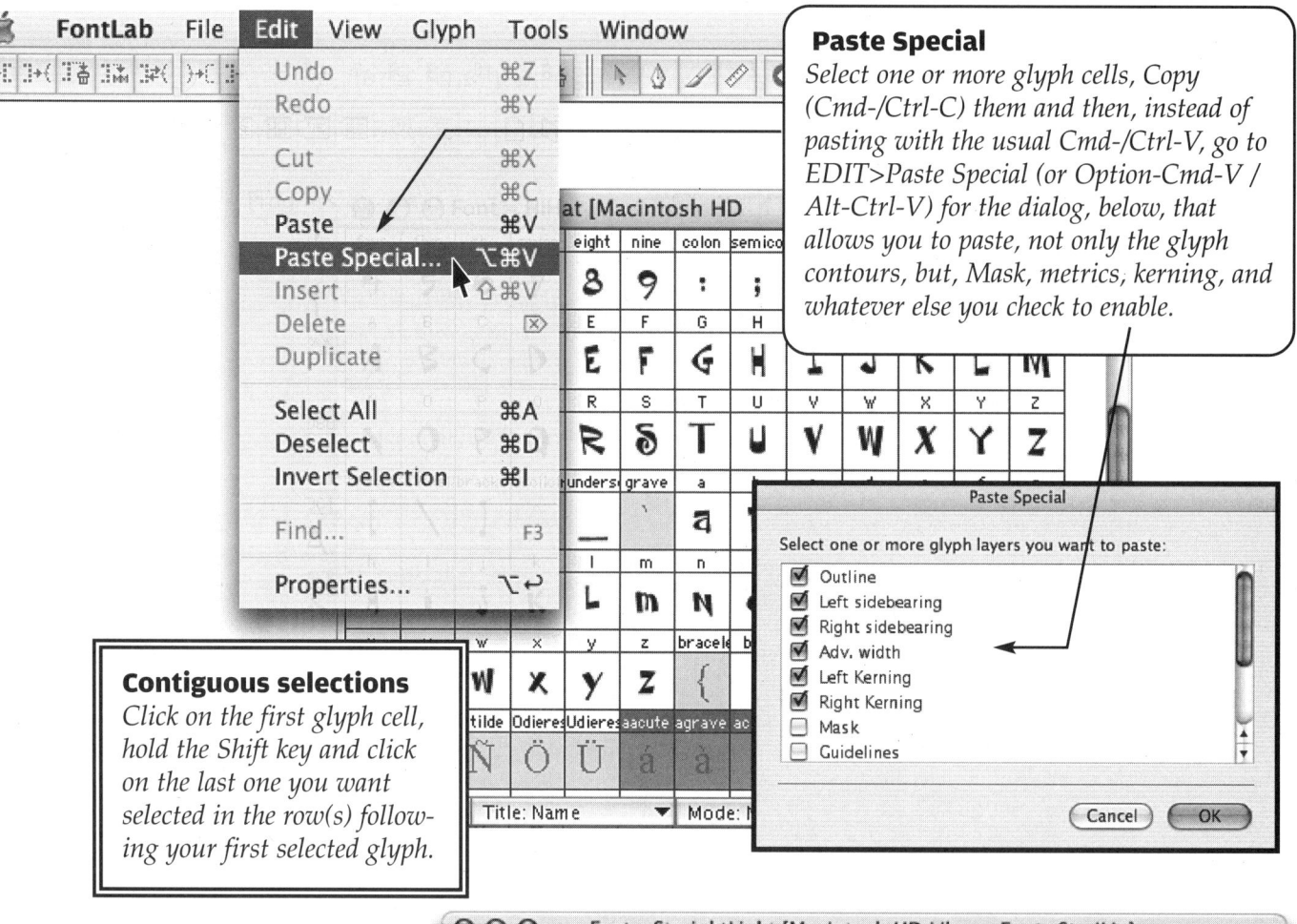

Paste Special

Select one or more glyph cells, Copy (Cmd-/Ctrl-C) them and then, instead of pasting with the usual Cmd-/Ctrl-V, go to EDIT>Paste Special (or Option-Cmd-V / Alt-Ctrl-V) for the dialog, below, that allows you to paste, not only the glyph contours, but, Mask, metrics, kerning, and whatever else you check to enable.

Contiguous selections

Click on the first glyph cell, hold the Shift key and click on the last one you want selected in the row(s) following your first selected glyph.

Colored Glyph cells

You can Mark *certain glyph cells or ranges/ categories of cells in the Font window with different colors to organize or call attention to them, as indicated, right. On the next page you'll see how to do it. The feature could be used to color-code all accent glyphs, or all math character glyphs, for example.*

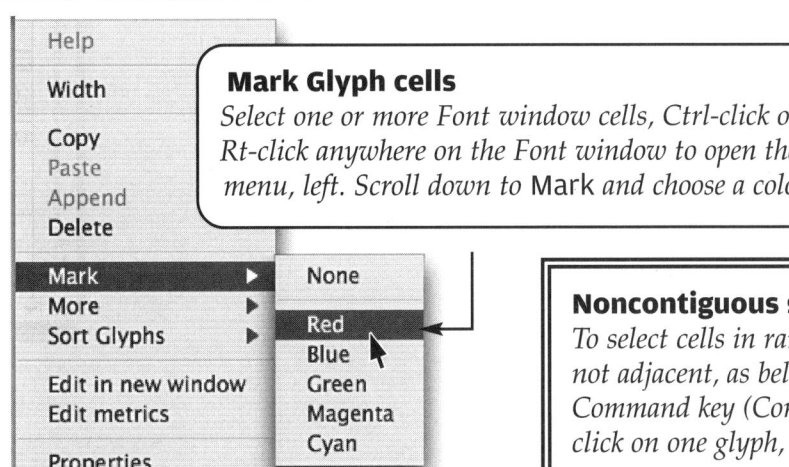

Mark Glyph cells
Select one or more Font window cells, Ctrl-click or Rt-click anywhere on the Font window to open the menu, left. Scroll down to Mark *and choose a color.*

Noncontiguous selections
To select cells in random order that are not adjacent, as below, hold down the Command key (Control, Win) as you click on one glyph, then the next.

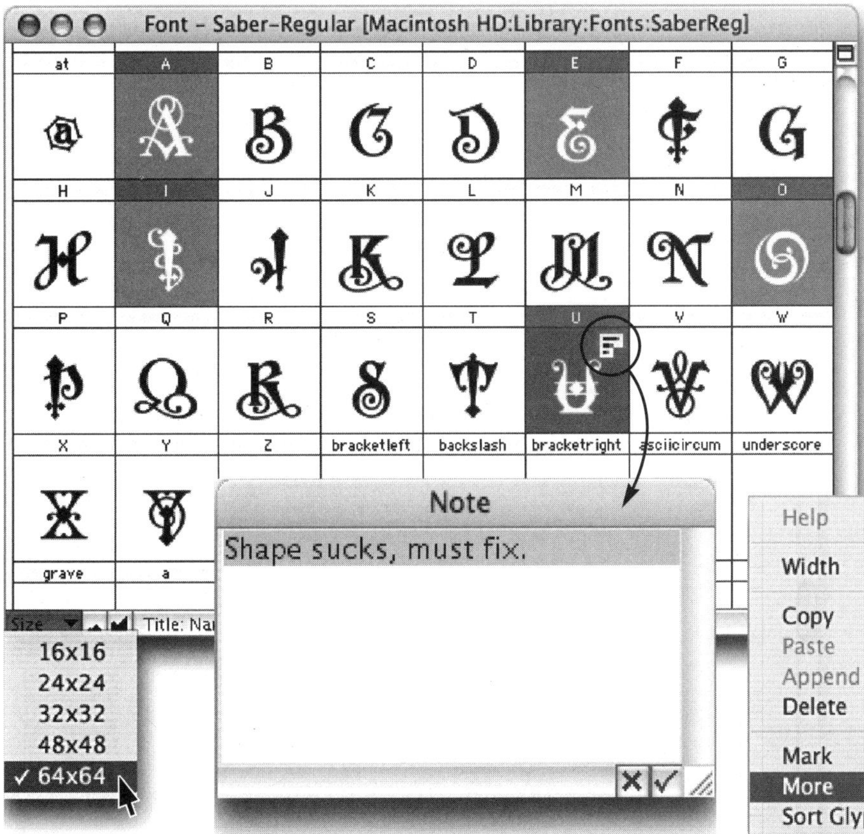

Annotate Glyph cells
You can add an annotation, called a Note, *to any number of glyph cells. Select one Font window cell, Ctrl-click or Rt-click anywhere on the Font window to open the menu, below. Scroll down to* More *and then to* Add Note. *A* Note, *left, will pop up into which you can type. Click the Check box to accept the note or the X box to scrap it. Since fonts sometimes take months of start-and-stop work,* Notes *are great ways of reminding us of tasks left half done, or of problems we intend to get around to fixing.*

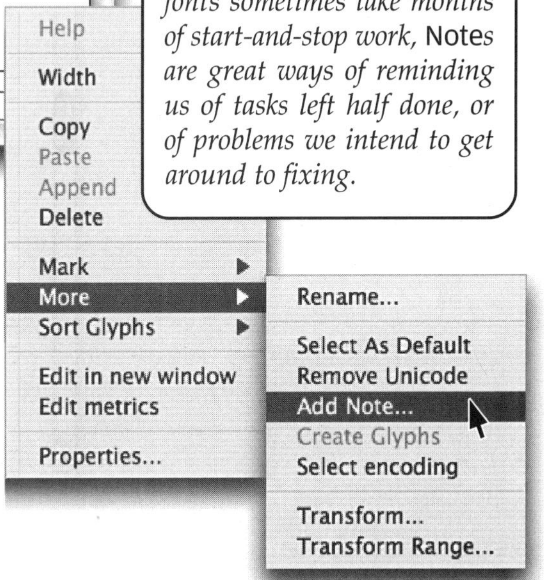

Note

Shape sucks, must fix.

Enlarging Glyph cells
If you want a better view of your Font window content, Click the Size *button, above and scroll to your pre-ferred cell size. The larger the viewing size, and depending upon the size of your monitor, the fewer cells you may be able to see at a glance. In FontLab 4.6 for Windows, cell size can be set in* Options>Font.

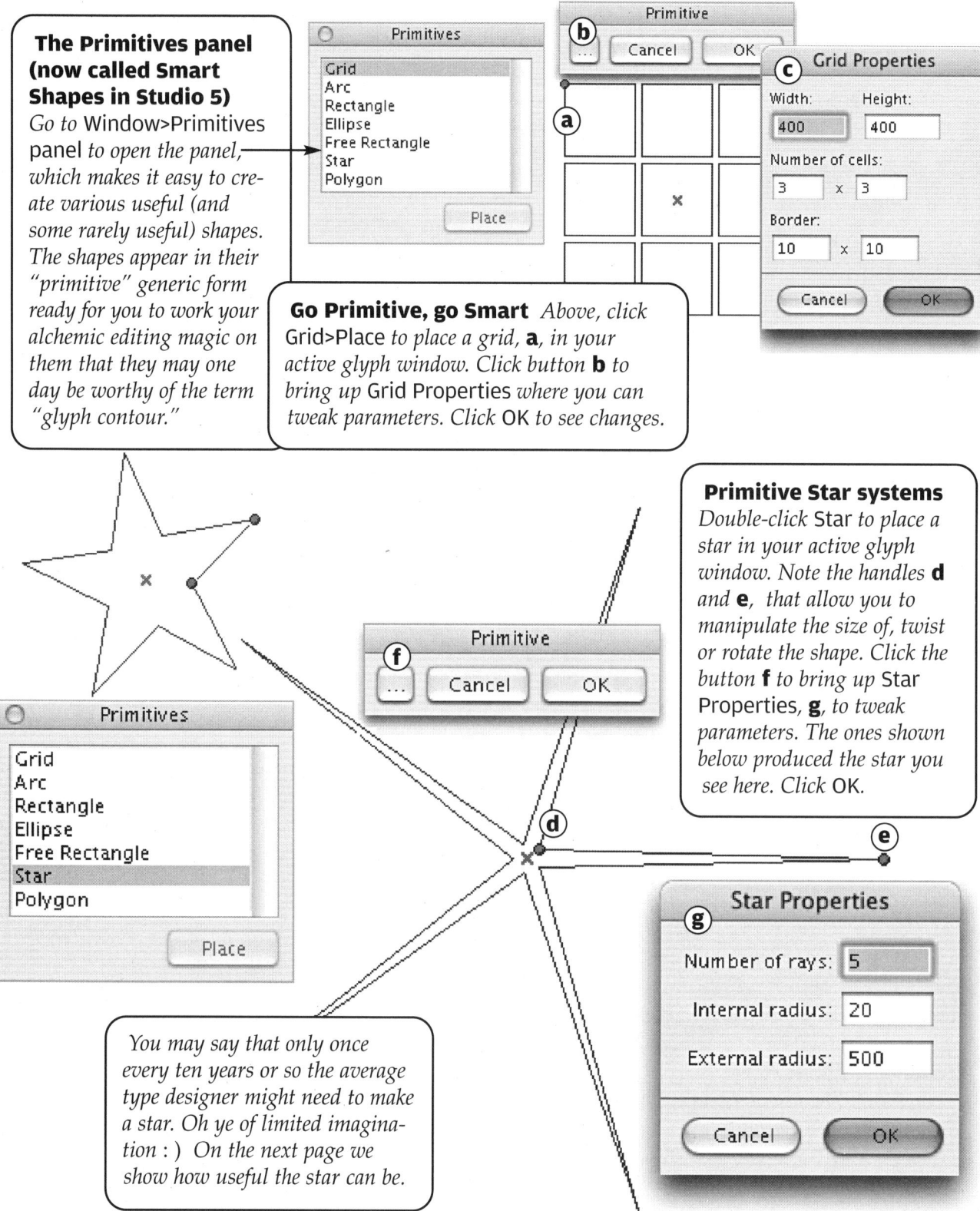

The Primitives panel (now called Smart Shapes in Studio 5)
Go to Window>Primitives *panel to open the panel, which makes it easy to create various useful (and some rarely useful) shapes. The shapes appear in their "primitive" generic form ready for you to work your alchemic editing magic on them that they may one day be worthy of the term "glyph contour."*

Primitives
Grid
Arc
Rectangle
Ellipse
Free Rectangle
Star
Polygon

Place

Primitive
... Cancel OK

Grid Properties
Width: Height:
400 400
Number of cells:
3 x 3
Border:
10 x 10
Cancel OK

Go Primitive, go Smart *Above, click* Grid>Place *to place a grid,* **a***, in your active glyph window. Click button* **b** *to bring up* Grid Properties *where you can tweak parameters. Click* OK *to see changes.*

Primitive Star systems
Double-click Star *to place a star in your active glyph window. Note the handles* **d** *and* **e***, that allow you to manipulate the size of, twist or rotate the shape. Click the button* **f** *to bring up* Star Properties, **g**, *to tweak parameters. The ones shown below produced the star you see here. Click* OK.

Primitives
Grid
Arc
Rectangle
Ellipse
Free Rectangle
Star
Polygon

Place

Primitive
... Cancel OK

You may say that only once every ten years or so the average type designer might need to make a star. Oh ye of limited imagination :) On the next page we show how useful the star can be.

Star Properties
Number of rays: 5
Internal radius: 20
External radius: 500
Cancel OK

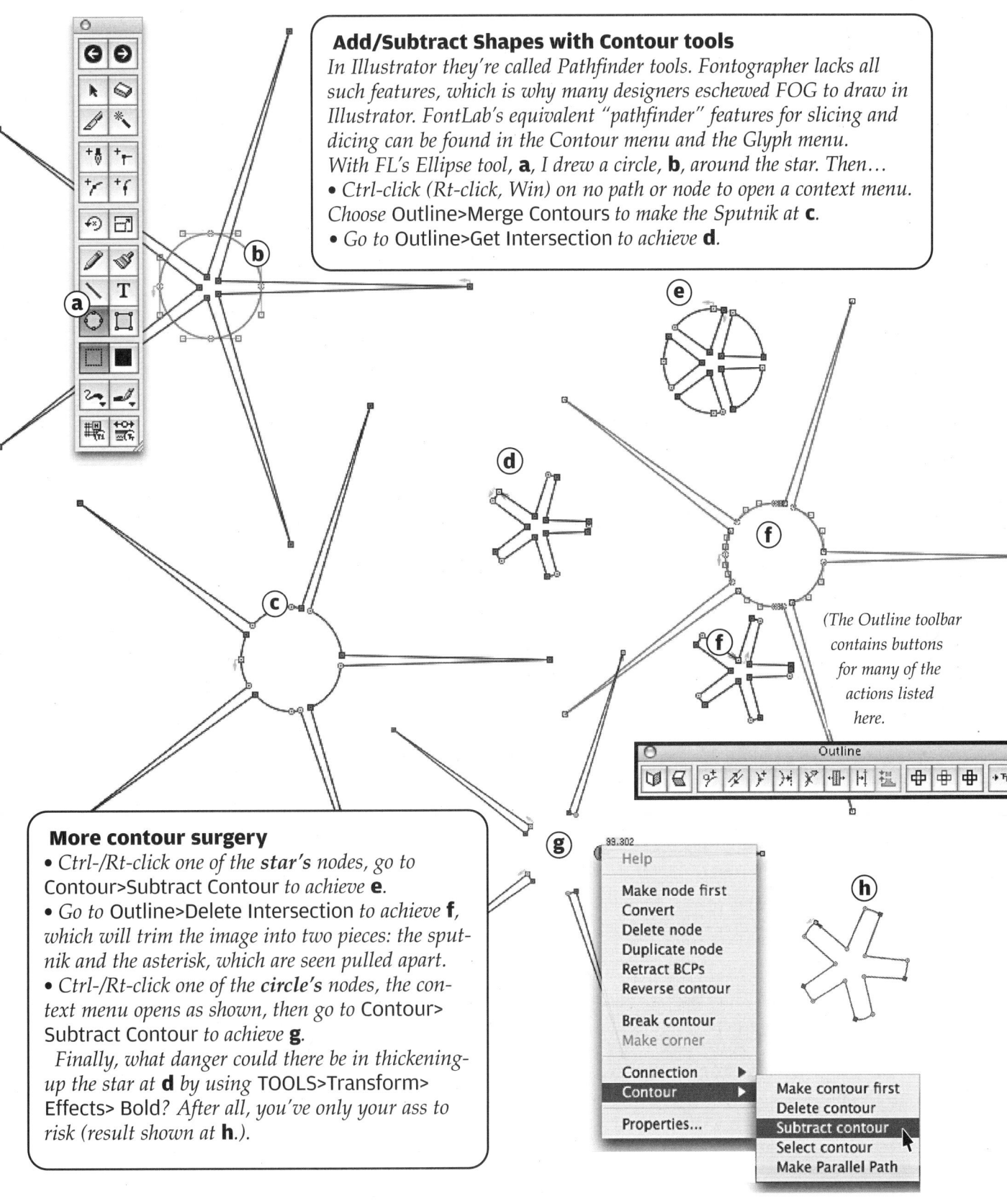

Add/Subtract Shapes with Contour tools

In Illustrator they're called Pathfinder tools. Fontographer lacks all such features, which is why many designers eschewed FOG to draw in Illustrator. FontLab's equivalent "pathfinder" features for slicing and dicing can be found in the Contour menu and the Glyph menu. Then…
With FL's Ellipse tool, **a**, *I drew a circle,* **b**, *around the star. Then…*
• *Ctrl-click (Rt-click, Win) on no path or node to open a context menu.*
Choose Outline>Merge Contours *to make the Sputnik at* **c**.
• *Go to* Outline>Get Intersection *to achieve* **d**.

(The Outline toolbar contains buttons for many of the actions listed here.)

Outline

More contour surgery

• *Ctrl-/Rt-click one of the* **star's** *nodes, go to* Contour>Subtract Contour *to achieve* **e**.
• *Go to* Outline>Delete Intersection *to achieve* **f**, *which will trim the image into two pieces: the sputnik and the asterisk, which are seen pulled apart.*
• *Ctrl-/Rt-click one of the* **circle's** *nodes, the context menu opens as shown, then go to* Contour> Subtract Contour *to achieve* **g**.

Finally, what danger could there be in thickening-up the star at **d** *by using* TOOLS>Transform> Effects> Bold? *After all, you've only your ass to risk (result shown at* **h**.*).*

99.302

Help

Make node first
Convert
Delete node
Duplicate node
Retract BCPs
Reverse contour

Break contour
Make corner

Connection ▶
Contour ▶
Properties...

Make contour first
Delete contour
Subtract contour
Select contour
Make Parallel Path

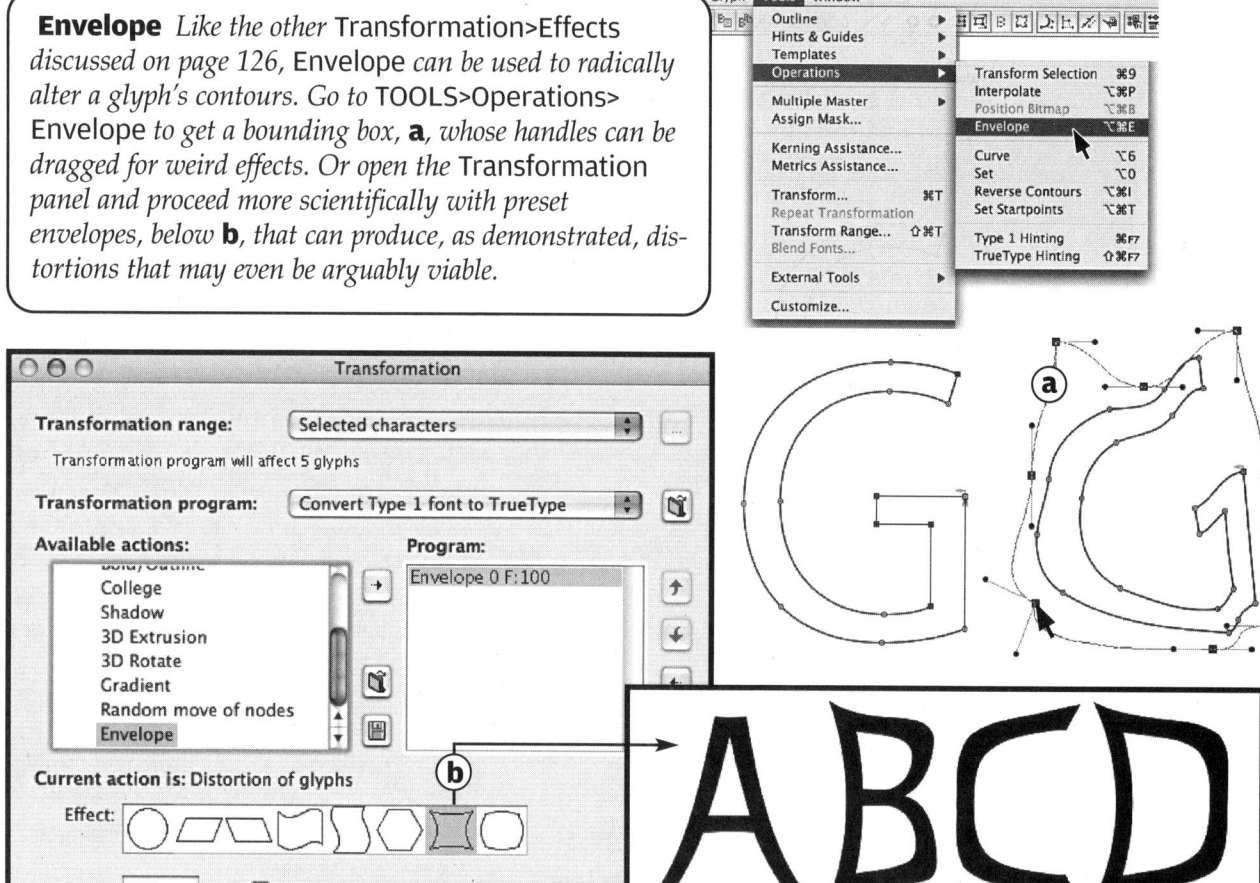

Envelope *Like the other* Transformation>Effects *discussed on page 126,* Envelope *can be used to radically alter a glyph's contours. Go to* TOOLS>Operations> Envelope *to get a bounding box,* **a***, whose handles can be dragged for weird effects. Or open the* Transformation *panel and proceed more scientifically with preset envelopes, below* **b***, that can produce, as demonstrated, distortions that may even be arguably viable.*

Twardoch's Tips: Setting family metrics

Font families should have consistent font family metrics (key dimensions) across all styles. This is important: with unharmonized vertical metrics, line heights may change when the user switches from regular to bold or italic. The following recommendations show an approach, but not necessarily the only one. Always plan a font family as a whole. It is helpful to start with the extreme characters. It is a good habit to make the distance between the ascender line and the descender line equal to the em square (or design space). This means that the distance between the descender line and the ascender line will be the same as the point-size of the font.

1. Setting Design Space

Assuming that our design space (em square) is the standard 1000 UPM, set all the styles of our family, in the Font Info>Metrics and Dimensions>Font's UPM is: 1000. Therefore, the sum of the absolute values of the ascender and descender should equal the UPM size. Also, the ascender line and the descender line in all styles of our family should be the same.

2. Calculating Automatic Metrics

Open all your styles in FontLab. Open Font Info

and go to Metrics and Dimensions>Key Dimensions. Go to the Regular style of your font, click on Recalculate. Now use the flyout menu or the arrows at the bottom of the Font Info dialog to iterate through all remaining styles of the family, clicking on Recalculate each time.

3. Calculating Average Metrics

Write down the auto-generated values of Ascender and Descender for each style. After all styles are processed, calculate the average ascender and descender value (sum of all the Ascender values you have written down and divide the sum by the number of styles, repeat the same for Descender). Let's assume that the average Ascender is 757 and the average Descender is –266. The sum of their absolute values is 757 + 266 = 1023. We have a difference of 23 units compared to the UPM size that is 1000.

4. Family Metrics

Therefore, we change our calculated average Ascender and Descender so that their sum equals the UPM size. The easiest way to do it is to divide the difference, that we just got, by half (23/2 = 11,5), and then subtract it from Ascender and Descender (rounding them up or down so that we get a "round sum"), to get the Family Ascender (757 – 12 = 745) and Family Descender (266 – 11 = 255). 745 + 255 = 1000. That's done.

Now iterate through all the styles in your family in the Key dimensions pane of the Font Info dialog, and enter the calculated Family Ascender into the Ascender field (745), and a negative Family Descender into the Descender field (–255). Check the little preview window for each style: the *b* glyph, with a thin red line, is shown for Ascender, the *g* glyph, with a thin red line, is shown for Descender.

5. Adjusting Family Metrics

Of course, for some styles, the actual drawings of the glyph may differ slightly from the ascender and descender lines. That's fine. In some cases, you may find that you would have done better by uniformly adjusting the ascender and descender

lines up and down for the entire family (e.g. 750 and –250 instead of 745 and –255). Simply remember that the sum of the absolute values should equal the UPM size, and that the values should be unified along the entire family.

You may also want to apply unified Caps height and x height across the family, but this is not necessary. If you choose to do so, just repeat steps 3–5 analogically.

6. Setting TrueType-specific Metrics

Move to the TrueType-specific metrics pane of the Font Info dialog. Iterate through all styles and click on both Recalculate buttons in that pane. You should always leave the WinAscent and WinDescent values auto-calculated for each style.

However, you should tweak the [OS/2] TypoAscender, TypoDescender and TypoLineGap values, as well as the [hhea] Ascender, Descender and LineGap values. Iterate through all styles and enter the Family Ascender value (that you have set in step 5, e.g. 745 in our case) into the [OS/2] TypoAscender and [hhea] Ascender fields. Similarly, apply the Family Descender value (255 in our case) into the [OS/2] TypoDescender and [hhea] Descender fields.

7. Setting Line Gap

In the [OS/2] TypoLineGap and [hhea] LineGap fields, enter a value that would correspond to the line gap that you would like to see for "automatic" leading. Since in most DTP applications automatic leading is set to 120% of the font size, the line gap would be 20%. Since the font size corresponds to the UPM size, the line gap should typically be 20% of the UPM size, i.e. equal 200. Note that you may also pick any other number (e.g. 0), but again, remember to apply the same value across the entire family.

You're done. Now you can export your font in OpenType-CFF or TrueType format. The recommendations above are only guidelines, there may well be other approaches to this issue.

—Adam Twardoch

What's NEW in FontLab Studio 5.0

Here is a rundown of some of the new features, and a description of the ways in which the interface has been upgraded for efficiency and ease of use. The beauty of this upgrade is that, refreshing as the changes it offers are, most users of FontLab 4.5 and 4.6 will still find themselves within familiar territory. It is not so much that there is now more to learn in Studio 5.0 as it is a case of learning to appreciate some really great changes. For additional Studio 5 updates earlier in this book, see Expanded printing on page 91, and Metrics on page 102.

(Screenshots are from the Windows version)

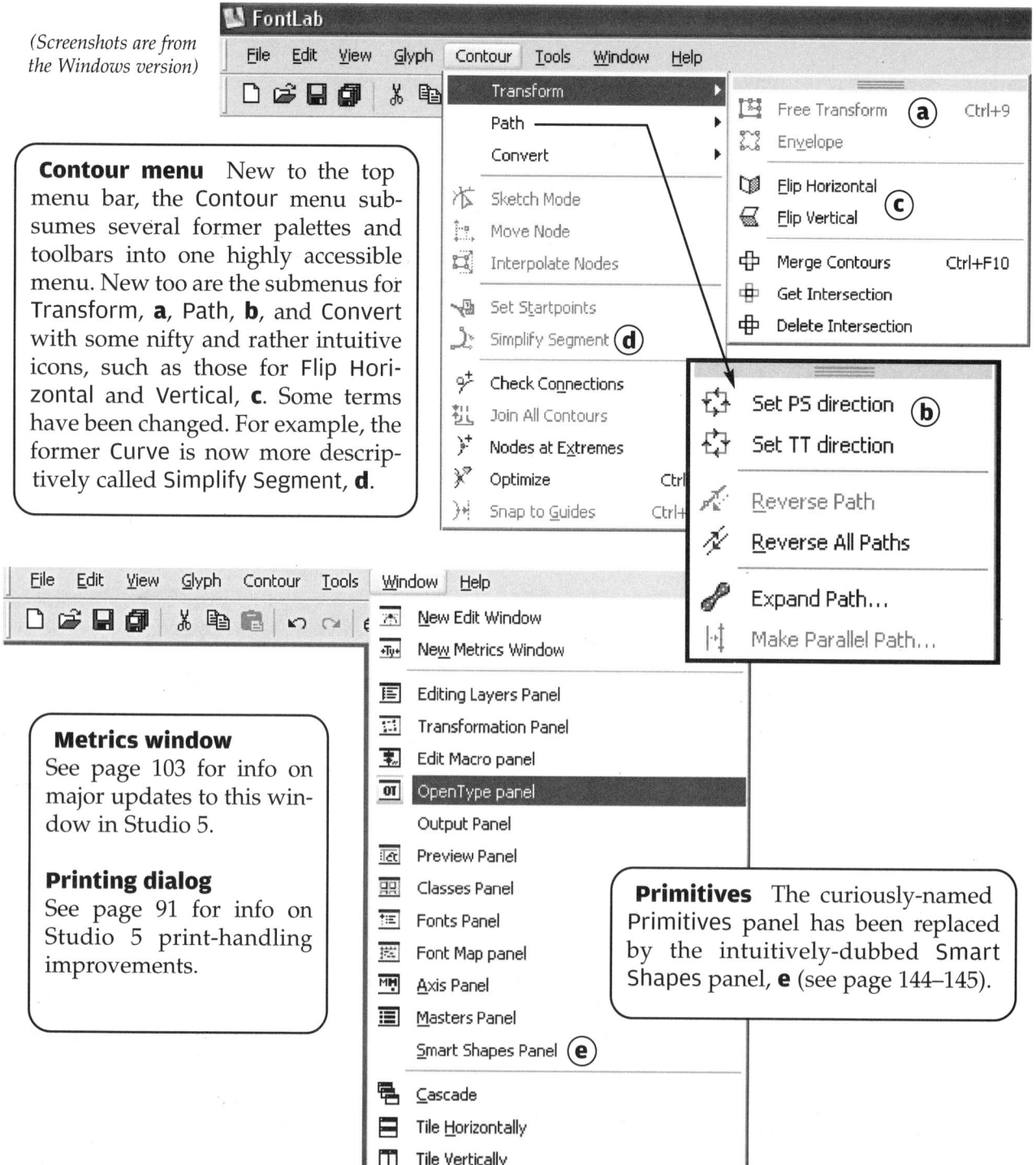

Contour menu New to the top menu bar, the Contour menu sub-sumes several former palettes and toolbars into one highly accessible menu. New too are the submenus for Transform, **a**, Path, **b**, and Convert with some nifty and rather intuitive icons, such as those for Flip Horizontal and Vertical, **c**. Some terms have been changed. For example, the former Curve is now more descriptively called Simplify Segment, **d**.

Metrics window
See page 103 for info on major updates to this window in Studio 5.

Printing dialog
See page 91 for info on Studio 5 print-handling improvements.

Primitives The curiously-named Primitives panel has been replaced by the intuitively-dubbed Smart Shapes panel, **e** (see page 144–145).

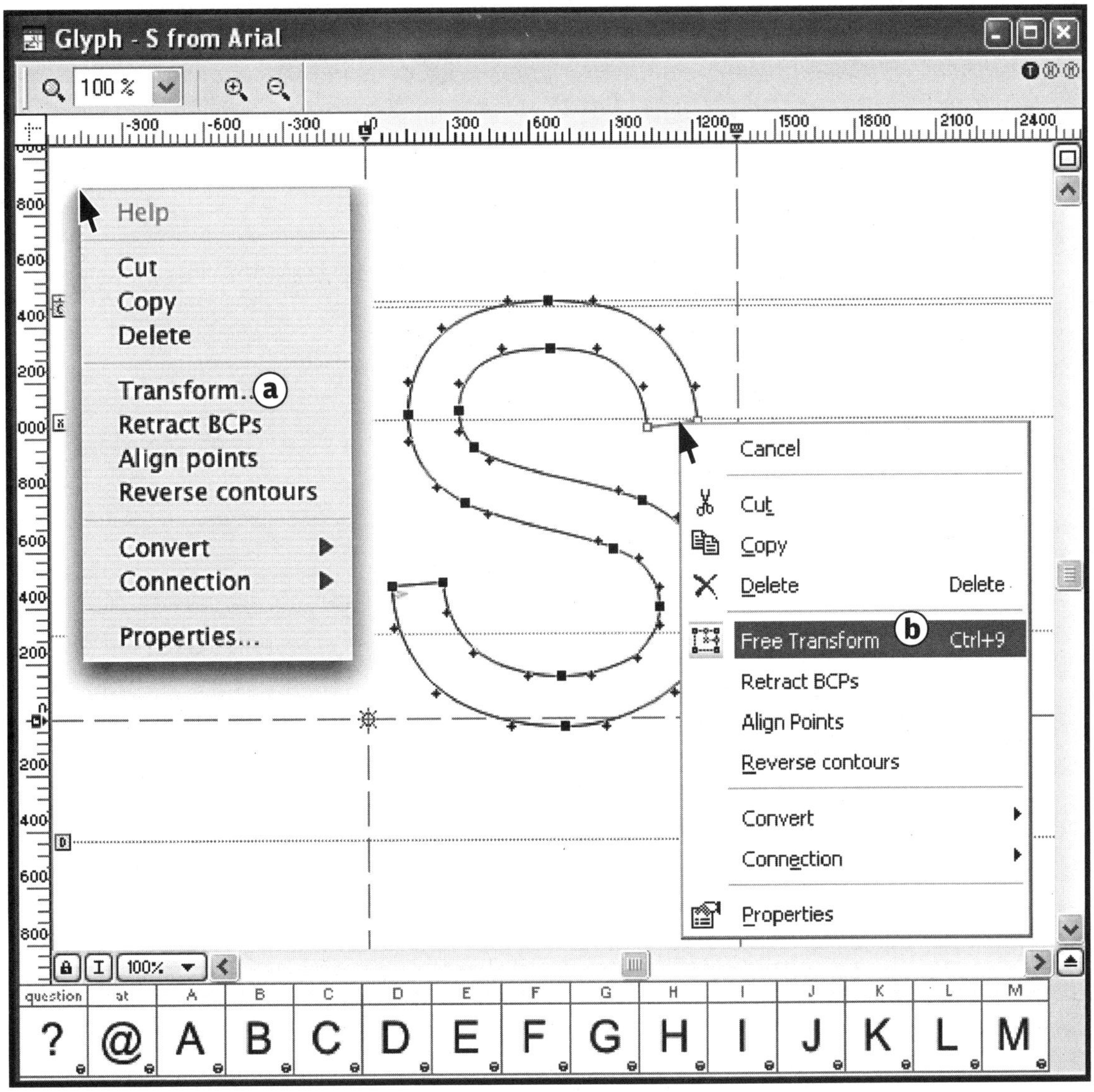

Glyph - S from Arial

Q 100 % ⊕ ⊖

Help

Cut
Copy
Delete

Transform. **(a)**
Retract BCPs
Align points
Reverse contours

Convert   ▶
Connection   ▶

Properties...

Cancel

Cut
Copy
Delete   Delete

Free Transform **(b)** Ctrl+9
Retract BCPs
Align Points
Reverse contours

Convert   ▶
Connection   ▶

Properties

question at A B C D E F G H I J K L M

? @ A B C D E F G H I J K L M

The Glyph window is familiar-looking, still. But use Ctrl-click, or Rt-click for Windows, to bring up one of the many contextual menus and you'll see that the Transform tool, **a**, as shown above in the 4.6 pop-up menu has come to be known as the Free Transform tool, **b**.

Toolbars are mostly the same in Studio 5 as they are in 4.6...with a few exceptions. The Edit toolbar is now called Tools. The Transform toolbar has been added, **c**.

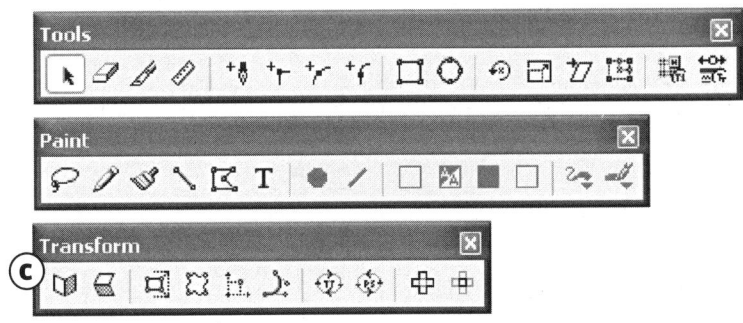

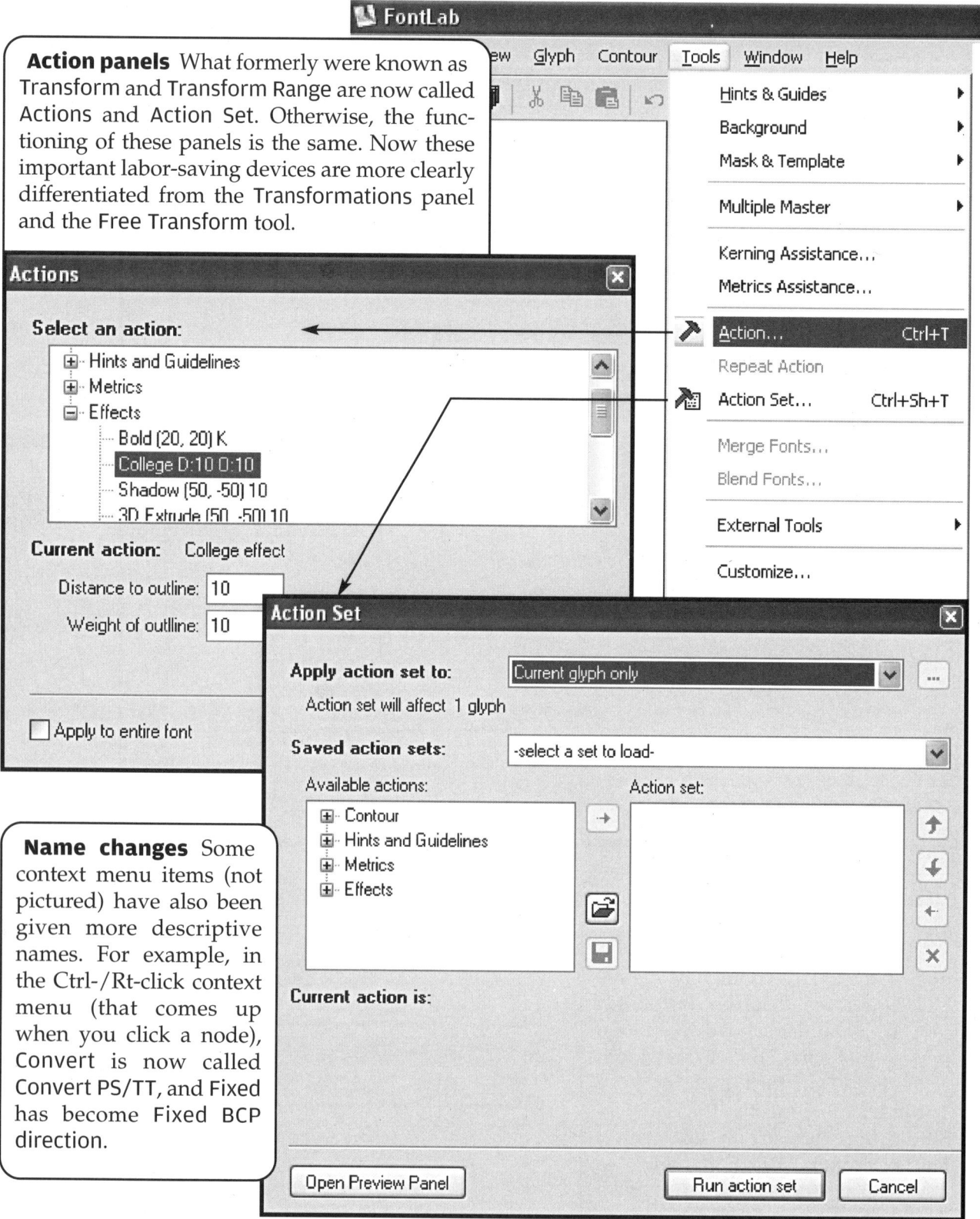

Action panels What formerly were known as Transform and Transform Range are now called Actions and Action Set. Otherwise, the functioning of these panels is the same. Now these important labor-saving devices are more clearly differentiated from the Transformations panel and the Free Transform tool.

Name changes Some context menu items (not pictured) have also been given more descriptive names. For example, in the Ctrl-/Rt-click context menu (that comes up when you click a node), Convert is now called Convert PS/TT, and Fixed has become Fixed BCP direction.

FontLab

ew Glyph Contour Tools Window Help

Hints & Guides ▶
Background ▶
Mask & Template ▶

Multiple Master ▶

Kerning Assistance...
Metrics Assistance...

Action... Ctrl+T
Repeat Action
Action Set... Ctrl+Sh+T

Merge Fonts...
Blend Fonts...

External Tools ▶

Customize...

Actions

Select an action:

⊞ Hints and Guidelines
⊞ Metrics
⊟ Effects
  Bold (20, 20) K
  College D:10 0:10
  Shadow (50, -50) 10
  3D Extrude (50, -50) 10

Current action: College effect

Distance to outline: 10

Weight of outline: 10

☐ Apply to entire font

Action Set

Apply action set to: Current glyph only

Action set will affect 1 glyph

Saved action sets: -select a set to load-

Available actions:

⊞ Contour
⊞ Hints and Guidelines
⊞ Metrics
⊞ Effects

Action set:

Current action is:

Open Preview Panel   Run action set   Cancel

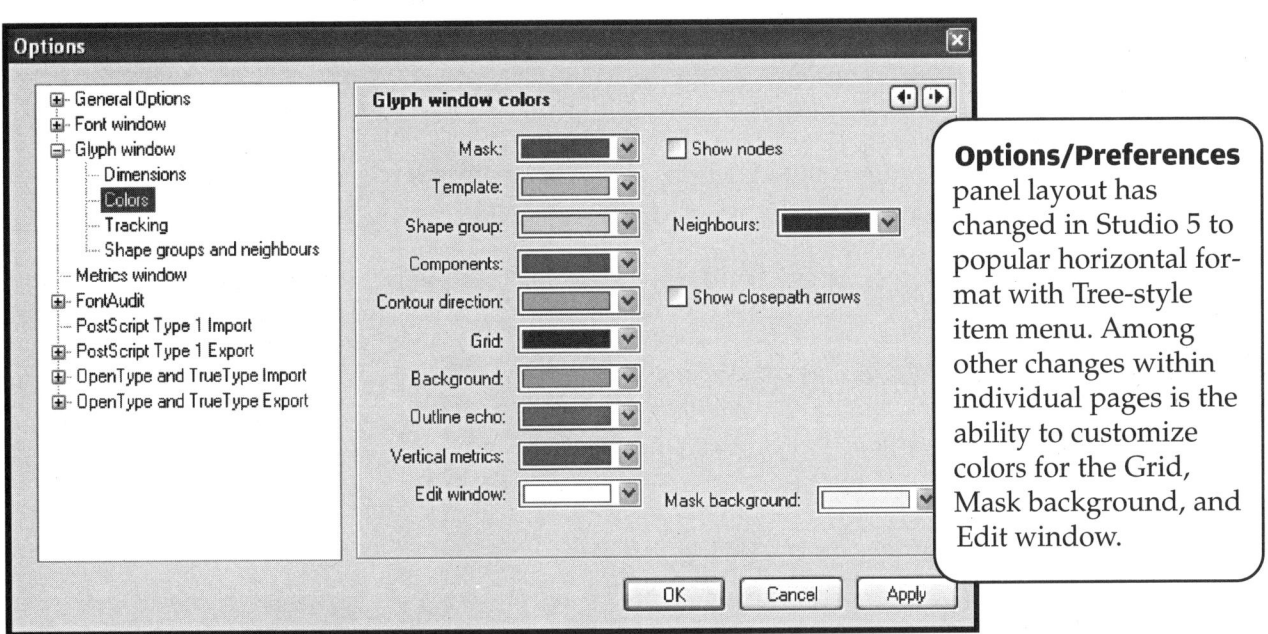

Options/Preferences panel layout has changed in Studio 5 to popular horizontal format with Tree-style item menu. Among other changes within individual pages is the ability to customize colors for the Grid, Mask background, and Edit window.

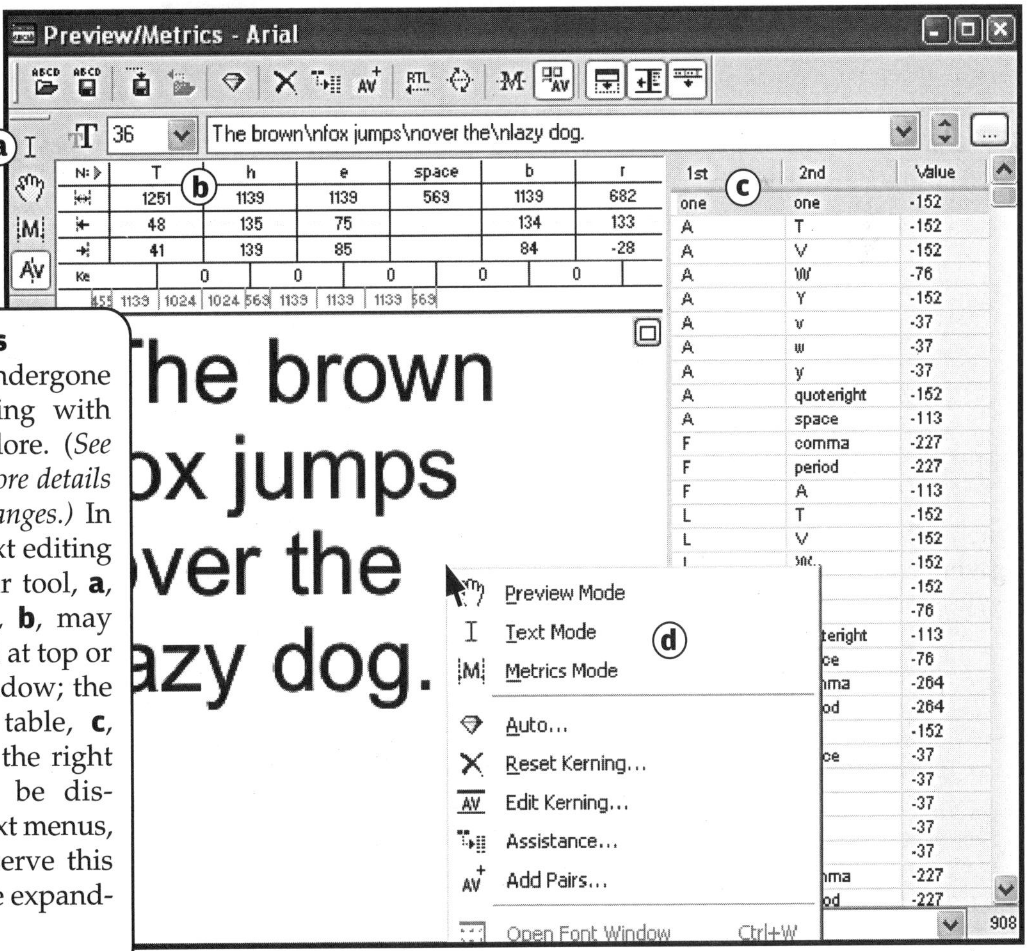

Preview/Metrics

This page has undergone a major remodeling with improvements galore. (*See also page 103 for more details on the Studio 5 changes.*) In addition to live text editing with the new I-bar tool, **a**, the editing panel, **b**, may now be positioned at top or bottom of the window; the Metrics/Kerning table, **c**, can be placed on the right and Classes can be displayed; The Context menus, such as **d**, that serve this window now have expanded options.

Using AsiaFont Studio

This program, in most respects—e.g. glyph-drawing features, menu items, toolbars, and dialog windows—is identical to its cousin, FontLab, so you will find the instructions in this book to be fully compatible with AsiaFont Studio. The differences, however, are that AFS enables designers of CJK (Chineses/Japanese/ Korean) fonts to create up to 64,000 glyphs within a font. With FL, you are restricted to a mere 6400 characters. Also, in AFS you can import CID keyed fonts; there is no limit to number of exported glyphs; and there is documented support for vertical glyph metrics.

Do you dongle? One never seems to forget the day one receives one's first dongle. There's an excitement in the air that's almost electric. Well, it *is* electric, actually, and without plugging the dongle into any convenient USB port, you can't use AsiaFont studio. But before you plug in your dongle—which must be done before installing AFS, and left in whenever the application is being used—write down its unique serial numbers (top right) so you may input them when asked during the installation process.

Access Code pages Enter Codepages mode by clicking the icon, **a**. Then choose one from column **b** that describes your language (*see also page 17 of this book, and page 85 of the free, AFS pdf manual*). If your font contains characters from one of the Far-East languages requiring one of the *double-byte* Codepages, an additional pulldown menu, **c**, will appear to the right of the codepage selection list. This menu allows you to select any "page" of the codepage (*theoretically, we may have 256 pages of 256 codes each, totaling 65,636 codes*). If you are not sure how to layout your CJK font, use AFS to open a competently-designed font from a reputable foundry so that you can study its construction.

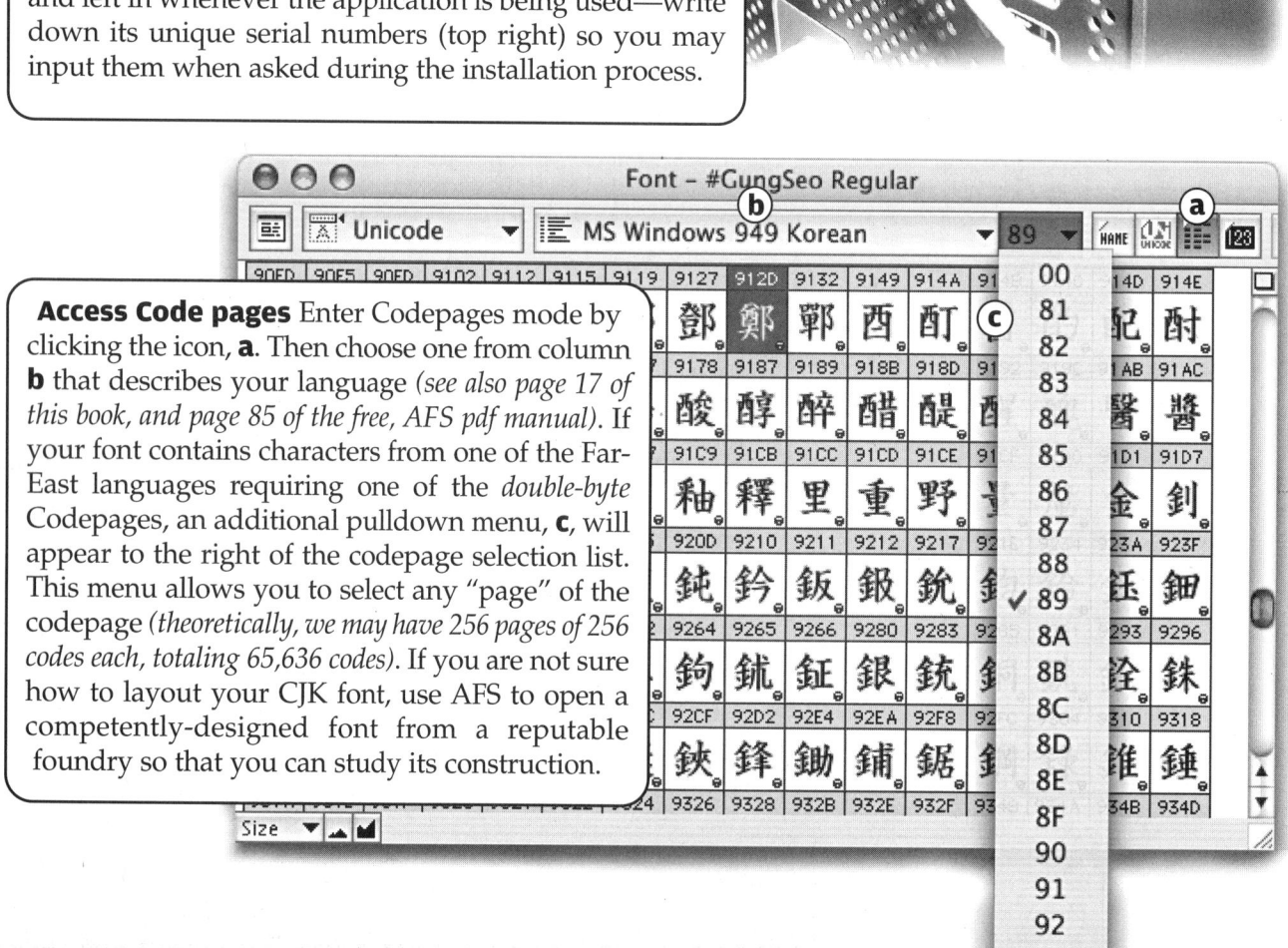

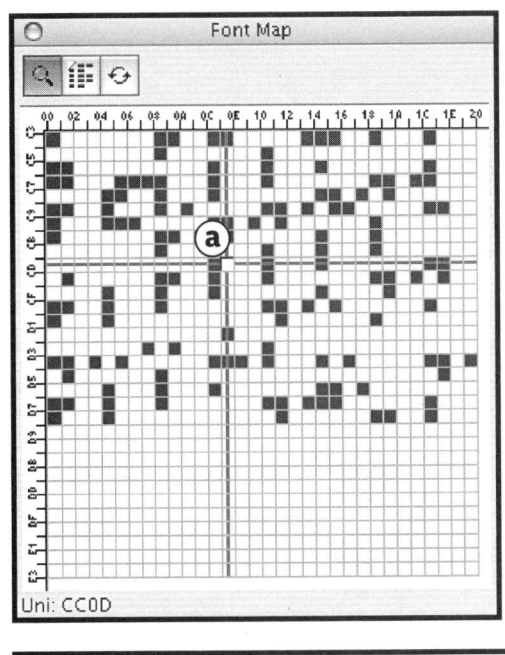

Font Map

Uni: CCOD

Font Map This feature is a navigation tool—which may also be found in FontLab—that is especially useful for tracking the glyph coverage of fonts containing thousands of characters. Go to WINDOW>Font Map Panel to open. Click with the Magnifing glass tool to increase the viewing scale of the map. Up close, as shown at left, filled-in squares show which glyphs are present. Click a square with the crosshair, **a**, and that glyph will pop up highlighted in the Font window. Read more about this in the AFS pdf manual, page 120.

Glyph – [7034] uni91CD from #GungSeo Regular

Remove some glyphs and try to save the font again.
FontLab cannot save or export a font containing more than 6400 glyphs.

OK

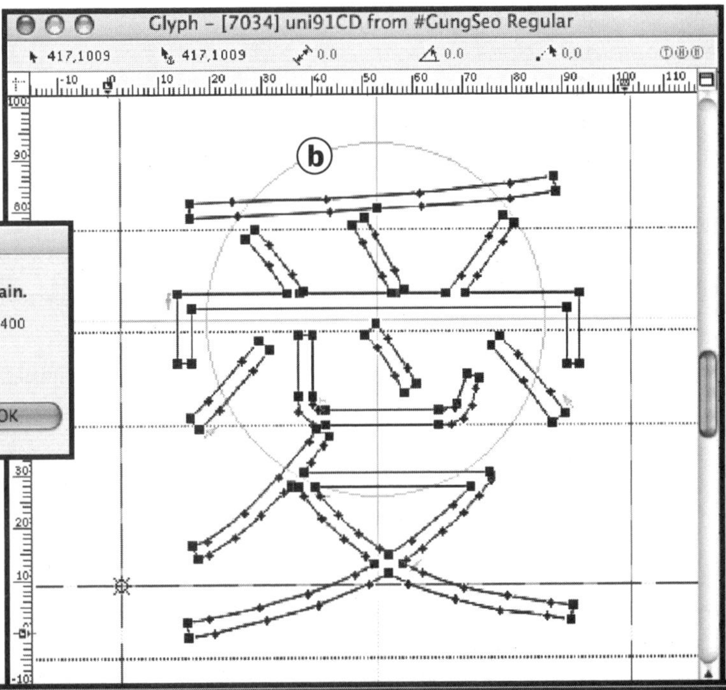

Warning: Try to save or export a font with more than 6400 glyphs in FontLab, and you get this message.
AFS Glyph window In AFS, you'll see the circle and crosshair, above right **b**, in the Glyph window background. This is fixed to force you to follow the strict CJK glyph construction rules (glyphs are monospaced in both directions). If you want to use a custom template, use the template layer (see page 79), just as in FontLab. Right, a Chinese font designed in AFS by Sammy Or who says, "Usually, I set the Chinese baseline at –18 to match the roman, (bilingual) glyphs in the font."

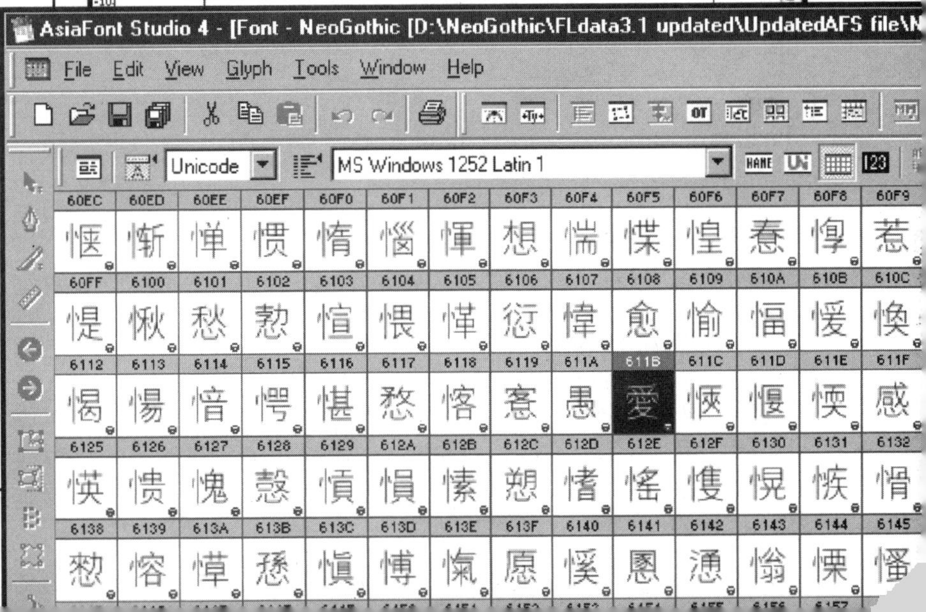

AsiaFont Studio 4 - [Font - NeoGothic [D:\NeoGothic\FLdata3.1 updated\UpdatedAFS file\N

File Edit View Glyph Tools Window Help

Unicode   MS Windows 1252 Latin 1

60EC	60ED	60EE	60EF	60F0	60F1	60F2	60F3	60F4	60F5	60F6	60F7	60F8	60F9
慲	慭	憚	惯	惰	恼	惲	想	惴	惵	惶	惷	悼	惹
60FF	6100	6101	6102	6103	6104	6105	6106	6107	6108	6109	610A	610B	610C
惿	愀	愁	愂	愃	愄	愅	愆	愇	愈	愉	愊	愋	愌
6112	6113	6114	6115	6116	6117	6118	6119	611A	611B	611C	611D	611E	611F
愒	愓	愔	愕	愖	愗	愘	愙	愚	愛	愜	愝	愞	感
6125	6126	6127	6128	6129	612A	612B	612C	612D	612E	612F	6130	6131	6132
愥	愦	愧	愨	愩	愪	愫	愬	愭	愮	愯	愰	愱	愲
6138	6139	613A	613B	613C	613D	613E	613F	6140	6141	6142	6143	6144
愸	愹	愺	愻	愼	愽	愾	愿	慀	慁	慂	慃	慄	慅

INDEX

FL is abbreviation for FontLab.
Bold page number indicates the best explanation of the feature.

A

Accented characters 119
Add
  a new point to a path 63
  Glyph Component 121
  -Corner tool 59, 63
  Glyph cells to a font 134
  Note ("Annotate" in Font wind.) 143
  -Tangent tool 59
Adjust sidebearings 71
Adobe Illustrator 28
  AICB clipboard 28, 29
  Glyphs palette 132
  importing art from 28
  importing art using ScanFont 36
  Pasting from FontLab 29
  Preferences in 28
  using OpenType in 133
Adobe InDesign 132
  using OpenType in 132
Alignment zones 14, **49, 109**
Align points 52, **62**, 63
Anchors **120**
  rename, delete or color 120
  to make composites 120
Apply to whole font (button) 125
Arc, a more perfect 51
Arrow keys
  increments
  to move paths 60
Asia Font Studio (AFS) **152-153**
ASCII characters 97
ATM (Adobe Type Manager) 87, 88
Auto hinting 108, 110
Auto kerning 101
Auto replacing (hints) 115
Automatic Metrics Generation **98**
Auto stems, 115
Autotracing
  in FL 39

B

Background layer **33**
  contours into 58
  create 33
  outline into 33
  traced with Drawing tool 46
BCPs (Bezier Control Points)
  change BCP direction 52

  retract 53
Bezier
  dragging out a handle 50
Bitmaps in FL 30
  enlarged, in hinting 114
  Scan tips 33
  scans with ScanFont 34
  tips for preparing scans 34
Break Contour 46, 56, 59
Brush tool 41–42
  body options 44
  calligraphic flat brush setting 41
  drawings with 43
  options 41
  shapes 44

C

Cap height comparison 23
Carpal tunnel 40
Carter, Matthew 107
Character
  strings into Metrics window 97
  vs. glyph (comparison) 11
CJK (Chinese/Japanese/Korean) 152
Class-based kerning 104
Classes
  entering in OT panel 138
  previewing 138
Clean up paths (see Optimize)
Clockwise (TrueType direction) 116
Close a path 51, 66, 69
Close a contour 59
Codepages 152
Compile (the OT features list) 135, 138
Components 119
  Adding from Select a Comp. panel 121
  centering 141
  Decompose 121
Composite glyphs 119
  Decompose 119
  viewing anchored 120
  making with Generate glyphs 121
Condense a font 125
Connection
  Break a smooth 52
  fixed **53**
  make a sharp smooth 53
  make a smooth sharp 53
  make sharp by removing handles 53
  smooth 52

Constrain
  BCP handles 57
  drag direction 57
Contextual (also: Pop-up) menus 52, 65, 115, 120, 121, 149
Control marks 14
Contour
  closing a 70
  >Delete Intersection 145
  direction 50, 69
  Menu in Studio 5 148
  Merge contour 42, 44, 63, 69, 145
  number of in hinting 112
  reversing 109
  scale the 125
  >Subtract Contour 145
Contours into Background 58
Convert Type 1 to TrueType 127
Color
  Font window cells 142
  Grid (in Studio 5) 151
Collection/Classes panel 104, 137
College (Effect) 126
Copy to Mask 64
Copy to Template 64, 79
Corner point 50
Counter-Clockwise direction 68–69
Create Background 58
Crosshair 14
  aligning nodes with 70
  Do not show crosshair 52
  straightening paths with 52
Curve (Simplify Segment) 148
Curve point 50
Curves, change to Type 1 109
Cut
  instead of deleting path(s) 46
  to break contour 68

D

Decompose composites 119
Default encoding 15
Delete
  a node, don't break contour 42
  a node, open the contour 56
  a path, leave contour closed 56
  Intersection 145
Digital pen tablet **40–42**
  freehand with 41
Dongle, for AFS 152

Double-click
to open cells in Font window 48
to select a path 55
a node to break smooth connection 52
a node to change BCP direction 52
a node to make smooth connection sharp 53
a node to make transition point 68
Drag and drop
a font to launch FL, 10
Drawing tool 43–46, **49-53**, 59, 62, 66, 70

E

Edit
*toolbar 10, **12***
Editing Layers palette 48
Hints layer 117
to expand it 48
to Show/Hide Mask layer 64
to Show, Snap-to, Lock layers 48
Edit tool 14
appearance changes 54
double-clicking a path with 55
toggle to 14
Effects
automate with Transform Range 127
Bold 137, 145
College 126, 127
Envelope 127, 146
3-D Extrude 126, 127
Encodings
for generating fonts 16
End of book 160
End point 51
Envelope 146
Ellipse tool 46, **58**, 145
using segments of ellipses 46
Export Options 86
Exporting
fonts (see generate fonts)
Illustrator into FL 29
Mac suitcase 83, 84
ScanFont into FL 37
Expand Stroke 59
Extrema
nodes in 39
nodes going out of 56

F

Families, font
general procedure for making 128
making with Effects 126
Metrics, setting 146

naming plan for 128, 129
naming for Mac Type 1 and TT, 128
"   *for OT, TT, and Win Type 1 129*
Find/Replace 141
Fixed connection 53, 150
Flash, hinting for 107
Flop (see Horizontal mirror)
Follow through 41
Font
best to open, 26
condense a 125
families, about 123
…is Italic button 129
…is Bold button 129
-loading pointers 87
unnamed 18
Font Audit 109
Font Book *(in Mac OSX.3)* 84
Font Map 153
Fontographer, Macromedia 27, 103, 145
Fonts used in book demos
Angle 89, 123
Augsberger Initials 106
Bernhard Modern 23
Brioso Pro 136
Cymbal 99
Delorita 99
Dispatch 123
Franklin Gothic 123
Georgia 94, 108
Gill Sans Light 23
Impact 94, 95
Interstate Regular 23
HiHat 136
Kobalt Black 27, 95
Love 123
Palatino 96
Popular 90
Progressiv 123
Rocket 100
Saber 98
Snell Roundhand 96
Stempel Garamond 123
Verdana 107
Font encodings
Latin-based 15
Non-Latin 17
Fonts Folder *(in hard drive)* 87
Font Format 16
comparison 81
Mac TrueType 82
Mac Type 1 82
OpenType 81
PC Type 1 82

TrueType 81
Font Info window **19**
Alignment Zones 49
Copyright information page 20
Embedding 21
Designer information 21
Font is Italic/Italic button 129
Hinting settings 110
Key Dimensions 23
Key Identification 22, 85
License Information 21
Metrics and Dimensions 22
Names and Copyright 84
OpenType specific names page 130
Standard Stems 111, 115
Synchronize slant 23
TrueType specific metrics 85
Unicode Ranges page 16
Unique ID number 22
Vender codes 22
FontLab Studio 5 *(see Studio 5)* **148–151**

FontLab team, above, left to right
Stas Zainchkovsky 155
Alex Simagin 155
Sasha Petrov 155
Cyril Murzin 155
Yuri Yarmola 155
Oleg Kozlov 155
Font window
Annotate cells in 143
contiguous selections in 143
enlarge cells in 143
gray images in (Template images) 15
Mark cells in 143
non-contiguous selections in 104, 143
reduce cell sizes in 11

Template images 17

G

Gauge ball, to make 79
Generate a font 80–86
 do before generating TT and OT 130
 Mac or PC TrueType font 85
 Mac Type 1 83
 Mac Type 1 and install it 83
 Mac suitcase 81
Generate Font dialog 85
Generate Glyphs 121, 134, 136
Glyphs Bar 13, 73
Glyphs
 compositing 119
 Decomposing composites 119
 drawing 58–71
 Generate Glyphs dialog 121, 134, 136
Glyph window
 about 12
 details 48
 double-click to open cell 12
 Editing Layers palette 48
 enhanced 13
 meter panel 48
Grabber hand 73
Grieshaber, James 9
Grid 77
 accessing in Editing Layers 77
 accessing in Show Layers 77
 changing color of 77
 rounding corners with 77
 setting dimensions of 77
 turning on the 77

H

Handles, bezier 50-53
 dragging out a 50
 dragging symmetrically 57
Hints
 deleting 115
 editing 114
 moving 114
Hinting 106–117
 Auto- 108
 Auto-replacing 115
 avoiding 106
 contours in 112
 Convert Hints to Links 114
 Convert Links to Hints 114
 entering mode 111
 Preview options 113
 removing existing 108

 replacement hints 114, 115
 slow-down during 113
 TrueType, beginning 116
 why should we? 106
Hinting settings 49
 toolbar 10
Horizontal (H) Mirror 64, 70
Horizontal (Hor.) scaling 124, 125

I

I-bar 48, 78
Illustrator (see Adobe Illustrator)
Import
 Adobe Illustrator, art from 28–29
 Fontographer, files from 27
Index 154
Inserting a new node 63
Installing
 a Mac font into Mac OSX 83
 by drag/drop into OSX 84
 Mac fonts into Mac OS8.x or 9.x 87
 PC fonts into Windows 88
Interface
 alternative for Win 10
 expand window button 13
 working suggestions 73

J

Jaybirds *(are not mentioned in this book)*

K

K (Kerning) button 72
Keep glyph's dimensions 137
Kerning 94, **99–103**
 about 99
 auto 101
 class-based 104
 common pairs 99
 erase existing 101
 K for Kerning mode 94
 Kern bar, dragging the 100
 Kerning Info panel 100
 remove existing 101
 reset existing 101
 setting in Transformation 102
Kerning Assistance panel 105
Key combinations
 Copy: Cmd-C
 Cut: Cmd-X
 Font Info: to open Cmd-F
 Magnifying glass: Z, X, Cmd-Space,
Option Cmd-Space
 New font: Cmd-N

 Open a font: Cmd-O
 Optimize: Cmd-E
 Paste: Cmd-V
 Preview, quick: ~ (tilde)
 Preview mode: Sh-Cmd-P
 Quit FontLab: Cmd-Q
 Save the Font: Cmd-S
 Save As: Sh-Cmd-S
 Select All: Cmd-A
 Undo: Cmd-Z
Key Dimensions 23
Knife tool
 appearance of 63

L

Lasso tool *(actually called: Select tool)* 41
 how to stop lassoing 43
Launch FL 10
Licho, Zuzana 8
Line tool 44
Links (in hinting) 114
Loading fonts (See Installing fonts)
Lock icon 48
Logo, Font & Lettering Bible 30
www.logofontandlettering.com 99

M

M (Metrics) button 72
Macintosh Roman 15
 preference for 16
Mac suitcase 83
Magic emerald button 19
Magic Wand 55
Magnifying Glass 13
Make Parallel Path **60, 62**
 close a parallel path 62
Making a usable font 81
Manual, FL's free pdf 20
Manual
 editing of metrics 96
 editing of kerning 72
Mark cells in Font window 143
Mask Layer **64**
 Clear 64
 Copy to 64
 Paste 64
 Show/Hide 64
Measurement Line 64, **71, 93**
Merge Contours 42, 44, 63, 69, 145
Meter Mode 78
Meter panel
 about 12
 show/hide with I-bar 48, 78

Metrics, setting family 146-147
Metrics Assistance panel 105
Metrics Layer 64
Metrics window **93–98**
  accessing through Editing Layers 93
  Automatic Metrics generation 98
  Auto or specified point size 97
  checking progress in 72
  Glyph window spacing 93
  Move glyph vertically in 98
  opening the 61
  RTL (Right to Left) orientation 97
  Studio 5, in 103, 151
  using 97
Move a node 56

N

Names title mode 11
Names mode 15
Naming a font family 19, **128–130**
New font, to open 11
  Key Command: Cmd-N, 11
Node connections **14, 53**
Node Properties palette 57
Nodes
  adding a new 63
  deleting 42
  moving 56
  overlapping 68
  *placing manually **50–53***
  same as points 14
  selecting to get pop-up menus 65
  selection states 14
  touching the guideline 60
  removing, leave path intact 56
  removing, leave contour closed 56
  *working with **56***
Notes (like *Sticky*, in Font wind.) 143

O

Oblique font **23**
  make in Transformation window 67
Off-curve points (*see TrueType curves*)
Open
  an existing font 26
  a .bmap font 26
  a Fontographer file 27
  recently opened fonts 26
OpenType
  about 132
  add OT features to existing font 134
  add OT features using Classes 136
  compile features list 135

create substitution list 135
failure, why? 138
features 139
naming plan for OT family 130
panel 135, 136, 138
preview panel 135
pros/cons 81
using in Adobe InDesign 132
using in Adobe Illustrator 132
Optimize 68, 109
Options window (*see Preferences wind.*)
Outline>
  Delete Intersection 145
  Get Intersection 145
  Merge contours 42, 44, 63, 69, 145
  Toolbar for 145
Outline into Background 33
Overlapping
  contours 44
  hints, fixing 114–115
  nodes 68
Overshoot 62
Overshoot suppression 110

P

Paint Options 41
Panther 84
Papazian, Hrant H. 17
Parallel Paths 44, **60**, 62
Parts, using 70
Paste Special 142
Pasting
  into FL from Illustrator 29
  into FL from Photoshop 30
Pathfinder (*equivalent in FL*) 145
Paths
  adjusting 52
  *closing **51**, 66, 69*
  closing a Parallel Path 62
  Deleting, opening contour 56
  deselecting 55
  dragging 54
  Magic Wand select 55
  marqueeing 62
  removing (deleting) 66
  Selecting All 55
  Shift-selecting a 54, 70
  Shortcut to breaking 56
  straightening with Align points 52
  straightening with crosshair 52
Pen tool 40, 43, 45, 46
Phinney, Thomas 9, 11, 138
Photoshop 30–32

bitmap scans importing to FL 30
hinting for 107
Points (also see "Nodes")
  clicking a new point 66
  same as nodes 14
  Snap to 63
Pop-up (also "Contextual") menus 65
PPM (point size) 113
Preferences ("Options," Win) window
  Add all glyph classes to OT… 137
  All BCPs are fixed 53
  Colors, changing in Studio 5 151
  Copy/Paste offset 60
  Do not fill open contours 69
  Do not show crosshair 52
  Don't show crosshair 70
  Edit/Delete command breaks contour 56
  Font Audit 109
  Give empty cells a template image 119
  Glyph window pane 42
  Show node's position 53
  TrueType pane 16
  Type 1 pane 16
Preview
  drawings in progress 61
  /Metrics (see Metrics window)
  Options dialog for Metrics window 97
  Options window 61
  panel 61, 127, 134, 135, 138
  quickie 61
  TrueType 117
Primitives panel (*Smart Shapes* in .5)
144
  Grid Properties 144
  Star properties 144
Printing
  a glyph table 89
  Print dialog 89
  Properties list 89
  test documents 89, 90
  in Studio 5 91
Proportional scaling 125

Q

Quit FontLab 18

R

Rectangle tool 29, 43, 46, 60
  if disabled 29
  location in Windows 29
Reflect (see Horizontal mirror)
Remove a node
  break open the contour 56

leave contour intact 56
Remove hinting 108
Remove kerning 101
Remove overlap *(see Merge Contours)*
Remove paths 66
Replacement hints 114
Reset kerning 101
Retract BCPs 53
Reverse Contour 68, 69, 109
Roman thick-thin, making 124
Rotate tool 46, 69
Round Cap strokes 43
Round corners 77, 124

S
Sandler, Stuart 8
Save the font 18
Script
  drawn with brush tool 41
  connecting ligatures of 96
ScanFont **34–38**
  cell tool 36
  exporting to FL 37
  exporting by drag/drop 38
  importing Illustrator files 36
  importing into FL 36
  placing into FL 37
  problems in Mac OSX 35
  scale tool 37
  Tracing options 38
  Twain, scanning with 35
Scans/Scanned images
  preparing 31
  resolution 31
  tips for preparing 34
  tracing over 46
Scale tool 28
Scale (in Transformation panel) 137
Schwartz, Christian 90
Screen font 26
Selecting
  All 55
  with Edit tool 54
  Font window, contiguous in 142
  Font wind., non contiguous in 104, 143
  multiple points 54
  points and paths 54–55
  Shift-select a path 54, 70
Select tool (lasso) 41, **43**
Shadow (Effect) 126
Show Contour Direction 50
Show Layers palette 48, 64
Sidebearings

adjusting 71, 94
enabling Metrics mode 94
LSB (Left Sidebearing) 94
negative 96
RSB (Right Sidebearing) 94
setting in Transformation 102
Simplify Segment (Studio 5) 148
Sketch mode 74–75
  Deleting, moving points in 75
  Previewing, leaving 75
  Optimizing 75
Slash before glyph in Metrics window 61
Slow-down during hinting 113
Small caps, making 137-138
Smooth connection 50–53
Snap to Points 63
  enabling in Editing Layers palette 63
Spacebar, pressing for Grabber hand 73
Space character
  adding to Metrics window 72
Spacing 71, 94
  how much, how little? 95
  manually edit spacing
  matches counters 95
  scripts 96
  serif spacing 96
  spacing the Space character 95
Standard Stems 111
Start-
  up FontLab 10
Start-point 50
Stems 111
Stone, Sumner 9
Stop
  lassoing 43
Strokes
  overlapped brush 41
Studio 5.0
  Actions panel 150
  Actions Set 150
  Alternate interface 11
  Class-based metrics 103
  Glyph window 149
  I-bar tool 103
  *Metrics/Preview window **103**, 153*
  Simplify Segment 148
  Smart Shapes (Primitives) 144, 148
  Preferences (Options, Win) 130
  printing 91
Style Name 128
Substitution list in OT panel 135
Subtract Contour 63

Suffixes (font format) 86
T
Template Layer 64
  copy to 79
  global image in 64
  method 79
  Template image in glyph cells 119
3-D Extrude 126
Toolbars
  dragging and stretching them 73
  Status bar 73
  in Studio 5 149
  Tools 149
  Transform 149
  Vector Paint 41
Tools
  Add corner 62
  Add Tangent 59
  Drawing tool 43–46, 50, 59, 62, 66, 70
  *Ellipse 46, **58**, 145*
  Pen 40, 43, 45, 46
  Rectangle 29, 46, 60
  Rotate 69
Tooltips 10
  showing caption 48
Tracing
  a scan 46
Transform 66, **67, 137**
Transform Range 127
Transformation panel 67, 116
Transformation window 124
  change weights in 124
  increase/decrease weights 125
  make Bold in 124, 137
  make roman thick-thin 124
  make round corners in 124
Transform tool 67
Transparent paint mode 41, 44
TransType 83
TrueType
  for Mac; pros/cons 81–82
  generating for Mac or PC 85
  hinting 116
  preparing for Type 1 hints 109
  Preview window 117
  Tools palette 117
TrueType curves 76
  converting to 76
  comparison to beziers 76
  rounding corners with 77
Twain software 35
Twardoch, Adam 16, 138, 146

Type 1
  for Mac; pros/cons 81
  for PC; pros/cons 81
  generating for Mac 83
  hinting 111-112
  preview panel 112
Type 1 Export Options 83

U

Undo 66
Unicode, entering in Metrics window 97
Unicode mode 17
Unnamed font 18

UPM, standard (1000) 22
UPM, TrueType (2048) 22

V

Vector Paint tools 43
  Pen, Polygon, Ellipse, Rectangle, Line, Drawing and Brush tools 43
Vendor code 85
.vfb 18

W

Weight values 20
Windows
  generating Mac fonts from 83

working suggestions 73

X

X-ray vision *(not mentioned in this book)*

Y

Yes, we have no bananas *(not mentioned, either)*

Z

Zoom In/Out 13

These products may be ordered from
www.fontlab.com

FontLab

The professional's font editor. Does hinting, kerning, glyph editing in TT, OTF or T1 and much more.

TypeTool

Our basic font editor. Good for quick, small jobs like accents, kerning pair adjustment, etc.

BitFonter

The first full-fledged bitmap font editor. Inputs, outputs and edits virtually every bitmap format, including Palm, HP, BDF.

SigMaker

Put your signature into a TT font (Windows only).

FONmaker

The bitmap font creator - generates bitmap fonts from outline.s

TransType

The universal font convertor. Convert between Mac and PC, TT and T1, MM to TT/T1 or multiple ways at once.

ScanFont

Turns bitmap or vector images into font glyphs. Great for handwriting fonts, logos, clipart, etc.

FontFlasher

A pixel font creator - converts any system font to a pixel font that is crisp in Macromedia Flash or Adobe Photoshop.

AsiaFont Studio

The best two-byte font editor for Mac or Windows. Edits T1, TT, CID and OpenType.

Books on fonts and lettering by Leslie Cabarga

Logo, Font & Lettering Bible

A Comprehensive Guide to the Design, Construction and Usage of Alphabets and Symbols

240 pages in full color;
8.5" x 11" trim
Hard cover, $32.95
5–11 copies: 20% off
12-plus copies: 30% off
FREE media mail shipping on all orders!
Educators can apply for a Free "desk copy" of this book at:
 http://www.fwpublications.com/exam books.asp?category=design

Learn FontLab Fast

A Simplified Guide to Creating Fonts with FontLab, TypeTool, ScanFont and AsiaFont Studio.

160 pages in black and white;
8" x 10" trim
Soft cover in full color, $23.95
5–11 copies: 20% off
12-35 copies: 30% off
36-plus copies: 40% off
Educators discount: 50% off
FREE media mail shipping on all orders!

The Lettering and Graphic Design of F.G. Cooper

The life and work of one of America's most influential lettering, poster, and advertising artists during the 1910s–1950s

128 pages in mixed sig two color
8.5" x 11" trim
Soft cover in full color, $19.95
FREE media mail shipping on all orders!

Also by this author:

The Fleischer Story; in the Golden Age of Animation
Dynamic Black and White Illustration
Letterheads; 100 years of Great Design
Progressive German Graphics; 1900–1937
Designer's Guide to Color Combinations
Designer's Guide to Global Color Combinations
Designer's Guide to Color Combinations CD-ROM
Talks with Trees; A plant psychic's interviews

Available from www.logofontandlettering.com
or call (323) 549 0700 from 8AM to 6PM PST
(and don't forget to visit www.flashfonts.com)